D1594351

The Survival of
Human Consciousness

ALSO EDITED BY MICHAEL A. THALBOURNE
AND LANCE STORM

Parapsychology in the Twenty-First Century:
Essays on the Future of Psychical Research
(McFarland, 2005)

The Survival of
Human Consciousness

Essays on the Possibility of Life After Death

Edited by LANCE STORM *and*
MICHAEL A. THALBOURNE

Foreword by James Houran

McFarland & Company, Inc., Publishers
Jefferson, North Carolina, and London

LIBRARY OF CONGRESS CATALOGUING-IN-PUBLICATION DATA

The survival of human consciousness : essays on the possibility of life
    after death / edited by Lance Storm and Michael A. Thalbourne ;
    foreword by James Houran.
            p.   cm.
    Includes bibliographical references and index.

    ISBN-13: 978-0-7864-2772-7
    ISBN-10: 0-7864-2772-8
    (softcover : 50# alkaline paper)

    1. Future life.   2. Near-death experiences.   3. Reincarnation.
I. Storm, Lance, 1958–   II. Thalbourne, Michael A., 1955–
BF1311.F8S87   2006
133.901'3 — dc22   2006020668

British Library cataloguing data are available

Cover images © 2006 Artville.

Manufactured in the United States of America

McFarland & Company, Inc., Publishers
  Box 611, Jefferson, North Carolina 28640
    www.mcfarlandpub.com

In memory of Robert L. Morris

Contents

Foreword
by James Houran

The most analytical and brilliant person I have ever met once tried to persuade me that the mystery of an afterlife or survival of bodily death was a moot and unimportant question. His perspective was grounded in the arguments that nothing can be done to prevent death, and nothing really can be done to answer the question as to the reality or nature of any afterlife. I basically agree with his first view, but I struggled to understand his second position. Specifically, humankind has adopted philosophical, anthropological, sociopsychological, medical, and parapsychological approaches to resolve the gnawing issue of survival. In the final analysis, we arguably are no closer to properly defining death physiologically — much less to knowing if any form of consciousness survives bodily death. Yet, insights from these and other disciplines are explored in this fascinating book. The fact that humankind — consisting of the lay public, scientists, skeptics, and true-believers — continues to debate the meaning and significance of such insights tells me that the reality and nature of bodily survival is anything but a moot and unimportant question.

Some research into the question of survival I consider laudable; other research laughable. You might ask, "Who are you to judge the merit of past and present approaches?" Well, I am probably just like you in many respects — a curious yet critical individual. And I should say that there is a deep-seated sense of hope in me as well. That hope refers to the anticipation that life as we know it is not the end. Before you write me off as a delusional, hyper-religious soul, you should know that my reputation in the academic community is one of a hardened critic of supernatural or paranormal interpretations for events that are currently inexplicable. Moreover, I am no armchair critic, having conducted a myriad of published studies and field research into phenomena and experiences that many people consider to be evidence of life after death.

My view is that most experiences related to survival tell us more about the living than the dead, but happily the contributors to this volume challenge that view with sobering arguments, data, and analysis. Personally, I hope that I am dead wrong in my thinking (no pun intended!). I have edited two academic books on apparitions, haunts, and poltergeist-like episodes, but Lance Storm and Michael Thalbourne are to be congratulated for going well beyond this limited set of experiences and phenomena. What they have done is brought together some extremely keen minds to present the case for why the question of survival is not simply an academic one. It is a relevant issue for all of us. Perhaps more importantly, it is an issue to which we can apply science and reason. In this sense, I feel we can gain ground, albeit slowly and cautiously, in understanding what might follow death.

I remain a hopeful skeptic, which is why I emotionally and academically appreciate the book you are about to read. It is not a passive collection of essays — rather this book is an active and boisterous call to action! I hope this book will make you so uneasy that you start taking the topic of survival seriously. My wish is that lay audiences gain a non-sensationalized understanding of the fascinating research that has dominated the issue of survival and that they demand from local colleges and universities the opportunity to learn more. My wish is that open-minded scientists and skeptics critically review this growing body of work and suggest new and improved studies and methodologies. And my wish is that parapsychologists and other motivated scientists take these constructive criticisms to heart and actually pursue advanced work in this area.

Already methodologies in psychical research have improved significantly. In my opinion, this is due to beneficial collaborations between mainstream scientists and parapsychologists. In my career in this field, I have strived to facilitate such collaborations. One of those collaborations, using advanced methodologies in particular, produced findings that actually changed the way I think about "near-death experiences" (NDEs). The results from that research were apparently compelling enough to merit publication in the prestigious *British Journal of Psychology.* Just when I thought I knew all about NDEs ... sophisticated analyses pulled the rug out from under me. Well, this book just might pull the proverbial rug out from under you. The editors do not claim that you will read a balanced set of viewpoints. Instead, the tremendous value of this book lies in its contribution to the debate. You see, to my knowledge no one has before assembled a collection of multidisciplinary perspectives on the reality and nature of bodily survival.

By assembling this book, my friends have given the scientific community and general public an entertaining and provocative gift. Read these chapters with critical eyes, but please make sure you have both eyes open. The question of survival ultimately impacts every academic discipline, not to mention personally affecting each of us in due course. Yes, I remain a hopeful skeptic. I am skeptical whether what we think we know about a possible afterlife is reliable or valid. But I am hopeful that this book, its contributors, and those it inspires will push the debate to a point where advances are made that give us undeniable insight and hints of truth. We may not arrive at definite answers in our lifetime, but the innovations and progress that come from the asking can hardly be considered moot or unimportant.

Preface

In 2005, we published *Parapsychology in the Twenty-First Century* (Thalbourne & Storm, 2005). In that book we argued that parapsychology should by now be a generally accepted scientific field of research. The book gave many reasons why the field should be received with open arms, especially by universities worldwide. Those reasons included a body of evidence accumulated over more than 100 years of serious investigation by numerous highly respected researchers with impeccable reputations. But acceptance of a science isn't won on evidence alone (which skeptics rebut anyway); it is the sociological forces at play inside and outside academia that determine its acknowledgment as a field *worthy of support* in every sense of that term as it applies in the university system. A few of us presented cogent arguments to that effect, the upshot being that if there ever was a double standard in our institutions, it is maintained in the universities. We can frankly assure our readers that if parapsychology enjoys some degree of tolerance in some universities, you can be sure that in other universities it experiences outright "hostility"—and that is not a word of our choosing.

So, we can say that outside religion and politics, there is no other area of human interest and experience that causes so much controversy as does the paranormal. If that is the case for mundane parapsychology—primarily, the innocuous study of the two major parapsychological domains of extra-sensory perception (ESP) and psycho-kinesis (PK)—what opinions must academics hold about the even more controversial and formal study in universities of survival after death?

Survival research was one topic we did not discuss in *Parapsychology in the Twenty-First Century*, and that is why we compiled the present volume, which we regard as a companion volume to *Parapsychology in the Twenty-First Century*. The book you are holding in your hands expands and extends our coverage of the field of parapsychology by dealing exclusively with the oft-forgotten, or at least marginalized, third domain in the study of the paranormal — afterlife research.

If there ever was a subject that divided the population it is the issue of survival — one either believes it is possible, or one does not. In 2000, the *New York Times Sunday Magazine* published the results of a poll conducted by Blum & Weprin Associates.* They reported that 81 percent of the sample believed in some kind of life after death. A more recent poll conducted in 2003 using over 2200 US citizens reported a survival belief-rate of 84 percent.[†] If these statistics are reliable, it is clear that the majority believes in life after death. But what does the majority think life after death means? What is a life after death supposed to entail? What is it that survives? How can life after death be anything like corporeal existence? Surely there must be some kind of change in our being. And if so, what will change, and what will stay the same? How much can change before who we *are*, is no longer who we *were*? And just where do we go exactly if we "leave" our bodies?

These questions, and the general question of our existence on this planet, and whether our existence can be maintained after we "shake off our mortal coils," are not only age-old questions of dire relevance and importance, they are just as pertinent today — in fact, more pertinent than ever before. From the very first chapter, and throughout the rest of this book, our authors will show that the issues concerning our existence here, and ostensibly in the hereafter, challenge our beliefs about what it means to live and die in the modern world.

The main purpose of this book is to present various aspects of afterlife research from diverse viewpoints. Some authors will discuss near-death experiences (NDEs), out of body experiences (OBEs), reincarnation, rebirth memories, psychomanteum research, mediumship, and channeling. Other contributors will look closely at what people have to say about surviving in the hereafter — they will even consider the ostensible evidence of dialogs with suicide victims. Consideration is also given to theoretical issues related to the survival hypothesis and alternative hypotheses, such as the superpsi hypothesis, and arguments from mainstream psychology and neuropsychology.

The Survival of Human Consciousness: Essays on the Possibility of Life After Death takes the reader into uncharted territory — Shakespeare's so-called "undiscover'd country." Throughout that journey, readers will discover that as human beings, it is not only what we think and feel that makes us unique as a species, but also what we believe. But whether or not one chooses to believe in a life hereafter, the great beyond is a domain that we might all one day

---

*See <http://www.parapsi.com/life_after_death.htm>
  [†]See <http://www.harrisinteractive.com/harris_poll/index.asp?PID=359>

encounter. This is a book that will provide much food for thought — it is a collection of essays that will provide constant insight.

The wide-ranging interests and expertise of all our contributors, covering fields such as medicine, psychology, parapsychology, sociology, and philosophy, have resulted in representative and professionally argued essays on afterlife research. On that basis we, the editors, give our personal thanks to all those who participated in the production of this book.

References

Thalbourne, M. A., & Storm, L. (Eds.). (2005). *Parapsychology in the twenty-first century: Essays on the future of psychical research.* Jefferson, NC: McFarland.

— Lance Storm and Michael A. Thalbourne

Section I: Historical Issues

1. Refutation of the "Denial of Death" Hypothesis
KEITH CHANDLER

In this opening chapter, Keith Chandler explores the origins of belief in an afterlife. He starts with the Neanderthals, and from there, leads us through the Early and Late Neolithic periods, up to the birth of civilization, as we know it. The modern era is next presented, which includes a look at religious ideas both in the East and in the West. Chandler seeks an answer to the question of what it is we think we believe when we say we believe in an afterlife. Chandler reveals a shocking dénouement to the afterlife issue that is the product of postcivilization.—*Editors*

> ... who would fardels bear,
> to grunt and sweat under a weary life,
> But that the dread of something after death,
> The undiscover'd country from whose bourn
> No traveler returns, puzzles the will,
> And makes us rather bear those ills we have
> Than fly to others that we know not of?
> *Hamlet* (Scene 1, Act 3)

Introduction

According to the venerable *Catholic Encyclopedia*:

Belief in a future life of some sort seems to have been practically universal at all times. Here and there individuals have rejected this belief, and particular forms of religion or systems of philosophy logically incompatible with it have had adherents; still, however vague and inconsistent may have been the views among different peoples as to the character of the life beyond the grave, it remains true that the persuasion of the reality of a future existence seems to have been hitherto ineradicable throughout the human race as a whole [Knight, 2003, Immortality section].

It seems to me that this observation is just about as true of the human species as any ever written. We have to recognize, however, that "future life of some sort" is far from specific. Particular care is needed not to conflate belief in survival with, for example, belief in immortality as defined in the remainder of the preceding paragraph from the *Catholic Encyclopedia*:

> The doctrine of immortality, strictly or properly understood, means personal immortality, *the endless conscious existence of the individual soul*. It implies that the being which survives shall preserve its personal identity and be connected by conscious memory with the previous life. Unless the individual's identity is preserved, a future existence has relatively little interest [Knight, 2003, Immortality section; emphasis added].

I will take it that any meaningful concept of life after death implies by definition connection with the previous life, possibly but not necessarily including conscious memory of that previous life, but not that it implies "the endless conscious existence of the individual soul" or of reincarnation or any other theological doctrine. Any future existence, even if it is not endless, has more than "relatively little" interest for most people. We need to be careful how we unpack the question of afterlife, extracting neither too much nor too little.

Hamlet speaks of existence after death as the country from which no traveler returns. Yet, earlier in the play, the young Prince has had an encounter with a ghost, who tells him,

> I am thy father's spirit;
> Doom'd for a certain term to walk the night,
> And for the day confined to fast in fires,
> Till the foul crimes done in my days of nature
> Are burnt and purged away.
>
> [*Hamlet*, Scene 5, Act 1]

In short, his father's ghost *has* returned from that "undiscover'd country" to inform his son about his own murder. He declares that he is "forbid to tell the secrets of my prison house," while having mentioned shortly before that, "My hour is almost come, when I to sulphurous and tormenting flames must render up myself." So the hapless father is a visitor released "for a certain term" from what, for Roman Catholics, is Purgatory to convey important information to his son. The play is, in fact, marbled with conceptions of life after death, often conflicting ones. It clearly takes the Catholic concepts of Hell, Purgatory and Heaven for granted. When Hamlet, convinced of his uncle's guilt, is ready to avenge the murder, he finds the king at prayer and withdraws, saying:

> Now might I do it pat, now he is praying;
> And now I'll do't: and so he goes to heaven;
> And so am I reveng'd. That would be scann'd:
> A villain kills my father; and for that,
> I, his sole son, do this same villain send
> To heaven.
>
> [*Hamlet*, Scene 3, Act 3]

Ironically, however, as the king rises from the altar in the same scene, he laments,

> My words fly up, my thoughts remain below:
> Words without thoughts never to heaven go.
>
> [*Hamlet*, Scene 3, Act 3]

So, having decided to "take arms against a sea of troubles," Hamlet is disarmed by a Christian belief that killing even a murderer at prayer would send him to heaven while at the same time the villain himself is acknowledging that his prayer is nullified because it lacked sincerity — nothing but words without thoughts. In short, Shakespeare's *Hamlet* is a real potpourri of notions about life after death, complete with angels and ministers of grace, spirits of health and goblins damned. Therein lies the profound irony of life after death. While it is, as Hamlet says, an "undiscover'd country," there is a surfeit of quite detailed but also vastly differing convictions about it.

I am well aware that there is a staunch "scientistic" orthodoxy living in an anachronistic Flatland of materialism that regards life after death as nothing more than a delusion serving only to hide from ourselves that we, in Djuna Barnes' words, are nothing "but skin about a wind, with muscles clenched against mortality" (Barnes, 1937/1961, p. 83). Psychiatrist Ernest Becker along with others such as Norman O. Brown, following faithfully if eccentrically in Sigmund Freud's footsteps, has argued that position. Becker (1973) contends that the belief in an afterlife is essentially an illusion supporting *Denial of Death* as he entitled his Pulitzer Prize–winning book. He claims:

> The knowledge of death is reflective and conceptual, and animals are spared it. They live and they disappear with the same thoughtlessness: a few minutes of fear, a few seconds of anguish, and it is over. But to live a whole lifetime with the fate of death haunting one's dreams and even the most sun-filled days — that's something else.... It is only if you let the full weight of this paradox sink down on your mind and feelings that you can realize what an impossible situation it is for an animal to be in. I believe that those who speculate that a full apprehension of man's condition would drive him insane are right, quite literally right [Becker, 1973, p. 27].

It would be well within the rules of debate to argue that Becker, presumably having himself "a full apprehension of man's condition" was "quite literally" insane when he wrote *Denial of Death*. That aside, however, it would be unfair to Becker to conclude from this passage that he is simply repeating the hackneyed materialist view that "life after death" is a delusion to shield us from the fearsome prospect of "the dying of the light." *His position is far more convoluted than that.* The human condition that death represents is, in Becker's view, actually our "creatureliness," the impotence of the ego in comparison to its drive to be omnipotent, i.e., to be God. Although I question whether there is either psychological or spiritual support for that Luciferian conception of the ego, it is unquestionable that triumph over ego cravings is the central issue in the teachings of spiritual masters in virtually every religious tradition, including theistic ones such as Christianity and Islam and nontheistic ones like Buddhism and Taoism.* What happens after death is secondary in all traditions to what the individual does in life. To many of the holiest people throughout history it simply does not matter at all. Becker, on the other hand, perversely sees life after death as a vicarious way for the individual to gain an infinite satisfaction that the ego can never find in life:

> In religious terms, to "see God" is to die, because the creature is too small and finite to be able to bear the higher meanings of creation. Religion takes one's very creatureliness, one's insignificance, and makes it a condition of hope. Full transcendence of the human condition means limitless possibility unimaginable to us [Becker, 1973, p. 204].

It is unfortunate that Becker is so ill-informed about the great spiritual teachings of even the Western tradition, let alone those of the East, and so saturated with the materialistic presuppositions of Freudianism that he cannot see what nonsense this is. "Full transcendence of the human condition" can only occur to the extent that possibilities "unimaginable to us" are left behind, because the "us" no longer matters. The only two theologians Becker seems to be somewhat acquainted with are Kierkegaard and Tillich, neither of whom anyone would suggest were masters of the spiritual life.

Setting aside Becker's notion that the Luciferian ego craves nothing less than divine omnipotence, the second problem with his view is the way he defines what "a full apprehension of man's condition" is. His stated assumption is that humans are nothing more than animals that have become reflective and conceptual enough to realize their mortal creatureliness. In my view, becoming human (cf. Chandler 2001, 2002a) entailed far more than merely self-awareness and the ability to apprehend the finality of death. I submit that Becker's view of the human condition is really based on the spiritual anorexia of modern skepticism, which has constricted our sense of self to the sensual and materialistic (in more than one sense) dimension, for which Freud bears

---

Buddhism is often referred to as atheistic *but Buddha himself was not so much atheistic as anti-mythological. Theological speculations, he taught, were simply not "conductive" to the practical quest for enlightenment* (buddhi).

considerable responsibility. I further submit that in the 150,000+ years that *Homo sapiens sapiens* has existed, until quite recently our species has never understood life in such skeletal terms. In virtually all times past, humans have been aware of and sensitive to dimensions of life that transcend their "animal" existence and have incorporated those dimensions into their worldviews. The reason I am raising these issues is not to deny Becker's position that life after death *can be* an illusion (one among many) to compensate for a fear of mortality. What I do most strongly deny is that such an illusion, when it occurs, is necessary *because we are human* rather than *because we are a particular variety of humans at a particularly fragile and disrupted stage of our evolution.*

Nevertheless, the profusion of different and often conflicting views about life after death might seem to lend some support to Becker's view that it is simply a compensatory illusion. After all, one might argue, since they can't all be right, why take any of them seriously? There are at least two possible retorts to that argument. First, we might simply seek to discover which view is right. After all, *one of them might be.* Second, we might offer the counterargument that belief in an afterlife is based on credible evidence, but that the evidence lends itself to many different interpretations. This situation is quite common in science. Scarcely a week goes by when some scientist, in fields from astrophysics to neurology, does not say, "Oops. We got that wrong — back to the drawing board." In April 2004, *Scientific American* published a lead paper entitled "The Other Half of the Brain," its short summary claiming evidence that hitherto overlooked *glial cells* in the brain may be nearly as critical to thinking and learning as neurons are. Considering all the theorizing that has been going on in cognitive science in the last half century, one could be fairly safe in saying that missing the importance of half the brain may lead to some significant reconsideration. The same thing has been pointed out in studies of mystical experience. For example, authority on mysticism Richard Jones says:

> A sense of having come into contact with a fundamental, undeniable reality (James's "noetic quality") is usually given in the experience, but these differences [in interpretation of the experience by mystics themselves or by philosophers and theologians] reveal that no complete interpretation of the mystical is dictated by the experience itself. No complete interpretation is a minimal description of what occurs, impervious to error. None is anything other than theory-laden in the stronger sense of being integrated into more elaborate conceptual systems which give meaning to the concepts [Jones, 1993, p. 37].

Mystical experience is, in fact, still open to new interpretations. I gave one myself as recently as the final chapter of my 2001 book, *The Mind Paradigm* (Chandler, 2001).

I confess to the reader that when I started this chapter, I did not know what final conclusions, if any, I would reach. Needless to say, had I not reached a conclusion, you would not be reading this chapter, but I never know the final result of anything I write, be it a paper, a chapter, or a book, because it is always a learning experience for me so that I ask the reader to indulge me, rather than expect knowledge to be handed down from a superior vantage point.* My opinion is that Becker's "Denial of Death" view is wrong, and some reasons for it have already been put on the table. But in this chapter, I will explore the evidence from anthropology and history as to how the human species has actually dealt with and conceptualized life and death in contrast to distorted views of human mentation that are so typical of Freud and his modern reconstructionists. What we will be looking for is any evidence that belief in life after death *was initiated by* the kind of terror of death that Becker describes or, if there is no such evidence, what did initiate a belief in life after death?

The Paleolithic and Early Neolithic Periods

The era in which we can start searching for the earliest evidence both of fear of death and belief in an afterlife is the Paleolithic, represented in the West by the Cro-Magnon humans of southern France and northern Spain.† The most vivid evidence of the concerns of humans living in this era comes from the cave paintings of the Cro-Magnon. However, in my recent review of Cro-Magnon paintings (Chandler 2002a), I found no suggestion of a concern about death or afterlife. On the contrary, the overriding obsession in those paintings is not death but *sexuality*. In Lascaux there is one image of a prone male figure, presumably killed by the bison shown towering over him. Or is it rather a symbolic image in which the male figure is not dead but lying prone with his erect penis pointing at the bison's head? The bison has clearly been established as a Paleolithic symbol of masculinity. That the composition is a symbolic image is further suggested by the presence of an enigmatic bird figure. There is simply no robust corpus of such symbols that would allow assigning the figure any definite meaning.

While the Paleolithic caves contain a profusion of highly accurate eidetic images of animals, there are no comparable renditions of humans. Depictions of male figures are rare. Those that do appear display features more associated

---

*For Chandler's constructive approach to the problem of life after death from the perspective of a mental realist in order to reach what seems to him to be the most plausible answer, see <www.keithchandler.com>.

†While we share the species name Homo sapiens with the Neanderthals, the latter are not our ancestors to any significant degree (except perhaps by misadventure). They were the last group that shared our hominid heritage, but they went down a dead-end road more than 50,000 years ago. The heritage they left in art and artifact, while not negligible, was far inferior both in quality and quantity to that of their "double-wise" successors.

with sexuality rather than death. On the other hand, images of female sexuality, stylized to the point of grotesquerie is one of the most distinguishing characteristics of middle Paleolithic cave paintings as well as free carvings. One such carving from Laussel is of a grossly pregnant female with her left hand over her swollen belly and her right hand holding a cervid (early species of deer) horn, one of a group of male symbols that included the horse, the bear, the rhinoceros, and the stag. Maleness and femaleness appear to have constituted the first archetypal polarity around which middle Paleolithic humans were beginning to organize their conceptual worlds. If they had a concern with death or afterlife in any way comparable to their obsession with sexuality it is certainly not evident in their cave paintings.

Paleoanthropologists have long seen evidence of a belief in an afterlife in the burial customs of Paleolithic humans. In his book, *Becoming Human,* paleoanthropologist Ian Tattersall says,

> The Neanderthals had occasionally practiced burial of dead, but among the Cro-Magnons we see for the first time evidence of regular and elaborate burial, with hints of ritual and belief in an afterlife. The most striking example of Cro-Magnon burial comes from the 28-year-old site of Sungir, in Russia, where two young individuals and a sixty-year-old male (no previous human had ever been known to survive to such an age) were interred with an astonishing material richness. Each of the deceased was dressed in clothing onto which more than three thousand ivory beads had been sewn; and experiments have shown that each bead had taken an hour to make. They also wore carved pendants, bracelets, and shell necklaces. The juveniles, buried head to head, were flanked by two mammoth tusks over two yards long.... Also found at Sungir were numerous bone tools and carved objects, including wheel-like forms and a small ivory horse decorated with a regular pattern of tiny holes. The elaborate interments at Sungir are only the most dramatic example of many; and taken together, these Cro-Magnon burials tell us a great deal about the people who carried them out.
>
> First, in all human societies known to practice it, burial of the dead with grave goods (and the ritual invariably associated with placing such objects in the grave) indicates a belief in an afterlife: the goods are there *because they will be useful to the deceased in the future.* Grave goods need not necessarily be everyday items, although everything found at Sungir might have been, since personal adornment seems to be a basic human urge that was expressed by the Cro-Magnons to its fullest. But whether or not some of the Sungir artifacts were made specifically to be used in burial, what is certain is that the knowledge of inevitable death and spiritual awareness are closely linked, and in Cro-Magnon burial there is abundant inferential evidence for both. It is here that we have *the most ancient incontrovertible evidence for the existence of religious experience* [Tattersall, 1999, pp. 10–11, emphasis added].

Tattersall's last sentence provokes a question that anthropologists have all too often failed to ask. Why is belief in an afterlife evidence, let alone incontrovertible evidence, of religion or religious experience? It patently is *not* such evidence for the simple reason that Cro-Magnons' entire lives were embedded in, and inseparable from their small communities and nothing they did could be designated as religious more than anything else. All activities were performed in accordance with the customs (social habits or mores) that had originated in a time beyond memory or record and continued without change. Death would have been dealt with in the same way without introducing any special religious experience. Religion, as its etymology suggests, emerges at a later stage when the consensual efficacy of the community had been or was in danger of being lost and rites and rituals performed by specialists called priests were required. I submit that that stage was reached during the Late Neolithic era in the milieu of the great agricultural collectives exemplified by the Minoans, the Incans, the Zimbabweans and the Mississippians.

It appears to me that afterlife was virtually a *presupposition* of Paleolithic and Neolithic cultures and that there is little if any evidence of "thanatophobia." We do not, however, have to rely on the past for evidence. Although there are no pre-linguistic Paleolithic societies extant today, evidence is available to us from "aboriginal" cultures, of which Australia is home to the most extensive. It would be absurd to claim that the Australian Aborigines are not "reflective and conceptual" except by defining those terms so narrowly that Becker's argument would become jejune.

The Aborigines are living examples of what I have termed Early Neolithic culture. While they have developed highly sophisticated and intricate methods for dealing with death, the evidence is clear that they are not in "denial" about it and certainly do not hope for individual survival as a hedge against insanity. The most striking thing about death among primitives is that it leaves a gaping rent in the tightly woven fabric of the community. For them death is not an isolated phenomenon as it seems to be for Becker and, tragically, for so many today — it is a communal issue, an accepted phase of life, the meaning of which is woven into the stories about the world into which that life is cast. Those stories — from the "Dreamtime" — undergird the Aborigines' identity as a community. Afterlife is not simply a matter of what happens to the ego of the departed as Becker construes it. For the Aborigines an individual's soul or identity is multidimensional and each dimension of identity has to be dealt with in order of priority. They acknowledge ritually the debt an individual soul owes to the (totemic) gifts of nature that sustained and nurtured it in life. They are also at great pains to reintegrate the soul with its ancestral clan identity, the source of which is spiritual energy patterns portrayed in stellar constellations.

The egoic soul or Trickster is the most difficult to deal with. I think it is fair to say that the Trickster is the part of human identity that is expressing itself in the hope for continuously conscious life after death because its principal purpose in life is to try to forge earthly immortality for itself. In the world of the Aborigine, that urge is seen as a disruptive and destructive force inimical to the benefit of the community as indeed it has been in the spiritual wisdom of societies throughout history. It is also seen as one that remains selfish and even spiteful after death, so much so that the Aborigines, like people of innumerable other cultures, do not fear death so much as *they fear the dead.*

For the Aborigines, the egoic soul's tendency is to return to its home ground and the artifacts that belonged to, or were used by it. The notion that goods buried with the dead "are there because they will be useful to the deceased in the future" is, I believe, too facilely assumed by paleoanthropologists. It seems equally, if not more likely true, that they were buried with the deceased so they could *not* be useful in the future and could not, if left behind, lead the trickster ghost back to the living. In some cases, as in the Sungir grave Tattersall mentions, the deceased were accompanied by especially lavish adornments but, as Tattersall admits, there is no way to know whether those beaded garments were prepared after death or worn during life. By his count, 9000 beads were attached to the garments and each bead was an hour's work, which means 1000 hours or 111.11 9-hour workdays. Unless there were a lot of bead makers or every bead maker worked feverishly, the corpses would have been very ripe by the time of burial. It seems far more likely that the deceased, at least the 60-year-old adult, had worn the garments while living. The fact that the adult was of such an unusually old age means he would probably have been held in great respect as well as awe during life and would be capable of inspiring considerable fear if he returned to angrily haunt the community.

There can be little doubt that among the Aborigines, while the egoic soul is being respectfully sent to its own final destination, every precaution is also being taken that it does not come back. Everything associated with the individual is destroyed, shunned or purified. The site where he died is deserted by his group and marked so it will be left deserted for many years (Lawlor, 1991). So that the dead will no longer have use of them, their bodies are often bound and weighted. The legs may even be broken so that they will not be able to travel. The burial party generally follows a meandering path to and from the gravesite or passes through a screen of smoke so that the deceased's spirit will not be able to follow the mourners (Elkin, 1964). Those who actually perform the interment are brushed with smoking twigs, and the wives who were close to the deceased during his lifetime, are usually separated from the rest of the camp for a prescribed period of time.

Certain traditional food taboos are observed as well as special ones adopted because the food was the deceased's totem or one of his favorites. In all these ways, the deceased, the thought of death and the rent caused by it are expelled from consciousness. When the various taboos have been lifted, widows or widowers are free to resume normal lives and society regains its equilibrium. According to Elkin, in this way the society "bequeaths to the past the associations of death, and faces the future with renewed hope and courage" (Elkin, 1964, p. 318).

The Late Neolithic Period

Paleoanthropologists have traditionally divided human prehistory (the time before civilization) into ages defined mostly by their distinctive styles of tools, especially weapons. However, in my view, the human mind did not change every time a new level of tool making or a new material was introduced. For my purposes, I use the term "Early Neolithic" to refer to the type of cultures that emerged between the latest of the Paleolithic caves, Chaffaud, around 10,000 BCE and the great agricultural collectives of the Middle East. Of course, in other parts of the world Early Neolithic culture appeared at different times and some of its exemplars, like the Australian Aborigines, are still with us today. I will use the term "Late Neolithic" to refer to the hierarchical but not exploitative cultures of the agricultural collectives, from about 5000–3500 BCE in the Middle East.

The Late Neolithic mind was among the most creative in human history. V. Gordon Childe credits the latter period, from about 5000–3500 BCE (in the Middle East), with all but two of the major inventions that made civilization possible:

> artificial irrigation using canals and ditches; the plow; the harnessing of animal motive-power; the sailboat; wheeled vehicles; orchard-husbandry; fermentation; the production and use of copper; bricks; the arch; glazing; the seal; and — in the earliest stages of the revolution [the urban revolution which initiated civilization] — a solar calendar, writing, numeral notation, and bronze [Childe, 1952, p. 180].

Childe credits civilization itself with only two noteworthy innovations down to 700 BCE: decimal notation and aqueducts for supplying water to cities. The introduction of the last four inventions, including writing, incidentally, are really on a cusp between pre-civilization and civilization, my own view being that fully syntactic and semantic writing marks the beginning of civilization just as comparable oral language marks the beginning of the Neolithic era.

As with the Early Neolithic, Late Neolithic cultures appeared elsewhere in the world besides the Near East at different times although probably none much earlier than 5000 BCE. On the other hand, unlike Early Neolithic cultures, no Late Neolithic cultures survive today because, as pointed out by Diamond (1960), civilizations first arose by the transformation and obliteration of typically primitive institutions. That observation is true of *all* Late Neolithic cultures as well as *many* Early Neolithic cultures. Many of the latter survived but became isolated and marginalized as did our own American Indian tribes.

Civilization

The Pre-Christian Era

Civilization began in the West, in what are now Iraq, Syria and Egypt, around 3500 BCE. The other three great streams of civilization emerged in sequence from west to east, separated by intervals of roughly a thousand years: ca. 2500 BCE in India, 1500 BCE in China, and 500 BCE across the Pacific Ocean in Mesoamerica — present day Central America and Mexico. The reason that it required "the transformation and obliteration of typically primitive institutions" was that civilization was a radical new form of socioeconomic organization based not on consensus, as were the agricultural collectives or their Early Neolithic predecessors, but on usurpation of power and monopolization of wealth and status by a small elite. So central was this mental saltation that I was able to provide the first comprehensive and organic definition of civilization in *Beyond Civilization*:

> Civilization is a type of social organization in which a relatively small power elite, in pursuit of its own goals, exercises authority over and preempts the production of a large, powerless majority through the monopolization of information, the sanctification of myth, the centralization of key institutions, and the utilization of regimented armed force [Chandler, 2002b, p.13].

The form of socioeconomic organization we call "civilization" was essentially a despotic oligarchy that not only dispossessed the masses of their share of the community's wealth and property but also of every skill and spiritual resource that had previously been parts of a common heritage. As I wrote in *Beyond Civilization*:

> In the end, the gods and their earthly surrogates owned everything, not only natural resources and their products but even skills and control over skills training. In a remarkable passage from the Sumerian civilization of 2000 BCE, the goddess Inanna, Queen of Heaven and Earth, lists the gifts her father, Enki, gave her. Besides those which we might expect a god to give his daughter — the high priesthood, godship, the noble, enduring crown, the throne of kingship, etc.— we also find he has given her the crafts of the woodworker, the copper worker, the scribe, the smith, the leather maker, the fuller, the builder and the reed worker.... In other words, every important skill came from and remained the property of the gods and hence of the rulers [Chandler, 2002b, p. 14].

The reason I am quoting this passage instead of simply repeating it in this context is that when I first wrote it in the late 1970s (the first edition was published in 1992), I overlooked something crucial, namely, that prior to civilization the existence of an afterlife had been *presupposed* by all humans as part of their common heritage. Civilization, however, not only dispossessed the masses of their material and temporal resources but of their spiritual ones as well. The priesthood of Sumerian Civilization no longer represented the interests of the whole society, as had the priests and priestesses of the Late Neolithic era. Instead, the priesthood supported the rulers' power even over the afterlife. The priests of civilized societies assured two things: (i) life after death for the rulers and their indispensable functionaries, the priests and scribes, and (ii) their own authority to set criteria for admittance to the afterlife by the underclasses. In other words, the priests had seized control of the road to life after death and could set up tollgates to block those they considered unworthy. *For the first time in human evolution the afterlife became a privilege to be earned instead of a phase in a natural life transition.*

The Egyptian god-kings and their priests were the first to define the afterlife as immortality. This was reflected in their building construction. Not only the pyramids but also later temples to the gods and divine rulers where literally intended to last forever. An inscription on a temple to Amon erected by Amenhotep III at Thebes reads:

> Behold, the heart of his majesty was satisfied with making a very great monument; never has happened the like since the beginning. He made it as his monument for his father, [the god] Amon, lord of Thebes, making for him an august temple on the west of Thebes, an eternal, everlasting fortress of white sandstone, wrought with gold throughout; its floor is adorned with silver, all its portals with electrum...; it is made very wide and large, and established forever [Casson, 1978, p. 120].

As the temple was "established forever," so was the god-king's afterlife. In an ancient text, a deceased king asks of the creator-god, "O Atum, what is my duration of life?" The deity replies, "Thou art destined for millions of millions of years, a lifetime of millions" (Casson, 1978, p. 17). And an inscription from the third millennium BCE "Papyrus of Ani" (the so-called Egyptian Book of the Dead) records joyfully, "Boundless eternity hath been granted to me, and, behold, I am the heir of eternity; to me hath been given everlastingness" (Budge, 1967, p. 310). The standards for the Egyptian elite to enter the afterlife were not very rigorous. The deceased appeared before the god Osiris who watched while Anubis weighed his/her heart (soul symbol) against a feather (purity symbol) on a scale. I think it would be fair to say that, except for a rogue pharaoh like Akhenaton, who defied and persecuted the priests of Amon, Osiris would never have found a member of the elite unworthy. It is notable as well that there is nothing horrific about Egyptian judgment scenes comparable, for example, to that of Michelangelo's "Last Judgment" in the Sistine Chapel. The inescapable impression one gets from the Egyptian paintings is that of an orderly, gentle and even reassuring process.

The tombs of the elite were furnished with valuable and useful items, as were the graves of Paleolithic humans thousands of years earlier, except that those furnishing were now often lavish beyond imagination as the tomb of the boy-king Tutankhamun revealed. The proliferation of lesser tombs that have been found on the plateau of Gizeh and elsewhere testify to that. The vast populace that had no way of earning a "blessed" afterlife was relegated to a kind of underworld that was dimly acknowledged throughout the Middle East by names such as Hades or Sheol where they lived as powerless "shades." Budge says:

> Of the condition of those who failed to secure a life of beatitude with the gods in Sekhet Aaru of the Tuat* the pyramid texts say nothing, and it seems as if the doctrine of punishment of the judgment which took place after death is a development characteristic of a later period [Budge, 1967, p. cvi].

The biblical book of Exodus relates the hallmark event in the history of the Hebrews. Although the Hebrews took many Egyptian ideas with them in the Exodus, Egypt's obsession with everlasting life was not among them. According to the Jewish Virtual Library:

> In Judaism, death is not a tragedy, even when it occurs early in life or through unfortunate circumstances. Death is a natural process. Our deaths, like our lives, have meaning and are all part of G-d's plan. In addition, we have a firm belief in an afterlife, a world to come, where those who have lived a worthy life will be rewarded.[†]

It should be noted that this accepting attitude toward death is not universal among Jews. Hasidic Jew Eli Wiesel, a survivor of the Nazi Holocaust or Hurban (whirlwind) has called death the ultimate negation. For Judaism, moderate or strict, death is faced squarely without invoking immortality. "A world to come, where those who have lived a worthy life will be rewarded" is far from eternal or everlasting life. One must note that if Becker is right in *Denial of Death*, it follows that nothing could satisfy the Luciferian ego except the immortality of God himself.

Tuat: the Underworld; Sekhet-Aaru, a privileged portion of the Tuat ruled by Osiris.

†<http://www.us-israel.org/jsource/Judaism/death.html>. *Jewish writers generally write "G-d" ("God" without the "o") in keeping with the tradition that the name of the deity not be spoken and only be written without vowels. No one really knows what the original vowels in the tetragammaton, YHVH or YHWH, spoken to Moses were anyway. Guesses as to its pronunciation include "Yahveh," "Yahweh" and "Jehovah."*

From this survey of views about the afterlife in chronological sequence, it is apparent that up to the most recent times in the Western world, life after death was never due to a need to deny death. Life and death were apperceived as parts of one continuous being-in-the-world. As cultures changed from Paleolithic to Early Neolithic to Late Neolithic, what that mode of being entailed was reinterpreted and elaborated upon. It was at the advent of civilization that the unity of life/death was sundered, and not only an afterlife, but also an *everlasting life* was claimed as the proprietary right of the elite and the right of whomsoever the elite selected to grant it. That claim was not only continued in Christendom but a sinister innovation was added.

The Christian Era

At the time of the apostle Paul's conversion, the afterlife dimension of human existence in the Roman Empire had found no satisfactory expression in the state religion. The idea of immortality was abroad in Mithraism and revivals of many of the ancient chthonic cults. But Mithra was a mythical being whose following was most widespread among the military and the Magna Mater (Great Mother) in her many guises was a deity whose native milieu was the preliterate, precivilized agricultural collectives that had long since ceased to exist. So Paul's cult of the risen Christ, a real human whose resurrection was allegedly well witnessed (although not by Paul) with its promise of *everlasting* life (cf. John 3:16) reinvigorated afterlife belief so powerfully in the Empire that within three centuries it became the official cult of the state. It was, however, a "trade off." Christianity supported the empire but the empire *romanized* Christianity, so, as in Egypt, access to immortality was again under the proprietary control of the elite. The Bishop of Rome became "the vicar of Christ," i.e., the direct representative of the risen God and took over the title previously reserved for the Emperor, *pontifex maximus,* the supreme "bridge builder" (between God and man) or highest priest. This new pontiff, the Pope, became both a temporal and spiritual ruler, surrounded by a College of Cardinals who were designated "princes of the church." And, finally, within a couple of centuries after Constantine, the Roman Church hierarchy acquired a new tool of suppressing dissent that even the Egyptian god-kings never dreamed of—*Hell.*

The doctrine of eternal torment in the afterlife is alien to Judaism and it was equally alien to the New Testament. Above all, it was completely contrary to the spirit of Jesus' own teaching. Of the three words translated in the New Testament as "hell"—*Hades* (11 occurrences), *Tartarus* (2 occurrences), and *Gehenna* (12 occurrences), none had any such connotation. There they are used mostly as terms of hyperbolic condemnation without specific content. (Cf.

Thayer 1855, an exceptional analysis even if written nearly 150 years ago.) In fact, the Christian doctrine of everlasting torment in Hell was not fully developed before the fifth century AD. Prior to that the "Church fathers," including St. Augustine, had been fighting about it like the lion and the unicorn all around nascent Christendom. The Nicene Creed, dating from 325 CE, the only one accepted today by all branches of the "Holy Catholic Church," does not mention it. However the "Athanasian" creed, probably from the early fifth century incorporates it explicitly at the very end, notably, however not mentioning faith in Jesus Christ but merely "good deeds" as the "get out of jail free" card: "And they that have done good shall go into life everlasting, and they that have done evil into everlasting fire. This is the Catholic Faith, which except a man believe faithfully and firmly, he cannot be saved. Amen" ("The Athanasian Creed, *Catholic Encyclopedia On-line*).*

The idea of the eternal torment of Hell-fire haunted "the dark ages" and several centuries of grisly imaginations provided Dante the basis for his *Inferno*. Dante, of course, had the privilege of choosing those who should occupy each of those tiers and what torments to subject them to. He even included a pope—Celestine V, who abdicated the papacy on December 13, 1294 after only five months and eight days in "the chair of St. Peter." Dante did not approve of a papal abdication.

The threat of interminable suffering in the afterlife as punishment for the sins of one short life is, in my view, the fiendish construction of sick minds. What made this monstrous fantasy possible, especially in the context of a religion that proclaims "God is love" was the radical departure of Paul from the perennial human intuition characteristic of Judaism that death is a natural occurrence transiting to some sort of afterlife. Paul interpreted the Genesis story of the first human's "original sin" to mean that death, rather than being a normal life phase, was a punishment for sin. Except for Adam's sin, humans, according to Paul, would not die. Given that premise, Paul's message is clear: "But in fact Christ has been raised from the dead, the first fruits of those who have fallen asleep. For as by a man came death, by a man has come also the resurrection of the dead. For as in Adam all die, so also in Christ shall all be made alive" (I Corinthians 15: 20–22 [RSV, 1952, p. 1]).

It appears that for Paul, those who refused to accept Jesus as Savior would simply die and stay dead or, if resurrected, be tossed back into the shadow world like inedible fish. However, for Romanized Christianity, anxious to maintain and extend its power, simply staying "asleep" or being barred from

---

According to the Columbia Encyclopedia *(6th ed.) The Athanasian Creed "is no longer believed to have been written by Athanasius, but rather by an unknown Western author of the 6th cent"— see <www.newadvent.org/cathen/02033b.htm> (Eds.).*

immortal bliss was not enough to dissuade its defiers (sinners, heretics, apostates, infidels, etc.), so it became necessary to counterbalance endless beatitude in Heaven with endless damnation in Hell. Interestingly, Islam, which originated about the same time as Christianity perfected Hell, did not follow the Judaic tradition of the Abrahamic religions but agreed with the Christian tradition about final judgment and Hell. As it is written in the Koran:

> O man! what has seduced thee concerning thy generous Lord, who created thee, and fashioned thee, and gave thee symmetry, and in what form He pleased composed thee?
> Nay, but ye call the judgment a lie! but over you are guardians set,—noble, writing down! they know what ye do.
> Verily, the righteous are in pleasure, and, verily, the wicked are in hell; they shall broil therein upon the judgment day; nor shall they be absent therefrom! [Koran, 1949, Surah LXXXII].

The Eastern View

Let us conclude this anthropological expedition into humanity's variations on the theme of life after death with a reminder that the fact that people have believed in an afterlife "of some sort" for 50,000 years does not mean that they have always wanted or hoped for it. A passage from the Tibetan Bardo Tödol warns:

> Those who are voraciously inclined toward this [i.e., temporal existence], or those who do not at heart fear it — O dreadful! O dreadful! Alas!— and those who have not received a guru's teachings, will fall down into the precipitous depths of the Sangsara in this manner and suffer interminably and unbearably [Evans-Wentz, 1976, p. 180].

This passage should not be confused with the Christian-Islamic conception of Hell. For Buddhism and Hinduism, sangsara (or samsara) is the temporal world of change, which includes but is not limited to our normal waking world. The Bardo Tödol is merely speaking about being reborn in further earthly lives, the concept that 18% of adult Americans now seem to find attractive. Evans-Wentz explains:

> Normally, existence in the Bardo ever tends to lead the deceased back to birth; and this is due to karmic propensities, which are the opposition, the forces opposing the Enlightenment of Buddhahood. Hence the deceased must oppose this innate tendency with every help available [Evans-Wentz, 1976, p. 176, n2].

I mention this example for three reasons. First, it is a reminder that life after death is by no means universally desirable.

Second, it highlights the fact that as long as we lived in societies structured by the civilized mindsets, our conceptualizations of life after death were as strongly determined by those mindsets as our behaviors during life or our worldviews. The Western world was always enabled as well as constrained in its attitudes by the presupposition that ultimate reality is that which is most perfectly ordered (structured, knowable, rational, quantifiable). The Indic world, on the other hand, presupposed just the opposite, that ultimate reality is unqualifiedly non-ordered (formless, ineffable, suprarational, undiscriminable). For the Hindu thinker one could only say that it is *neti, neti,* "not this, not that." For the Buddhist it was *sunnya,* void. Chinese and Mesoamerican civilizations had their own distinctive presuppositions about reality as well, based on their mindsets.

Third, one should never overlook the part religious doctrines played in maintaining the rule of the power elite. As I mentioned earlier, the doctrine of "Hell" was a powerful means of social control in Christendom as well as Islam but karma played a similar role in Indic society, which was organized on transcendent principles, that is, in ladder-like stages. Each person's relative position on the ladder leading to ultimate release was his *caste* and that depended on his accumulated beneficial karma. A person was born into one of the castes and with that caste went a well-defined status and equally well-defined obligations and proscriptions. One never went upward in the caste system in the present life, although there were countless ways, through his own dereliction of duty, in which a person might sink to a lower caste or even find himself with no caste at all. The position into which one was born depended on his karma in past lives and his position in the next life would depend on his adherence to dharma (religious law or duty) in this life.

There was no question about anyone making a judgment as to your past karma. The cosmic system took care of that. You automatically were born into the caste position you deserved. But if your present status depended on your past merit or lack of it, you were also a passive victim of what Manu stated to be the real reason for the caste system: "the protection of the universe" (Manu, 1969, p. 24). What he meant by that, in simplest terms, is that the Indic social system ("the universe" to a Hindu) with its complement of priests, warriors, merchants and servants needed to be perpetuated. The caste system, supported by the doctrine of karma, assured there would always be a supply — especially of servants. It is noteworthy that Buddhism eventually lost favor in India and emigrated to other lands because the Buddha taught that escape from karma was possible in *this life*, that the caste system was irrelevant, and that the fundamental social structure should be the *samgha,* the community of seekers for enlightenment. His teachings, therefore, were seen as a serious threat to the traditional power structure of Hindu society.

The Afterlife Question Re-Considered

If it is our intention to consider the issue of life after death anew, then we must first understand that we are no longer bound by the mental structure of civilization. We are beginning postcivilization *now* and that means our minds have the capability of being *unset,* postcivilized minds. I explained what this means in *Beyond Civilization*:

> In terms of our earlier analogy of the mindset as a cognitive lodestone, the contemporary revolt is based on ignoring, abandoning or rejecting the single direction of the Occidental Mindset. That opens up the possibility of kinds of behavior and experience that were traditionally off limits to the Occidental Mindset but within the familiar ambit of other mindsets. But we should not make the mistake that those involved in the revolt are adopting one of the other mindsets. On the contrary, what is happening is that their minds have become unset, free of any mindset. Freedom from any mindset implies that the whole circumference of possible experience is open. The mind can go in any direction [Chandler, 2002b, p. 402].

Let us be clear about the fact that we have no choice about whether to be postcivilized or not. We simply can no longer count on our societies or our religions to provide us with clear, indubitable answers. *Everything is dubitable!* Our choice is what stance we take toward that fact. There could hardly be any stronger proof of our unset minds than a telephone survey conducted by the Barna Research Group of Ventura, California (2001–2003) to learn contemporary Americans' attitudes about life after death. Even with all the centuries of effort the churches have put into getting Christians to believe in the rewards of Heaven and the punishment of Hell, Barna finds that today:

> Most Americans do not expect to experience Hell first-hand: just one-half of 1% expect to go to Hell upon their death. Nearly two-thirds of Americans (64%) believe they will go to Heaven. One in 20 adults (5%) claim they will come back as another life form, while the same proportion (5%) contend they will simply cease to exist. Even though most Americans believe in life after death and the existence of the soul, not everyone is clear about their own ultimate destination. One in every four adults (24%) admitted that they have "no idea" what will happen after they die. Those who felt their eternal future is undefined were most likely to be Hispanics, singles, men, atheists and agnostics, residents of the West, and 18- and 19-year-olds (i.e., young adults who also happen to be the first members of the Mosaic generation to enter adulthood). Among those who expect to go to Heaven, there were differences in how they anticipate such an end would be attained. Nearly half of those who say they are Heaven bound (43%) believe they will go to Heaven because they have "confessed their sins and accepted Jesus Christ as their savior." Others felt they will get to Heaven because "they have tried to obey the 10 Commandments" (15%) or because "they are basically a good person" (15%). Another

6% believed their entrance to Heaven would be based upon the fact that "God loves all people and will not let them perish" [Barna Research Group on line, 2003].

Furthermore:

> George Barna, the president of the company that conducted the research, pointed out that "Americans' willingness to embrace beliefs that are logically contradictory and their preference for blending different faith views together create unorthodox religious viewpoints." For instance, he noted that among born again Christians — who believe that they will experience eternal existence in Heaven solely because they have confessed their sins to God and are depending upon Jesus Christ to spare them from eternal punishment or rejection —10% believe that people are reincarnated after death, 29% claim it is possible to communicate with the dead, and 50% contend that a person can earn salvation based upon good works [op. cit.].

The Barna survey indicates that traditional religious certainty about life after death is breaking apart like a ship in a cyclonic sea and those who think about it are grasping at every bit of flotsam they can find to keep afloat. Or are they? One thing the survey does not tell us is how important an existential concern the afterlife issue is for the people surveyed. My guess is *not very.* There are just too many ways to avoid the issue altogether. Few really want to take on the burden of such an enormous and unprecedented mental freedom. It is not facing death but facing the awesome responsibility of making choices in a world with no clear answers or values that is terrifying to so many people. The fear incites two major responses in those not ready to accept it: *reaction* and *escapism.*

The horrendous results of reaction are seen everyday in the actions of militant Islamic "jihadist" organizations arising in country after country but, lest we overlook the log in our own eye, they are also evident in the political machinations of Christian fundamentalists such as Pat Robertson, Jerry Falwell and, quite recently, Justice Roy Moore.*

In economically privileged countries like the USA, by far the preferred response to the critical challenge posed by freedom from mindsets is escapism. In *Beyond Civilization* I mentioned drugs, religion, television, sports, and physical fitness as the principal modes of escape from mental freedom. At that time, however, I lived in Jamaica where I had a Macintosh computer but no access to the Internet or the World Wide Web. I would not change those five modes were I writing that book today; they are vastly more potent than I ever dreamed in my island reclusiveness. However, I would have to add "surfing the Internet" not only as a sixth mode of escapism but as a kind of hypermode that connects them all.

*Cf. *The Roy Moore case: American law vs. biblical law* (see <www.keithchandler.com>).

It may seem surprising that I mentioned physical fitness as a mechanism of escape. The renewed affirmation of the body is indeed an important and healthy component of the postcivilized mind. But I was pointing to a second and more somber reason for our current interest in physical discipline. That is that our liberated generation, to which the civilized religious traditions no longer provide a credible conception of the afterlife, has to face death more nakedly than people at any other time in the history of the world. Djuna Barnes' (1937/1961) cynical words in *Nightwood*, "We are but skin about a wind, with muscles clenched against mortality " (p. 83), reflects a vacuous view of life that underlies much of our modern fitness craze. We tan the skin, massage it, tighten it with surgery or botulinus, and diet the "cellulite" out from under it. We save the wind by giving up smoking and practicing aerobics. We restore the strength and resilience of the muscles by calisthenics, yoga and t'ai chi.

Yet, even with all that strenuous effort we often remain terribly afraid — afraid of the microscopic virus, afraid of the trace of toxic chemical, afraid of the invisible radiation which can bring all our strident attempts to preserve youth and deny death to naught, afraid of cancer, afraid of AIDS. Precisely because our lives are completely defined in the "materialistic" terms of authors like Ernest Becker and Norman O. Brown, death has become something to fear and we go to extraordinary lengths to subdue premonitions of it. In her excellent book, *Women Coming of Age*, Jane Fonda tells us:

> The passing of my father placed all of this [thoughts about middle age] into a far deeper context. While living, our parents are the barriers between us and mortality. When they pass on, we step up to the head of the line. Being with my father during the months of his decline, shattered any childhood illusion of living on forever. I realized then, sitting at his bedside those many days, that it was not so much the idea of death itself which frightened me as it was being faced with the "what ifs" and the "if onlys" when there's no time left, arriving at the end of the third act and discovering too late it hasn't been a rehearsal [Fonda, 1984, p. 14].

To suppress those "what ifs" and "if onlys," Fonda proposes we get ourselves in shape to get as much out of life as we can while we can. And, although she doesn't say it, the implication is clear that the more we are concentrating on how well our body feels and looks, the less we will be dwelling on death. In the wake of twentieth-century scientism's lethal assault on the idea that there is more to humanness than our life spans can contain, physical fitness with its emphasis on remaining young, vigorous and sexy, will undoubtedly continue to provide an escape from thinking about the inevitability of death. Yet, what is happening among that group which is at the very peak of youth, vigor and concupiscence? In the United States:

— Every hour and forty-five minutes another young person commits suicide.
— Suicide is the second leading cause of death among college students and the third leading cause of death among youth overall (ages 15–24).
— Teen/youth suicide rates have tripled since 1970.
— Evidence indicates that for every suicide, there are 50 to 100 attempts at suicide.*

The obvious conclusion is that an alarming number of Americans at the very height of their vivacity not only have no fear of dying but actually seem to have more fear of living and deliberately choose death over life — *if and when all the available modes of escapism no longer work.* The essential question that is raised by all these concerns about an afterlife, when the churches, mosques and synagogues no longer provide trustworthy guidance, is whether such concerns are "natural" to humankind as Becker suggests, or whether they are cultural artifacts of the age in which we live. *The evidence from the history of our species indicates they are the latter.*

Conclusion

We have now seen as full a review of how our ancestors confronted with death and afterlife as space will allow but we are still only on the border of the undiscover'd country. Even if we are not afraid to cross the line we are not sure we would be able to communicate any of our findings back to our readers, so we will have to content ourselves with looking through the fence and catching what glimpses we can.

As I delved into the question of "what comes next," I kept in mind the fact that I was writing as a postcivilized human and writing to other postcivilized humans. I started this chapter with a quotation from Shakespeare, so it is fitting to end it with another. Shakespeare wrote: "What is past is prologue," but what is past is also *resource.* It is important to bear in mind that the past is not something behind us. Both personally and historically it is always *with us,* producing both pernicious and salutary influences on our lives. It is only as a living structure in the universal holopresent that it exists at all and it has only those effects that it is allowed to have. It can be an indispensable trove of our species' wisdom if we are prepared to look at it, not impassively but appreciatively, scrub off the encrustations deposited on it by previous minds, and restore its insights to as useful a condition as possible.

*Source: <http://www.1-teenage-suicide.com/>.

References

Anonymous translators (1952). *The Holy Bible (Revised Standard Version)*. NY: Thomas Nelson & Sons.

Barna Research Group (2003). Americans describe their views about life after death. *Barna research on line*. December, 2004, from <http://www.barna.org/cgi-bin/PagePressRelease.asp?PressReleaseID=150&Reference=A>

Barnes, D. (1937/1961). *Nightwood*. NY: New Directions.

Becker, E. (1973). *The Denial of Death*. New York: The Free Press.

Budge, E. A. (1967). *The Egyptian book of the dead (The Papyrus of Ani)* (trans. E. A. Wallis Budge). NY: Dover.

Casson, L. (1978). *Ancient Egypt*. Alexandria, VA: Time-Life.

Chandler, K. (2001). *The mind paradigm: A central model of mental and physical reality*. San Jose, CA: Author's Choice.

Chandler, K. (2002a). *The android myth: How humans think and why computers can't*. San Jose, CA: Author's Choice.

Chandler, K. (2002b). *Beyond civilization—the world's four great streams of civilization: Their achievements, their differences and their future*. San Jose, CA: Author's Choice.

Childe, G. (1952). *Man makes himself*. NY: Mentor Book, The New American Library of World Literature.

Diamond, S. (Ed.) (1960). *Primitive views of the world*. NY: Columbia University Press.

Elkin, A. P. (1964). *The Australian aborigines*. Garden City, NY: Doubleday.

Evans-Wentz, W. Y. (1976). *The Tibetan book of the dead* (trans. W. Y. Evans-Wentz). London: Oxford University Press.

Fonda, J. (1984). *Women coming of age*. New York: Simon & Schuster

Jones R. H. (1993). *Mysticism examined: Philosophical inquiries into mysticism*. NY: State University of New York Press.

Knight, K. (2003). *Catholic encyclopedia*. Retrieved June 4, 2005, from <http://www.newadvent.org/cathen/07687a.htm>

Lawlor, R. (1991). *Voices of the first day: Awakening in the aboriginal dreamtime*. Rochester, VT: Inner Traditions.

Manu (1969). *The Laws of Manu* (Georg Buhler, trans.). NY: Dover.

Palmer, E. H. (1949). *The Holy Koran* (trans. E. H. Palmer). London: Oxford University Press.

Tattersall, I. (1999). *Becoming human: Evolution and human uniqueness*. NY: Harcourt Brace & Co.

Thayer, T. B. (1855). The biblical doctrine of hell. In *The origin and history of the doctrine of endless punishment*. Retrieved December, 2005, from <http://www.auburn.edu/~allenkc/tbhell.html>

Wiesel, E., & de Saint-Cheron, P. (1990). *Evil and exile* (trans. Jon Rothschild). Notre Dame: University of Notre Dame Press.

2. Mystical Experience and the Afterlife

CHRISTOPHER M. MOREMAN

Dr. Christopher Moreman reviews survival-related phenomena as they occur throughout history in the various religions and cultures. Though a body of evidence of an afterlife supposedly exists, it is a taboo area amongst the major religions. Nevertheless, closely related to these religions are mystical experiences from which emerges the mystical school of thought, or mysticism. Mystical experiences tend to be religious or spiritual in nature. Dr. Moreman argues the case that mysticism provides a key to understanding that all minds are somehow united, even in death. Through mysticism, the Universal Mind hypothesis is a way of treading a path between the afterlife hypothesis and the alternative viewpoint that phenomena that suggest survival (e.g., so-called discarnate entities) are really manifestations of paranormal information transferred between the living.—Editors

The great religions of the world have confronted the issue of death throughout recorded history. It is often pointed out that stone-aged graves containing specially arranged bodies buried with whatever provisions might aid a person on a long journey indicate pre-historic notions of a continued existence after death. While such ideas are intriguing, they remain speculation. On the other hand, recorded history reveals to us that the mystery and fear of death were questions as important for the ancients around the world as they are for us today. Given the centuries that have been available to humans to ponder their own mortality and the possibilities of some continued existence, it may not be surprising for me to admit that what I propose in this chapter is an age-old theory. Mysticism has shared an uneasy partnership with religion since the beginnings of the latter, and can be supposed to have predated even the establishment of the earliest religions. Below, it will be my attempt to demonstrate how this antediluvian wisdom can be applied to a modern understanding of what happens to us all after death, while also accounting successfully for the evidence for survival stemming from the past hundred-plus years of psychical research.

Huston Smith, who has argued ceaselessly for co-operation between science and religion, quotes Oliver Wendell Holmes in his defence: "Science gives us major answers to minor questions, while religion gives us minor answers to major questions" (Smith, 2001, p. 200). Still, answers are answers, however incomplete, and the small answers offered by religion have remained the only answers to such big questions as that of death and what lies beyond. For its part, science's response to the question of human survival of death has been roundly negative, in effect a non-answer. Every major religion has dealt, to some extent, with the problem of death. Most have posited some kind of a continued existence beyond this life. The Judaeo-Christian-Islamic position has evolved to offer now some kind of personal resurrection in the distant (or perhaps not so distant, according to some) future, guaranteeing the eternal survival of the faithful individual. Eastern religions, like Hinduism and Buddhism, also posit the continuation of individuality in successive lifetimes through reincarnation, eventually reaching a state of blissful dissolution of the individual as we know it. Even Confucius, who refused to discuss the possibility of an afterlife until all the questions of this life had been answered, urged his followers to venerate the ancestor spirits. While individual differences exist between traditions in terms of the nature of the afterlife, they at least all agree that some form of personal survival is possible if not guaranteed.

Similarities do exist, however, in the experiences relating to death of people across these traditions, and the phenomenological similarities cross the boundaries of history and culture. I am speaking, of course, of those experiences most often seen as proof for the continued survival of humans beyond death: apparitions, near-death and out-of-the-body experiences, mediumistic communications, and past-life memories. Each of these experiences can be found commonly across cultures regardless of religious doctrines. Though past-life memories do tend to appear much more frequently in communities that already accept the possibility of reincarnation, they can also be found across cultures.

The writings of the Ancient Greeks refer constantly to the ability of humans to have contact with the spirit world, whether seeing ghosts awake and in dreams or communicating through mediums (for example, see Dodds, 1959; Felton, 1999). The Old Testament book of Samuel (Chapter 28) recounts the story of a purported witch who can summon up spirits of the dead. Along with the Biblical admonitions against communicating with the dead, the Koran also warns against such otherworldly contact. In fact, the Koran has an entire chapter devoted to discussion of the *jinn*, ethereal creatures who can maliciously masquerade as spirits of the dead (Koran 72; see also Ibn Taymeeyah, 1989). The scriptures of Hinduism and Buddhism are replete with ghostly tales and it is common for many Hindus and Buddhists to incorporate shamanistic rituals involving communication with the dead and astral travel to a spiritual realm into their own religious practice (Crooke, 1896/1968; Freed & Freed, 1993; Parry, 1994; Thurman, 1994). Further, in the Far East, contact with the ancestors has been a part of society for millennia (Cheu, 1988; Emmons, 1982; Jordan, 1972; Paper, 1995; Willoughby-Meade, 1928). Apparitions and mediums are common experiences for humans and have been throughout time.

Out-of-the-body experiences have been found to be surprisingly common human experiences, as well. Combined with normal dreaming, the experience of being dissociated from one's body certainly compels the experient to a belief in some kind of a spirit-body. Lucid dreams would only further encourage the association. OBEs are quite common across cultures, and accounts of them show up in the writings of practically every group of people in history. In a religious context, the writings of mystics regularly include such experiences of separation from the body.

The near-death experience is a special area of concern for several reasons, including both the potential for a descriptive experience of the afterlife as well as the fact that it has received a great deal of attention from scientists who normally operate outside the bounds of psychical research. For the purposes of evidential merit, NDEs can be distilled down to a couple of important features. In fact, the descriptive elements of NDEs have been found to be almost entirely culturally determined, and thus of little value in determining the nature of a possible afterlife (Kellehear, 1996; Pasricha & Stevenson, 1986; Zaleski, 1988). Apart from the culturally induced aspects, we are left with two key components: the OBE, and the emotional impact of the experience.* As noted above, the OBE is commonly reported in mystical texts. Interestingly, however, there is often an emotional component to the NDEs that has a life-changing effect on those who have them, with results similar to those reported by mystics or religious converts. Several writers have examined in detail the relationship between near-death experiences and other mystical experiences (for example, see Cressy, 1994; Fox, 2003). This relationship will be discussed again below.

Normally, in discussing the variety of evidence for the survival of bodily

---

*Grosso (1982) points out three problematic areas in NDE research, adding the universality of the experiences to the list, but a review of the texts mentioned above (i.e., Koran 72; Taymeeyah, 1989) will reveal that the universality of NDEs has often been over-stated.

death, there are two sides put forth — three if you include those who simply prefer to ignore the evidence altogether. The weight of evidence certainly tends to indicate that there is something strange going on, to say the least. To shrug the evidence aside smacks of dogmatism. In fact, it is not only the materialistic skeptics who are guilty of this ignorance, but mainstream religious institutions as well. Ancient prohibitions against communicating with the dead have seen all of the Abrahamic religions deny its possibility. Christians blame demons for appearing as the dead, Muslims blame the *jinn*, and Jews generally simply deny the phenomena in question when they don't agree with a demonic interpretation. Hindus and Buddhists, for their part, advise against necromancy as a distraction from ultimate enlightenment; the masses who incorporate these rituals into their religious life will simply have to get over their ignorance in future lifetimes. So, while all of these great traditions are forced to accept the facts of human experience, they all refuse to accept the common-sense assumptions towards which one tends to be led. Each of the world's religions has its own take on what happens when we die, and human experience has little impact on dogma.

So, the question then becomes one of what exactly the afterlife according to these experiences might be like. We can take the collection of evidence from psychical research and surmise from the various pieces just what kind of an afterlife they suggest. The philosopher H.H. Price (Price, 1953) most famously constructed a theory of the afterlife based upon a careful consideration of the evidence, though he wrote before Stevenson began accumulating his massive data on past-life memories. Price suggests that the afterlife might be a mental realm, akin to the dream state. Certainly, such an idea would have been familiar in ancient times when dreams were actually thought to occur as the soul travelled in another plane of existence. The dream-like qualities of OBEs and apparitions are adequately accounted for in this thesis. Price further argues that this mind-based afterlife frees the mind to access more easily the psychic powers of the mind, thus enabling spirits to have just those extreme powers of paranormal cognition that have been assumed according to the evidence. He further adds a moral element to his theory in positing that minds will exist in self-developed mental realities. For example, if a person was an evil person in life, their mental afterlife will be filled with images that accord with how they lived life, thus creating a kind of personal hell.

Price's theory has some merit, especially in the emphasis on the dream-like quality of the afterlife depicted by such phenomena as apparitions and mediumistic communications, but it relies too heavily on speculation without evidence to back it up. From an analysis of the raw experiences, however, the kind of afterlife we can look forward to is substantially different. OBEs and NDEs certainly lend credence to the idea that the spirit and body are not connected and that the individual can exist apart from the physical form. From the evidence on apparitions and mediums, it would appear that the existence of a spirit in the afterlife is in a shade-like state of half-confused wanderings where the individual has very little ability for new thought, if any at all. Apparitions in haunting cases tend to repeat actions in an almost mindless way, sometimes for decades. Mediumistic communications have been found to contain a good deal of personal information known only to the deceased and some other person who recognizes the significance of the given statements beyond what the medium herself is capable of realizing. On the other hand, these messages tend to be filled with errors as well. Some of these can be explained as error on the part of the medium, or perhaps as some problem with the method of communication itself. The medium Mrs. Holland channelled the purported spirit of Frederic Myers, who described his efforts to communicate from the other side saying, "I appear to be standing behind a sheet of frosted glass which blurs sight and deadens sounds — dictating feebly — to a reluctant and somewhat obtuse secretary" (Johnson, 1909, p. 208). Other cases, however, are inexplicable as the spirit insists on information that is blatantly incorrect. Furthermore, of all the great thinkers, poets, musicians, etc., none has succeeded in creating a masterpiece from beyond the grave (see Brown, 1971; 1974).*

The existence thus depicted is dreary at best, though it does mesh closely with the afterlife conceived of by ancient civilizations from the Greeks to the Jews to the early Chinese. John Hick (1976) made the same observation in his study of death across cultures. Before parting ways through a variety of philosophical and theological deliberations, all of these cultures held a similar view of the afterlife as a dismal, anonymous place. The Greeks called it *Hades,* the Jews *Sheol,* for the Chinese it was *The Yellow Springs,* and still others held similar views. In these early days, people were familiar enough with their own experience to acknowledge the implications of them for the afterlife. I would imagine that just as the countless thinkers of more sophisticated times developed new and improved notions of the afterlife, so too modern philosophers like Price and others are not looking forward to such an existence when they argue for survival after bodily death.

For what it is worth, both the evidence for past-life memories and NDEs offer some indication of a more hopeful existence. Past-life memories suggest that the dreariness of the spirit-world would be only temporary, and the thought of eternally being alive in a body is comforting for some, especially

---

The medium Rosemary Brown produced compositions claiming to come from a group of famous composers, though reviews of these compositions are mixed, and certainly none has achieved any notoriety.

Western materialists.* Many NDEs depict a journey to an afterlife beyond this world that is blissful, beautiful, and full of love and loved ones. Given the cultural differences in these accounts, though, it is unreasonable to draw conclusions other than that these visions represent expectation more than reality. Of course, the possibility that there might be some kind of a life after death is at least more than nothing at all. Plus, such a possibility leaves the door open further that there may yet be another, even better existence lying beyond that spiritual one even if we accept the dreariness of its apparent being.

The alternative usually presented to so-called survivalist theories is the unfortunately named super-psi theory. Stephen Braude (2003) has recently made a very good analysis of both sides of this debate. Though he ends up coming down on the side of survival, his defence of super-psi and his discussion of many of the problems surrounding the entire debate are very fair for the most part. Braude acknowledges that one of his main aims is to rectify the lack of significant defence that has been brought to bear on the super-psi hypothesis. While it is true that the super-psi theory has not received the kind of in-depth treatment that Braude provides, his argument fails the theory from the outset. Braude privileges Western notions of individual survival over Eastern ideas of a collective existence. By allowing this significant hole in his argument, Braude significantly weakens the potential of the super-psi theory, leading him to his pro-survivalist conclusion.

Early in his argument, Braude discusses the meaning of survival beyond bodily death. Here, he briefly mentions Eastern conceptions of the afterlife as a merging of the individual with some Absolute in a kind of World Soul, or *anima mundi*. He quickly shrugs off the conception of the afterlife:

> No doubt that would count as a kind of *life after death*, but it wouldn't be personally interesting, and it's certainly not the *survival of death* that has intrigued humankind for centuries and which many either anticipate or desire. Unlike merging with the infinite, personal postmortem survival would be a condition that *preserves* (rather than obliterates) who we are — or at least something we consider essential to who we are (many say it's our mind or soul) [Braude, 2003, p. 1].

This is not the first time such an argument has been made to defend a certain approach to the evidence for an afterlife, but it remains a fallacious one. Michael F. Brown, in a study of New Age spirituality, echoes this line of reasoning in saying, "if the idea of oneness is pushed too far, the self would dissolve into the totality of everything. That might be acceptable to

---

It is worth noting that many of those from cultures that believe in reincarnation describe the prospect of limitless future lives as tiresome and frustrating, looking forward instead to the time when they can cease being reborn and finally "rest."

Buddhists, but it is unappealing to Americans convinced that each of us is unique in the universe" (Brown, 1997, p. 24). The pragmatist, F. C. S. Schiller found the notion of a World Soul to be, "the genuine and logical outcome of every dualistic view of the relations of body and soul," but then goes on to argue against it on the basis of personal satisfaction:

> ... it is pretty clear that the eternity of Universal Soul is not what men bargained for, nor anything that men desire, or perhaps ought to desire; it may or may not be an excellent doctrine philosophically, but it will hardly do duty instead of a personal immortality [Schiller, 1910, pp. 377–378].

Whatever happens after our deaths surely happens without any correspondence to our desires, personal interests, or how appealing the outcome may or may not be. That some people, probably the vast majority of Westerners, feel that the afterlife must involve the continued existence of our individual selves in no way influences the reality of what actually happens after death. This simply illustrates a typically Western bias towards individualism.

Aside from this bias, there appears also a serious misunderstanding of the Eastern view of the afterlife. Braude states that an acceptable form of afterlife would be one that preserves our individual identity, or the essential components thereof, as opposed to an Eastern view that he describes as the obliteration of the self. This is a common error made by Westerners approaching Eastern philosophy. In fact, when looking at the afterlife, there is no talk of destroying the self. It can more accurately be described as a realization of the true essence of the self. In eventually merging each self with a World Soul, the essential component of the self is preserved, it is only that what we presently perceive of as the essential component of a self is actually mistaken.

Ambrose Bierce's tongue-in-cheek spin on Descartes' old maxim is an appropriate syllogism for this idea: "I think that I think, therefore I think that I am" (Bierce, 1911/1958, p. 21). According to these Eastern philosophies, our belief in ourselves as a distinct individual is the result of ignorance on our part, and through a succession of lifetimes, we might become sufficiently enlightened that we recognize this. Once this recognition is attained, then the dissolution of the illusory individual is achieved, and the essential components of the true, inner self are revealed in a union with everything and everyone.

All of this to point out that Braude, and others, erroneously ignore Eastern ideas of a communal afterlife because it goes against closely held Western notions of the importance of the individual. Certainly, the egocentric impulse is strong, particularly in an increasingly materialistic world where the instant gratification of individual desires is commonplace. However strong this impulse, though, it cannot be used as an argument for what will happen to each of us when we die. In fact, this Eastern world-view is actually much better suited to dealing with the evidence from psychical research than is the materialistic Scientism of the West.

Mysticism runs across cultures and religions, though it is often closely associated in peoples' minds with the Eastern traditions. While it can be said that mysticism is often a major part of Eastern religion, especially Buddhism, mystics and mystical experience are important to all established religions. The great monotheisms of Christianity, Judaism, and Islam all contain streams of mystical thought that echo the Eastern philosophies hinted at above. Mystical experience is, actually, as universal a human experience as the phenomena studied by psychical researchers. Such experiences might be described as a range of spiritual experiences that instil religious feelings while transcending all established religions and their doctrines. As a universal human experience, mysticism can be seen as a source for understanding the nature of our reality just as much as can the experiences directly relating to an afterlife discussed throughout this text. As such, the reality defined by mysticism bolsters the case for a kind of super-psi hypothesis that does not fall victim to the criticisms levelled at it by Braude and others. So, we must understand more clearly what is meant by the term mystical experience if we are to understand how best to explain apparitions, mediums, OBE, past-life memories, and what happens to us after we die.

Since the turn of the twentieth century, William James' *Varieties of Religious Experience* has garnered a lasting respect within the study of religion and religious experiences. In it, James sought to demonstrate the common elements of mystical states in order to better understand them. He delineated four characteristics, being the noetic quality, ineffability, transiency and passivity (James, 1902). The noetic quality refers to that aspect of the experience that implies a certainty of some knowledge learned through it, often to the point that the experience is seen as being even more real than every-day life. Confounding the explication of this knowledge is the second characteristic delineated by James, ineffability. Mystical experience defies words, forcing most mystics to resort to poetic and metaphorical language. The final two aspects describe how such experiences come upon individuals unexpectedly and without their control. While these four characteristics certainly appear in all mystical states, the core component of the experiences is what makes them truly unique. This element is best described as a unitive experience between the self and the Absolute, the sense that all things are one and the same within infinitude and eternity. Walter Stace, in his *Mysticism and Philosophy*, identifies the unitive experience as what he calls a "common core" of all mystical experience (Stace, 1961).

If one reads through the theological interpretations which pervade mystics' accounts, one cannot fail to realize the same conclusion.* William James states it thus:

> This overcoming of all the usual barriers between the individual and the Absolute is the great mystic achievement. In mystic states we become one with the Absolute and we become aware of our oneness. This is the everlasting and triumphant mystical tradition hardly altered by differences of clime or creed. In Hinduism, in Neo-Platonism, in Sufism, in Christian mysticism, in Whitmanism, we find the same recurring note, so that there is about mystical utterances an eternal unanimity which ought to make the critic stop and think [James, 1985, 410].

Abraham Maslow takes this observation even further, emphasizing not only the cross-cultural importance of mystical experience to even atheistic religions, but also to humanity as a whole.

> This private religious experience is shared by all the great world religions including the atheistic ones like Buddhism, Taoism, Humanism, or Confucianism. As a matter of fact, I can go so far as to say that this intrinsic core-experience is a meeting ground for [every human being] [Maslow, 1970, p. 28].

One need not see the mystical experience as necessarily religious in the sense of pertaining to any specific established religion, but as an experience that is available to any human being, anywhere in the world, at any point in time. The unitive experience, then, is a common human experience in which individuals have had the sense of not only a personal union with some form of divinity, but have actually experienced a unity of all things in the cosmos. Within the context of mystical experience, it is important to keep in mind, there remains a wide spectrum of actual experience, culminating in the total union of the individual with the Absolute. Stace describes a range rising to the highest forms of mystical experience, what he calls introvertive and extrovertive. The former — that which Stace argues to be the higher of the two — involves the actual experience of union, whereas the latter involves the perception of everything as one, thus perceiving requires a

---

It must be pointed out that there is some debate on the universality of experience, namely from the likes of Stephen Katz. His argument revolves around the idea that each mystic experiences their own personal mystical experience in entirely culturally and personally bound ways, so that when a Buddhist experiences nirvana, the Buddhist actually experiences a oneness in Void, whereas when a Christian experiences a union with God, there is actually a union with God. The problems with such a claim are many. For one thing, if one accepts Katz's position, one is left with no objective reality whatsoever as each person's experience is identified as primarily subjective. Such a line of argument may be amusing, and perhaps even useful, in some circles, but it does nothing to aid in the pursuit of an understanding of objective reality (see Katz, 1978).

separate self.* So, at the very basic level, a common out-of-the-body experience can be seen as the beginnings of mystical experience in its suggestion that our individuality is not as we normally perceive it in day-to-day life.

We can now speculate upon how such unitive mystical experience can account for the phenomena studied by psychical researchers. First, the reality depicted by mystical experience is one in which every human is in actuality united on some spiritual level with every other human. To go even further, this union transcends humanness to include the universe as a whole. Some branches of science, particularly quantum physics, tend to agree with this mystical world-view in describing the cosmos as an inter-mingling of indistinct particles and energy. For many, this quantum interconnectedness is seen as a solution to many of the problems posed by paranormal phenomena, from the instantaneous transfer of information to the influence of mind over matter. However, the evidence from psychical research does not necessitate a universe-wide interconnectedness, as the evidence from psychical research and parapsychology relates almost exclusively to phenomena appearing on Earth. Any psychic claims relating to places more distant than our world cannot be verified, and those that have been tested have been found to be wrong.† So, while fields such as quantum physics may provide the theoretical framework in which both mystical experiences and paranormal phenomena might be explained, the evidence from psychical research supports only a scaled down version of this universal inter-connection. Instead, the evidence for psi in general certainly suggests an interpersonal connectedness among humans here on Earth, but the union need not extend beyond the limits of the human race.

Still, in terms of the relationship between human beings, we have a clear connection between the experiences of mystics (and the physics that agrees with them) and the paranormal. For psi in general, the interconnectedness proffered by mystical experience allows a conduit for the transfer of information. Whereas for many the main problem of psi is to explain how information moves from one mind to the other, or from mind to matter, if all are one and the same then there is no more mystery of information transference *between* mind and mind as there is *within* an individual mind. That is to say, the problem of psi can be reduced to the problem of consciousness. An individual can access

---

*Aside from the distinction outlined by Stace, other great minds have similarly seen layers of experience. Stace's extrovertive mysticism corresponds directly to Zaehner's nature mysticism as well as Otto's Unifying Vision and the spontaneous peak-experience described by Maslow. Introvertive experience finds its correspondence in Zaehner's monistic and theistic mysticisms combined, as well as Otto's mysticism of introspection and Maslow's more controlled plateau-experience (see Maslow, 1970; Otto, 1957; Zaehner; 1967, 1970).

†The most famous example of which can be found in Flournoy (1900).

long-forgotten memories spontaneously and without effort, though the process behind this act is not understood. If all minds are in fact unified beyond the veil of physical reality, then it is no greater mystery if the same individual can access information from the mind of another individual, whether living or dead. The process in both cases will be the same, though in neither case has the problem of how the mind works been adequately explained.

William James discussed such possibilities at length, referring to the brain's function as being one of transmission rather than production — as materialism would have us believe. James talks of each individual consciousness separated from what he calls a "mother sea" — a vague notion of World Soul, Universal Mind, or Collective Consciousness — by the barrier of the brain. Within this mother sea exists the information that is spread from one mind to the next, so that each individual is in actuality connected one to another through this great sea of consciousness. James, in describing consciousness in this way, backs off from any claims to universal monism and the existence of a World Soul. His move is seemingly done, in part at least, for reasons similar to those of Schiller, Braude, and others who are uncomfortable either with the idea of a loss of individuality, or perhaps the public reaction to such a suggestion. In an attempt to salvage some possibility for individuality in the afterlife, James (1956) allows for the possibility of multiple transcendent minds existing within the mother sea.

Specifically in the context of phenomena relating to life after death, the same process can be applied. The key evidence in all evidence for survival of bodily death involves the transfer of information. The most common forms of such information are of the "knowledge-that" type (Braude, 2003, pp. 9–10). "Knowledge-that" is basically raw data in the form of memories transferred ostensibly from the dead to the living. Super-psi has long posited the possibility that such information could be transferred between living minds, removing the dead from the equation. Various kinds of data have appeared that seem to tax the super-psi hypothesis, such as the cross-correspondences and drop-in mediumistic communicators. Further complicating matters for a super-psi theory are instances of "knowledge-how," in which someone, a medium for instance, gains knowledge of a skill that normally requires training versus simple data, such as the ability to speak a foreign language. As Braude has shown, it is in these instances that the super-psi theory as commonly developed fails. A super-psi hypothesis incorporating mystical experience does not meet the same resistance, however, and can easily account for all of the problems faced by the traditional person-to-person model of information transference.

In a unity of minds, the information from any given individual, whether alive or dead, need not travel from one specific mind to another, but instead simply exists within the Universal Mind, accessible to all transient minds that walk the Earth. Anyone, in this model, has access to all of the information ever known to any human being, though actually gaining that information is no easy task. The most successful parapsychological experiments, using the Ganzfeld technique, are based upon the notion that effort tends to have a negative influence on psychic functioning, and that instead one must cease to try and simply allow psychic impressions to come seemingly of their own accord. This is analogous to the functioning of memory, as anyone who has ever tried desperately to remember a phone number can attest to. Braude (2003) also acknowledges the importance of "passive volition" (p. 38). However, he mentions it only in arguing against the problem of complexity in relation to superpsi. He argues further that a psychological approach to case studies might be taken in order to discover the underlying needs being addressed by the phenomena at hand. In relation to a theory of a Universal Mind, passive volition makes sense in terms of giving one's self over to what might be deemed a transcendent agent. Without trying, the information that we need, whether we realize it or not, arrives.

Consider Raymond Moody's (Moody, 1993) observations with his psychomanteum — a device designed to induce apparitions of the dead. In conducting his study, he found a very high rate of success in inducing visions in his subjects. While all subjects were instructed to seek a specific deceased person, there were cases where a different, but no less familiar, apparition appeared. These instances led Moody to conclude that witnesses often perceive the apparition that they personally need to perceive at that moment in time, rather than the one they consciously wish to perceive. And the reason for this, according to Moody, is due to the presence of unresolved emotions, which are dealt with by words of consolation from these visions. If such nonveridical apparitions can be caused by unconscious needs, then surely the possibility must exist for similar needs being met through more complex phenomena. The experience occurs without any knowledge of the actual need's having even existed in the first place, and can run quite contrary to conscious effort and desire. This is not a point that is not out of line with Braude's contention that underlying needs should be addressed, but it is not necessarily the case that such needs must come from the individual.

Several authors have correctly identified the need for meaning in the paranormal acquisition of information. In particular, questions about why a given drop-in communicator might appear or why a child might remember a given past-life over any other seem to imply some kind of specific need or meaning to explain their appearance. The survivalist would argue that the need comes from the dead, while traditional super-psi proponents might argue that the need comes from the individual having the memories. The theory from mystical experience implies meaning and need on a far greater scale, transcending the boundaries of either the living or the dead. In any event, it is clear that the needs being discussed stem from the farthest reaches of the unconscious. It is ideological to limit meaning to the individual. In the face of mystical experience, it is likely that meaning transcends the individual and comes from without rather than from within. While this may sound like an odd proposition in this modern, secular age, the reality of transcendent meaning has been at the root of religious thought for millennia, and it is mystical experience that has led humans to conclude the reality of implicit meaning in this world throughout time.

We then find that with mystical experience as a universal, cross-cultural human experience, we have the answer to the problems plaguing the super-psi hypothesis. All of us as humans are interconnected with everyone else. Jesus' commandment to "love thy neighbor as thyself"* could be no more true since my neighbor and myself are one and the same, despite outward appearances. Just as memories and thoughts percolate up from my unconscious mind for reasons unknown to me consciously, so too can memories, thoughts, and information in general surface from even deeper within the Universal Mind. Whether a medium communicates with spirits, a ghost appears to the living, a person has the sensation of leaving the body, or when one remembers aspects of a past-life, information enters the subject's mind from what might be described as an unknown source. The survivalist notions that the information comes directly from spirits, from the actual separation of body and soul, or from verifiable memories have been shown to fail to account for many of the problematic features of these experiences. The alternative super-psi hypothesis, which argues that the information comes from the minds of other living beings combined with various other psychic faculties somehow working unconsciously, has likewise failed to account for some of the more complicated cases. The Universal Mind hypothesis might be said to take the middle path between the two, positing that the information comes to the individualized mind from within and from without at once, so to speak. By this theory, every mind is linked, facilitating the transfer of information among the minds of the living, as witnessed through apparent cases of telepathy. By extension, the minds of the dead are also linked, as they, having lived, remain a part of the *anima mundi* even in death.

Aniela Jaffé (1979), one of Jung's disciples, describes the analogy of consciousness as pyramids. The tips are the conscious minds of individuals, but as the bases widen, they eventually overlap one another, merging into a

Matt. 19:19.

collective. Extending this analogy for the context of a life after death, I might add that these pyramids should be imagined as stemming from a large piece of rubber, like a broken balloon. Pulling at the balloon will create a pyramid of sorts, the pinnacle of which is the individual mind. Any number of such pyramids can be formed by pulling at different parts of the balloon. When a person dies, however, the pinnacle might be released and the pyramid will thus snap back into the flat surface of the rubber. The individual is lost in terms of its individualized nature, but remains as a part of the whole. The pinnacle of the conscious self is only a very small part of the larger whole.

Jaffé describes apparitions as archetypal images of the unconscious appearing to reveal meanings of critical importance to the witness, or witnesses. Some need or meaning is being addressed by the unconscious of the observer, and the image of some spirit appears in order to transmit best this necessary idea. Similarly, all of the paranormal phenomena associated with life after death can be viewed in the light of unconscious meaning bubbling up in the form of archetypal images and symbols. In this way, verifiable information is conveyed by constantly occurring "meaningful coincidences," to borrow Jung's own term. Coincidences which strike us as somehow important can be analyzed for their implicit meaning, according to Jung's (1955) theory of synchronicity.

Just as meaning can be found in dreams, so too can meaning be found in everyday experiences, from meaningful coincidences of a more mundane variety to legitimate paranormal experience. The hallucination of a deceased loved one might appear to correct some previous wrong. A medium may gain some insight ostensibly from the dead in order to help in the bereavement process. A child may remember the life of some person who lost their life unjustly in order to learn an important moral lesson, or perhaps to complete whatever tasks that previous person left unfinished. Evidence from psychical research invariably includes some element of meaning, and it is up to the individuals in each case to determine what the meanings of their own experiences are. Above all, such experiences convey the common message that death is not to be feared, while appearing to the average person in such a way so as not to fracture the carefully individualized personality working in the physical universe towards what ends no one knows. In relation to experiences of the dying and those near-death, Jung was surprised at just this observation, noting, "On the whole, I was astonished to see how little ado the unconscious makes of death. It would seem as though death were something relatively unimportant, or perhaps our psyche does not bother about what happens to the individual" (Jung, 1960, pp. 410–411).

The reality described by mystical experience is one in which the individual that we each believe ourselves daily to be is, in fact, not as solid and independent a thing as we think. The transiency of our individuality becomes immediately apparent within the greater context of an infinite universe. The theosophist Arthur Osborn puts it nicely in stating, "The question of survival ... seems trivial when the timeless Self is known" (Osborn, 1974, p. 316). On the one hand, we are each of us temporary beings living apparently independent lives, while on the other hand we are also eternal in our oneness with everyone and everything else.

Transcendent meaning seems to guide a forward evolution of some kind, with each transient individual playing an important, meaningful role. Mystics have been aware of this built-in meaning since the beginning of history, but it is clearly up to the individual to determine how it applies to his or her own life at any given moment. Paranormal phenomena can be seen as markers and indicators of this transcendent meaning. Evidence for survival is particularly effective in conveying meaning as it most often involves highly emotional subject matter. In this light, every experience must be considered individually for the implied meaning, for it is only through the manifestation of transcendent meaning that temporal life has any value.

In considering the life after death, then, the mystic's message is that we must each focus upon this life and endeavor to live it appropriately, within the context of the meanings we can find from day to day. In the grand scheme of things, the individual that I am is no more than a drop in a bucket, with form for but a brief fall before merging back into the whole. But, rather than see this as a pessimistic state of affairs as most Westerners are wont to do, the truth of the matter is that each drop is essential, for without the constant drip there would be nothing but an empty, meaningless void. And a drop with no bucket to catch it is simply wasted.

References

Bierce, A. (1911/1958). "Cartesian." In A. Bierce, *The devil's dictionary* (p. 21). NY: Dover.

Braude, S. E. (2003). *Immortal remains: The evidence for life after death.* NY: Rowman & Littlefield.

Brown, M. F. (1997). *The channeling zone: American spirituality in an anxious age.* Harvard, MA: Harvard University Press.

Brown, R. (1971). *Unfinished symphonies: Voices from the beyond.* New York: William Morrow.

Brown, R. (1974). *Immortals at my elbow.* London: Bachman & Turner.

Cheu, H. T. (1988). *The nine emperor gods: A study of Chinese spirit-medium cults.* Singapore: Times Books International.

Cressy, J. (1994). *The near-death experience: Mysticism or madness.* Hanover, MA: The Christopher Publishing House.

Crooke, W. (1896/1968). *Popular religion and folklore of Northern India* (vol. 1). Delhi, India: Munshiram Manoharlal.

Dodds, E. R. (1959). *The Greeks and the irrational.* Berkeley, CA: University of California Press.

Emmons, C. F. (1982). *Chinese ghosts and ESP.* Metuchen, NJ: Scarecrow.

Felton, D. (1999). *Haunted Greece and Rome: Ghost stories from classical antiquity.* Austin, TX: University of Texas Press.

Flournoy, T. (1900). *From India to the planet Mars: A study of a case of somnambulism, with glossolalia* (trans. D. B. Vermilye). New York: Harper & Brothers.

Fox, M. (2003). *Religion, spirituality and the near-death experience.* London: Routledge.

Freed, R. S., & Freed, S. A. (1993). *Ghosts: Life and death in North India.* Seattle, WA: University of Washington Press.

Grosso, M. (1982). Toward an explanation of near-death phenomena. In Craig R. Lundahl (Ed.), *A collection of near-death research readings* (p. 207). Chicago, IL: Nelson-Hall.

Hick, J. (1976). *Death and eternal life.* London: Collins.

Jaffé, A. (1979). *Apparitions: An archetypal approach to death, dreams and ghosts.* Irving, TX: Spring p. 116–126.

James, W. (1956). *The will to believe and other essays in popular philosophy: Human immortality.* New York: Dover Publications.

James, W. (1985). *The varieties of religious experiences.* Cambridge, MA: Harvard University Press.

Johnson, A. (1909). On the automatic writing of Mrs. Holland. *Proceedings of the Society for Psychical Research, 21,* 166–391.

Jordan, D. K. (1972). *Gods, ghosts, and ancestors.* Berkeley, CA: University of California Press.

Jung, C. G. (1955). *Synchronicity: An acausal connecting principle* (trans. R. F. C. Hull). London: Routledge & Kegan Paul.

Jung, C. G. (1960). The structure and dynamics of the psyche (trans. R. F. C. Hull). Princeton: Princeton University Press.

Katz, S. T. (Eds.) (1978). *Mysticism and philosophical analysis.* London: Oxford University Press.

Kellehear, A. (1996). *Experiences near death.* Oxford: Oxford University Press.

Maslow, A. H. (1970). *Religions, values, and peak-experiences.* New York: Viking/Penguin.

Moody, R. (1993). *Reunions: Visionary encounters with departed loved ones.* New York: Ivy Books.

Osborn, A. W. (1974). *The superphysical.* New York: Harper & Row.

Otto, R. (1957). *Mysticism east and west* (trans. B. L. Bracey & R.C. Payne). New York: Meridian.

Paper, J. (1995). *The spirits are drunk.* New York: SUNYP.

Parry, J. P. (1994). *Death in Banaras.* Cambridge, England: Cambridge UP.

Pasricha, S., & Stevenson, I. (1986). Near-death experiences in India: A preliminary report. *Journal of Nervous and Mental Disease, 174,* 165–170.

Price, H. H. (1953). Survival and the idea of another world. *Proceedings of the Society for Psychical Research, 50,* 125.

Schiller, F. C. S. (1910). *Riddles of the Sphinx.* London: Swan Sonnenschein.

Smith, H. (2001). *Why religion matters: The fate of the human spirit in an age of disbelief.* San Francisco, CA: HarperSanFrancisco.

Stace, W. T. (1961). *Mysticism and philosophy.* London: MacMillan.

Taymeeyah, Ibn. (1989). *Essay on the Jinn (Demons)* (trans. Abu Ameenah Bilal Philips). Riyadh, Saudi Arabia: Tahweed.

Thurman, R. A. F. (trans.) (1994). *The Tibetan book of the dead.* New York: Bantam.

Willoughby-Meade, G. (1928). *Chinese ghouls and goblins.* London: Constable.

Zaehner, R. C. (1967). *Mysticism sacred and profane.* London: Oxford University Press.

Zaehner, R. C. (1970). *Concordant discord.* London: Oxford University Press.

Zaleski, C. (1988). *Otherworld journeys.* Oxford: Oxford University Press.

Section II: Theoretical and Experimental Issues

3. Mind, Matter and Death

DOUGLAS M. STOKES

In this chapter Dr. Douglas Stokes takes us on a whirlwind travelog through the many and various viewpoints surrounding the issues of self, mind, matter and death. The central question which he implies is "What is consciousness?" and depending on the answers given to this question he contemplates the meaning of "death." He appears to favor an Eastern model in which the essential datum is (contentless) pure consciousness, of which we partake, but which is independent of our bodies and personalities, and which may therefore survive the dissolution of the latter.—Editors

Introduction

The question of whether the human mind or spirit survives the death of the physical body is one of the oldest and least tractable problems to confront human (and other hominid) philosophers, scientists and theologians. In more recent times, it was the central occupation of investigators in the early days of psychical research, the field that gave rise to parapsychology. This problem has, however, since receded into the murky background, due to its intractability, the existence of alternative explanations of the evidence for survival and to advances in modern cognitive neuroscience that have revealed the intimate dependence of the human personality on the state of the physical brain. Writers such as Patricia Churchland (2002) have suggested that

47

such dependence is so complete as to rule out the possibility that any souls or any nonphysical aspects of the mind exist. This would seem to shut the door on the case for survival; however, I will argue below that any such door slamming is at best premature.

In this chapter, I will be arguing for the existence of a persisting self in each person or (or more likely) a myriad of persisting selves. However, such persisting selves may not in fact persist in the commonly understood sense of lifelong and continuous association with one particular physical body, yet may persist long beyond the deaths of the bodies they currently inhabit. This seemingly paradoxical position will hopefully become clearer as the chapter goes on. It will also be argued that such persisting fields of consciousness enjoy an ontological status that is not inferior to that of elementary particles such as electrons and quarks, as is commonly supposed, but may play a fundamental role in determining the outcomes of quantum processes and possibly even in the design and creation of the universe itself.

The Persisting Self

Most of us (at least most of us who are not professional philosophers) believe that we have some sort of continuing self, a field of consciousness that persists from our birth to our death. While this self may be thought to lapse during deep sleep and under conditions such as surgical anesthesia, most of us generally believe that the self that wakes up after each lapse is the same as the self that preceded the lapse. There is perhaps no rational basis for such belief. The self that wakes could be an entirely different entity from the self that inhabited the body prior to the loss of consciousness. After all, if a self can somehow become "stuck" in a human body sometime after conception and released somehow at death, it stands to reason that such a self could also become stuck in the body well after the body's birth and to depart long before its death.

However, if the self that wakes is only able to access memories stored in the current brain, it would naturally come to believe that it experienced the events corresponding to these memories and hence is the same self that inhabited the body prior to the lapse in consciousness. Meanwhile, the prior self (field of consciousness) might be waking up in a new body and quickly forming the belief that it had inhabited the (new) body all along. In view of the occasional experience in which one is unsure of one's location or even one's identity for a few brief moments after waking, this "realization" (or possibly this delusion) may not be so sudden after all.

The Denial of the Self

Of course there are those, such as Daniel Dennett (1991), Susan Blackmore (1991, 1993, 2002), Galen Strawson (1997), Patricia Churchland (2002) and Thomas Metzinger (2003), among others, who deny the very existence of any continuing self, or "Cartesian theater," as Dennett calls it, even over a limited time-period. The self, they maintain, is a convenient "story" we tell ourselves in an attempt to render our experiences coherent and consistent. As such, the self is an entirely fictional concept, and "we" are nothing more than the scattered contents (fleeting sensations, thoughts, and emotions) of "our" minds. However, to most people, the existence of a continuing self is immediately given and obviously true. It is an integral part of our essential existence as commonly understood.

The Zen doctrine of "No Mind" also denies the existence of a continuing self. However, the Buddhist doctrine seems more directed at the concept of the self as one's personality, comprising one's aspirations, motivations, cravings for material possessions, lusts, pride, and so forth, rather than at the existence of a field of pure consciousness. A goal of Buddhist practice is to distance oneself from these transitory elements. In order to achieve a state of peace and tranquility, the Buddhists teach that one must suppress and eliminate one's cravings and greed, which, unfulfilled, are the root of all human misery and suffering.

Most branches of Buddhism and Hinduism teach that the true self is pure consciousness, not the contents or objects of consciousness. Thus, the Eastern philosophies teach that our personalities are transitory and not our true selves. One's true self in this view is the pure consciousness that in Hindu philosophy is taken to be identical with all consciousness, including that of the World Soul or Brahman. It is thus not clear that these Eastern philosophies deny the reality of a persisting self in the sense of a field of consciousness, as opposed to the contents of one's consciousness or one's personality or motives (which obviously do not persist unchanged even from moment to moment).

Also, it has been amply demonstrated that one's sensations, feelings, thoughts, emotions, ideas, and even personality can be radically altered through electromagnetic, surgical, chemical, and accidental interventions in the brain. If relatively minor modifications of brain states can substantially alter the nature of one's experience and personality, how could your personality and experiences manage to continue on in a more or less uninterrupted fashion after the far more drastic event of the destruction of the entire brain? Also, many of the concerns that drive the structure of your personality have to do with the preservation of your own physical body and those of people who are closely related to you (or perhaps to the propagation of your "selfish genes"). What would be the point of the continuance of these concerns once your physical body has been returned to dust and your ability to intervene in the physical world perhaps radically curtailed?

"Downloaded" into Heaven

Some philosophical functionalists, such as Hans Moravec (1988), Grant Fjermedal (1987), and Frank Tipler (1994) among others, have suggested that one's thoughts, memories and personality could be "downloaded" into a computer or robot, allowing one's essential self to survive after death in a cybernetic world or as a cybernetic simulacrum operating in the physical world. Of course, it would be just as easy to create multiple simulacra of oneself rather than just one. It is counterintuitive to think that one's "self" could really inhabit all the copies simultaneously, providing another indication that one's self cannot be identified with one's emotions, thoughts, memories and personality.

Hart's "I-thinker"

The self that (seems to) persist over long time-periods (from birth to death in the popular, common view) would appear to correspond to what Hornell Hart (1958) called the "I-thinker," that entity that thinks one's thoughts (although it may not have a primary role in generating them), feels one's feelings, remembers one's memories and senses one's sensations, rather than being the conglomerate of the thoughts, feelings, memories, and sensations themselves. After all, these contents of consciousness are fleeting and do not persist from one moment to the next. One outlives one's current emotional state, and one's self may survive the demise of myriad personalities. After all, how could we be the contents of our streams of consciousness when these contents change from moment to moment while we ourselves seem to persist unchanged from moment to moment, day to day and even from year to year?

What seems to persist, at least from an introspectionist point of view, is the (contentless) field of consciousness itself. Perhaps, as suggested above, our real selves are fields of pure consciousness, the "contentless consciousness" of Indian philosophy, as described by Rao (2002), among others. In other words, we are the vessel of consciousness rather than the contents of that vessel.

In fact, a persisting self not only cannot be identified with the fleeting and ever-changing contents of consciousness, it also cannot be identified with the particular configuration of material particles that constitute one's physical body or brain, as these too are continually undergoing change and replacement. Due to the constant exchange of material substance with your environment, your present physical body shares few if any molecules with your body of 20 years ago. You have already survived the death and dissolution of that earlier body. Thus, any self or field of consciousness associated with the physical body that persists unchanged from birth to death cannot be identified with any particular physical body (configuration of material particles) or conglomeration of mental contents such as thoughts, feelings and personality traits, as neither of these (the body or the contents of consciousness) persists unchanged from moment to moment.

The fact that you have apparently survived the dissolution of your body of several years ago suggests that you may likewise survive the ultimate death and dissolution of your present body as well. It is, however, unlikely that you would survive death with your personality traits and memories intact as suggested in the Western religious traditions (and by much of the research on survival conducted by psychical researchers), due to the dissolution of the brain activity and neural structures underlying your current personality traits and memories. It is conceivable, however, that a field of pure consciousness might survive the ultimate death of the physical body much as it seems to have survived the "death" of the prior bodies that have been "shed" through a process of molecular replacement and recycling.

Modern Dualists

The postulation of a continuing contentless field of consciousness brings us perilously close to Cartesian dualism, a once dominant philosophical position that has become increasingly out of favor in the current intellectual climate, which is dominated by several remarkably successful scientific disciplines that largely adopt a materialistic or reductionist stance toward the realm of mental events. The postulation of a self or field of consciousness that is in some sense independent of, or external to, the brain, immediately raises the question of how such a self and brain could interact.

One of the last holdouts for a dualistic position during the latter half of the twentieth century was the Nobel laureate neurophysiologist Sir John Eccles (Eccles, 1979, 1980, 1983, 1987, 1989; Eccles & Robinson, 1984; Popper & Eccles, 1977), who proposed the existence of a conscious self lying outside (in a nonspatial sense) of the physical brain. Eccles viewed this conscious self as being capable of receiving information from the brain and acting upon the brain. At one point, Eccles (1977) used the term "psychokinesis" to describe the mediating vehicle whereby the mind or self influenced the brain.

Modern science is generally at a loss to explain how a nonphysical mind could interact with a physical brain; hence, its general denial of the existence of the former. Thus, the terms "internal psychokinesis" and "internal clairvoyance" may be as good as any to describe such mind-brain interaction (assuming the existence of a nonphysical mind). The use of the terms "internal psychokinesis" and "internal clairvoyance" in this context does not necessarily commit one to affirming the existence of psi phenomena as usually defined, which involve anomalous interconnections between internal and *external* events. The provisional use of the terms "internal psychokinesis" and "internal clairvoyance" in the present context is intended merely as a way of recognizing our current state of bafflement as to how a nonphysical mind could interact with a physical brain.

The "Shin" Model

Two writers to take Eccles' suggestion that mind-brain interaction may be mediated by "internal psychokinesis" literally (albeit nearly three decades before Eccles got around to making the suggestion) were Thouless and Wiesner (1948). They proposed that each brain has associated with it an entity they termed the "Shin." They used the Hebrew letter shin (ש) to denote this entity rather than the terms "mind" or "soul" as they wished to avoid the connotations and other general baggage that would accompany the use of the latter terms. They proposed that the Shin becomes aware of brain states through a type of "internal clairvoyance" and that this awareness manifested itself in consciousness as various forms of "cognita" (to use Carington's, 1949, term), such as sensations, emotions, memories, and impulses. Conversely, the Shin controls the physical body and brain activity through internal psychokinesis. Thouless and Wiesner postulated that psi phenomena as traditionally defined correspond to an "externalization" of the mind's usual relation with the brain.

Clearly, under the view that physical bodies are associated with immaterial minds that are conceived as fields of "contentless consciousness," with virtually all of the activity underlying cognition and motor activity being embodied by material brain processes, some sort of theory analogous to that proposed by Thouless and Wiesner commends itself, if one wishes to adhere to a dualistic model in which consciousness is conceived as a component of the world that is in some sense "external to" (i.e., not identical with any part of) the physical brain.

Of course, such dualistic terminology may only be provisional. Should a "Shin-o-scope" be invented allowing the physical location and activity of Shins to be measured, it is likely that Shins would come to be viewed as physical components of brains. We are, however, a long way from a complete, partial, or even minimal understanding of consciousness, and "Shin-o-scopes" do not appear to be in the immediate offing. To the extent that such hypothetical Shins cannot at present be identified with any particular component of the physical world, it may be appropriate to continue to use the word "nonmaterial" to describe them, recognizing that such attribution of nonphysicality is provisional and may need to be withdrawn in the light of subsequent scientific discoveries. Indeed, the fact that Shins seem to get "stuck," however temporarily, in physical brains suggests that they exist in spacetime and therefore correspond to some sort of quasimaterial objects. At the same time, if psi phenomena exist, this is an indication that minds may have nonlocal aspects and direct access to a "higher dimension" or at least a wider region of spacetime than is encompassed by the brain. But the same could be said of all quantum objects and hence all matter.

The Problem of Epiphenomenalism

Fields of consciousness, including the Shins postulated by Thouless and Wiesner, cannot be merely passive spectators of brain states. If one assumes that mental events or qualia such as sensations, feelings, and memories are brought about through the Shin's "clairvoyant" perception of (i.e., conscious awareness of) brain states, one must assume that Shins or fields of consciousnesses are also capable of influencing the activity of the brain. Otherwise, one falls into the trap of epiphenomenalism, the doctrine that physical brain events cause mental events but that the latter have no causal influence on the former. A prominent champion of the position of epiphenomenalism was the nineteenth century biologist T. H. Huxley (the grandfather of the noted writer Aldous Huxley), famous for his tireless defenses of Darwin's theory of evolution.

Several writers, including Penrose (1987) and Popper and Eccles (1977) have noted that epiphenomenalism in fact runs counter to Darwinism. Why should consciousness have evolved, they ask, if it did not play an active role in benefiting the organism?

Also, and perhaps most amusingly, the mere existence of epiphenomenalist theories is in itself sufficient to refute the doctrine of epiphenomenalism. After all, epiphenomenalism is an attempt to explicate the role of mental events; therefore, the theory has been created in response to (i.e., has been caused by) mental events. Thus, mental events (i.e., qualia) have played a causal role in influencing the behavior of the epiphenomenalists, which is in direct refutation of their own theory. (It should be noted that this argument works largely because epiphenomenalism is a dualistic theory, positing that mental events exist in a realm separate from physical events. Such arguments based on causality are less effective in the case of monistic, or at least quasi-monistic, theories as panpsychism, double-aspect theory, neural identity theory and neutral monism, the first of which is discussed more extensively below.)

Thought and Brain Activity

The Thouless and Wiesner Shin theory does carry one advantage over classical Cartesian dualism in that the apparatus of thought and cognition may be ascribed largely to the physical brain, whereas under many interpretations of Cartesian dualism, much cognitive activity is carried out in the nonphysical realm. Descartes' "I think, therefore I am" may need to be replaced by "I am aware of my thoughts from time to time, therefore, I am." This is perhaps not as catchy a phrase, but does recognize the implications of modern research in cognitive neuropsychology showing the intimate connections between mental events, such as thoughts, emotions and perceptions, and brain processes. If such research has not yet established the identity of mental events with physical events, it has certainly revealed the intimate dependence of the former on the latter.

Naive Dualism and Split Brains

The results of research on split-brain patients (which was largely conducted after the publication of Thouless and Wiesner's paper but is now well emblazoned in the brains of all veterans of introductory psychology courses) pose devastating problems for any naive version of the Shin theory. A split-brain patient is someone who has undergone a callosectomy, or severing of the corpus callosum, the bundle of fibers that connect the two cerebral hemispheres of the brain. This operation generally disrupts the direct lines of communication between the two cortical hemispheres, and is often performed in order to prevent epileptic seizures from spreading from one hemisphere to the other. A typical finding is that such a patient is verbally unable to describe an object held (out of sight) in the left hand, because the left hand provides neural input primarily to the right hemisphere, whereas verbal skills reside in the left hemisphere in most patients. Such a patient is, however, able to use his or her left hand to pick up the previously held object from among a collection of objects scattered on a table, showing that the right hemisphere (which controls the left hand) did have knowledge of the object, but that knowledge was not able to be transferred to the left hemisphere due to the severing of the corpus callosum. (Sometimes, after the object is revealed, the left hemisphere dissembles and pretends that it knew its identity all along.)

Such findings pose grave difficulties for Thouless and Wiesner's Shin theory. A single Shin should be able, through "clairvoyant" perception of the right hemisphere, to gain knowledge of the object held in the left hand and then be able to describe the object through "psychokinetic" influence of the language centers in the left hemisphere. Thus, the findings of split-brain research would seem to directly refute the single Shin theory. In fact, these findings are precisely the evidence Patricia Churchland uses to refute the existence of a nonphysical self or soul (Churchland, 2002, pp. 46–47).

Thalbourne (2004) has responded to this argument by Churchland by proposing that "a callosectomy causes one portion of the self to become unconscious to the main center" (p. 17). He then goes on to propose that one portion of the brain is controlled by the conscious aspect of the self and that the other portion is controlled by the unconscious self. Thalbourne asserts that in such cases, "the self would maintain an overall unity, but be divided with respect to consciousness or unconsciousness of process" (p. 17). However, instances of conflict between the hemispheres and the ability of the right, presumably unconscious, hemisphere to respond to verbal commands and to communicate itself (sometimes through such devices as a Scrabble set) makes it seem unreasonable to deny consciousness to that hemisphere. Indeed, in the following sections it will be argued that many spheres of consciousness may somehow reside within a single human brain.

Thalbourne further suggests that the single self or Shin might be able through practice to reacquire the ability to "clairvoyantly" acquire information from one hemisphere and "psychokinetically" influence the other. However, if such reacquisition occurs, it is likely only partial, as a full functional recovery from a severed corpus callosum would be nothing short of miraculous and would be widely reported in the scientific literature. In view of the evidence for psi phenomena, I would not rule out a partial reacquisition (indeed, a partial reacquisition might be achieved through the remaining subcortical neural channels connecting the hemispheres). However, the existing neurological evidence suggests that inter-hemispheric information transfer likely depends primarily on neural pathways. Also the instances of motivational conflict between the hemispheres alluded to above, as well the "minor" hemisphere's ability to communicate messages sometimes at odds with its partner's motivations, strongly suggest that there are multiple selves or Shins in split-brain patients that are likely to be, to use Morton Prince's term, coconscious. Indeed, as argued below, it may be that there are multitudinous

Shins lurking in a single brain, with many or most of them "buying into" the delusion that they are the Person and the sole center of consciousness residing in the body. If in fact they are transient residents in the brain, as suggested below, it would not do from an evolutionary perspective for this fact to be widely recognized among the Shins. The service of the genes may require that the Shins fall into the delusion that they are the Person (i.e., the body, memories, personality, etc.).

In fact, the scientific and philosophical community has found it difficult to agree on a clear line of demarcation between conscious and nonconscious beings. Some (e.g., Descartes) would draw the line at humans and deny consciousness to animals. This seems to me to involve a retreat to the pre-Copernican view that humankind stands at the center of the universe. Others (e.g., the panpsychists) would extend consciousness all the way "down" the evolutionary chain to amoeba or even to plants and elementary particles, as discussed in more detail below.

We are complex organisms; each of our brains is composed of billions of amoeba-like neurons, much like a "Woodstock" for single-celled creatures. Perhaps, as argued below, our brains may harbor multiple, perhaps countless "selves" (i.e., fields of consciousness), with the majority of them identifying with the body as whole and quickly falling under the pre-Copernican delusion that each of them is the sole "self" or consciousness inhabiting the body. This identification of our "selves" with the body or the personality (the "Person") is natural but, as we have seen above, a false identification. To identify our true "selves" with our bodies and personalities is to fall into the same delusion that the Buddhists (and to some extent Blackmore and Dennett) have warned us against. Our selves (conceived as centers of pure consciousness) persist unchanged, while our bodies (and our personalities) grow, blossom, metamorphize, wither and die. From an introspectionist perspective, it seems clear that we are centers of consciousness that persist over macroscopic time intervals (contra Blackmore and Dennett). If the self as a center of consciousness does not even exist, the problem of survival does not arise — there is simply nothing left to survive. However, it is more plausible that, like the physical particles that make up our bodies, these centers of consciousness are continually entering and exiting the brain. If memories are stored in the brain, a newly entering Shin would quickly come to believe that it had been there all along, its memories of its former incarnations lost like a misplaced scrap of paper on which an important phone number was scrawled. The view that we are a single self that persists in the same body from day to day and year to year likely arises from the false identification of one's self with one's body and personality. We may be constantly recycled, awakening in a new body in each morning with no memories of our real adventures the day before.

This view may be depressing to many, in that it does not involve the survival of the Person. However, despite the fact this process may be random and "meaningless," like so much else in this universe, it is "fair" in the sense that we all may share the experiences of being deformed and poor or handsome and wealthy. Despite their centering in seemingly moral Agents and Principles, the "will of God" of the Judeo-Christian-Islamic tradition and the karmic principle of Hinduism (responsible in part for the "caste wars" in India) seem much less fair than the purely random and frequent reassortment I am proposing here. The latter view may also promote the values of kindness and altruism (if only out of egoism), as you may find yourself housed in (or stuck to) the other's body tomorrow. The main downside is that such a view may promote a "seize the day" form of hedonism in which one would elect to maximize one's pleasure now, with no thought of the consequences to the body or the "Person" the next day.

Multiple Selves

As intimated above, one way around the difficulty posed by split-brain patients would be to propose that the right and left hemispheres are associated with separate Shins or selves. It could be postulated that the two Shins were present prior to the callosectomy or that a second Shin was acquired during or shortly after the callosectomy. Each Shin would be restricted to interaction with its own hemisphere. As Eccles (1980) notes, many prominent split-brain researchers, including Puccetti, Sperry, Bogen and Gazzaniga, have postulated the existence of two spheres of consciousness in split-brain patients, although Gazzaniga has since modified this view (Gazzaniga, 1992). Libet (1994) has postulated the existence of "conscious mind fields" (CMFs), which he sees as being produced by brain activity. CMFs are capable of causal action upon brain activity and provide the means whereby diverse neural activity is synthesized into unified perceptions and experiences. He notes that the existence of CMFs would be compatible with a variety of philosophical positions on the mind-body problem. Following the lead of the above researchers, Libet speculates that there may be two CMFs in split-brain patients.

Incidentally, not all may be sweetness and light between the selves of the two hemispheres. Spence and Frith (1999) report on two cases of "alien hands" in which the left hand of patients who exhibited lesions or pathology in the corpus callosum actually attempted to strangle the patient. They also report on instances of motivational conflict between the hands of such patients, such as when the one hand fastens a button, which is then immediately unfastened by the other hand.

Perhaps the most convincing line of evidence for the existence of separate selves in the two cerebral hemispheres comes not from research on humans but rather from research on our cetacean friends. As pointed out by Patricia Churchland (1986, p. 181), dolphins sleep one hemisphere at a time.

A Proliferation of Selves

Two conscious selves may, however, not be enough, as there are more ways to divide up (or dissociate) a brain than are dreamt of in the classical split-brain paradigm. Take for instance the phenomenon of blindsight. "Blindsight" is a term coined by Lawrence Weiskrantz to describe a syndrome in which cortically blind subjects respond appropriately to visually presented stimuli even though they report no conscious awareness of such stimuli (Sanders et al., 1974; Weiskrantz, 1986; Marcel, 1988; Rafal et al., 1990). Cortical blindness refers to blindness that is a result of damage to the visual cortex in the occipital lobes of the brain. Even though the eyes of such patients may be normal, they may be blind in part of their visual field because of such damage to their visual cortex. If you present a small dot of light to such patients in the blind areas of their visual fields, they will say that they saw nothing. However, if you ask them to just take a guess by pointing to where the dot of light might have been, they frequently point at the exact location that the dot occupied. If you present erotic pictures to such a patient in the blind area of the visual field, the patient may blush or giggle or say things such as "That's quite a machine you've got there, Doc!" They will still, however, deny having consciously seen anything. Interpretations of words may be biased by information presented in the blind area of the visual field, and eye movements may be altered by such stimuli (Rafal et al., 1990). Many researchers have speculated that blindsight is mediated by a secondary visual center in a subcortical area of the brain known as the superior colliculus, although some researchers have challenged this view. Francis Crick (1994) has noted that other areas must be involved as well, in that blindsight sometimes involves responsiveness to color differences, and there are no color-sensitive neurons in the superior colliculus.

The phenomenon of blindsight might lead one to postulate the existence of a secondary center of consciousness, perhaps located subcortically in the superior colliculus. However, some writers, such as Flanagan (1992) and Marcel (1988), have argued against any attribution of full consciousness to this secondary center, insofar as information acquired through blindsight is not generally acted upon. For instance, the patient may be thirsty, but will not respond to the sight of a water fountain presented to the blind area of the visual field. It would be possible to argue that this secondary center cannot move the patient's body of its own accord, as it is a subordinate "module." (Actually, most researchers feel that the primary function of this secondary center is to guide eye movements, and perhaps this is not a role that one would want to associate with consciousness.)

In fact, in addition to the superior colliculus, many other regions of the brain have been nominated as "centers of consciousness." Indeed, it would almost seem that no region of the brain has been omitted from the list of brain regions that form the primary center of consciousness according to one researcher or another. These proposed centers of consciousness or mind/brain interaction have included the "liaison" brain (the "liaison" being between mind and brain) predominately located in the cerebral cortex of the left hemisphere (Eccles), the higher brain stem, or diencephalon (Penfield, 1975), the frontal lobes of the brain (Ramachandran, 1980), the linguistic apparatus of the brain (Ledoux, 1985), the septohippocampal region involved in mental representations of the world and memory formation (O'Keefe, 1985), the hippocampus and neocortex (Oakley, 1985a, 1985b), the supplementary motor area of the cerebral cortex (Libet, 1989, 1991), the thalamus (Cotterill, 1995), more specifically the intralaminar nucleus of the thalamus (Churchland, 1995), the right parietal lobe (Damasio, 1994), the temporal lobes (Ramachandran & Hirstein, 1997), patterns of synchronous firings of neurons (Burns, 1993, Crick, 1994), nonrandom, coherent deviations of the brain's electromagnetic field from its resting state (John, 2003), and, last but not least, water in the microtubules composing the cytoskeletons of neurons (Penrose, 1994; Hameroff, 1994). Each of these authors presents a cogent argument in favor of their candidate for the area of the brain (or brain process) that is the center of consciousness (or of the interaction between consciousness and mind).

With this many candidates for the *primary* center of consciousness (or of interaction between the conscious mind and brain), it may begin to seem that no center is primary and that many different brain centers and processes may be associated with their own conscious activity, and that these centers of consciousness may not be mutually accessible to one another, at least in a direct sense.

A Hierarchy of Selves

The notion that the human mind may be composed of an assembly of interacting centers of consciousness is an old one. It may be traced as far back as Aristotle, who postulated the existence of "vegetative soul," a "sensitive soul" and a "rational soul" in each person. William McDougall (1926) proposed that the normal human mind is composed of a hierarchy of "coconscious personalities," each carrying out its own separate function. McDougall used Morton Prince's term "coconscious" rather than the usual terms "subconscious" or "unconscious" to describe such secondary personalities in order to emphasize their self-awareness. Ostensible cases of multiple personality (if genuine) may represent instances in which one or more of these subordinate personalities has rebelled against the primary, executive personality.

In support of McDougall's view, many lines of psychological research, including studies of subliminal perception, posthypnotic suggestion, preattentive filters, and automatic motor performance suggest that the human mind is capable of conducting a great deal of sophisticated mental activity outside of the field of awareness of the primary personality. For instance, his investigations into hypnotic phenomena led Ernst Hilgard (1977) to propose what he called the "neodissociation" theory of hypnosis. Hilgard asserted that the hypnotized person was associated with a subconscious "hidden observer" that was aware of events for which the primary, conscious personality had no knowledge because of hypnotically induced amnesia, anesthesia, or negative hallucinations (e.g., when a hypnotized subject is instructed *not* to see a particular person or object). Hilgard was able to hold conversations with such "hidden observers," and the latter frequently reported knowledge of events (posthypnotic suggestions, pain, etc.) for which the primary personality claimed no knowledge.

In the decades since the "cognitive revolution" in psychology, research into the "cognitive unconscious" has led to the creation of many hierarchical models of the mind, such as the "Massachusetts modularism" proposed by Jerry Fodor (1983), in which the mind is seen as being split into modular "computational" components.

Michael Gazzaniga (1985, 1989) likewise rejected the notion of a unitary consciousness in favor of the view that the mind is composed of a collection of independently-functioning modules that he, following William McDougall, describes as "coconscious." As evidence for this modular view of the mind, Gazzaniga cites post-hypnotic suggestions, apparent unconscious (or coconscious) problem-solving activity (in which the solution to a complex problem suddenly emerges full-blown into consciousness), blindsight, the existence of separate procedural and episodic memory systems, and split-brain research.

Gazzaniga tends to identify the "conscious self" with the module that is in control of the language centers of the brain, and he refers to this module as the "executive module." He cites many instances in which the executive module uses confabulation to explain behavior that was in fact generated by other modules. For instance, a person who acts under a posthypnotic suggestion to close a window may claim that he or she was cold. Gazzaniga also cites several instances of confabulation by the left hemisphere to explain actions performed in response to directions given to the right hemisphere in split-brain patients. It might not be far-fetched to suppose that all or most modules might likewise maintain the illusion that they were the sole center of consciousness or in sole control of the body. For instance, modules hearing the mouth issue verbal utterances may be under the illusion that they were primarily responsible for producing those utterances. They might naturally identify with the body as a whole rather than with the particular brain region in which they are located.

In general it seems that fields of consciousness are blissfully ignorant of their physical location and sphere of activity. After all, Aristotle and many other ancient philosophers located the seat of consciousness in the heart rather than the brain. Also instructive is a short science fiction story entitled "Where am I?" by Daniel Dennett (1981). In Dennett's "story," sensory information is transmitted to a human brain from a robot or decerebrated human body, and the brain's motor commands are in turn relayed to the remote body or robot, thus controlling its activity. Dennett's story leaves no doubt that the brain would locate its center of consciousness in the remote body or robot under these circumstances and not in its "real" location in the physical brain. Our centers of consciousness may thus not be located where we think they are.

Each "module" or center of consciousness may subscribe to a "unitararian" philosophy of the self or soul, in which it believes itself to be unitary and indivisible and in sole control of the body. If such modules in fact correspond to centers of contentless consciousness that are fundamental constituents of the universe existing prior to the evolution of complex organisms, they may be correct in regarding themselves as unitary and indivisible but sadly mistaken in the view that they are in sole control of the body.

Thus, one means of addressing the problems posed by split-brain research and other neurological findings (e.g., blindsight) would be to propose that each person is composed of an aggregation of selves or fields of consciousness associated with local brain regions. This raises the question of what characteristics are necessary for a brain region to "host" (or comprise) a field of consciousness. Must the region be large (an assembly of thousands of neurons)? Or could it be "medium-sized" (a single neuron) or small (a single quark)? Perhaps, as some writers (e.g., Beck, 1994; Bohr, 1958; Eddington, 1935; Hameroff, 1994; Hodgson, 1991; Leggett, 1987a, 1987b; Margenau, 1984; Penrose, 1994; Squires, 1990; Stapp, 1992, 1996; Walker, 2000) have suggested, consciousness may reside in the "hidden variables" that govern the collapse of quantum mechanical state vectors in the brain. In fact, Eccles (1953) noted that the brain is just "the sort of machine a 'ghost' could operate" (p.

285), as its functioning is dependent on minute electrical potentials and the motions of neurotransmitters and calcium ions. Thus, in Eccles' view (as expressed in his later writings), changes in macroscopic brain activity may be brought about without violating the limits of indeterminacy allowed under the theory of quantum mechanics.

It should be noted, however that contrary views have been expressed by Mohrhoff (1999) and Wilson (1999), who have argued that any action of a nonphysical mind on the brain would entail the violation of physical laws, such as the conservation of energy and momentum and the requirement that the outcomes of quantum processes be randomly determined. However, conscious selves might turn out to be physical or quasi-physical entities possessing physical energy. Also, it might turn out that the outcomes of quantum processes inside complex systems such as brains are not randomly determined but are governed by fields of consciousness, whereas those in simpler systems are not so governed. Also, many parapsychological researchers, going back to Schmidt (1969, 1970), have produced evidence that conscious minds may be capable of determining, or at least biasing, the outcomes of quantum processes.

The world may have many surprises in store for those scientists who think that their work is nearly done and their understanding of the world is virtually complete. After all, *Science's* "Breakthrough of the Year" for 2003 was the discovery that 96% of the energy in the universe is comprised of dark matter and dark energy, the existence of which was not even suspected a few decades ago, rather than the matter-energy that is visible to us, which comprises a mere 4% of the energy in the universe. A full 73% of the universe is comprised of dark energy, the existence of which was not even suspected until 1998 (Seife, 2003). Many more surprises may be in store for us.

Panpsychism

How small a brain region could be represented by a center of consciousness? Many of the writers listed above have suggested that a relatively large "suborgan" of the brain (such as the cortex of the left hemisphere or the thalamus) is the center of consciousness. However, David Skrbina (2003) has recently provided a comprehensive and brilliant defense of the philosophical tradition known as "panpsychism." Under this doctrine, all matter is imbued with consciousness. Skrbina argues for instance that an electron must somehow sense the presence of a proton in order to respond to its attractive force. (An electron may even enjoy a certain degree of freedom of action due to quantum indeterminacy and may be able to sense a quantum field that is highly complex and global in nature.)

More complex forms of consciousness may be associated with aggregates of matter, such as single neurons, or large assemblies of neurons such as hippocampi and cerebral hemispheres. (However, it should be noted that such aggregates of matter, much like one's personality and physical body do not persist over time and thus cannot form the basis of a continuing self. Also, fields of consciousness appear to be unitary and indivisible, much more like a quark than like a molecule or a neuron.)

As Skrbina points out, the panpsychist position solves the problem of "emergence" or the need to account for how organisms acquired consciousness in the course of evolution. As he notes, there is no definitive line of demarcation that can be drawn between conscious and nonconscious organisms, in either the present world or in the course of evolution. If all matter is imbued with consciousness or if fields of consciousness are fundamental constituents of the universe that have existed throughout its history, then the problem of evolution of consciousness does not arise.

Quantum "Hidden Variables"

For many writers, such as Walker (2000), who equate consciousness with the "hidden variables" that govern the collapse of the quantum mechanical state vector, the physical arena over which consciousness works is often assumed to be restricted to local areas of the brain (such as Eccles's "liaison brain") or specific networks of entities within the brain (e.g., water molecules in microtubules, as proposed by Penrose, 1994). If the area is deemed to be a wide region, encompassing virtually the entire brain, such a theory might be based on the influence of nondeterministic events governing synaptic transmission, as proposed by Eccles, Walker and others. In this case, the conscious mind (if assumed to be single and unitary) would be unable to overcome the effects of a severed corpus callosum in split brain-patients and might be supposed to experience a field of consciousness fluctuating between awareness of one hemisphere and the other.

However, as is by now well known to any consumer of the literature on "new age" physics, quantum systems exhibit nonlocality. For instance, the quantum state of a proton may be instantaneously influenced by measurements made on another proton light years away from it, if their quantum states are entangled. It might be thought that local areas of the brain might be "connected" or "entangled" with larger areas of the brain through such nonlocal quantum interconnections and thus local regions might in some sense be "aware of" or have "knowledge" of a wide array of brain activity. If the quantum wave governing its activity is presumed to be sufficiently complex and to contain substantial nonlocal information, perhaps even a single proton could be said to possess awareness of large portions of brain activity. Thus, even a proton could constitute one of a myriad of selves, each under the illusion that it is was the sole self associated with the body. However, it should be noted that Penrose (1994) has proposed that the collapse of quantum state vectors may require a minimal amount of mass-energy or gravitational potential that would likely exceed that of a single proton.

Panexperientialism

What could form the physical basis of a "self," conceived as a field of consciousness that seems to persist despite rapid turnover in the contents of consciousness, such as sensations, thoughts and feelings, and despite the constant turnover of physical matter in the underlying brain region? If the self is a proton or a quark, it would be expected to survive the physical death of the body and thus to constitute a "soul-like" entity (although it would likely retain no memory of its previous life once it became disentangled from the brain state).

The self might instead be an aggregate self or "compound individual" of the sort proposed in the "panexperientialism" of David Ray Griffin (1988a, 1988b, 1994, 1997). Such compound individuals are composed of, or arise from, a hierarchical collection of more primitive selves or "individuals." For instance, a neuron would be a compound individual in relation to its individual constituents such as molecules, and a "suborgan" such as the hippocampus that is composed of neurons would be a compound individual somewhat further up the hierarchy. All such "individuals" would have both mental and physical aspects under the panexperientialist view, although only hierarchically ordered structures would be assumed to have a highly organized and structured consciousness. Less well-organized structures, such as rocks, would be ascribed only vague "feeling responses" according to Griffin's panexperientialist theory. Again, it is doubtful that conscious selves can be identified with aggregates of matter in that selves seem to persist through time periods in which the configuration and composition of such aggregates change and the fact that fields of consciousness seem to be unitary and indivisible whereas such aggregates are not.

Mini-Shins

A compound individual (in the panexperientialist sense) would only be able to survive death (of the body or its associated neural structure) if its identity is not dependent on the aggregate structure that supports it remaining intact (e.g., if it is a field of consciousness associated with or acquired by the structure rather one emerging from the structure and depending on the latter's exact composition for its existence). Such a view would be analogous to postulating mini-Shins (in the sense of Thouless and Wiesner) associated with localized brain regions. Such mini-Shins could be thought to possess global awareness of brain activity both through entanglement with complex and global quantum states as well as through classical (neural) connections. If its awareness of brain activity were sufficiently global, each such mini-Shin might develop the delusion that it was the supreme executive module governing the activity of the body (as it is likely that its primary identification would be with the entire body rather than with the local brain region with which it was directly associated). For instance in Libet's famous experiment (see Libet, 1991), subjects believed that their "will" spontaneously controlled the flexing of their hands, even though the neurological record showed a "readiness potential" building in their brains for 350 milliseconds prior to the time the subject's "will" decided to act. Thus, the subjects' "fields of consciousness" in Libet's experiment may only have thought they were in control of the entire body and could move it at will, when really their "wills" were at least in part the result of prior brain activity outside of their knowledge or control. Thus, each person may be composed of a multitude of fields of consciousness, with many of them under the illusion that they are the "executive module" controlling the entire body. Should these fields of consciousness be comprised of elementary particles such as quarks or of mini-Shins in the sense of Thouless and Wiesner (1948), they might be supposed capable of surviving the death of the body. Indeed, such mini-Shins may frequently transit in and out of the body during its physical lifetime.

The idea that one's self or soul becomes attached to one's body shortly after conception and remains attached until death is likely the result of the false identification of one's self with one's body and one's personality (i.e., ongoing saga of brain states). This self is, perhaps as Blackmore and Dennett insist, likely to be a story that we tell ourselves. The "purpose" of such a story in an evolutionary sense might well be to preserve the physical body and combination of one's genes. Such stories and the fear of death they engender would serve to preserve the organism and thus may be the result of evolutionary processes. However, our true selves (fields of pure consciousness) should not be confused with these "heroes" of our own personal fables. One source of the fear of death is precisely the identification of selves with "persons" in the sense of physical bodies conjoined with personalities. The "person" is not likely to survive the death of the physical brain. But we are at once much more and much less than persons.

If mini-Shins are identified with the "hidden variables" that underlie the collapse of quantum mechanical state vectors, they may persist after the death of the physical body. In either case, it is unlikely that they would retain much in the way of memory for events occurring during their association with their former bodies, traces of former personalities, or other contingent psychological characteristics.

Note that the identification of the self with the quantum mechanical wave function itself or with some other sort of field surrounded the brain is also likely to be a false one, just as is the identification of the self with the physical body and personality. Such functions and fields undergo constant change and are in essence divisible into parts, unlike fields of pure consciousness, which appear to be changeless and unitary.

Some physicists (e.g., Walker, 2000) have proposed that quantum processes do not give rise to a definite outcome unless such outcomes are witnessed by a conscious observer. Indeed, some physicists (e.g., Wheeler, 1983) have suggested that the universe itself, conceived as a quantum process, could not have come into existence without some conscious observer to collapse state vectors and thus to give rise to a definite history of the universe. Wheeler terms this view the "participatory universe." Wheeler notes that this view may explain the "Anthropic Principle," the fact that the initial state and physical laws of the universe seem finely tuned to support the existence of conscious observers. Potential universes that do not support the presence of conscious observers could not become actualized in Wheeler's view, as there would be no conscious observers to collapse their state vectors in the proper "direction" to create such a history.

The mini-consciousnesses or "proto-consciousnesses" proposed by Walker (2000) to govern the collapse of state vectors corresponding to events that are remote from human observers might be thought to correspond to mini-Shins in the sense of Thouless and Wiesner, if such mini-Shins are viewed as corresponding to, or containing, some of the "hidden variables" that determine the outcomes of quantum processes (whether in a human brain or elsewhere).

Indeed, physical bodies may continually be acquiring and expelling such mini-Shins, much as they do material particles. Such mini-Shins might then be reacquired by new bodies or incorporated into new "compound individuals" in Griffin's sense. Thus, each of us, if a mini-Shin, may be "dead" long before we suspect we will and possibly even long before the death of our current physical bodies, the good news being that we won't in fact suspect our deaths or remember our lives for that matter, having no access to the memories stored in our former brains and being completely absorbed in new cognitive tasks. Thus, life and death may equally be illusions.

Hill (2005) notes that the vast emptiness of space is totally hostile to the existence of humanity (i.e., strong radiation, lack of air, poor access to fast-food establishments). Thus, he suggests that if the Anthropic Principle (the hypothesis that the universe is designed to support the presence of conscious observers) is true, the evidence would suggest that the universe was "designed" for beings that exist in the vacuum of space, not beings that are confined to rarely occurring sponge-like brains found on one tiny speck of matter in one remote corner of a cold and desolate universe (or more likely a number of such tiny specks sparsely populating a virtually empty space-time continuum). Indeed recent scientific photography has uncovered the startling beauty of the inanimate physical world, from the microscopic domains such as electromagnetic fields to the haunting beauty of the cloud-like nurseries of infant stars. The mini-Shins discussed above may in fact correspond to the empty-space-dwelling beings postulated by Hill. Such beings may be lost in an artwork universe of their own creation.

Alternatively, if the Eastern tradition's view that all consciousness is One is correct, the One may be wandering through Its creation one lifetime at a time, contemplating it from all angles, lost in its beauty and drama. The noted physicist Richard Feyman noted that a positron (the antimatter analogue of the electron) might be regarded as an electron traveling backwards in time. He once joked that the reasons all electrons look identical to one another is that they are in fact the same particle zig-zagging its way backward and forward in time. Perhaps, the conscious self is much like Feynman's electron (a.k.a. positron).

A Quasi-Bayesian Argument

If centers of consciousness are indeed fundamental components of the universe, whether being identified with elementary physical particles, the "hidden variables" that determine the outcomes of quantum processes, or mini-Shins à la Thouless and Wiesner (these possibilities not being necessarily mutually exclusive), one fundamental mystery would be solved. If each of us is identical with his or her physical body, it is most surprising that we would find ourselves conscious at the present moment of time. A human lifespan is only several decades long. On the other hand, the universe has existed for approximately 13.5 billion years and will likely exist for billions more to come (to say nothing of the age of any "multiverse," of which the universe may be only a part). Thus, the probability that the moment in time that has somehow been mysteriously selected to be the "present" would correspond to a moment in one's lifetime would seem to be vanishingly small. Also, if one is to be identified with a particular physical body, the probability that the set of genes that formed the blueprint for that body would ever have come into combination is virtually zero (and still smaller is the probability that the particular configuration of material particles that comprises one's *present* physical body would ever have formed, much less exist at the present moment). Yet here you find yourself (a field of consciousness that is unique and special to you at any rate) existing at the present time. This is most surprising (indeed virtually impossible) based on the view that you are identical with, or dependent on, the presence of a particular collection of material particles at a particular moment in time. Hence, by a quick pseudoapplication of Bayes' theorem in statistics, the probability that the standard view (that you are your physical body) obtains is also virtually zero. However, on the view that fields of consciousness or mini-Shins are fundamental constituents of the universe, it is conceivable that they may be somehow "breathed out" and "breathed in" by physical bodies in much the same way as those bodies acquire and expel material particles. Under this view, the probability that your conscious self would exist now may be something approaching one.

In passing, it should be noted that many lines of parapsychological research have suggested that psi phenomena are spacetime independent (i.e., their strength is not diminished by increased spatial and temporal separations). Also, known physical signals are inadequate to account for psi phenomena (see Stokes, 1987, for a review). The existence of psi phenomena would thus suggest that persons are quite possibly associated with nonphysical components in addition to their physical bodies. (Here, the term "nonphysical" may be either interpreted literally or in the sense of lying outside of the range of phenomena explained by current theories of physics, leaving open the possibility that a radically expanded theory of physics may one day encompass such components.)

The Self as "Recyclable"

In the oft-quoted words of Voltaire, it is no more surprising to be born twice than it is to be born once. On the view advocated here, it may not even be surprising to be born (and die) every several hours, as one's center of consciousness is acquired by and expelled from various physical bodies and other material systems. (During its association with a particular brain, the field of consciousness might even be under the illusion that it is in sole control of the body, as discussed above, not realizing that a "team effort" is likely involved.) One would of course have no memory of one's former (possibly fleetingly brief) "lives," as such memories (and former personality traits for that matter) are presumed to be located in, or at the very least highly dependent on, the activity and structure of brains to which one no longer has access. Of course, many such lives may consist of associations with animal brains, quantum computers, and possibly even plants or other material or nonmaterial systems deemed to possess consciousness (such as Walker's"proto-consciousnesses" that govern the collapse of state vectors remote from physical observers). Such survival of consciousness after dissociation from a particular human brain would thus not correspond to the sort of afterlife proposed in traditional Western religious traditions, in which memories and personalities are presumed to survive relatively intact (or perhaps only partially intact, as in the shades that inhabited the realm of Hades in ancient Greek mythology). But it would go a long way toward explaining the amazing fact that one finds oneself conscious "now" (which is highly improbable on the basis of the standard materialistic view as noted above). Just because we cannot explain consciousness does not imply that consciousness plays any less fundamental a role or enjoys less of a permanent status in the universe than do material particles. We may not be ontolologically inferior to protons after all. (Indeed, we might even be quite proton-like ourselves, in light of the above discussion. Or perhaps we might be much more, as noted below.)

Ian Stevenson's research into children who report memories of past lives (see Stevenson, 1987) has uncovered little in the way of evidence of the operation that a moral principle such as karma governs the process of reincarnation (even assuming for the moment the unlikely possibility that memories can be transferred from life to life). However, the idea that we are mini-Shins housed only temporarily in our present bodies does, as noted above, introduce an element of fairness. We may not be trapped for long in suffering bodies and may not for long enjoy the pleasure of bodies born into luxuriant circumstances. We each may sample many (and possibly all) of the human and nonhuman lives open to us, thus spreading around not only the suffering but also the pleasure. Also, we should treat others well, if only out of self-interest. It might not be long before we find ourselves guests in their "body hotels."

The Universe

As the noted mathematician and physicist Sir James Jeans once observed, the "universe begins to look more like a great thought than a great machine" (Jeans, 1937, p. 122), or as another great physicist, Sir Arthur Eddington, remarked, "the stuff of the world is mind-stuff" (Eddington, 1920/1959, p. 200).

Indeed, the base reality of the world appears to be one of quantum probability waves inhabiting an abstract, multidimensional mathematical space rather than the solid, marble-like electron and protons zipping around in the four-dimensional spacetime continuum that we imagine to be the firm under-pinnings of our material existence. The mathematical complexity and beauty of the laws of the quantum mechanics are remarkable. It does indeed seem as though the Creator is, as both Jeans and Einstein thought, a great math-ematician. (Of course it could well be that the creation of the universe was a group effort, a kind of Manhattan Project involving trillions of mini-Shins embedded in an unimaginably complex "computer" in the "preuniverse," whatever that was.)

But if the universe is a thought, whose thought is it anyway? As noted above, many physicists have observed that the laws of the universe and the initial conditions set at the time of its creation seem extraordinarily finely-tuned to support the evolution of complex life forms and hence conscious observers (see Barrow & Tipler, 1986). This seeming evidence of intelligent design is often referred to as the Anthropic Principle. Was the universe created as a vast cosmic amusement park or "art gallery?" And why go to the trouble of designing such an elaborate "roadside attraction" unless One intended to enjoy it Oneself, if only vicariously? Are our individual consciousnesses just aspects of the Creator's (or Creators') consciousness, lost in an unimaginable form of contemplation of the myriad creatures It has managed to generate from Its mathematical inventions, much as we may become lost in the adventures of a goldfish in the bowl in our living room or in the adventures of the cybernetic "life" forms we may create when we implement the mathematician John Conway's "Game of Life" on our com-puter?

Of course, the Anthropic principle is based on the observation that the laws and initial conditions of the universe must be extremely fine-tuned to support life as we know it (i.e., carbon-based life forms). But there may be other forms of life (e.g., nucleon based) that may arise under different con-ditions. Also, there may be multiple universes created, so that we necessarily find ourselves in a universe capable of supporting conscious observers, with initial conditions and laws that would seem improbable had only one uni-verse been created with a random assortment of physical laws and initial con-ditions. Guth and Kaiser (2005), for instance, note that cosmic inflation (the currently favored model of cosmogenesis) may produce "pocket universes" in each of which the fundamental laws of physics might be different. Again, we of necessity inhabit a pocket universe that is capable of supporting the exis-tence of conscious observers. Also, as remarked above, given the vast realms of empty space hostile to life as we know it, the primary observers may well be drifting mini-Shins that just happen to become stuck in physical bodies from time to time. And still one must explain the laws and initial conditions that gave rise to cosmic inflation in the first place.

Consciousness and Cosmos

One's true self in the Eastern view is the pure consciousness that in Hindu philosophy is taken to be identical with all consciousness, including that of the World Soul or Brahman. Under the Vedantic worldview, there is only one pure consciousness, and we are the entire Universe looking at itself from different perspectives. Thus, when persons temporarily abandon their individual identities and perceive themselves as merging with the Cosmos or as being in perfect union with God, as in the mystical experiences described by James (1902), they are seeing directly into their true selves, according to this view. All consciousness is the one Consciousness that underlies this and all other worlds. In this view, we are fragments of the World Soul, our selves at once separate from, and yet identical to, one another.

One might imagine that a consciousness so complex and vast as to be able to create (perhaps literally dream up) such a startlingly wonderful (and frightening) world as this one might well become bored with its omniscience and may wish to lose itself in its creation, if only temporarily. It may need to fragment itself and temporarily shed much of its omniscience to accomplish this. We too might well begin to stagnate and become bored if we were to somehow become immortal and become trapped in our present bodies and mired in our present personalities and situation for all eternity. Death may be the rope thrown to free us from the quicksand of our current identities.

If these thoughts are correct, each of us, as centers of consciousness, will be around for a long time to come. But the lengths of our associations with our present personalities may be much shorter than we think. Our true selves, however, may be both much less than and much greater than we think.

References

Barrow, J. D., & Tipler, F. S. (1986). *The anthropic cosmological principle.* New York: Oxford University Press.

Beck, F. (1994). Quantum mechanics and consciousness. *Journal of Consciousness Studies, 1*(2), 153–255.

Blackmore, S. J. (1991). Beyond the self: The escape in reincarnation in Buddhism and psychology. In A. S. Berger & J. Berger (Eds.), *Reincarnation: Fact or Fable?* (pp. 117–129). London: Aquarian.

Blackmore, S. J. (1993). *Dying to live.* Buffalo, NY: Prometheus.

Blackmore, S. J. (2002). There is no stream of consciousness. *Journal of Consciousness Studies, 9*(5/6), 17–28.

Bohr, N. (1958). *Atomic physics and human knowledge.* New York: Wiley and Sons.

Burns, J. E. (1993). Current hypotheses about the nature of the mind-brain relationship and their relationship to findings in parapsychology. In K. R. Rao (Ed.), *Cultivating consciousness: Enhancing human potential, wellness and healing* (pp. 139–148). Westport, CT: Praeger.

Carington, W. (1949). *Mind, matter and meaning.* New Haven: Yale University Press.

Churchland, P. M. (1995). *The engine of reason, the seat of the soul: A philosophical journey into the brain*. Cambridge, MA: MIT Press.

Churchland, P. S. (1986). *Neurophilosophy*. Cambridge, MA: MIT Press.

Churchland, P. S. (2002). *Brain-wise: Studies in neurophilosophy*. Cambridge, MA: MIT Press.

Crick, F. (1994). *The astonishing hypothesis: The scientific search for the soul*. New York: Charles Scribner's Sons.

Cotterill, R. M. J. (1995). On the unity of conscious experience. *Journal of Consciousness Studies, 2*(4), 290–312.

Damasio, A. (1994). *Descartes' error: Emotion, reason and the human brain*. New York: G. P. Putnam's Sons.

Dennett, D. C. (1981). Where am I? In D. R. Hofstadter & D. C. Dennett (Eds.), *The mind's I: Fantasies and reflections on self and soul* (pp. 217–231). New York: Basic Books.

Dennett, D. C. (1991). *Consciousness explained*. Boston: Little, Brown.

Eccles, J. C. (1953). *The neurophysiological basis of mind*. Oxford: Clarendon.

Eccles, J. C. (1977). The human person in its two-way relationship to the brain. In J. D. Morris, W. G. Roll & R. L. Morris (Eds.), *Research in parapsychology, 1976* (pp. 251–262). Metuchen, NJ: Scarecrow Press.

Eccles, J. C. (1979). *The human mystery*. New York: Springer International.

Eccles, J. C. (1980). *The human psyche*. New York: Springer International.

Eccles, J. C. (1983). Voluntary movement, freedom of the will, moral responsibility. *Perkins Journal, 36*(4), 40–48.

Eccles, J. C. (1987). Brain and mind, two or one? In C. Blakemore & S. Greenfield (Eds.), *Mindwaves: Thoughts on intelligence, identity and consciousness* (pp. 293–304). New York: Basil Blackwell.

Eccles, J. C. (1989). *Evolution of the brain: Creation of the self*. New York: Routledge.

Eccles, J. C., & Robinson, D. (1984). *The wonder of being human*. New York: The Free Press.

Eddington, A. S. (1920/1959). *Space, time and gravitation: An outline of the general relativity theory*. New York: Harper & Row,

Eddington, A. S. (1935). *New pathways in science*. Cambridge, England: Cambridge University Press.

Fjermedal, G. (1987). *The tomorrow makers*. New York: MacMillan.

Flanagan, O. (1992). *Consciousness reconsidered*. Cambridge, MA: MIT Press.

Fodor, J. (1983). *The modularity of mind*. Cambridge: MIT Press/Bradford Books.

Gazzaniga, M. S. (1985). *The social brain: Discovering the networks of the mind*. New York: Basic Books.

Gazzaniga, M. S. (1989). Organization of the human brain. *Science, 245*, 947–952.

Gazzaniga, M. S. (1992). *Nature's mind*. New York: HarperCollins.

Griffin, D. R. (1988a). Introduction: The reenchantment of science. In D. R. Griffin (Ed.), *The reenchantment of science* (pp. 1–46). Albany: State University of New York Press.

Griffin, D. R. (1988b). Of minds and molecules: Postmodern medicine in a psychosomatic universe. In D. R. Griffin (Ed.), *The reenchantment of science* (pp. 141–163). Albany, New York: State University of New York Press.

Griffin, D. R. (1994). Dualism, materialism, idealism and psi. *Journal of the American Society for Psychical Research, 88*, 23–29.

Griffin, D. R. (1997). Panexperientialist physicalism and the mind-body problem. *Journal of Consciousness Studies, 4*(3), 248–268.

Guth, A. H., & Kaiser, D. I. (2005). Inflationary cosmology: Explaining the universe from the smallest to the largest scales. *Science, 307*, 884–890.

Hameroff, S. R. (1994). Quantum coherence in microtubules: A neural basis for emergent consciousness. *Journal of Consciousness Studies, 1*, 91–118.

Hart, H. (1958). To what extent can the issues with regard to survival be reconciled? *Journal of the Society for Psychical Research, 39*, 314–323.

Hilgard, E. (1977). *Divided consciousness*. New York: Wiley.

Hill, T. (2005). [Letter to the Editor.] *Skeptical Inquirer, 29(1)*, 61.

Hodgson, D. (1991). *The mind matters.* New York: Oxford University Press.
James, W. (1902). *The varieties of religious experience: A study in human nature.* New York: Longmans, Green & Co.
Jeans, J. (1937). *The mysterious universe.* Cambridge, England: Cambridge University Press.
John, E. R. (2003). A theory of consciousness. *Current Directions in Psychological Science, 12,* 244–250.
LeDoux, J. E. (1985). Brain, mind and language. In D. A. Oakley (Ed.), *Mind and brain* (pp. 197–216). New York: Methuen.
Leggett, A. J. (1987a). Reflection on the quantum measurement paradox. In B. J. Hiley & D. F. Peat (Eds.), *Quantum implications: Essays in honour of David Bohm* (pp. 85–104). London: Routledge & Kegan Paul.
Leggett, A. J. (1987b). *The problems of physics.* New York: Oxford University Press.
Libet, B. (1989). Neural destiny: Does the brain have a mind of its own? *The Sciences, 29*(2), 32–35.
Libet, B. (1991). Conscious functions and brain processes. *Behavioral and Brain Sciences, 14,* 685–686.
Libet, B. (1994). A testable field theory of mind-brain interaction. *Journal of Consciousness Studies, 1,* 119–126.
Marcel, A.J. (1988). Phenomenal experience and functionalism. In A. J. Marcel & E. Bisiach (Eds). *Consciousness in contemporary science* (pp. 121–158). New York: Oxford University Press.
Margenau, H. (1984). *The miracle of existence.* Woodbridge, CT: Ox Bow Press.
McDougall, W. (1926). *An outline of abnormal psychology.* London: Methuen.
Metzinger, T. (2003). *Being no one: The self-model theory of subjectivity.* Cambridge, MA: MIT Press.
Moravec, H. (1988). *Mind children: The future of robot and human intelligence.* Cambridge, MA: Harvard University Press.
Mohrhoff, U. (1999). The physics of interaction. In B. Libet, A. Freeman & K. Sutherland (Eds.), *The volitional brain* (pp. 165–184). Thorverton, UK: Imprint Academic.
Oakley, D. A. (1985a). Animal awareness, consciousness, and self-image. In D. A. Oakely (Ed.), *Mind and brain* (pp. 132–151). New York: Methuen.
Oakley, D. A. (1985b). Cognition and imagery in animals. In D. A. Oakley (Ed.), *Mind and brain* (pp. 99–131). New York: Methuen.
O'Keefe, J. (1985). Is consciousness the gateway to the hippocampal cognitive map? A speculative essay on the neural basis of mind. In D. A. Oakley (Ed.), *Brain and mind* (pp. 59–98). New York: Methuen.
Penfield, W. (1975). *The mystery of the mind.* Princeton, NJ: Princeton University Press.
Penrose, R. (1987). Quantum physics and conscious thought. In B. J. Hiley & F. D. Peat (Eds.), *Quantum implications: Essays in honour of David Bohm* (pp. 105–120). London: Routledge & Kegan Paul.
Penrose, R. (1994). *Shadows of the mind.* New York: Oxford University Press.
Popper, K., & Eccles, J. (1977). *The self and its brain.* New York: Springer International.
Rafal, R., Smith, J., Krantz, S., Cohen, A., & Brennan, C. (1990). Extrageniculate vision in hemianopic humans: Saccade inhibition by signals in the blind field. *Science, 250,* 118–120.
Ramachandran, V. S. (1980). Twins, split brains and personal identity. In B. D. Josephson & V. S. Ramachandran (Eds.), *Consciousness and the physical world* (pp. 139–163). New York: Pergamon Press.
Ramachandran, V. S., & Hirstein, W. (1997). Three laws of qualia: What neurology tells us about the biological functions of consciousness. *Journal of Consciousness Studies, 4*(5/6), 429–457.
Rao, K. R. (2002). *Consciousness studies: A cross-cultural perspective.* Jefferson, NC: McFarland & Co. Inc.
Sanders, M. D., Warrington, E. K., Marshall, J., & Weiskrantz, L. (1974). "Blindsight": Vision in a field defect. *Lancet* (April 20), *1*(7860), 707–708.
Schmidt, H. (1969). Precognition of a quantum process. *Journal of Parapsychology, 33,* 99–108.

Schmidt, H. (1970). PK tests with animals as subjects. *Journal of Parapsychology, 34*, 255–261.

Seife, C. (2003). Illuminating the dark universe. *Science, 203*, 2038–2039.

Skrbina, D. (2003). Panpsychism as an underlying theme in Western philosophy: A survey paper. *Journal of Consciousness Studies, 10*(3), 4–46.

Spence, S. A., & Frith, C. D. (1999). Towards a functional anatomy of volition. In B. Libet, A. Freeman, & K. Sutherland (Eds.), *The volitional brain: Toward a neuroscience of free will* (pp. 11–29). Thorverton, UK: Imprint Academic.

Squires, E. (1990). *Conscious mind in the physical world.* New York: Adam Holger.

Strawson, G. (1997). "The self." *Journal of Consciousness Studies, 4*(5/6), 405–428.

Stapp, H. P. (1992). A quantum theory of consciousness. In B. Rubik (Ed.), *The interrelationship between mind and matter* (pp. 207–217). Philadelphia, PA: The Center for Frontier Sciences.

Stapp, H. P. (1996). The hard problem: A quantum approach. *Journal of Consciousness Studies, 3*(3), 196–210.

Stevenson, I. (1987). *Children who remember past lives.* Charlottesville, VA: University Press of Virginia.

Stokes, D. M. (1987). Theoretical parapsychology. In S. Krippner (Ed.), *Advances in parapsychological research, Volume 5* (pp. 77–189). Jefferson, NC: McFarland.

Thalbourne, M. A. (2004). The Thouless-Wiesner shin theory: Can it be saved? *Paranormal Review*, No. 31, 16–17.

Thouless, R. H., & Wiesner, B. P. (1948). The psi process in normal and "paranormal" psychology. *Journal of Parapsychology, 12*, 192–212.

Tipler, F. J. (1994). *The physics of immortality.* New York: Doubleday.

Walker, E. H. (2000). *The physics of consciousness.* Cambridge, MA: Perseus Books.

Weiskrantz, L. (1986). *Blindsight: A case and implications.* Oxford: Oxford University Press.

Wheeler, J. A. (1983). Law without law. In J. A. Wheeler & W. H. Zurek (Eds.), *Quantum theory and measurement* (pp. 182–213). Princeton, NJ: Princeton University Press.

Wilson, D. L. (1999). Mind-brain interaction and the violation of physical laws. In B. Libet, A. Freeman, & K. Sutherland (Eds.), *The volitional brain* (pp. 185–200). Thorverton, UK: Imprint Academic.

4. Conversations About Survival: Novel Theoretical, Methodological, and Empirical Approaches to Afterlife Research

WILLIAM BRAUD*

During the last days of a conference on death and dying, Dr. William Braud's protagonistic alter-ego Alan starts an informal debate with his antagonist Erica, who adopts a somewhat skeptical point of view about survival. Erica's stance, however, is quite constructive because it not only challenges, but also presents some interesting interpretations and implications of ideas expressed by Dr. Braud. This deceptively simple conversation produces some fresh re-conceptualizations of the afterlife, and some innovative methods of testing, and even working with, discarnate entities are proposed.—Editors

Introduction

In this chapter, a fictional, storied, conversational format is used to address various alternative and novel approaches to survival/afterlife issues. Among the treated topics are ideas on the possible nature and modes of survival (including possibilities that only some survive, that survival may be "contentless," "witness-ing," or even "unconscious"); the role of thoughts, beliefs, and expectations in influencing the nature and experience of survival; and suggested expansions of research methods and empirical approaches for exploring survival (including a novel experimental design that addresses both investigator and participant

*I thank Jennifer Clements, Jerry Posner, Peter Raynolds, Nancy Rowe, Judy Schavrien, and Rhea White for helpful suggestions.

75

expectancies, new uses of hypnotic regression and evocation, experience-simulation contrasts, and life-impacts of "acting as if" with appropriate follow-ups). The discussion also addresses extensions and limitations of "super-psi" arguments (including typically-ignored time-displaced aspects), personification and dramatization (mythopoetic) aspects; selective suggestions relevant to several varieties of afterlife evidence (e.g., apparitions, hauntings, mediumship, OBEs, NDEs), and alternative conceptualizations of the nature of "reincarnation."

> In mystical literature words are frequently confused with things, and symbols with realities; so that much of this literature seems ... to refer to some self-consistent and exclusive dream-world, and not to the achievement of universal truth.... What elements are due to the suggestions of tradition, to conscious or unconscious symbolism, to the misinterpretation of emotion, to the invasion of cravings from the lower centers, or the disguised fulfillment of an unconscious wish? And when all these channels of illusion have been blocked, what is left? [Evelyn Underhill, 1920/1960, pp. 1–2].

Erica and I arrived at our pre-arranged lunch site almost simultaneously. It was good to see her again. We had known each other since graduate school days, when we had been fellow students in a very behavioristic psychology department. We often joked that we were recovering behaviorists. Erica had left her behaviorism behind to move into cognitive research and teaching. I had added other approaches in following my path as a clinical psychologist.

Erica was in town to attend a four-day conference sponsored by the National Research Academy (NRA) and devoted to research and issues involving death and dying. The last day of the conference had been set aside for presentations and discussions of survival and afterlife research. Knowing my long-term interest in parapsychology and psychical research, Erica had told me about the conference, thinking I might wish to attend. I was able to shift some appointments, making it possible for me to attend the last day and a half of the conference.

We spent the first part of our lunchtime catching up on each other's lives since Erica's last visit to California. As we sipped our coffees, I turned the conversation to the topic of the conference.

"I'm surprised that the National Research Academy is including sessions on survival/afterlife research in its program," I commented.

"Yes; curious, isn't it?" Erica replied. "I suppose that, since the conference is in San Francisco, the conference organizers must have assumed there would be a lot of interest in such a topic, among both professionals and the public."

"Now, Erica, I hope you haven't bought into that stereotype of California." I grinned.

"Well, Alan, you must admit," she paused for a moment. "Your beloved state has given birth to a lot of very strange ideas and practices."

Erica was an eternal skeptic — but, fortunately, an open-minded one. She was suspicious of even slightly outlandish ideas. However, in the face of sufficient evidence, she could change her mind and eventually embrace "strange" ideas — sometimes tentatively, sometimes even enthusiastically.

An Overview of the Subject Matter

"You know I've never understood your keen interest in life after death and all this psychic stuff."

"Erica, believe it or not, I'm skeptical about a lot of it myself, as are many parapsychologists. Many experimental parapsychologists accept the reality of different forms of psychic functioning — telepathy, clairvoyance, precognition, and psychokinesis — in the living, but they draw the line at the possibility that some aspect of ourselves might survive the death of the physical body. Some parapsychologists — actually, it would be better to call them psychical researchers — are willing to explore the possibility of some sort of survival of aspects of our personality or individuality after physical death. They have devoted considerable effort to studying the evidence for phenomena consistent with survival or an afterlife — phenomena such as apparitions, hauntings, mental mediumship, physical mediumship, poltergeist incidents, past-life recall, near-death experiences, and out-of-body experiences."

Erica interrupted, "I noticed that many of those things are mentioned in the program for tomorrow's sessions."

Erica extracted a program from her thin leather satchel and handed it to me. This part of the program seemed well-organized, with sessions devoted to theory, research methods, empirical findings, interpretations, implications, and even possible practical applications. From the names of the presenters and discussants, it seemed the conference organizers had achieved a reasonable balance of views. I recognized some well-respected researchers and advocates of survival, along with some thoughtful skeptics and counter-advocates.

* * *

"It's almost time for the afternoon sessions," I said, glancing at my watch. "What's next, and what do you think of the conference thus far?"

Relevance to Bereavement Applications

Erica replied, "This afternoon's sessions will address various approaches to working with the dying, and there will be some presentations on bereavement and ways of helping people in their bereavement processes. About the first two and a half days, there've been the usual boring conference presentations, with a few exciting and memorable ones interspersed."

Erica had described earlier, in an e-mail, her own conference contribution. She had presented her research on lucidity preceding death and summarized findings that indicated greatly increased cognitive, intellectual functioning just before death. I had been impressed with these findings, which were not at all consistent with the accepted view that our mental life is completely dependent on healthy and optimally functioning brain and body systems.

We left the coffee shop and made our way to the rooms where the afternoon sessions were to be held. I was pleased that my freed schedule had allowed me to partake of these dying and bereavement presentations, and I hoped that I might learn new approaches to use with my own bereaved clients.

One of the most exciting presentations — and one that even had parapsychological implications — was by a team of researchers at the Institute of Transpersonal Psychology in nearby Palo Alto. The researchers explored a so-called "psychomanteum process" that involved remembering a deceased friend or relative, sitting in a darkened room gazing into a mirror while thinking of the person, and finally discussing and musing over the experience. The study's main finding was a significant reduction in bereavement responses for the entire group of research participants. These included unresolved feelings, loss, grief, guilt, sadness, and need to communicate. Participants also reported significant impacts on their lives following the session. About half of the participants reported contacts with the sought deceased person. These took the forms of a variety of images appearing in the mirror, experiences of dialogue, sounds, light, body sensations, and smell. Several participants reported specific messages that they believed were from the sought persons.

The final portion of the conference began with an early evening presentation for both conference attendees and the general public that provided a good overview of the major methods, findings, and theories of survival/afterlife research. Erica and I had arranged to have a late dinner after the presentation. I hoped I would be able to help bring Erica up to speed on this topic. In earlier meetings, she had shared the latest information about what was happening in her field of cognitive psychology. I always appreciated these briefings, and I hoped to return the favor.

*   *   *

It turned out, however, that it was Erica who did most of the talking. The evening presentation had triggered many thoughts for her, and she was eager to share them with me. While waiting for and then nibbling on our appetizers, she launched into what turned out to be a lengthy and useful discussion of some of the foundational aspects of psychical research.

"That presentation was interesting," she said. "I scribbled a few notes to help me remember some things I wanted to ask you about." She removed a couple of sheets of paper from her always-present satchel and placed them on the table. "I suspect many of these things will be covered in tomorrow's more technical sessions. I hope so, because I have quite a few questions at this point."

I encouraged her to go on.

"OK," she said. "I want us to discuss three main points, and they are interrelated. The first has to do with the nature of survival, the second involves reincarnation, and the third concerns alternative interpretations of the evidence suggestive of survival."

I smiled, knowing I was in for a treat. Erica always had been good at generating possible alternative explanations of things. In fact, she was almost too good at this — violating a kind of Occam's Razor of theorizing by positing plurality without necessity. She was especially good at exposing hidden assumptions, questioning them, sometimes turning them on their heads, 180 degrees. This always reminded me of quantum physicist Niels Bohr's comments about two kinds of truth. To one kind, he said, belonged statements so simple and clear that the opposite assertion obviously could not be defended. The other kind, the so-called "deep truths," are statements in which the opposite also contains deep truth (Bohr, 1959).

On the Nature of Survival

"I can only discuss these things from the viewpoint of my training and work in cognitive psychology, of course," Erica began. "It's important that one's constructs be defined carefully. So, when we speak of 'survival,' what are we talking about? Just what is it that is supposed to survive?"

"I might be able to help out here," I offered. "The usual referent for survival is some recognizable aspect of personality or individuality. Of course, the body's matter and energy 'survive' in some form, and eventually undergo various changes and transformations. And the deceased's progeny and works survive — as actual persons, cultural artifacts, or memories in the minds of others. These sorts of survival are obvious, but trivial in relation to the kind of personal survival that we're addressing here. This personal survival should be such as to be recognizable by the person herself or himself, in alleged past life recall or reincarnation instances, or by others, in cases of ostensible communications from the deceased. The latter might be extended to identifiable physical or behavior characteristics of the deceased — things such as appearance, mannerisms, behaviors, and perhaps things such as attitudes or preferences."

"For such things to be identifiable," Erica pointed out, "there would have to be persistence of certain physical or quasi-physical forms or patterns, in cases of apparitions, or persistence of certain specific cognitive content or memories, in cases of communications."

"Yes," I agreed, "that would be necessary."

"As an aside," Erica added, "there does exist evidence that at least certain forms of individually acquired learning and memory actually can 'survive' the death of the individuals that initially acquired these. This evidence comes from so-called memory transfer studies that were conducted back in the 1960s and 1970s. These findings always were quite controversial, and they tend to be forgotten or dismissed nowadays. However, if one examines them carefully and objectively, one cannot but conclude that quite specific information could, indeed, survive transfer from one organism to another in some of these studies. In summary, naïve recipient animals injected with brain extracts from trained donor animals showed signs of the types of learning and memory that had been acquired by the donor animals. The best of these studies included proper controls to rule out various artifacts. It seemed that the carriers of the transferred and 'surviving' information were small-chain proteins, polypeptide molecules. These findings were too much for those who oversubscribed to the views that were prevalent at the time. Additionally, I think such work was about 5 or 10 years ahead of its time, being done before the various neuropeptides such as the endorphins and encephalins were discovered. So, for various reasons, the work was not accepted. I mention this because, if we assume for a moment that these findings were real, such studies did demonstrate survival of knowledge and memory. Of course, there was a physical substrate for such survival — the physical chemicals served to encode, carry, or catalyze the surviving information. Yet, these studies provided proof of principle — the principle being that knowledge or memories of one individual might survive the death of that individual and show up elsewhere, provided the detection system were appropriate. It occurs to me that the various pathways through which the knowledge and memories could be 'revived' in other, naïve organisms, in these memory transfer studies, could be studied as possible analog methods in which survival of individuality or personality might manifest in these human afterlife investigations."

"Hmmm. I think I see what you mean. The key would be how the survival evidence tends to be manifested — as a kind of passive, direct presentation to be 'discovered' by just about anyone or, instead, as a more active creation — or catalyzing, as you put it — of the information in the percipients or investigators. The first case would imply a kind of continuation of the personality or individuality of the deceased, whereas the second case would suggest a kind of re-creation of a simulacrum of the deceased or partial characteristics of the deceased. This is a subtle distinction, but it seems an important one."

"Yes, this is very similar to something I was going to mention later. But could you say more about what these psychical researchers think might survive, and in what forms?"

"Well, there's a view that the specific mind, for want of a better word, or individual consciousness of the deceased continues to survive death. It might do this for a lengthy period — perhaps indefinitely — or, more likely, some believe, it might persist for a while and then gradually fade away, like the prolonged echoes that can occur in certain mountainous regions. Another view, that is gaining in prominence, is that what survives might be a form of pure consciousness or witnessing consciousness — present and aware, but devoid of content. This would be analogous to a searchlight beam that is not illuminating anything particular."

"Ah," Erica interjected, "this suggests an interesting possibility: that what survives might not be "conscious" in the usual sense of self-conscious; that there might be some contentless awareness, without individual memories — in which case, would it even make sense to say that this would be a form of individual or personality survival? It might even be the case that something survives, but that something could be completely unconscious."

"What we're now addressing," I mentioned, "are areas where psychical research overlaps topics in Hinduism-Buddhism and mystical studies — each of these concerns itself with different forms of consciousness: some very content-determined and local, others content-free and nonlocal. These are areas where these various disciplines can cross-communicate and mutually enrich one another."

I continued, "Other than a first-person appreciation of the nature of surviving consciousness, I think the closest we might come to determining its possible form might be through studies of responsive apparitions, which seem to be aware of and respond to particulars in the environment, and through studying cases in which particular motives or needs seem to be present in apparitions or in communications ostensibly from the deceased."

"I suppose," said Erica, "there might be quite a range of forms of survival. They needn't be all of the same kind. Perhaps only some 'persons' survive, but not others."

"Yes," I agreed, "and it also seems possible that the thoughts, beliefs, and expectations of individuals might influence the nature of their survival or survival experiences or whether they even survive at all."

"Regarding the nature of survival," I added, " I know many feel that it would be a shame if nothing specific were retained — knowledge, memories, perhaps aspects of important relationships. They feel that the meaning and significance of life and of existence itself might be reduced if something 'individual' did not survive. I certainly appreciate that view. On the other hand, I have to recognize that such a form of survival might be what we wish would happen, rather than what might actually occur."

This reminded me of a concern that had haunted me for a long time — that the presumed nature of survival seemed too much like business as usual, that the usually-presumed form of afterlife existence was human, all too human, as Nietzsche might have put it. It seemed presumptuous to assume that the afterlife would so closely resemble our physically embodied life and our familiar lived experiences. Perhaps there would be continuity — but to some variable extent. Perhaps an afterlife, if such indeed existed, might be very, very different from our customary experiences — difficult or impossible for us to conceive or appreciate while still in our present, embodied form. It also might be possible that the nature of what might survive death, and the nature of the afterlife itself, might not be static. There might be change, development — even degradation. These change possibilities didn't seem to be addressed much by survival researchers.

I continued to ponder these things as we slowed our discussion to better concentrate on the main course of our seafood dinner. As we were finishing our light desserts, Erica returned to our survival topic. She mentioned that she was tired, and that she would postpone her other two points — about reincarnation and evidence interpretations — until tomorrow.

"I do want to mention two thoughts that pestered me as I listened to this evening's overview presentation," she said. "One thing is that psychical researchers and others might be taking the idea of 'life after death' too literally. Perhaps that should be taken symbolically or analogically: There are many ways of 'dying,' 'surviving,' and even being 'reborn' other than literally and physically. There are many ways of leaving old ways of being behind and taking on new ones. Exploring these could be just as interesting, exciting — and probably more useful — than focusing so much attention on what might happen after physical death.

"Another thing that bothered me is the seduction toward reification in all of this," she continued. "These psychical researchers, and many, many others, use terms such as 'mind' and 'consciousness' so frequently — and, I fear, so thoughtlessly — that these come to be considered as very concrete entities, rather than as dynamic processes; as nouns, rather than as verbs or gerunds. I wonder if views would change if gerund forms such as 'minding,' 'consciousing,' 'individualing,' or 'personing' were used rather than noun forms such as 'mind,' 'consciousness,' 'individuality' or 'personality'? Such terminology changes might allow us to emphasize processes more than entities (for example, conscious minding or unconscious minding, rather than conscious mind or unconscious mind), and this might allow us to think about psychic functioning, survival, and consciousness itself in alternative, and possibly more useful, ways. Immediately, this would raise the question of which other processes or entities — especially, possible physical or other supporting substrates — might be necessarily or sufficiently involved in the minding processes and, hence, in the possible survivaling processes."

"Erica, these thoughts are making my head hurt! Or maybe it's a sugar rush from this dessert!"

With that, we paid our bill, left the restaurant, walked out into the clear, chilly evening, and said our goodnights.

* * *

The next morning, I arrived at the conference center only minutes before the first session was about to begin. I looked for Erica but didn't see her. I found an empty seat near the front of the room just as the first speaker was being introduced for what was to be a set of presentations on the various research methods currently being used in survival/afterlife investigations. The presentations were pleasant enough, but because I had been keeping up with such things through the years, I didn't learn anything that was really new or exciting, methodologically.

A few minutes into the break, I spied Erica at the end of the short line of people standing before the coffee urns, and I joined her. We commented briefly on the session that had just ended.

"Before I forget, Erica, I have a synchronicity to report. Last night, after our discussion, I was reading Barbara Hannah's (1991) biography of Carl Jung. There were sections that seemed to speak to what we were discussing last night, about whether what survives might be conscious, semi-conscious, or unconscious. I copied some of these. Let me read them to you."

"The eternal Self needs the limited ego in order *to experience itself in outer reality*. It can thus, in earthly form, 'pass through the experiences of the three-dimensional world, and by greater awareness take a further step toward realization'" (p. 171).

"But we can also see here just how important the ego is to the Self, for it was the former that became *conscious* of the impression, that gave it three-dimensional existence, *definite* existence, whereas five thousand years are as yesterday to the Self, whose knowledge may indeed even be absolute, without ever registering in the here and now, in this moment, and thus giving it definite or objective existence" (p. 173).

"Thank you," said Erica as we reached the coffee urns and helped ourselves to two large cupfuls. "Those two quotes are quite apropos. They're also relevant to my point about certain substrates being necessary for the realization of certain processes. And if something is considered a process, rather than an entity, there is less temptation in thinking that something might 'survive' on its own, without its substrate(s)."

"That's a forceful argument, Erica, provided one has identified the true substrate. In the case of survival, for example, advocates of survival often like to present an analogy. In watching a television program, there is a tendency to think of the program as being intimately connected with the television set itself. Yet, if the television receiver (like your 'substrate'?) is smashed, that does not destroy the program; the program still exists 'in the air' (like your 'process'?). The TV receiver allows the expression of the program — the signal — but is not necessary for its generation or its existence. A similar argument often is proposed for the mind/body issue — that the brain may be necessary for the *read-out* of consciousness but not for its generation or existence. In such a view, consciousness is not an epiphenomenon of brain functioning. Rather, the brain might be a kind of transmitter or expressor of consciousness."

"That's an interesting position, Alan, but it isn't taken far enough. If there were no television sets, the signal never could be received; the program never could be known or experienced. It would be like the Self— in that Jung quotation you just shared — that cannot be known or realized without an ego. This is not unlike the nonlocal Schrödinger wave before it collapses and is localized or particularized by an observation. Without a detector, read-out device, or substrate — to use my term again — the 'process' would have no recognizable characteristics. To extend this to survival research, without a 'detector' of some sort, what 'survives' would have no individual, unique, or definite qualities that could be experienced — in either a third person or first person manner.

"We could take this analogy even further. In the case of the television program, there still are *other* physical substrates for the signal: There is a physical transmitter and antenna, and there is an electromagnetic carrier of the signal. Without those, the signal vanishes. So, in a sense, the perceived and appreciated TV program still is an epiphenomenon of the *entire system* of transmitter, carrier, and receiver. To shift this to a computer analogy, both hardware and software are necessary for information exchange, for intelligibility."

We had to stop at this point, for the next session — another one on research methods and representative findings — was about to begin.

*   *   *

Following the second morning session, Erica had promised to have lunch with some of her colleagues, and so we couldn't continue our conversation until just before the first afternoon session began. We decided to visit a room where several posters of research projects were on display. As we walked slowly along the aisles, stopping to read the posted findings, Erica mentioned her luncheon meeting:

"While Marsha, John, and I were having lunch, we talked a bit about how survival research methods might be extended. I told them you might be interested in the four of us getting together at the end of today's sessions, to explore these further."

I agreed that that would be interesting, and Erica said she would make arrangements for us to meet after the last session.

Regarding Reincarnation

"Erica, we still have a few minutes before the next session begins. You had mentioned earlier that you had some thoughts about reincarnation and about alternative explanations of some survival findings. What did you have in mind?"

"Regarding reincarnation, I was thinking of two ways of understanding *another life*. One way is to conceive of the very same entity — soul, spirit, personality, individual consciousness, or what have you — participating in both (or several) lives. According to this view, individual survival would make sense: Some aspect of the individual would continue, would persist in time, and that entity or aspect would be recognizable in the second life or in subsequent lives. According to another view, the second life would not be a persistence of the first, but would be made fresh, out of new ingredients, as it were, and would only *resemble* the first life — and the resemblance, in some cases, could be extremely close, could sometimes be virtually identical. The *pattern* would be the same or very similar, but it would be a different life, with different constituents, not a recycling of the original constituents. I don't think 'survival' would be an appropriate way to characterize this second possibility.

"Let me try to clarify all of this with some examples. Imagine the countless waves that continuously emerge from the sea. If you looked long enough and carefully enough, you probably would find quite a few wave patterns that are virtually identical. Let's suppose you observed one of these forming then disappearing, and then, shortly thereafter, you observed an identical one appearing nearby. You could say that one wave actually 'died' and then 'was reborn as' or 'became' the second wave — that is, the same substance survived, persisted, transferred itself from one to the other. But we know that did not happen. The second wave really was a new one, made up — afresh — from new materials, new water molecules. The only identical aspect is the form, the pattern, the appearance. Two different waves, but having virtually identical form, happened to emerge from a common ground.

"Even wave motions in general confirm the principle I'm describing. Drop a stone into a pond, and it seems that the same wave, the same set of water droplets and molecules, moves across the pond from one point to another, but in reality the individual droplets and molecules stay in one place and simply move up and down; the pattern moves horizontally, but the constituents don't; the moving wave is created (then disappears) afresh, out of new materials, at each point. Continuity is an illusion.

"Applying this same principle to human reincarnation can yield a different view of the process: What reincarnates is a *pattern*, not necessarily a persisting, continuing individual 'entity' of some sort that survives and is reborn. What might be happening, in cases of the reincarnation type, could be multiple but fresh instantiations of a certain pattern, template, or archetype, rather than the persistence and recycling of a particular being."

Once again, our discussion was cut short by the beginning of the next session. All this talk about sea waves had reminded me of an old Tennyson poem I had memorized in high school. As I walked to my seat in the meeting room, the last stanza ran through my mind and seemed particularly apropos:

> Break, break, break,
> At the foot of thy crags,
> O Sea! But the tender grace of a day that is dead,
> Will never come back to me.

*   *   *

As I waited for the first afternoon presentation, Erica's wave analogies continued to flow through my head. The idea of waves replaced by other waves reminded me of an old Buddhist text in which King Milinda was questioning the sage Nagasena. Among many similes that Nagasena used to help the King's understanding was one about whether the flame of a lamp that burned later in the night was the same at the flame that burned earlier. The answer was yes and no. One flame ceased and another immediately took its place — simultaneously, continuously. The simile could be applied to "rebirth" or even to consciousness after death. The "new" consciousness might be neither new nor the same, or both new and the same.

There were three sessions that afternoon — a short one in which additional findings were presented, a lengthy session devoted to various theories and interpretations that might (or might not) account for various types of evidence, and another short session devoted to possible practical applications and implications of this kind of research. During the breaks between sessions, Erica and I had brief discussions about theory, explanations, and applications.

Alternative Explanations
and Practical Applications

We covered three major interpretations of survival findings — that these were actually what they appeared on the surface, that is, manifestations and communications of the discarnate; that the findings might be the results of very accurate, complex psychic functioning on the part of the living persons involved in providing and collecting the evidence and only simulated survival (the so-called "superpsi" interpretation); and that the findings might be productions of the personifying, dramatizing, mythopoetic tendencies of our "unconscious minds"— ways of communicating with ourselves in the service of providing needed lessons and satisfying important wishes.

Regarding superpsi, I suggested that this might account for some, but not necessarily all, survival evidence, and that a wise approach would be to evaluate the evidence on a case-by-case basis, to make judgments about when superpsi might or might not reasonably account for the given findings. I mentioned that there were well-documented cases in which psychic functioning in the living could be unconscious, accurate, and complex, and that it might, indeed, account for some afterlife findings. Additionally, we don't know the range or limits of what might be possible through psi in the living, so it would be unwise to place limitations on it in the face of such ignorance. I also pointed out that even advocates of the superpsi hypothesis did not devote sufficient attention to the possible actions of time-displaced (forward-in-time and backward-in-time) forms of psychic functioning in accounting for how and when crucial survival-simulating information might be acquired.

I shared my disappointment that parapsychologists and psychical researchers tended to view superpsi and survival in an either/or manner. I preferred a combinatorial, both/and appreciation of the matter. I saw no reason for psi in the living not to be mixed with the actual existence of some afterlife process. It seemed that aspects of the three processes — some afterdeath residuum, psi in the living, and the mythopoetic propensity of our psyche — were very likely to be mixed, happening all at once. The triggering source for living psi could be some surviving residuum. The trigger might also be some latent trace in the physical environment that suddenly became apprehended, as William Roll had suggested, in his notion that consciousness was embodied and also emplaced. And the mythopoetic skills of our psyche could weave their tales, personifications, and dramatizations — perhaps triggered by living psi, but perhaps also triggered by subtle, invisible contact with some surviving residuum — as ways of bringing those triggering aspects into our awareness.

In discussing practical applications, I felt it important to tell Erica that although I had had a nearly lifelong interest in psychic phenomena, this interest had been bolstered by the reports I almost constantly received from my clients about their own psychic experiences. What had struck me most forcefully were the profound impacts that such experiences had had on my clients' lives. Although I had once been most keenly interested in the veridicality of these unusual experiences, through the years it had become increasingly important for me to study and appreciate the meanings and life-impacts of these experiences for those who had them. Certainly, it is a lot easier to study the side effects and aftereffects of such experiences, and to reach some fairly unambiguous conclusions about these, than it is to explore the reality status of the phenomena themselves. Each approach has its place, of course. But I had been increasingly thinking that psi researchers and psychical researchers — with a few notable recent exceptions — generally have overemphasized the need to establish the "reality" of their studied phenomena, as *events*, and have, usually, underemphasized the life-impacts of these experiences, as *experiences*. They have been behaving like para*ontologists* rather than para*psychologists*.

It also struck me that psi researchers and psychical researchers have been subscribing to a very narrow view of "reality"— equating this with *physical* reality. It seemed much more reasonable, especially for psychologists, to honor William James' view of reality as anything that we find ourselves obliged to take into account in any way. If an experience of X, whatever that might be, has a meaningful impact on a person, then X is real to that person. And if the effects of X on the person are important to us, as professionals or as friends or loved ones of that person, then X obviously becomes real to us, as well.

Whether occurrences such as apparitions, hauntings, mental and physical mediumship, poltergeist incidents, past-life recall, near-death experiences, and out-of-body experiences might be "real" in the physical reality sense is, of course, an important question to ask and to attempt to answer. Equally important, especially for those in the psychological, human, and social sciences, is the question of the functions such occurrences might serve in the lives of the experiencers.

I was pleased that some of these functions had been identified in the day's final session. A number of investigators had summarized effects of survival-/afterlife-related experiences that they had found in their studies. The experiences can open the experiencers to greater possibilities, prompting them to consider whether — and, sometimes, allowing them to *firmly know* that — there is something More to reality than they previously assumed or understood. The experiences can provide affirmations, confirmations, and sometimes specific directions regarding courses of action that are being considered or undertaken. Sometimes the experiences provide warnings or help prepare the experiencer for future challenging events. If they involve deaths of family, friends, or loved ones, the experiences often help the experiencers deal with feelings of loss and grief, and help them deal more effectively with issues of unfinished business with the deceased. In general, the experiences appear to foster feelings of, and appreciation of, linkages, connections, and community — with others and with all aspects of nature.

Of course, these experiences sometimes are accompanied by "negative" side effects or aftereffects — feelings of fear, bewilderment, even guilt in some cases. It is important to understand these reactions, as well, in order to help persons better deal with these. Indeed, simply sharing what is known and not known about such experiences often serves to greatly diminish strong feelings of anxiety or uncertainty about the nature and meaning of these experiences. People often are greatly helped simply by learning that they are not alone or unique in having such experiences, that the experiences are much more common than previously assumed. Even in these relatively enlightened times, there are still many who consider these experiences signs of craziness or works of the devil. Removing such misapprehensions often can be extraordinarily healing.

*   *   *

After the day's final session, Erica, John, Marsha, and I joined one another in a small room to the right of the main conference area. After introductions and some general talk about the conference as a whole, we began discussing ways in which survival research methods might be extended. It turned out that John was a health psychologist, with a strong background in hypnosis; he was able to offer some interesting suggestions for novel uses of hypnosis in survival research. Marsha had expertise in both cognitive science and neuropsychology, and she, too, was able to offer some novel suggestions for research designs.

Novel Research Approaches

"I'll start with something obvious," Erica began. "In any research project, it's important to work with experienced and well-motivated research participants. After all, if one is interested in learning whether white crows exist — to paraphrase William James — one doesn't set out by studying brown sparrows. Purposive sampling — as is done as a matter of course in qualitative research, nowadays — is an appropriate approach. I noticed, in many of today's presentations, that experimental parapsychologists still seem to be following quantitative design drummers, with random samples of unselected participants, and so on. This might be useful if one were interested in discovering general, universal laws, but if one simply wishes to learn or demonstrate whether a particular phenomenon exists, it is not necessary to prove that it exists in everyone or is inevitably present at the .05 level of significance."

"Speaking of purposive or focused sampling," I added, "I find it curious that there has been so little research, among psychical researchers, in trying to 'contact' recently deceased psychical researchers. Quite a few very dedicated parapsychologists and psychical researchers died recently; many of these had very keen interests in survival. Of all people, it would seem they would be highly motivated to contact the living, if they did, indeed, survive in some form. It's strange that there have been so few concerted efforts to contact such persons. This stands in stark contrast to what was attempted, in the early days, when some of the founding members of the Society for Psychical Research, such as Myers, Sidgwick, and Gurney, passed away."

"Something else that could be done," Marsha contributed, "is to simply 'listen' more often. If the discarnate continue to exist in some form, and are trying to communicate, how many of us are really listening? We keep our time and our minds filled to the brim, 99.9 percent of the time. Our phones are either busy or off the hook nearly all the time; if someone were attempting to call, it would be almost impossible for them to get through! What might happen if psychical researchers simply quieted themselves, unbusied their minds, and simply made themselves available for possible messages, for some reasonable time periods each day?"

"And that also would require increased sensitivity and preparation on the part of the listeners," added John. "The researchers themselves would have to become more adequate to the task, more skilled in becoming aware of and understanding subtle thoughts, feelings, and images that might carry information relevant to afterlives."

"I was thinking," said Marsha, "that one of the most direct ways to explore survival would be to find persons who might be really skilled at telepathic attunement, have them connect with the mentation of persons who are near death, and monitor this mentation as closely and as continuously as possible. If this would be done, keeping the telepathists 'blind' as to the time of death of those they were monitoring, it might be possible to note what happened at the time of death — whether the mentation continued, and in which form, and for how long. This seems far out, but I think such a study actually could be conducted, with the help of persons in hospitals, hospices, and so on."

"I think this brainstorming is exciting. Thank you, Marsha," I said.

"In the interest of further brainstorming," John offered, "let me share some thoughts about how hypnosis might be used in novel ways. Hypnotic regression could be used to help people who have had near-death experiences, out-of-body experiences, past-life recall, or other afterlife-related experiences relive, recall, and better integrate those experiences. Another approach would be to hypnotically regress persons to early childhood ages, to help them recall possible past lives — given that past life memories tend to occur early, then disappear with age. Note that this differs from using hypnosis and suggestions for recall of past lives themselves. Still another approach might be to simply hypnotize persons and suggest that they be more receptive and less resistant to possible afterlife phenomena. This could increase their sensitivity and allow them to become better detectors of survival evidence."

"In terms of gathering more and better information about experiences, persons with similar histories of experiences could be brought together for group phenomenological sessions," Erica added.

Marsha offered the following: "The typical way of dealing with the possibility of investigator or participant bias or influence upon research findings is either to ignore this factor or to reject findings entirely. My suggestion is to deal with possible investigator and participant biases more directly by maximizing them, manipulating them, and assessing their possible roles and interactions. For example, we could use a 2 × 2 design to compare and contrast the types of past-life recall findings that emerge from participants with two types of belief systems (reality of a past-life existence versus subconscious construction of 'memories') who are studied by two types of investigators (those with strong beliefs in the reality of survival and past-life recall versus those who attribute the information to subconscious construction). By studying the types of information that emerge within each of the four 'cells' of this 2 × 2 design, and by studying themes and details that seem invariant or variant across the conditions, we could emerge with a better idea of possible interactions of findings with the belief systems of investigators and participants. The principle could be extended to explore other types of experiences, as well."

John contributed another interesting research idea: "Hypnotic, waking suggestion, and experience-simulation work could be done in which participants are asked to imagine and fill themselves fully with the cognitive, emotional, evaluative, volitional, and expectational accompaniments of three survival alternatives or scenarios, and then act and function on the basis of those different belief patterns, so that we might be able to observe commonalities and differences associated with three 'as if' answers to the survival question. The three patterns could be (a) consciousness is an epiphenomenon of brain functioning that ceases when the body dies; (b) consciousness may persist after death in a form in which fragments of individuality, specific memories, and personality characteristics may still be recognizable and which may fade after some duration; and (c) consciousness continues in a much more persistent but depersonalized, attribute-free, and nonlocal form. We could study possible life-impacts of acting as if each of these scenarios was true, and there could be appropriate follow-ups after various time intervals. Findings might suggest new insights about the three answers to the survival question that could lead to new research directions and possibilities not yet obvious to us."

I offered another thought of my own: "There's a very interesting assessment tool that could be used in survival research — the Projective Differential (PD), developed by Peter Raynolds. The PD uses choice responses to very briefly presented pairs of carefully designed, abstract images in order to register holistic, intuitive, affective (nonverbal, "unconscious") reactions, preferences, and attitudes. It has features similar to those of Charles Osgood's more familiar Semantic Differential; it resembles a tachistoscopic Rorschach presentation. The rapid and projective nature of the procedure serves to minimize deliberate, conscious distortions, and, therefore, the PD results may have greater validity than do many deliberate, verbal assessments. The PD procedures also include built-in indicators of the discrepancy or incongruence between its own novel (imagistic, intuitive, affective) measures and more traditional (verbal, consciously and deliberately considered) measures. It can be used to provide profiles of idiosyncratic meanings of various target referents (e.g., myself, my home environment, my view of life after death). My thought is that the PD could be administered to various persons before their deaths. Later, should any of the deceased be channeled or their personalities taken on by mediums, the channelers or mediums could be asked to retake the PD when representing the deceased. The pre-death and post-life PD profiles could be compared — as an additional indicator of the possible identity of the source of the post-life PD. As far as I know, the PD has not yet been used in psychical research, but I think it holds great promise."

A conference official approached us, indicating that they would be closing the rooms for the day. We gathered our belongings and thoughts and brought them with us — to continue our discussion elsewhere.

Coda on Reincarnation

Upon returning home, after the conference, I recalled that I once had read something similar to some of what Erica had shared in her discussion of reincarnation. After some searching I was able to find it. It was part of a letter that the Indian philosopher and spiritual teacher, Sri Aurobindo, had written to a student in 1933:

You must avoid a common popular blunder about reincarnation. The popular idea is that Titus Balbus is reborn again as John Smith, a man with the same personality, character, attainments as he had in his former life with the sole difference that he wears coat and trousers instead of a toga and speaks in cockney English instead of popular Latin. That is not the case. What would be the earthly use of repeating the same personality or character a million times from the beginning of time till its end? The soul comes into birth for experience, for growth, for evolution till it can bring the Divine into Matter. It is the central being that incarnates, not the outer personality — the personality is simply a mould that it creates for its figures of experience in that one life. In another birth it will create for itself a different personality, different capacities, a different life and career.... It is not the personality, the character that is of the first importance in rebirth — it is the psychic being who stands behind the evolution of the nature and evolves with it. The psychic when it departs from the body, shedding even the mental and vital on its way to its resting place, carries with it the heart of its experiences — not the physical events, not the vital movements, not the mental buildings, not the capacities or characters, but something essential that it gathered from them, what might be called the divine element for the sake of which the rest existed. That is the permanent addition, it is that that helps in the growth towards the Divine. That is why there is usually no memory of the outward events and circumstances of past lives ... [Aurobindo, 1970, pp. 451–452].

References

Aurobindo, S. (1970). *Letters on yoga.* Pondicherry: Sri Aurobindo Ashram Trust.
Bohr, N. (1959). Discussion with Einstein on epistemological problems in atomic physics. In P. A. Schilpp (Ed.), *Albert Einstein: Philosopher-scientist: Vol. 1* (pp. 201–241). New York: Harper Torchbooks.
Hannah, B. (1991). *Jung: His life and work: A biographical memoir.* Boston: Shambhala.
Hastings, A., Hutton, M., Braud, W., Bennett, C., Berk, I., Boynton, T., Dawn, C., Ferguson, E., Goldman, A., Greene, E., Hewett, M., Lind, V., McLellan, K., & Steinbach-Humphrey, S. (2002). Psychomanteum research: Experiences and effects on bereavement. *Omega: Journal of Death and Dying, 45*(3), 211–228.
James, W. (1911). *Some problems in philosophy.* New York: Longmans, Green.
James, W. (1969). What psychical research has accomplished. In G. Murphy & R. O. Ballou (Eds.), *William James on psychical research* (pp. 25–47). New York: Viking. (Original work published 1890).
Osgood, C. E., Suci, G. J., & Tannenbaum, P. H. (1957). *The measurement of meaning.* Urbana: University of Illinois Press.
Raynolds, P. A. (1997). On taming the evaluation monster: Toward holistic assessments of transformational training effects. *Simulation and Gaming: An International Journal of Theory, Practice and Research, 28*(3), 286–316.
Rhys Davids, T. W. (Trans.). (1963). *The questions of King Milinda* (2 vols). New York: Dover. (Original work published 1890–1894).
Roll, W. G. (1995). Psyche and survival. In L. Coly & J. D. S. McMahon (Eds.), *Parapsychology and thanatology.* New York: Parapsychology Foundation.
Underhill, E. (1960). *The essentials of mysticism and other essays.* New York: E. P. Dutton & Co. (Original work published 1920).

5. Hallucination Proneness and Experiences Related to Survival

Michael A. Thalbourne

Results from two questionnaire studies by Dr. Michael Thalbourne show that hallucination proneness is a predictor of hearing the voice of a dead person; and that belief in, and experience of paranormal phenomena is a predictor of three single items—(a) "I have had veridical, nonhallucinatory visionary experience," (b) "In the past I have heard the voice of a dead person speaking to me," and (c) "I have felt, heard or seen a ghost or spirit." These results were replicated in a follow-up study. However, Dr. Thalbourne's post hoc analysis suggests that there is no direct relationship between paranormal belief/experience and hallucination proneness.—Editors

This chapter is divided into two parts. In Part One, 244 psychology undergraduates were administered the 12-item, true/false Launay-Slade Hallucination Scale (LSHS), together with the Rasch Australian Sheep-Goat Scale (RASGS; a paranormal belief scale), Tellegen's Absorption Scale,* and three single items ("I have had veridical, nonhallucinatory visionary experience," "In the past I have heard the voice of a dead person speaking to me," and "I have felt, heard or seen a ghost or spirit"). Pearson correlations suggested relationships between all these variables, and so multiple regression analysis was carried out in an attempt to predict each of the three single items. Hallucination-proneness proved to be a significant predictor for hearing the voice of a dead person; the Sheep-Goat Scale was a predictor for all three single items, while Absorption predicted none. In Part Two, 60 psychology students in a replication study were administered a disguised version of the LSHS (it was embedded in the Absorption Scale), as well as the RASGS. After filling

*(see Appendix)

94

out the combined questionnaire, participants were asked to describe what immediately entered their consciousness when they encountered the word "orange," and then the word "democracy," in counterbalanced order. It was predicted that persons scoring *high* on the Hallucination Scale tend to give *sensory* associations to both words, while persons scoring *low* on the Scale report the *word* or concept without images. This prediction was not significantly confirmed. However, the results of Part One were replicated. Moreover, post hoc analysis suggested that after controlling for the influence of absorption, there is no relationship between paranormal belief/experience and hallucination-proneness.

Introduction

The Launay-Slade Hallucination Scale (hereinafter LSHS) is a 12-item true/false questionnaire scale designed to measure predisposition to hallucination. According to the authors' summary, the Scale "includes both pathological items and other items which appear to represent sub-clinical forms of hallucinatory experience" (Launay & Slade, 1981, p. 221).

The LSHS was constructed by first listing 30 potential items. A normal control group and a patient (hallucinating) group were then compared on these items. Then, after combining with a prisoner group, factor analysis, classical item analysis, and goodness of fit to the Rasch model were applied. In this way, 12 items passed the tests and were ranked for endorsement frequency: "of the first seven items three are concerned with 'vivid' or 'intrusive thoughts,' three with 'vivid daydreams' and one with overt 'auditory hallucinations,' while of the latter five items, four are concerned with overt 'auditory hallucinations' and one with overt 'visual hallucinations'" (Launay & Slade, 1981, p. 226). The visual item correlated positively and significantly with all the other 11 items, auditory and imaginative. In a book chapter concerning hallucinatory experiences, Bentall (2000, p. 90) refers to this questionnaire favorably and cites two studies that have used it (viz., Bentall & Slade, 1985; and Rankin & O'Carrol, 1995).

The main finding in the initial Launay-Slade study was a significantly positive correlation with the P scale (i.e., Psychoticism: Eysenck & Eysenck, 1975). The researchers also noted that no items were concerned with dream experience, a finding which "tends to go against the general theory of hallucinations proposed by West (1962) who suggests that dreams represent a sleeping manifestation of waking hallucinations, lying on the same continuum" (Launay & Slade, 1981, pp. 230–231).

In a study by Bentall, Claridge and Slade (1989), 14 "schizotypal" or psychotic scales were administered along with the four subscales of the Eysenck Personality Questionnaire (Eysenck & Eysenck, 1975). One of these schizotypal scales was the LSHS, scores on which were found to be lower in older people (*r* with age = -0.28). Factor analysis was carried out (at first excluding four delusion scales), and the LSHS loaded on the first of three factors, suggesting "more active or positive forms of psychotic symptomatology" (Bentall et al., 1989, p. 367), in particular delusions and hallucinations.

Also presented was a table of intercorrelations between all 18 scales. The correlations with the LSHS and their significance were noted for the present chapter and are given in the appropriate column in Table 5.1.

As to moderately large correlations, high scorers on the LSHS tended to score higher on Magical Ideation, Schizotypal Personality Disorder,* Hypomanic Personality, Delusions of Disintegration, Borderline Personality Disorder,* Delusions of Contrition, Perceptual Aberration, Delusions of Grandeur, the Nielsen-Petersen Schizophrenism Scale, and Neuroticism. The LSHS was weakly correlated with Psychoticism (P), Delusions of Persecution, Schizoidia, and negatively with the Lie Scale, indicating some social desirability responding.

Note that a large replication study (*N* = 1095) was carried out by

Table 5.1— Correlations between the LSHS and 17 Variables Measured by Bentall et al. (1989), and by Claridge et al. (1996)

Variable	*r*	
	Bentall et al. (1989) $N = 180$	Claridge et al. (1996) $N = 1095$
Magical Ideation Scale	.63***	.70***
Schizotypal Personality Disorder	.58***	.73***
Hypomanic Personality	.58***	.63***
Delusions of Disintegration	.52***	.64***
Borderline Personality Disorder	.49***	.52***
Perceptual Aberration Scale	.46***	.65***
Delusions of Contrition	.45***	.36***
Delusions of Grandeur	.43***	.45***
Nielsen-Petersen Schizophrenism Scale	.32***	.38***
Neuroticism	.31***	.40***
Psychoticism	.28***	.21***
Delusions of Persecution	.26***	.32***
MMPI Schizoidia Scale	.24***	.30***
Social Anhedonia	.05	.15***
Extraversion	.02	.15***
Physical Anhedonia	−.10	−.12***
Lie Scale	−.16*	−.08**

*: $p < .05$; **: $p < .01$; ***: $p < .001$ (all p values are two-tailed)

*For this and various other technical scale names, see the Appendix.

Claridge *et al.* (1996). The correlations that they obtained with the LSHS together with their significance are given in the last column of Table 1. (Note parenthetically that the rank-order correlation for these two columns of correlation coefficients is extremely high, r_s = .95, p = .001, indicating a similar order, though it must be borne in mind that the data from Bentall *et al.* are *included* in Claridge *et al.*) Note that the LSHS in Claridge *et al.* again loaded most strongly on the first of four factors, this factor being called "Aberrant perceptions and beliefs" (p. 103).

In the meantime, McCreery and Claridge (1995) surveyed the out-of-the-body experience and its relation to personality. One of the scales they used was the LSHS, and it was found that those who had an out-of-body experience (i.e., OB-experients) scored significantly higher than non-OB-experients.

Thalbourne (1998) administered the LSHS and three schizotypal scales and others, plus some single-items, to 244 students studying psychology at various levels. The correlations between the LSHS and these variables, together with their significance, were specially calculated for the present chapter from these data, and are shown in Table 5.2.

Moderately high correlations were found with Schizotypal Personality Disorder, the Questionnaire on Dissociative Experience, Fantasy-Proneness, the Dissociative Experience Scale, Magical Ideation, the 29-item Transliminality Scale, Tellegen's Absorption Scale, the Rasch Manic-Depressiveness Scale, Hyperaesthesia, the Rasch Australian Sheep-Goat Scale (paranormal belief/experience), frequency of dream-interpretation, synesthesia, neuroticism, and the Rasch Mystical Experience Scale. Weak relationships were found with (positive) attitude towards dream-interpretation, the Creative Personality Scale, report of an out-of-body experience, Psychoticism (P), religiosity, and the Lie Scale (this latter being significantly negative).

Where the three studies overlap — namely, on Magical Ideation, Schizotypal Personality Disorder and Neuroticism — there is replication of the Bentall *et al.* study in terms of both significance and magnitude of the relationships.

While the Bentall *et al.* (1989) study and the Claridge *et al.* (1996) study were mostly concerned with psychopathology, the Thalbourne (1998) study included a large number of non-pathological scales, and it is interesting to note that in addition to pathological scales such as Psychoticism, dissociative experience and manic-depression, the LSHS also has relevance to such areas as the study of belief in and experience of the putatively paranormal (e.g., having an out-of-body experience), to absorption and synaesthesia, to religiosity and mystical experience, to creativity and fantasy-proneness, and the practice of dream-interpretation.

In Part One of this study, correlates of 3 of the above-mentioned

Table 5.2 — Correlations between the LSHS and 21 Variables Measured
by Thalbourne (1998) in Order of Magnitude (*N* = 244)

Variable	r
Schizotypal Personality Disorder	.71***
Questionnaire on Dissociative Experience	.68***
Inventory of Childhood Memories & Imaginings (Fantasy-Proneness)	.65***
Dissociative Experience Scale	.59***
Magical Ideation Scale	.59***
29-item Transliminality Scale	.58***
Tellegen Absorption Scale	.53***
Rasch Manic-Depressiveness Scale	.45***
Hyperaesthesia Scale	.38***
Rasch Australian Sheep-Goat Scale	.35***
Frequency of dream-interpretation	.34***
Synaesthesia	.33***
Neuroticism (*N* = 83)	.32**
Attitude toward dream-interpretation	.28***
Creative Personality Scale	.27***
Have had an Out-of-the-body Experience	.25***
Rasch Mystical Experience Scale	.24***
Psychoticism P (*N* = 83)	.23*
Religiosity	.23***
Extraversion (*N* = 83)	.02
Lie Scale (*N* = 83)	−.28*

*: $p < .05$; **: $p < .01$; ***: $p < .001$ (all p values are two-tailed)

scales were sought for 3 single-item variables of psychological and parapsychological interest, namely, question #8 of the Rasch ASGS on having veridical, nonhallucinatory visionary experience; a specially composed item similar to the LSHS statements: "In the past I have heard the voice of a dead person speaking to me"; and "I have felt, heard or seen a ghost or spirit." In Part Two an additional experiment was devised with the aim of investigating more closely what the LSHS is measuring.

Part One

Method

PARTICIPANTS. Two hundred and forty-four students of first-year and third-year psychology were surveyed. Twenty-eight percent were male. Age ranged from 17 to 63, with a mean of 25 years (*SD* = 10 years).

MATERIALS. The participants were administered a lengthy questionnaire, but for the purpose of the present analyses it suffices to say that the questionnaire included the LSHS, the Absorption scale (Tellegen & Atkinson, 1974), and the Rasch Australian Sheep-Goat Scale (Rasch ASGS; Lange & Thalbourne, 2002), which measures belief in, and alleged experience of, the paranormal. These were chosen as the predictor variables.

Also measured were three dependent variables: (1) on a scale where 0 was interpreted as "false," 1 as "uncertain," and 2 as "true," was the item: "I am completely convinced that I have had at least one vision that was not an hallucination and from which I received information that I could not have otherwise gained at that time and place" (item #8 on the Rasch ASGS); 21% participants said "true"; (2) the true/false item "In the past I have heard the voice of a dead person speaking to me"; 11% said "true"; and (3) from the Inventory of Childhood Memories and Imaginings (ICMIC; Myers, 1983) was the true/false item #33, namely, "I have felt, heard, or seen a ghost or spirit," to which 37% said "true."

PROCEDURE. First-year participants were given half of the combined questionnaire on one occasion, and the other half a week later. Third-year participants were given a copy of the combined questionnaire to take away, fill out and return in their own time.

Results

Descriptive statistics for the LSHS, the Absorption scale, and the Rasch ASGS are given in Table 5.3.

INTERCORRELATIONS. The (Pearson) intercorrelations between the three multi-item scales and the three single items are shown in Table 5.4.

Note first that all the correlations are significant ($p < .001$). It can be seen that the LSHS correlated moderately with absorption and the sheep-goat scale, and to a lesser degree with having veridical visionary experience, hearing voices and sensing ghosts. Of these latter three items, the intercorrelations were

Table 5.3 — Descriptive Statistics for the Sample of 244 (Thalbourne, 1998)				
Variable	*Minimum*	*Maximum*	*M*	*SD*
Launay-Slade Hallucination Scale	0.00	10.00	4.04	2.53
Absorption Scale	5.00	34.00	21.94	6.75
Rasch ASGS	8.13	43.39	24.84	6.58

Table 5.4 — Pearson *r* Intercorrelations for the Three Scales and Three Single Items (*N* = 244)					
Variable	*LSHS*	*Absorption*	*Rasch ASGS*	*Vision*	*Voice*
Absorption	.53	–	–	–	–
Rasch ASGS	.33	.58	–	–	–
Vision	.27	.41	n/a	–	–
Voice	.30	.25	.35	.33	–
Ghost	.24	.28	.45	.47	.30

Note: All correlations are significant at better than the $p < .001$ level

moderate, especially for having had veridical visionary experience and having sensed a ghost.

REGRESSION ANALYSES. The predictor variables were entered into a standard multiple regression analysis for each of the three single item variables:

1. For having a veridical visionary experience, using the three predictor variables Rasch ASGS,* the LSHS and Absorption, the $R = .61$ ($R^2 = .38$), and the multiple correlation was significant, $F(3, 234) = 47.22, p < .001$. The only significant Beta† was .56 for the Rasch ASGS.

2. For hearing the voice of a dead person, $R = .39$, ($R^2 = .15$), and the ANOVA was significant, $F(3, 236) = 14.28, p < .001$. Betas were significant for the LSHS (.20) and the Rasch ASGS (.31).

3. For sensing a ghost, $R = .46$, ($R^2 = .21$), and the ANOVA was significant, $F(3, 234) = 21.21, p < .001$. The only Beta to be significant was that for the Rasch ASGS (.43).

In summary, the most consistent predictor variable — on three out of three occasions — was the Rasch Australian Sheep-Goat Scale. The Launay-Slade Hallucination Scale yielded a significant Beta value on just one occasion out of three (predicting the hearing of the voice of a dead person), while the Absorption Scale yielded no significant Betas. The amount of variance accounted for (R^2) ranged from 15% to 38%, which may be regarded as modest.

*Note that since "veridical vision" is a part of the Rasch ASGS the two should not be correlated with each other, lest spurious part-whole correlations be found. Therefore, to enable an approximate result, the visionary experience item was removed from the Rasch ASGS before the three predictor-variables were entered into the multiple regression for visionary experience.

†Beta is known as the standardized regression coefficient, and the closer it is to ±1.00 the more influence is being exerted by its parent variable in the prediction equation.

Part Two

It was sought, first, to replicate where possible the results in Part One. Second, another task was added: in giving verbal feedback to participants in Thalbourne (1998) with respect to the LSHS, it was noticed serendipitously that high scorers on the scale tended to give sensory associations to the word "orange," while low scorers tended to respond simply with the word "orange" itself. With the word "democracy," high scorers still gave sensory associations (like the image of a ballot box, of the American flag, Parliament in session, etc.), while, again, low scorers tended to say "What comes into my consciousness is the *word* itself, with no imagery." This anecdotal observation was the basis for that part of the present experiment that sought to understand more clearly what was being measured by the LSHS.

Method

PARTICIPANTS. A total of 60 first-year psychology students participated in this study. Age ranged from 17 to 48, with a mean of 21 years ($SD = 7$ years). Males comprised just 17%.

MATERIALS. It was thought that presentation of the 12-item LSHS by itself might give away the variable that was being measured. Therefore, to minimize demand characteristics, it was presented embedded in Tellegen's 34-item, true/false Absorption Scale (Tellegen & Atkinson, 1974), whose items are not dissimilar to those of the LSHS. Indeed, the Absorption Scale correlates .53 ($N = 240$, $p < .001$) with the LSHS (Thalbourne, 1998; see Table 5.2 above). In the combined scale there were thus a total of 47 true/false items. Also available were scores on the Rasch ASGS, but not for the ICMIC, so the "sensing a ghost" item was not used. Thus, there were just two dependent variables, namely, having had veridical visionary experience (claimed by 20%), and "hearing the voice of a dead person speaking to me" (claimed by 7%).

PROCEDURE. Approval for this study was obtained from the Departmental Ethics Subcommittee; the mild deception about the existence of the Hallucination Scale was not deemed unethical. The participant filled out a consent form. They then filled in a combined questionnaire, containing the Rasch ASGS (including also the visionary experience item), Absorption, and the LSHS, as well as the item about hearing the voice of a dead person. Upon completion of that inventory, and in advance of scoring it, the participant was asked: "When I say the word 'orange,' *what* immediately comes into your consciousness?" They were also asked "When I say the word 'democracy,' *what* immediately comes into your consciousness?" (Presentation of the stimulus word was counterbalanced across participants.) The responses were noted and clarified where necessary, and categorized as sensory or purely conceptual, after which the participant's score on the LSHS was calculated.

Results

Descriptive statistics for the LSHS, the Absorption scale, and the Rasch ASGS are given in Table 5.5.

Table 5.5 — Descriptive Statistics for the Sample of 60

Variable	Minimum	Maximum	M	SD
Launay-Slade Hallucination Scale	1.00	10.00	5.17	2.62
Absorption Scale	5.00	33.00	18.87	7.13
Rasch ASGS	8.13	39.55	24.39	5.62

INTERCORRELATIONS. The intercorrelations (Pearson) between the 5 variables are to be found in Table 5.6.

It can be seen from Table 5.6 that despite a dramatically smaller sample size than in Part One, all but one of the correlations reached significance. The LSHS was positively and significantly correlated with Absorption and the Rasch ASGS, and with having had visionary experience, but not with hearing the voice of a dead person, although that variable correlated significantly with Absorption, the Rasch ASGS, and having had visionary experience.

Table 5.6 — Pearson *r* Intercorrelations for the Three Scales and Two Single Items (*N* = 60)

Variable	LSHS	Absorption	Rasch ASGS	Vision
Absorption	.56***	–	–	–
Rasch ASGS	.30*	.49***	–	–
Vision	.44***	.46***	.64***	–
Voice	.14	.32*	.44***	.35**

*: $p < .05$; **: $p < .01$; ***: $p < .001$ (all p values are two-tailed)

MULTIPLE REGRESSION ANALYSES

1. For having a visionary experience, using the three predictor variables, viz., (adjusted) Rasch ASGS, the LSHS and Absorption, $R = .63$, ($R^2 = .37$), and the multiple correlation was significant, $F(3, 56) = 12.28$, $p < .001$. Two of the three Betas were significant, for the LSHS (.27) and at a rather higher level, for the adjusted Rasch ASGS (.42).

2. For hearing the voice of a dead person, using the three predictor variables again, $R = .46$, ($R^2 = .21$), and the multiple correlation coefficient was significant, $F(3, 56) = 4.99$, $p = .004$. Only one of the Betas was significant: that for the Rasch ASGS (.38).

In summary, while Hallucination Proneness gave a significant Beta on one of the two occasions, the Rasch ASGS proved to be a superior predictor, its Beta being significant on both occasions and at a rather high level.

A POST HOC ANALYSIS ON PARANORMAL BELIEF/EXPERIENCE. A standard multiple regression was performed *post hoc* in an attempt to predict Paranormal Belief/Experience on the basis of the other two scalar variables, Absorption and the Hallucination Scale (LSHS). For the sample of 244, $R = .58$, ($R^2 = .33$), and the multiple correlation coefficient was significant, $F(2, 237) = 59.11$, $p < .001$. Of the two predictors, only Absorption had a significant (and very high) Beta (viz., .56); the LSHS contributed nothing further to the prediction.

The Sample of 60 yielded a perfectly consistent outcome: R was .49, ($R^2 = .24$), and the multiple correlation was again significant, $F(2, 57) = 9.22$, $p < .001$. Of the two predictors, again, only Absorption produced a Beta that was significant (.48), while the Hallucination Scale contributed nothing to the prediction.

Thus, given these two analyses, it would seem that once Absorption is controlled for there is no further relationship between the Rasch ASGS and the LSHS. That is, while believers/experients in the paranormal may be higher on absorption (cf., Irwin, 1985), they are no higher on hallucination-proneness.

THE SUB-EXPERIMENT WITH THE LSHS. As regards the responses to "orange" and "democracy," it turned out that 90% of responses to "orange" were visual images, and only 10% abstract concepts. The mean LSHS score was higher for the image responders than for the concept respondents, but the difference was not significant.

Of the responses to "democracy," 47% were visual images, and 53% abstract concepts. The mean LSHS score was higher for visual responders than for conceptual respondents, but, again, the difference was not significant.

Thus, in the case of both stimulus words, there was no significant association between type of response and a person's score on the LSHS.

Discussion

The main purpose of this two-part study was to investigate the relationship between hallucination-proneness and three single-item variables, namely, veridical visionary experience; hearing the voice of a dead person; and sensing a ghost. In Part One, it was found that the Hallucination Scale correlated significantly and positively with the three single items, but only to a weak degree. Since the Rasch Australian Sheep-Goat Scale and Absorption likewise correlated with these three variables, three standard multiple regression analyses were undertaken to see which scalar variables were the most important. In the case of (i) veridical visionary experience, the (slightly abbreviated) Rasch ASGS gave the only significant Beta; (ii) hearing the voice of a deceased person, the Beta values were significant for the Hallucination Scale, but more strongly so for the Rasch ASGS; and (iii) sensing a ghost, the Rasch ASGS was again significant, while neither the Hallucination Scale nor the Absorption Scale was.

Considering both the Pearson intercorrelations (Table 5.4) and the regression analyses, an association between the three single items and the Hallucination Scale is present, but only to a very weak degree. More important for predicting these three dependent variables is paranormal belief and alleged paranormal experience, as measured by the Rasch Australian Sheep-Goat Scale.

The results obtained in Part Two were consistent with those found in Part One. While the LSHS again entered the regression equation as a weak predictor of hearing the voice of a dead person, the Rasch ASGS entered it in both regressions and at a relatively high level. The conclusion would seem to be, from both Parts One and Two, that hallucination-proneness is not a major predictor of the single items. Those who argue that having veridical visionary experience, hearing the voice of a dead person, and sensing ghosts are merely the result of hallucinations find only a little support for this position in this study. The Rasch ASGS is the major predictor variable in this investigation. However, whether high Rasch ASGS scores lead to the survival-related phenomena, or whether the survival-related phenomena lead to high scores on the Rasch ASGS, cannot be decided on the basis of this correlational study.

A subsidiary aim was to examine the correlations between the Hallucination Scale, the Rasch ASGS, and Absorption. The Hallucination Scale correlated positively, moderately, and significantly with Absorption and with the Rasch ASGS in both studies: those participants who scored high on the Hallucination Scale tended also to experience more absorption, and to report more paranormal belief and more paranormal experience. Does this mean, for example, that paranormal experients are more likely to have hallucinations? The results of the two post hoc analyses show that there is no relationship between belief and hallucination proneness when the effects of Absorption are controlled.

In the second part of the study, psychological reactions to the words "orange" and "democracy" were studied. It was hypothesized that responders reporting imagery would score significantly higher on the LSHS than responders reporting abstract concepts. For neither prompt did this occur. If this line of research is to be undertaken in future it is suggested that it would be better to use a *number* of stimulus words of a sensory or abstract nature, in case responses to "orange" and "democracy" are in some way idiosyncratic. For example, the word "orange" could refer to a fruit and/or a color, and these two aspects are confounded (L. Storm, personal communication, May 27, 2005). A better stimulus word might have been "banana." Future research of a methodologically superior kind is desirable to investigate whether there is any evidence for the hypothesis and what implications we may validly draw from the use of the Launay-Slade Hallucination Scale.

Appendix: A Brief Glossary of Terms

Absorption: A psychological dimension defined by Tellegen and Atkinson (1974) as "a 'total' attention, involving a full commitment of available perceptual, motoric, imaginative and ideational resources to a unified representation of the attentional object" (p. 274). According to Harvey Irwin (1985), the "inherent correlates of a state of absorption are posited to be an imperviousness to normally distracting events and a heightened sense of the reality of the object of attention" (p. 2).

Borderline Personality Disorder: "[A] pattern of instability in interpersonal relationships, self image, and [emotions], and marked impulsivity" (American Psychiatric Association, 1994, p. 629).

Hyperesthesia: An acute sensitivity to sensory stimulation, such as to light, sound and smell.

Hypomanic Personality: An overactive, gregarious style of behavior in which episodes of sub-clinical euphoria occur.

Schizoidia: A scale for measuring schizoid personality disorder, which "is a pervasive pattern of detachment from social relationships and a restricted range of expression of emotions in interpersonal settings" (American Psychiatric Association, 1994, p. 638).

Schizotypal Personality Disorder: "[A] pervasive pattern of social and interpersonal deficits marked by acute discomfort with, and reduced capacity for close relationships as well as by cognitive or perceptual distortions and eccentricities of behavior" (American Psychiatric Association, 1994, p. 641).

Synesthesia: A perceptual phenomenon in which "an inducing stimulus produces, at the same time, two kinds of sensory response: the primary sensory experience that is normally associated with that stimulus and, anomalously, a secondary experience in another modality," such as seeing a color in response to hearing a sound (Marks, 2000, p. 121).

References

American Psychiatric Association (1994). *Diagnostic and statistical manual* IV. Washington, DC: Author.

Bentall, R. P. (2000). Hallucinatory experiences. In E. Cardeña, S. J. Lynn, & S. Krippner (Eds.), *Varieties of anomalous experience: Examining the scientific evidence* (pp. 85–120). Washington, DC: American Psychological Association.

Bentall, R. P., Claridge, G. S., & Slade, P. D. (1989). The multidimensional nature of Schizotypal traits: A factor analytic study with normal subjects. *British Journal of Clinical Psychology, 28*, 363–375.

Bentall, R. P., & Slade, P. D. (1985). Reality testing and auditory hallucinations: A signaldetection analysis. *British Journal of Clinical Psychology, 24*, 159–169.

Claridge, G., McCreery, C., Mason, O., Bentall, R., Boyle, G., Slade, P., & Popplewell, D. (1996). The factor structure of "schizotypal" traits: A large replication study. *British Journal of Clinical Psychology, 35*, 103–115.

Eysenck, H. J., & Eysenck, S. B. G. (1975). *Manual of the Eysenck Personality Questionnaire.* London: Hodder & Stoughton.

Irwin, H. J. (1985). Parapsychological phenomena and the absorption domain. *Journal of the American Society for Psychical Research, 79*, 1–11.

Lange, R., & Thalbourne, M. A. (2002). Rasch scaling paranormal belief and experience: The structure and semantics of Thalbourne's Australian Sheep-Goat Scale. *Psychological Reports, 91*, 1065–1073.

Launay, G., & Slade, P. (1981). The measurement of hallucinatory predisposition in male and female prisoners. *Personality and Individual Differences, 2*, 221–234.

Marks, L. E. (2000). Synesthesia. In E. Cardeña, S. J. Lynn, & S. Krippner (Eds.), *Varieties of anomalous experience: Examining the scientific evidence* (pp. 121–149). Washington, DC: American Psychological Association.

McCreery, C., & Claridge, G. (1995). Out-of-the-body experiences and personality. *Journal of the Society for Psychical Research, 60*, 129–148.

Rankin, P., & O'Carrol, P. (1995). Reality monitoring and signal detection in individuals prone to hallucinations. *British Journal of Clinical Psychology, 34*, 517–528.

Tellegen, A., & Atkinson, G. (1974). Openness to absorbing and self-altering experiences ("absorption"), a trait related to hypnotic susceptibility. *Journal of Abnormal Psychology, 83*, 268–277.

Thalbourne, M. A. (1998). Transliminality: Further correlates and a short measure. *Journal of the American Society for Psychical Research, 92*, 402–419.

West, L. J. (1962). A general theory of hallucinations and dreams. In L. J. West (Ed.), *Hallucinations.* New York: Grune & Stratton.

6. Constructing Time After Death: The Transcendental-Future Time Perspective

JOHN N. BOYD AND PHILIP G. ZIMBARDO*

Doctor John Boyd and Professor Philip Zimbardo, foremost researchers on time perspective, have developed a scale that measures the "transcendental-future." Their scale assesses individual time perspectives on life after death. Boyd and Zimbardo find that the motivations of many religious people may have more to do with their transcendental-future time perception, and less to do with religious belief per se. High-scorers on the scale believed that rewards and punishments would be meted out in the afterlife. Transcendental-future is a factor in its own right, and the authors state that it is, therefore, a unique dimension of personality.—Editors

Overview

This chapter reports on an extraordinary time perspective that partitions the future into pre and post death time frames. Based on data from 1,235 individuals, the "transcendental-future" extends from the point of imagined death of the physical body to infinity, yet may influence present behavior. Related

Reprinted by permission of Sage Publications Ltd. from J.N. Boyd and P.G. Zimbardo in Time and Society, vol. 6, pp. 35–54, SAGE Publications, 1997.

*The first author would like to thank George Parrott for introducing him to time perspective. The authors would like to thank David Rosenhan, Nicholas Herrera, Progga Choudhury and three anonymous reviewers for their helpful and insightful comments on drafts of the article which became the current chapter, and Christina Maslach, Julie Goldberg, Anita Fisher, and Forest Jourden for graciously allowing access to their data.

to numerous psychological variables, the transcendental-future is a component of, but not synonymous with, many religious beliefs. When seen from the perspective of the transcendental-future, behaviors often seen as irrational, such as suicide, extreme heroism, and excessive tithing, are transformed into rational behaviors expected to lead to fulfillment of transcendental-future goals.

Introduction

Humans the world over behave in complex and often baffling ways, ways that make the motivation for their behavior difficult to ascertain. When a behavior is not well understood, people commonly marvel at it, assume some special motivation underlying it, and infer that the actor is unique in some way. People may come to believe that special people have unusual motivations for behaving in extraordinary ways. But this may not always be the case. When soldiers sacrifice themselves for their comrades, suicide bombers drive trucks loaded with explosives into crowded buildings, cult members follow their leaders to the death, and individuals take their own lives, these newsworthy behaviors may be performed by ordinary people. Social psychology has shown that an individual's construal of reality, what they believe reality to be, can cause ordinary people to behave in extraordinary ways (Milgram, 1974; Ross & Nisbett, 1991; Zimbardo, 1969). In addition, there are examples in which vast numbers of people behave in less exciting but equally exceptional ways. Muslims cease all secular activity five times a day, face Mecca, and pray, and millions of Americans make weekly pilgrimages to church services. What motivates such behaviors? What do these people seek? Or, put less dramatically, for what are people willing to forgo sex, money, family, friends, and work? "Religious belief" may be an obvious answer, but it is an incomplete one. Religious belief labels the motivation; it does not explain it. This chapter will suggest that it is not religious belief per se that accounts for such behavior, but an aspect common to many religious beliefs, an extraordinary time perspective, that one can maintain in the absence of religion.

Based on evidence presented in this chapter, we believe that for many people the psychological future is partitioned into pre- and post-death time frames. The traditional, or mundane, future begins in the present and extends to the point of imagined death of the physical body. It contains lifetime goals such as graduating from college, becoming a parent, owning a home, and living out one's life with a mate. The "transcendental-future" time perspective, postulated to be distinct and separate from the traditional future, encompasses the period of time from the imagined death of the physical body to infinity.

The transcendental-future may contain goals such as reunion with deceased loved ones, eternal life, reincarnation, the avoidance of eternal damnation, and the elimination of current poverty, pain, suffering, and shame. As a psychological construct, the transcendental-future time perspective exhibits attributes similar to those associated with the other more conventional time perspectives of past, present, and future orientation. Extending this reasoning to include the past before birth may yield a transcendental-past time perspective, which we speculate may be related to beliefs such as reincarnation, the existence of past lives, and the collective unconscious. Our current research, however, is limited to the transcendental-future and reports on the nature of this unstudied temporal perspective, on the scale developed to assess this new psychological variable, and on the comparison of the results of this scale with other psychological instruments and variables.

Social-cognitive theories of motivation have long acknowledged the role that future-orientation plays in motivation (Bandura, 1986, 1991; McClelland, 1985a, 1985b; Nuttin, 1985; Rotter, 1954; Tolman, 1932, 1948). These theories share the assumption that an individual's view of the future feeds back to influence present behavior. According to Kurt Lewin (1951), this influence occurs through the psychological construct of "time perspective." Lewin defined time perspective to be "the totality of the individual's views of his psychological future and psychological past existing at a given time [in the present]" (p. 75). Joseph Nuttin (1985), continuing Lewin's thought, wrote, "future and past events have an impact on present behavior to the extent that they are actually present on the cognitive level of behavioral functioning" (p. 54). Not only do present beliefs, thoughts, and feelings influence behavior, but so do memories and expectations. Nuttin (1964, 1985) went on to assert that the future is our primary motivational space and that the past and present are of only minimal importance in motivational processes.

Future time perspective, as one's preferred temporal orientation, has been associated with a host of motivational processes and outcomes, such as attributions (Miller & Porter, 1980), locus of control (Koenig, 1979), delay of gratification (Mischel, 1974), academic achievement (DeVolder & Lens, 1982), and achievement motivation (McClelland, 1985b). Consideration of Future Consequences (CFC), a construct related to future time perspective, was recently demonstrated to affect susceptibility to persuasive communication (Strathman, Gleicher, Boninger & Edwards, 1994). In addition, lack of a well defined future has been associated with juvenile delinquency (Barndt & Johnson, 1955; Brock & Del Giudice, 1963; Landau, 1975, 1976; Oyserman & Markus, 1990a, 1990b; Stein, Sarbin & Kulik, 1968), risk behaviors such as alcohol use, drug use, and smoking (Keough, Zimbardo, & Boyd, 1996), and sexuality, aggression, and thrill-seeking (Zimbardo, Boyd, & Keough, 1996).

This body of research supports the assumption of social-cognitive theories of motivation that the manner in which individuals view the future is closely related to their goal-directed behaviors.

While acknowledging the importance of the future in motivation, psychology has traditionally been constrained by the mortality of its subjects. Psychology's interest in the individual has revolved around overt and covert behavior and has ended with the last breath, ended when the individual ceased to be a behaving organism. Religious belief systems, in contrast, typically explain the delayed consequences of current behavior on outcomes expected to be experienced after death. Since religious belief, especially fanatical belief, is often associated with the kinds of extraordinary behavior noted previously, mainstream psychology may benefit by expanding its domain of interest to include the motivational implications of beliefs in life after death.

In random surveys of thousands of Americans (Associated Press, 1982) and Western Europeans (Goldman, 1993), the majority of respondents disclosed that they believe in life after death. From a different perspective, in their expansive random sample of 113,723 Americans, Kosmin and Lachman (1993) report that only 8.2% of Americans consider themselves atheists, agnostics, humanists, or other religious "nones." Such self-reports, however, are likely to be a minimal estimate of belief in life after death. Freud (1915/1962) noted that even when individuals imagine their own death, they survive it as spectators. He insisted that, "In the unconscious every one of us is convinced of his [or her] own immortality" (Freud, 1915/1962, p. 289). Freud continued, "Our unconscious, then, does not believe in its own death; it behaves as if it were immortal" (p. 296). The ubiquity of post-death beliefs and the importance of the future in social-cognitive theories of motivation suggest that, just as beliefs about the traditional future feedback to affect individual decisions and actions, beliefs about post-death existence may also feedback to influence present behavior.

The little empirical research conducted on belief in life after death has been done from a religious perspective in response to Becker's (1973) theory of the denial of death. These researchers felt that Becker's psychological view of death was narrow and unidimensional and sought to demonstrate that people expect to transcend death in multiple ways, not just through denial. Spilka and his colleagues (Spilka, Stout, Minton & Sizemore, 1977) showed that the process of death means different things to different people, and Hood and Morris (1983; Vandecreek & Nye, 1993) developed a scale designed to assess the ways that people believe they can achieve transcendence. In Hood and Morris's view, transcendence can be accomplished through biosocial, creative, religious, natural and mystical methods. For instance, the biosocial method allows transcendence of death through the legacy of children and families, the creative method accomplishes transcendence by bequeathing works of art and projects to posterity, the natural method allows transcendence through identification with natural cycles that are greater than the individual, and the mystical method allows transcendence through communion with a higher power. This previous research was conducted with religious samples and proceeded on the assumption that transcendence of death is possible. While tangentially related to this earlier work, our research represents the first attempt to investigate belief in life after death within the framework of time perspective and to stress not the plausibility of these beliefs, but their possible impact on present behavior.

While the question of immortality stands as a profoundly important issue for many people, from a social psychological perspective it is the *belief* in immortality, not its reality that is relevant. For the social psychologist, reality is what individuals believe it to be, or construct it to be (Griffin & Ross, 1991; Ross & Nisbett, 1991). As with belief in repressed memories of childhood abuse, UFO abductions, near death experiences, and past lives, the social psychologist is interested in the influence of the belief, not the verity of the belief. Religion, theology, parapsychology, and the judicial system investigate the question of existence; social psychology explores the nature and implications of belief, whether or not what is believed is objectively verifiable. It is the social representation of a given phenomenon in the minds of individuals, true or not, that comes to influence their collective and personal behavior (Moscovici, 1984).

The influence of the representation of a future beyond death has remained consistently absent from social-cognitive theories of motivation, yet the psychological conception of the traditional future is little more objectively real than the idea of existence after death. Only the present is real in any tangible, empirical way. The future exists only as a psychological construct, an invention of human imagination. As such, the imposition of a psychological barrier to the investigation of beliefs at the point of imagined death may be more an avoidance of the metaphysical than a reflection of the manner in which individuals actually view their futures.

The difference in the traditional conception of the mundane-future and the conception of the transcendental-future after death lies in partitioning the future into pre- and post-death time frames. Mundane-future goals consist of events at a discrete, finite period of time while an individual is alive. In the mundane-future, nothing lasts forever; careers end, rewards are exhausted, and people die. A property of goals expected to be reached in the transcendental-future, however, may be their continuous, enduring nature. The reward of goals to be achieved after death, eternal life for instance, may extend to infinity, raising the intriguing possibility of a source of infinite motivation. Once individuals expect to exist after death, they may become eternally accountable for their behavior. Due to this accountability (see Tetlock, 1989, 1994 for the effects of accountability in other domains), they may behave according to eternal, possibly divine, laws. When eternal reward or punishment is thought to be predicated on present behavior, behavior may assume a new significance. For individuals with goals expected to be reached after death, the statute of limitations may never expire on sins or saintly behavior. They may expect to reap the fruits of their present behavior from here to eternity.

Method

Investigation into the possible existence of a Transcendental-Future Time Perspective (TFTP) began by examining how time perspective was traditionally assessed. Among the many methods that have been used, the most common have been projective measures that are subjectively interpreted, such as the Thematic Apperception Test (TAT), Cottle's circles test (Cottle, 1976), the Motivational Induction Method (Nuttin, 1985), and time lines (Rappaport, 1990). Another measure is the Zimbardo Time Perspective Inventory (ZTPI; Rothspan & Read, 1996; Gonzalez & Zimbardo, 1984; Gonzalez & Zimbardo, 1985). Developed over the span of ten years by Zimbardo and his collaborators at Stanford University, internal consistency of the ZTPI is satisfactory (Cronbach's alphas range from .68 to .83 for the five sub-scales), and test-retest reliability over 4 weeks is good (ranging from .70 to .80 for the sub-scales).

Scores on the five sub-scales of the ZTPI — future, present-hedonistic, present-fatalistic, past-positive, and past-negative — have been shown to be related to many important behaviors. The future-orientation sub-scale, the scale most relevant to this chapter, has consistently had the greatest internal consistency (.80) and test-retest stability (.80). Future-orientation is associated with conscientiousness, academic achievement, health maintenance behaviors, and energy (Zimbardo, Boyd, & Maslach, 1996). Some of the 14 items thought to measure future-orientation on the ZTPI include: "I complete projects on time by making steady progress"; "Meeting tomorrow's deadlines and doing other necessary work comes before tonight's play"; "I am able to resist temptations when I know that there is work to be done"; and "Before making a decision, I weigh the costs against the benefits." High present-hedonistic scores on the ZTPI, in contrast, are related to drug and alcohol use, unsafe sexual practices, omission of preventive health maintenance behaviors, and risk taking (Keough, Zimbardo & Boyd, 1996, in submission). Past orientation, as measured by the ZTPI, is related to self-esteem and emotional stability (Boyd & Zimbardo, 1995). As an objective and reliable assessment instrument related to many psychological variables, the ZTPI was used as the starting point for investigation into the dichotomous nature of the future and as a model for the development of the scale designed to measure the TFTP.

Transcendental-Future Scale Development

As an initial attempt to explore the possible differentiation between a psychological conception of the mundane-future and a transcendental-future, items thought to reflect a transcendental time perspective were developed and added to a version of the ZTPI. An attempt was made to exclude items that reflected a Judeo-Christian bias and include items that reflected a more ecumenical belief in existence after death. Transcendental items included: "I will be held accountable for my actions on earth when I die"; "Humans possess a soul"; "Only my physical body will ever die"; and "Death is just a new beginning" (see Appendix for the complete scale). Items were mixed and then evaluated by respondents on a five-point Likert scale assessing the degree of belief in each one, from "Very Uncharacteristic" to "Very Characteristic" of me.

Respondents

Over the past three years, 1,235 individuals have completed successive versions of this modified time perspective inventory. Populations sampled include introductory psychology students at the College of San Mateo; California State University, Sacramento; University of California, Berkeley; and Stanford University. For our Sacramento sample, we had introductory psychology students complete our materials themselves and also had them recruit two additional people to complete our materials. These people had to be five years younger or ten years older than the student. This procedure gave us a sample with larger variance in age than our college student samples. We also collected data at three community schools in the San Francisco Bay Area. Community schools are the last stop for troubled juveniles before incarceration. All of the students in these schools had been expelled from traditional high schools and most were on probation or parole. We have combined the data from the community schools and other samples when the samples are commensurate and the materials used were identical. Respondents ranged in age from 13 to 73, included both genders, and encompassed a wide range of socioeconomic classes, ethnic groups, and religious beliefs. Because different versions of the transcendental scale and different supplemental materials were used, the results presented may represent a subset of the total 1,235 respondents. When this is the case, means and standard deviations for the relevant group are clearly identified and reported. See Table 6.1 for demographic information.

Table 6.1 — Sample Demographics and Transcendental-Future Differences

Sample	N	Sex Male (%)	Female (%)	Mean Age (SD)	Ethnicity (% of N)	Sex Differences	Age Differences	Ethnic Differences
A	174	37	63	29.5 (13.3)	White = 59; Black = 4; Hispanic = 9; Asian = 20; Other = 8	Yes**	Yes*	Yes[†]
B	50	76	24	16.7 (0.9)	White = 19; Black = 21; Hispanic = 32; Asian = 19; Other = 8	No	No	Yes*
C	287	43	57	19.0 (1.3)	White = 51; Black = 6; Hispanic = 13; Asian = 23; Other = 6	Yes***	Yes*	Yes***
D	588	40	60	20.6 (4.7)	White = 40; Black = 5; Hispanic = 9; Asian = 35; Other = 11	Yes***	No	Yes***
E	136	45	55	n/a	n/a	Yes*	n/a	n/a

A = California State University, Sacramento introductory psychology students, their friends, and relatives; B = Community School / juvenile delinquents; C = Stanford University introductory psychology students, Fall 1994; D = Stanford; University of California, Berkeley; and College of San Mateo psychology students; E = Stanford University introductory psychology students, Spring, 1995
[†] $p < .10$; *: $p < .05$; **: $p < .01$; ***: $p < .001$; (all p values are two-tailed)

Factor Analysis and Scale Reliability

At this early stage of our investigation, exploratory principal components factor analysis and varimax rotation have revealed a distinct transcendental time perspective as the first factor for every sample, as shown in Table 6.2.

Table 6.2 — Results of Factor Analysis of Transcendental-Future Items & ZTPI Items: Six-Factor Solution

Sample	N	% Variance Explained by Transcendental Factor	Total Variance Accounted for by Six Factor Solution	Transcendental Factor Rank
A	174	9.9	34.5	First
B	50	11.5	45.5	First
C	287	10.3	37.6	First
D	588	9.6	34.4	First
E	136	12.6	43.9	First
Totals	1235	10.2	36.6	First

A = California State University, Sacramento introductory psychology students, their friends, and relatives; B = Community School / juvenile delinquents; C = Stanford University introductory psychology students, Fall 1994; D = Stanford; University of California, Berkeley; and College of San Mateo psychology students; E = Stanford University introductory psychology students, Spring, 1995

Questions thought to reflect an orientation toward a transcendental time perspective cohere well, consistently accounting for 10% of total variance. Scores on the transcendental scale are slightly related to present-fatalistic, past-positive, and past-negative orientations, but not to traditional future or present-hedonistic orientations, suggesting that the transcendental-future is a distinct time perspective (see Table 6.3).

Table 6.3 — Correlations between Transcendental-Future Time Perspective and the Five Time Perspective Categories (Sample D)

Time Perspective Category	r	p
Present-Fatalistic	.19	< .01
Past-Positive	.18	< .01
Past-Negative	.11	< .01
Future	.06	.17
Present-Hedonistic	.06	.17

$df = 530$

Internal reliability (Cronbach's alpha) of the transcendental-future scale is .87, and test-retest reliability (over a four-week duration) is a robust .86. These psychometric properties have remained relatively stable throughout the years of scale development. From this analysis, it is reasonable to conclude that this large sample of respondents views the transcendental-future as a distinct and meaningful psychological construct and, furthermore, that the scale developed to assess this construct possesses satisfactory reliability.

Results

After establishing the discrete nature of the transcendental-future and verifying the reliability of our assessment instrument, our research investigated the relationship of the scale to other established measures and to basic demographic variables.

Demographic Characteristics

The youngest and the oldest members of our samples score highest on the transcendental-future scale (see Table 8.1). In the sample with the largest variance in age (Sample A), endorsement of transcendental items differs significantly by age group, $F(4,157) = 3.31$, $p < .05$ ($\eta = .28$). Respondents in their 20's score lowest in transcendental-future, while those over 50 score highest. Teenagers score above average on the 1 to 5 point scale ($M = 3.7$), as do those between 30 and 39 ($M = 3.8$), those between 40 and 49 ($M = 3.9$), and those over fifty years old ($M = 4.0$). In contrast, those 20–29 years old score below average ($M = 3.4$).

The group mean for Sample A was 3.6, with a standard deviation of .72. The age range was 13 to 79 years old. Although significant differences in transcendental scores by age group were not found in every sample, this may be explained by the restricted age range of some of our samples, which can hamper the detection of differences. In our sample of juvenile delinquents (Sample B) all of our respondents were between 15 and 18 years old, and, in our samples of only college students (Samples C, D, & E), over 85% of the respondents were between 17 and 22 years old.

Females score significantly higher on the transcendental scale than do males (Sample D), $F(1,539) = 20.1$, $p < .01$ ($\eta = .19$). In Sample D, our largest sample, the mean female score was 3.2, while the male mean was 2.7. Sample D's overall mean was 3.0 ($SD = 0.9$). Females, on average, felt the items on the transcendental-future scale were slightly characteristic of them (3 is neutral), while males felt the items were slightly uncharacteristic. Gender differences, however, were not found in our juvenile delinquent sample. Restriction of range and self-selection biases may explain these results. Juvenile delinquents may be delinquent because they have similar time perspectives, or they may develop similar time perspectives because they are delinquent. Regardless of the causal process, previous research has shown that juvenile delinquents have both a foreshortened future time perspective and a greater reliance on a present time perspective. They may, therefore, also possess a more homogenous TFTP than our other samples.

Across all samples, African-Americans and Hispanics score higher in transcendental-future beliefs than either Asians or Caucasians (Sample D), $F(4, 540) = 5.2, p < .01$ ($\eta = .19$). Again in Sample D, Caucasians scored lowest at 2.8, Asians 2.9, Hispanics 3.2, and African-Americans topped the scale at 3.9. The sample mean was 3.0, with a standard deviation of .9. A least-significant difference (LSD) post-hoc analysis revealed that Caucasians differed significantly from both Hispanics and African-Americans and that Asians and Hispanics differed significantly from African-Americans. Caucasians and Asians, on average, felt that the items on the transcendental-future scale were slightly uncharacteristic of them, while Hispanic and African-Americans felt that the items were characteristic.

Values, Beliefs and Personality Measures

Although an effort was made to ensure that the transcendental scale does not reflect a specific Western religious bias, scores on the transcendental scale do correlate highly with both self-reported religiosity (Sample C), $r(203) = .50, p < .01$, and with the value placed on salvation as terminal value (Sample A), $r(159) = .54, p < .01$, as assessed using a modified version of the Rokeach Value Scale (Rokeach, 1973). The modified Rokeach Value Scale asked respondents to rank 14 instrumental and 14 terminal values in order of importance. Terminal values are characteristics valued as an end state, such as equality, freedom, and social recognition. Instrumental values are characteristics valued as means leading to fulfillment of terminal values, such as ambition, courage, and responsibility. As mentioned, the transcendental-future scores correlate positively with one terminal value, salvation, but not above .30 with any other terminal or instrumental value. This strong correlation was expected because many religions espouse beliefs, such as life after death, in the temporal region that we call the transcendental-future.

People of different religious persuasions (as indicated by self-report in a 280 respondent subset of Sample D that completed a special questionnaire), however, differ significantly in transcendental scores, $F(6,140) = 11.9, p < .01$ ($\eta = .58$), as seen in Figure 6.1.

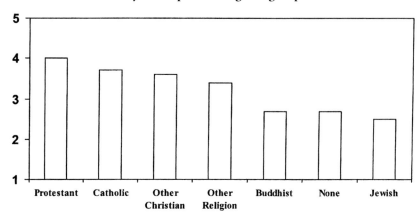

Figure 6.1— Transcendental-Future scores
by self-reported religious group.

Protestants score highest, followed by Catholics, other Christians, and other religions. At the low end are Buddhists, those reporting no religious affiliation, and Jews. An LSD post-hoc test revealed that Protestants, Catholics, other Christians, and those with "other" religious affiliations differ significantly from Buddhists, those with no religious affiliation, and Jews in transcendental-future scores. The overall group for this subset of Sample D mean was 3.2 (SD = 0.9).

Although transcendental-future scores are highly correlated with religiosity, there is significant variation among religious groups. Some religions appear to believe the items on the scale are characteristic of them, while others tend to believe that they are uncharacteristic. In addition, while those with no religious affiliation tend to be lower in transcendental-future than religious individuals, there is considerable variation among non-religious individuals as well. Transcendental-future scores for individuals with no religious affiliation ranged from 1.1 to 4.7, with a mean of 2.7 (SD = .72). While the transcendental-future and religiosity appear to be closely related, they do not appear to be synonymous or entirely overlapping constructs.

Scores on the transcendental scale are closely related to attendance of religious services and performance of religious rituals at home. Within a subset of Sample D, individuals that attend services weekly (M = 4.0), monthly (M = 3.7), on special occasions (M = 3.1), and never (M = 2.7) scored significantly different on the transcendental scale, $F(3,142)$ = 24.1, $p < .01$ (η = .58). In addition, individuals that perform rituals at home daily (M = 4.0), weekly (M = 3.8), monthly (M = 3.2), on special occasions (M = 3.2), and never (M = 2.7) also scored significantly different on our TFTP scale, $F(4,142)$

= 20.4, $p < .01$ ($\eta = .60$). Scores on the transcendental-future scale are related to self-reported attendance of religious services and self-reported perform-ance of rituals at home, and, therefore, we may assume those scale scores are related to actual religious practice. Again, the sample mean for this subset of Sample D was 3.2 ($SD = 0.9$).

Research on personality has consistently shown that the Five Factor Model (FFM) provides the most accurate and useful characterization of individual personalities (Caprara, Barbaranelli, Borgogni & Perugini, 1993; Costa & McCrae, 1992, 1995). The five personality factors that comprise the FFM are energy, conscientiousness, friendliness, emotional stability, and openness. Scores on the transcendental scale do not correlate above .30 with any facet of the Big Five Questionnaire (BFQ) Personality Inventory (Caprara, Barbaranelli, Borgogni & Perugini, 1993). The BFQ measures the FFM of personality, assessing personality characteristics in nonclinical adult populations. Although the BFQ was developed in Italy, it shows similar psychometric properties for American and Spanish populations, and correlates highly with the NEO-PI (Costa & McCrae, 1992, 1995), another well-known measure of the FFM.

The lack of correlation between transcendental-future scores and factors of the BFQ suggest that the transcendental-future scale may be a personality factor not accounted for in the standard FFM. To investigate this hypothe-sis, the 10 items from the transcendental scale were factor analyzed along with the 132 items that comprise the BFQ Inventory using a subset of 399 psy-chology students from Sample D. When confined to six factors, an exploratory principal component analysis with varimax rotation revealed that the 10 tran-scendental scale items all loaded at .30 or better on factor five. Nine of the items loaded at over .50. Only three items from the BFQ loaded above .30 on the fifth factor along with the transcendental scale items. The BFQ items that loaded with the transcendental items are: "I believe that there are no uni-versally valid values or customs" (-.34); "I hold my colleagues' point of view in great esteem" (.31); and "I hold that there's something good in everyone" (.33). Factor five accounted for 3.4% of the variance with an Eigen value of 4.8. Total variance accounted for by the six-factor solution equaled 28.4%. This pattern suggests that the transcendental scale may measure a personal-ity dimension unaccounted for within the standard FFM framework, thus meriting recognition as a significant index of individual differences.

Discussion

While "religious belief" is often cited as the motivation for extraordinary behavior, our analysis proposes an alternative, yet compatible explanation, one centered on a TFTP. The research summarized in this chapter suggests that (i) the transcendental-future is an important psychological construct, (ii) the scale developed to assess this construct is both reliable and valid, and (iii) beliefs about the transcendental-future may influence behavior. A TFTP appears to be a common characteristic of many religions and, as one's view of the remote future, may feedback to influence behavior just as beliefs about the traditional future have been demonstrated to affect behavior.

Goals in the transcendental-future, unlike traditional future goals, however, are not bounded by death, can extend infinitely, and may be a source of enduring motivation. Although closely associated with religiosity, a TFTP does not appear to be the exclusive domain of the devout and may even be held by those with no religious affiliation. We conclude that the modal transcendental-future person is an older, Protestant woman of Hispanic or African-American origin; who values salvation; and who attends religious services and performs religious rituals at home. Because those between 10 and 20 years old appear to be higher than average in the transcendental-future, the transcendental-future may also be useful in understanding some of their extreme behaviors. The high-risk behaviors often associated with youth, such as reckless driving, unsafe sexual practices, and abuse of drugs, may reflect a belief that they are immortal, that existence will continue for them after death.

Returning to the extreme behaviors mentioned in the introduction, our characterization of those high in the transcendental-future may seem incompatible with the common conception of people that behave extraordinarily. The transcendental-future however, transforms extraordinary behaviors from the irrational acts of special people into the rational acts of the ordinary. It allows current social-cognitive theories of motivation to be extended past the point of imagined death and to be used to explain what were often thought of as irrational, incomprehensible behaviors. Irrational acts become rational attempts to secure rewards or avoid punishment in the transcendental-future. One doesn't need to be special to behave rationally. Ordinary people do it all the time.

Although experimental research will be needed before causality can be established, clearly many people view the transcendental-future as a distinct and meaningful dimension of their temporal orientation. The relationships between the transcendental-future, values, self-reported religious practices, and personality factors should provide direction and impetus for future research — research that promises to clarify the transcendental-future's role in human motivation.

While the goal of the studies presented in this chapter was to determine whether people conceived of the transcendental-future as a distinct time perspective and to explore its relationship to other relevant variables, speculation on the implications of the transcendental-future may be provocative and useful to other researchers. Issues to be discussed and speculated upon in the remainder of this chapter include the implications of the transcendental-future for learning theory, the role of the transcendental-future in behavioral compliance, and the relationship between the transcendental-future and the phenomenon of religious conversion.

Learning Theory and Infinite Reinforcement

In a sense, learning based on views of the transcendental-future can be thought of as vicarious trial and error learning (Tolman, 1932, 1948) without reality testing. Individuals with goals in the transcendental-future have a cognitive map of a foreign land that they can never visit. There are no reality checks built into the transcendental-future belief system, no means of disconfirming any propositions. Because individuals cannot fail to reach a goal in the transcendental-future while alive, and because the only feedback that individuals receive concerning their progress toward goals is their own subjective interpretation, all life events are eligible for construal as positive reinforcement. Negative events can be interpreted as divine tests, such as those endured by Job, and positive events can be construed as rewards for proper behavior. Both can be interpreted as markers on the path to enlightenment, and can therefore be positive reinforcers.

As for punishment, the specter of eternal damnation can be imagined to exert a powerful force on behavior. Unlike punishment in the traditional future however, belief in punishment in the transcendental-future cannot be eliminated by objective reality testing and, therefore, may not be subject to extinction. The only information feeding back into the present is an individual's interpretation of the future. Such a closed, self-reinforcing system could conceivably lead to greater and greater levels of motivation and may lead quickly from initial belief to fanaticism, or, in the case of Protestants, to the tremendous motivation reflected in the Protestant work ethic. As Weber (1904/1956) and Tawney (1926) pointed out, the Protestant reformation and the rise of capitalism were inextricably intertwined. Promoting some types of transcendental-future beliefs may generate powerful pro-social motivation.

The Transcendental-Future as Opiate of the Masses

Karl Marx suggested that religion numbed the people to the injustices of this world and kept the masses from rising against the bourgeoisie (Marx, 1844/1970). Marx wrote, "Religion is the sigh of the oppressed creature, the heart of a heartless world and the soul of soulless conditions. It is the opium of the people" (p. 131). Minorities and women, groups that have traditionally been subjugated by the dominant class, score highest on the transcendental-future. The promise of transcendental-future rewards far exceeding any obtainable during this lifetime may make life among the proletariat, in the ghetto, or in the dysfunctional home easier to bear. Nirvanic beliefs about the transcendental-future may make present inequities less painful to endure and rebellion less imperative, especially when spilling blood in this life may result in an eternity of punishment. If individuals believe that they will be eternally punished for violence and that they will be eternally rewarded for turning the other cheek, it is not surprising that they tolerate mistreatment and subjugation. We predict that individuals high in the transcendental-future may have a propensity to comply with authority and a reluctance to dissent and rebel against unjust authority.

Religious Conversion and the Transcendental-Future

Development of a belief in the transcendental-future may be related to the "born again" Christian phenomena and may be especially appealing to those individuals for whom the mundane-future holds little hope. Beliefs in the transcendental-future may offer an absolution of sins committed in the past, a new accountability for behavior in the present, and the promise of future rewards without the threat of disappointment in this life, as rewards can only be reaped after death. At the extreme, the phenomena of criminals sentenced to life in prison undergoing a religious conversion may reflect the exchange of goals that they can no longer hope to accomplish during this life for goals that can be fulfilled in the transcendental-future. This conversion may represent three psychological processes at work: (i) the transformation of a present or future temporal orientation into a transcendental-future orientation; (ii) the desire to maintain a set-point level of motivation in light of the loss of motivation provided by previous traditional future goals; and (iii) the change in motivational focus from negative hopelessness to positive hope. We would expect the transcendental-future to be negatively related to length and severity of depression.

The influence of transcendental-future beliefs, as presented in this chapter, may partially explain the motivation underlying extreme behaviors noted in the introduction. Soldiers that sacrifice themselves for their comrades may not believe that they are ending their life but simply moving to a new phase of existence. Zealots that die in suicide bombings may not be altruistically sacrificing themselves for a cause but selfishly seeking personal gain in the afterlife. Cult members that follow their leaders to the death may not be irrationally ending their lives but rationally pursuing transcendental-future goals.

And individuals that end their own lives may not be desperately trying to avoid suffering but striving for promised rewards in the transcendental-future. Although these examples are dramatic, the transcendental-future may also exert a more subtle, yet powerful, influence on the way individuals lead their daily lives. Eighty million Americans attend religious services each week (Kosmin & Lachman, 1993), possibly out of concern for transcendental-future consequences of their present behavior.

While far from conclusive, this chapter has proposed that a pervasive yet unstudied temporal perspective, a TFTP, may play a prominent role in determining an array of motivated behaviors, both individual and collective. With the reliable assessment instrument presented in this chapter and the encouraging initial pattern of interrelationships, research on the TFTP should be stimulated, and may prove rewarding.

At best, the development of goals in the transcendental-future may elicit a potent source of motivation and allow the "transcendental" conversion of what were "incorrigible" or hopeless humans into productive citizens. Such individuals may be made both more productive and happier. For many people without material success in this lifetime, existence is made bearable by creating illusions. Such positive illusions are psychological mechanisms that soften their harsh reality, enhance their self-worth, and infuse their lives with meaning (Taylor, 1989). Many established religions offer positive illusions or visions of the transcendental-future, and new age beliefs may provide a more individualistic avenue for developing transcendental beliefs. These beliefs may make behavior more understandable, more rational, both to observers and the person performing the behavior. As for the exact determination of the extent to which transcendental-future beliefs influence present behavior, of course, only time will tell.

Appendix: The Transcendental-Future Time Perspective Scale

Read each item and, as honestly as you can, check the box corresponding to how characteristic you believe the statement to be of you. Please answer ALL questions using the following scale:

1 = Very Characteristic
2 = Uncharacteristic
3 = Neutral
4 = Characteristic
5 = Very Characteristic

1. Only my physical body will ever die.
2. My body is just a temporary home for the real me.
3. Death is just a new beginning.
4. I believe in miracles.

5. The theory of evolution adequately explains how humans came to be.

6. Humans possess a soul.

7. Scientific laws cannot explain everything.

8. I will be held accountable for my actions on earth when I die.

9. There are divine laws by which humans should live.

10. I believe in spirits.

References

Associated Press. (1982). Survey finds work rated high in U.S. *The New York Times*, May 19, 23.

Bandura, A. (1986). *Social foundations of thought and action: A social cognitive theory*. Englewood Cliffs, New Jersey: Prentice-Hall.

Bandura, A. (1991). Self-regulation of motivation through anticipatory and self-reactive mechanisms. In R. Dienstbier (Ed.), *Perspectives on motivation* (pp. 69–164). Lincoln, NB: University of Nebraska Press.

Barndt, R. & Johnson, D. (1955). Time orientation in delinquents. *Journal of Abnormal and Social Psychology*, *51*, 343–345.

Becker, E. (1973). *The denial of death*. New York: The Free Press.

Boyd, J. & Zimbardo, P. (1995). Correlations between the Zimbardo Time Perspective Inventory and self-esteem. Unpublished raw data.

Brock, T. & Del Giudice, C. (1963). Stealing and temporal orientation. *Journal of Abnormal and Social Psychology*, *66*, 91–94.

Caprara, G., Barbaranelli, C., Borgogni, L., & Perugini, M. (1993). The "Big Five Questionnaire": A new questionnaire to assess the Five Factor Model. *Personality and Individual Differences*, *15*(3), 281–288.

Costa, P. & McCrae, R. (1992). Four ways five factors are basic. *Personality and Individual Differences*, *13*, 653–665.

Costa, P. & McCrae, R. (1995). Domains and facets: Hierarchical personality assessment using the Revised NEO Personality Inventory. *Journal of Personality Assessment*, *64*(1), 21–50.

Cottle, T.J. (1976). *Perceiving time: A psychological investigation with men and women*. New York, NY: John Wiley.

DeVolder, M. & Lens, W. (1982). Academic achievement and future time perspective as a cognitive-motivational concept. *Journal of Personality and Social Psychology*, *42*, 566–571.

Freud, S. (1962). Thoughts for the times on war and death: Our attitude towards death. In J. Strachey (Ed. and trans.), *The standard edition of the complete psychological works of Sigmund Freud* (Vol. 14, pp. 289–300). London: Hogarth Press. (Original work published 1915).

Goldman, A. (1993). Religion notes. *The New York Times*, May 22, p. 25.

Gonzalez, A. & Zimbardo, P. (1984). A Psychology Today reader survey. *Psychology Today*, February, pp. 53–54.

Gonzalez, A. & Zimbardo, P. (1985). Time in perspective. *Psychology Today*, March, pp. 21–26.

Griffin, D. & Ross, L. (1991). Subjective construal, social inference, and human misunderstanding. In M.P. Zanna (Ed.), *Advances in experimental social psychology* (pp. 319–359). New York, NY: Academic Press.

Helmreich, R. & Stapp, J. (1974). Short forms of the Texas social behavior inventory (TSBI), an objective measure of self-esteem. *Bulletin of the Psychonomic Society*, *4*(5A), 473–475.

Hood, R. & Morris, R. (1983). Toward a theory of death transcendence. *Journal for the Scientific Study of Religion*, *22*, 353–365.

Keough, K., Zimbardo, P. & Boyd, J. (1996). Who's smoking, drinking, and using drugs? Time perspective as a predictor of substance use. Manuscript submitted for publication.

Koenig, F. (1979). Future-orientation and external locus of control. *Psychological Reports*, *44*, 957–958.

Kosmin, B. & Lachman, S. (1993). *One nation under God: Religion in contemporary American society*. New York, NY: Harmony Books.

Landau, S. (1975). Future time perspective of delinquents and non-delinquents. *Criminal Justice and Behavior, 2*, 22–36.

Landau, S. (1976). Delinquency, institutionalization, and time orientation. *Journal of Consulting and Clinical Psychology, 44*, 745–759.

Lewin, K. (1951). *Field theory in the social science: Selected theoretical papers*. (D. Cartwright, Ed.). New York, NY: Harper & Brothers.

Marx, K. (1844/1970). *Critique of Hegel's philosophy of right* (A. Jolin & J. O'Malley, trans.). (J. O'Malley, Ed.). London: Cambridge University Press. (Original work published 1844).

McClelland, D. (1985a). How motives, skills, and values determine what people do. *American Psychologist, 40*, 812–825.

McClelland, D. (1985b). *Human motivation*. Glenview, IL: Scott, Foresman & Co.

Milgram, S. (1974). *Obedience to authority*. New York, NY: Harper.

Miller, D. & Porter, C. (1980). Effects of temporal perspectives on the attribution process. *Journal of Personality and Social Psychology, 39*, 532–541.

Mischel, W. (1974). Processes in delay of gratification. *Advances in Experimental Social Psychology, 7*, 249–292.

Moscovici, S. (1984). The phenomenon of social representations (S. Rabinovitch, trans.). In R. Farr & S. Moscovici (Eds.), *Social representations*. Cambridge, England: Cambridge University Press.

Nuttin, J.R. (1964). The future time perspective in human motivation and learning. *Acta Psychologica, 23*, 60–83.

Nuttin, J.R. (1985). *Future time perspective and motivation: Theory and research method*. Hillsdale, NJ: Lawrence Erlbaum.

Oyserman, D. & Markus, H. (1990a). Possible selves and delinquency. *Journal of Personality and Social Psychology, 59*, 112–125.

Oyserman, D. & Markus, H. (1990b). Possible selves in balance: Implications for delinquency. *Journal of Social Issues, 46*, 141–157.

Rappaport, H. (1990). *Marking time*. New York, NY: Simon & Schuster.

Rokeach, M. (1973). *The nature of human values and value systems*. New York, NY: The Free Press.

Ross, L. & Nisbett, R. (1991). *The person and the situation*. New York, NY: McGraw-Hill.

Rothspan, S. & Read, S. J. (1996). Present versus future time perspective and HIV risk among heterosexual college students. *Health Psychology, 15*, 131–134.

Rotter, J. (1954). *Social learning and clinical psychology*. Englewood Cliffs, NJ: Prentice-Hall.

Spilka, B., Stout, L., Minton, B., and Sizemore, D. (1977). Death and personal faith: A psychometric investigation. *Journal for the Scientific Study of Religion, 16*, 169–178.

Stein, K. & Sarbin, T., & Kulik, J. (1968). Future time perspective: Its relation to the socialization process and the delinquent role. *Journal of Consulting and Clinical Psychology, 32*, 257–264.

Strathman, A., Gleicher, F., Boninger, D., & Edwards, C. (1994). The consideration of future consequences: Weighing immediate and distant outcomes of behavior. *Journal of Personality and Social Psychology, 66*, 742–752.

Tawney, R. (1926). *Religion and the rise of capitalism*. New York, NY: Harcourt Brace.

Taylor, S. (1989). *Positive illusions: Creative self-deception and the healthy mind*. New York, NY: Basic Books.

Tetlock, P. (1989). Accountability: A social magnifier of the dilution effect. *Journal of Personality and Social Psychology, 57*, 388–398.

Tetlock, P. (1994). Accountability amplifies the status quo effect when change creates victims. *Journal of Behavioral Decision Making, 7*, 1–23.

Tolman, E. (1932). *Purposive behavior in animals and men*. New York, NY: Naiburg.

Tolman, E. (1948). Cognitive maps in men and rats. *Psychological Review, 55*, 189–208.

Vandecreek, L. & Nye, C. (1993). Testing the death transcendence scale. *Journal for the Scientific Study of Religion, 32*, 279–283.

Weber, M. (1956). *The Protestant ethic and the spirit of capitalism* (T. Talcott, trans.). New York, NY: Charles Scribner's Sons. (Original work published 1904).

Zimbardo, P. (1969). The human choice: Individuation, reason and order versus deindividuation, impulse and chaos. In W. J. Arnold & D. Levine (Eds.), *Nebraska symposium on motivation* (Vol. 17). Lincoln, NE: University of Nebraska Press.

Zimbardo, P. (1995). *The Zimbardo Time Perspective Inventory.* Unpublished inventory, Stanford University.

Zimbardo, P. Boyd, J. & Keough, K. (1996). *The relationship between time perspective, sexuality, aggression, and thrill-seeking.* Manuscript in preparation.

Zimbardo, P., Boyd, J., & Maslach, C. (1995). *Time perspective and the Five Factor Model of personality.* Manuscript in preparation.

Section III: Evidential Issues

7. Evidence for Survival from Recent Research into Physical Phenomena

DAVID FONTANA

Paranormal physical phenomena, in their various forms suggesting survival, have been treated with suspicion for some three quarters of a century. David Fontana considers some sources of the most evidential phenomena of this kind, from Eusapia Palladino, D. D. Home, Etta Wriedt, John Sloan and the Scole investigation. The widespread suspicion has therefore not always been warranted. Dr. Fontana expresses the hope that the physical evidence for survival will now emerge from its position of neglect.—Editors

Distrust of Physical Phenomena

Physical phenomena — that is, phenomena that involve the supposedly paranormal manipulation of the material environment by spirit energies — were a focus of interest for psychical researchers in the years from the first events at Hydesville, USA in 1842 until the 1930s, but since then have been largely ignored. The reasons are clear. Physical phenomena typically take place in séances and many consider the possibilities for fraud are all too obvious.

Magicians have frequently claimed they can reproduce séance room effects with sleight of hand and insisted they have actually unmasked numerous fraudulent practitioners. Harry Houdini (1924), the most famous magician of his day, was particularly vocal in his claims of detecting fraud, and his testimony, as a member of the committee set up by the *Scientific American* to test anyone claiming to produce a "visible psychic manifestation," was influential in ensuring in 1924 that Boston medium "Margery" (Mina Crandon) was not awarded the $2,500 prize offered by the journal to anyone who satisfied the committee.

Worse was to come in 1927 when J. B. Rhine was appointed by Professor William MacDougal to head the first newly established laboratory devoted to psychical research at Duke University. Rhine, with his wife Louisa, had a sitting with Margery in 1926 and concluded she was fraudulent (Louisa, impressed initially, agreed with him on the grounds he had been sitting closer to Margery and thus could watch her more closely). Supported by MacDougal, who had been on the *Scientific American* committee and who remained doubtful about Margery, Rhine set his face against experimental work with physical mediums. In his view the risk of fraud was too great, and if psychical research (re-named *parapsychology*) was to become acceptable to fellow scientists, then it must avoid any association with spiritualism and the séance room. Rhine was not against the possibility of survival of death (Rhine, 1954), but considered research into the matter should be confined to collecting first-hand accounts of relevant spontaneous psychic experience out of general interest — a job given to Louisa Rhine (see L. Rhine, 1961, 1967).

Inevitably, the fact that physical séances usually take place in near or absolute darkness has also been seen as a cause for deep suspicion. Darkness and trickery go together. The reply to this has been that light actually prevents the manifestation of physical phenomena, and can even be dangerous for the medium. Light, it is argued, is a form of energy, and as such interacts with and sometimes inhibits other forms of energy. Most seeds require darkness in which to germinate. Mammals gestate their young in the near-darkness of the womb. Strong sunlight destroys some forms of life. If physical phenomena are a reality, then it is not impossible that they can be adversely affected by light. In addition, it is claimed that some physical phenomena (such as materializations) are formed by spirit energies from a semi-physical substance called ectoplasm said to be extruded from the medium's body. In the presence of light, ectoplasm is described as recoiling violently back into the medium, producing great pain and potential injury (in support, red wheals have been observed on the medium's abdomen when light has been allowed into the séance room — for example, see Gaskill, 2001).

The Case for Physical Phenomena

Thus, it is possible there is a valid case for darkness after all. Even notable physical mediums such as Daniel Home and Eusapia Palladino, who often worked in subdued light, sometimes insisted on complete darkness, supposedly on instructions from the spirits. It is also argued that if the medium's movements are fully restricted by the investigators, or if for other reasons fraud would seem a physical impossibility, darkness should not lead us automatically to dismiss the physical séance as unworthy of attention. Similarly it is said that discovery of occasional fraud should not lead us automatically to dismiss all of a medium's work. The Italian medium Eusapia Palladino (1854–1918) was several times caught out in crude cheating on the occasions when her own powers seemed inadequate. Hereward Carrington, one of the leading psychic investigators of the early twentieth century, who researched Palladino's mediumship over a number of years (e.g., Carrington, 1909) was, like most European researchers, well aware she would use fraud if she could. Palladino herself warned investigators to watch her or she would cheat, claiming that John King, her spirit guide, forced her to do so. Carrington considered that her "strong impulse to produce phenomena" was the underlying cause, but was convinced that "if she is restrained, genuine phenomena will result" (p. 328).

In one of the most extensive investigations ever into physical mediumship, the three leading members of the SPR who were dispatched to Naples to test her over eleven sittings, many in good light, shared this conviction. The three concerned, the Honorable Everard Fielding, W. W. Baggally and Carrington himself, were highly experienced at investigating physical phenomena and deeply skeptical as to their reality. In addition, all three had an extensive knowledge of the conjuring arts (Baggally in particular was also an accomplished practitioner), and Carrington had already written the standard text on investigating physical phenomena (Carrington, 1908). While carefully controlled by the investigators, Palladino produced no less than 22 different types of phenomena, including table levitations, raps, touches by spirit hands, movement of objects, ringing of bells, and materializations of spirit hands. Like all the mediums discussed in detail in this chapter she sat in the open rather than in a cabinet. In their report (Fielding, Baggally & Carrington, 1909) concluded "that some force was in play that was beyond the reach of ordinary control, and beyond the reach of the most skilful conjuror ... to explain Eusapia's manifestation some agency of a kind wholly different from mere physical dexterity on her part must be invoked" (pp. 340- 341). The investigation remains a classic in psychical research, and the various attempts to discredit it have been easily defeated (for example, see Fontana, 1992a, 1992b, 1998).

In fact, despite the efforts to dismiss it from Rhine onwards, research into physical phenomena has not been killed off. The advantage of physical phenomena is that they provide objective experiences that can be witnessed and potentially agreed upon by all those present. It challenges our view of the relationship between the physical and the spiritual worlds in that it suggests beings from the latter can directly influence — seemingly on a macro scale — the behavior of matter in the former. Laboratory results such as those at the Princeton Engineering Anomalies Research Unit (e.g., Jahn & Dunne, 1987) at Princeton University — to say nothing of the many dice-throwing and other experiments detailed by Louisa Rhine (L. Rhine, 1967) — have established beyond reasonable doubt that the mind appears able directly to influence material objects, if only on a micro level.

This demonstration of the existence of PK in the laboratory provides us with a further basis for looking at the physical phenomena of the séance room. And the more one studies the accounts of these phenomena (and seeks personal experience of them) the more it become clear that the prejudice against them is not only unwarranted but has actively handicapped an area of research that may have important implications for the question whether or not we survive physical death. For although the history of physical mediumship is not free from well-grounded accusations of fraud, there are many instances where such accusations are unfair. Houdini's supposed systematic and frequent unmasking of fraud (Houdini, 1924) turns out in fact, as with many magicians who have scorned physical mediumship, to focus mainly upon how fraud *could* have taken place rather than upon solid proof that it actually did take place. Even in the *Scientific American* investigation of the Margery mediumship, Houdini (who failed to attend most of the test séances held by the investigating committee) produced no conclusive evidence of fraud. Again his charges were based upon supposition rather than demonstrable fact (there were even claims, although never properly substantiated, that Houdini tried to frame Margery by instructing his assistant to hide a ruler in the fraud-proof cabinet he designed to restrict her movements during the test séances). As I pointed out in connection with the Scole investigation (discussed more fully later), in order to substantiate claims of fraud mediums must first demonstrate the phenomena concerned under the same conditions that obtained during the séance. In spite of our challenges to magicians to demonstrate the Scole phenomena under such conditions, we had no takers (sadly, both my two fellow investigators, Montague Keen and Professor Arthur Ellison, are now deceased and the opportunity for this demonstration has been lost).

Critics of physical phenomena have supported accusations of fraud by pointing to the fact that physical mediumship is now rare. The reason, they suggest, is that modern methods of detection are so sophisticated that no medium would any longer get away with trickery. However, it is untrue that the research methods of yesteryear were inadequate. For example, modern methods of fraud detection could hardly improve over those used by the late Harry Price with Rudi Schneider (Price, 1930) and with Stella C. (Turner, 1973) or even over those many years earlier by William Crookes with Daniel Home (Crookes, 1871 etc., re-published Medhurst, 1972). A more credible reason for the decline in physical mediumship is that few people have the time in the distractions of modern living and the cultural emphasis upon immediate results, to devote the years required for the development of physical mediumship abilities. Such abilities are by all accounts rare, and the financial returns, if one wished to earn a living from them, meager in the extreme. A mental medium can have many sittings with clients every day with much better returns (although I have never met a good medium who was in it for the money). In addition, as physical mediums are frequently in trance during séances, they cannot themselves appreciate the phenomena for which they are responsible. And whereas mental mediums can, when necessary, be charged with incompetence they rarely attract the accusations of fraud leveled at physical mediums. The mystery is not why there are so few physical mediums, but why there are any at all.

However, in spite of the difficulties, physical mediumship is undergoing something of a revival in the UK. This may be part of the reaction against the materialism of the present age. Scientific materialism, undermined on the one hand by the discoveries of quantum physics and on the other by a recognition that scientific advance has hardly yielded the secret of happiness, no longer holds the commanding position in human thought that it did in the early decades of the twentieth century. Perhaps physical phenomena now seem less inherently unlikely than they once did. The question therefore is: "Are such phenomena genuine, and if they are, what light do they throw upon the possible survival of physical death?"

Crookes and Home

To answer these questions we must look at some of the details of the cases to which I have already referred, commencing with Crookes' work with Daniel Home (see Crookes, 1871, re-published by Medhurst, 1972). Home's phenomena were, by all accounts, among the most remarkable on record. One of the best descriptions of them is given by Lord Adare (later the Earl of Dunraven, who worked intensively with Home for over two years) in a privately circulated monograph later published as a complete edition of the SPR *Proceedings* and in book form (Dunraven, 1924). A more frivolous account, relying upon published material, is by Burton (1948). But it is Crooke's investigations with Home that provide us with the most carefully controlled evidence for his gifts. No brief summary of these investigations can do them justice, and those interested should read them in their entirety, together with Lord Adare's account. Home, who was presumably in the best position to know, insisted throughout his life that these gifts were due not to powers of his own but to those of the spirits, and that his own mediumship was a gift from God. Summing up his conclusions on Home, Crookes (1871) wrote that "During the whole of my knowledge of D. D. Home, extending for several years, I never once saw the slightest occurrence that would make me suspicious that he was attempting to play tricks" (p. 225). The only direct accusation of fraud ever made against him was in a letter by a Mr. Merrifield published in 1903 in the *Journal* of the SPR in which he claimed that in a séance he had witnessed a connection between Home's shoulder and arm and a "spirit hand," and the charge was repeated by Frank Podmore (collaborator with Myers and Gurney of their book *Phantasms of the Living* of 1882), in his *Newer Spiritualism*, posthumously published in 1910. However, the flimsy nature of this evidence and Podmore's known prejudice against any form of physical phenomena render the accusation of little value.

The great majority of Home's phenomena took place in candlelight, sometimes subdued, sometimes bright. With the exception of the direct voice, he was reported as producing all the effects associated with physical phenomena. Levitations (of heavy tables and of himself), materialization of spirit hands, touches by spirit hands, movement of objects, large-scale elongations of his own body (measured under controlled conditions), the ability to handle burning coals without harm, impressive alterations in the weight of objects (certified by Crookes using fraud-proof weighing apparatus), the full materialization of his first wife (witnessed by Lord Adare), spirit raps, and tunes played by spirits on an accordion provided by Crookes and encased in a cage that prevented access to the keys. Lauded and vilified in turn throughout his career, Home frequently gave invited séances to many of the crowned heads of Europe (e.g., the French Emperor Napoleon III, the King of Naples, the Queen of Holland, the German Emperor, and the Russian Czar), all of whom seemed suitably impressed. In spite of hostility from many scientists who preferred not to influence themselves by actually attending a séance, not only was he never detected in fraud, no-one (as even the suspicious Frank Podmore admitted) was able to explain how he effected his tricks, if tricks they were, and effected them moreover in unfamiliar surroundings and in adequate light. In addition, no magician has, to my knowledge, ever attempted to duplicate any of them.

In the absence of any evidence or fraud or of duplication by normal means, we have to accept Crooke's conclusion that Home was genuine. In which case we are left with only two alternatives: either the phenomena were the product of PK by Home, or they were the work of discarnates. As we have seen, Home claimed the latter was the case. In his autobiography *Incidents of My Life* (1872) he tells us that at age 13, he experienced his first vision — that of a deceased school-friend Edwin who appeared to him in a bright cloud one night, thus keeping a promise that whichever of the boys died first would appear to the other. His next vision occurred four years later when, while in America, he was told, to the hour, of the death of his mother, in far off Scotland. If his own account is to be believed he was thereafter in constant mental contact with the spirits. Although prone to ill-health (probably tubercular) throughout his life, he firmly believed the spirits kept him alive. He never charged for his séances, though he received many gifts for his services and enjoyed financial independence thanks to his two marriages.

If we set his varied phenomena and his belief in the reality of the spiritual world against the possibility of PK, it is hard not to favor the former. The PK effects demonstrated in the laboratory are miniscule when compared to Home's phenomena. Could one man, sometimes in trance, produce these phenomena by his own unaided psychic abilities? And if he could, would he be unaware of the fact? We must be cautious in attributing motives to others, but if Home knew he was responsible, why would he have maintained to his death that the spirits were responsible? Possibly he might think that mention of spirits would ensure greater attention, but all who knew Home spoke of his honesty on one hand and his vanity on the other. Possessed of these two qualities it is not easy to accept he would have failed to claim the credit for himself if his it was.

Direct Voice Mediumship

I have discussed Home at length because he is in many ways the yardstick against which all physical mediumship is measured. If Home was genuine, as the evidence suggests, then his phenomena provide strong support for survival, even though his spirit friends made little attempt to give details of their identities and of their earthly lives. Evidence of this kind is associated particularly with physical mediums who produce the direct (or independent) voice — that is, supposedly spirit voices that come from disembodied positions around the séance room (sometimes through a trumpet that circles the room touching people and presenting whispered voices to their ears) rather than through the medium him or herself.

One of the most outstanding direct voice mediums was Etta Wriedt from

Detroit in the USA, who paid five visits to the UK between 1912 and 1919 giving over 200 séances, and who was exhaustively studied by Admiral Usborne Moore (Moore, 1913). Sir William Barrett, founder of the SPR along with respected journalist Dawson Rogers, also had sittings with her and vouched for the fact that she was genuine. Often working out of trance, Etta Wriedt (who never charged more than a dollar for her séances) is reported as producing trumpet and other voice phenomena during which communicators spoke, sometimes at length, in nine different languages (Dutch, French, German, Italian, Norwegian, Serbian, Arabic, Spanish and Croatian) although she herself spoke only English.

Countess Nora Wydenbruck, an experienced researcher, reports hearing no fewer than three voices speaking simultaneously at a Wriedt séance, sometimes from the floor, sometimes from overhead. Her grandmother communicated and gave her name, Isabella, and then in materialized form kissed the Countess' husband on the forehead. A voice then addressed him in German, French and Italian and claimed convincingly to be the man who had recognized his artistic talents when he was a boy. Most remarkable of all a voice addressed Wydenbruck (1938) and her husband in German "with a most peculiar accent impossible to imitate" (p. 97) which they recognized as that of an officer in one of the Austrian frontier regiment whose members were usually of Slav extraction.

Usborne Moore, whose book contains testimony after testimony from sitters, reports hearing three voices addressing him simultaneously, one in each ear and one through the trumpet in front of him. Mrs. Wriedt, when operating out of trance is reported as conversing with sitters and with communicators while direct voices could be heard. Like Home she never sat in a cabinet, and in addition to the direct voice phenomena her séances were reported as including the materialization of luminous forms, touches by spirit hands, flowers taken from vases and placed in the hands of sitters, spirit lights in the form of discs brilliant as the full moon that moved freely around the room, wafts of cool air, the displacement of heavy objects and drops of water that fell upon sitters.

The only claim of fraud made against Etta Wriedt was that the noises in the trumpet were caused by the mildly inflammable powder lycopodium. In the light of the numerous testimonies in her favor by experienced investigators this can hardly be taken seriously, and we are left once again with the choice between PK and the action of surviving spirits. It is hardly credible that, with no knowledge of the languages concerned, Mrs. Wriedt's own abilities allowed her to use nine languages with sufficient skill to convince native speakers. If the phenomena depended on her own abilities we would have to assume that in addition to using PK she obtained data telepathically from sitters, then fed it back into the séance room in the form of direct voices. As with Home, the survival explanation surely seems the more credible.

The same is true of other direct voice mediums such as Arthur Ford and John Sloan, neither of whom was reliably detected in fraud. Space allows me to deal only with Sloan, who was investigated exhaustively by Arthur Findlay (Findlay, 1951), and who also impressed Sir William Barrett, who urged the SPR (unsuccessfully) to mount a research program to explore his gifts. Sloan, a simple workingman with no pretensions and little interest in his own gifts, took no money for his séances, which were usually carried out in the various homes of members of his home circle. Like Etta Wriedt he often worked out of trance, and could be heard conversing with the direct voice communicators himself. One of the best of the many good pieces of survival evidence associated with Sloan was the dialogue during one of his séances between John Findlay (Arthur Findlay's brother, who was unknown to Sloan at the time) and a communicator who claimed to be one of the soldiers who had attended a machine gun training course under Findlay during the First World War. In the course of the dialogue and in response to questions posed by John Findlay the soldier gave his own name (Eric Saunders), the location of the training course (an obscure village called Kessingland), the name of his Company Commander, the type of machine gun on which he trained, the date he was posted to France, and other personal details. John Findlay was unable to remember the man, but checking later with the NCO who kept records of the trainees, every one of the details was confirmed as correct. The only disappointment was that John Findlay failed to ask Saunders for the name of his regiment. Enquiries at the War Office by Arthur Findlay revealed that many men with the same name had been killed during the war, and without knowing Saunder's regiment no further checks on his identity could be made.

Sloan held literally thousands of direct voice séances over 50 years, and Arthur Findlay discusses what would have been needed if trickery was involved. Sloan would have had to compose a new "script" for each séance, to research personal details of his sitters (including many who, like John Findlay, came as guests) and their deceased friends and relatives, and to use accomplices to impersonate voices from various parts of the room and smuggle them into and out of the many houses in which séances were held. Furthermore the accomplices would have had to keep two trumpets flying around the room at great speed, produce dancing spirit lights, ring the bells that were also a feature at the sittings, and find sitters unerringly in the dark and touch (often on request) their faces and bodies. Finally, the accomplices would have had to do all this in rooms where most of the space was taken up by sitters, avoid detection, and make themselves scarce before the lights were turned on. To this we should add that, as with Home and with Etta Wriedt, many of the sitters at Sloan's séances were highly educated professional people not given to superstition, and in many cases initially skeptical.

By any reasonable standards it is hard to accept that hundreds of such people would, over 50 years, have been deceived by Sloan and his hypothetical accomplices. It is equally hard to accept that the phenomena witnessed over the 50 years were the consequence of PK and other psychic abilities on the part of Sloan. Once again, the balance of probabilities must come down firmly in favor of communications from individuals who claim to have survived physical death and who wish to convey the fact to their family and friends.

It is of course one thing to accord these various cases a kind of detached theoretical acceptance, and quite another to accept fully that physical phenomena really do happen. In order to arrive at genuine conviction there is in fact no real substitute for personal experience. Sadly there are certain constraints against seeking personal experience and even more against publishing positive results. Scientific laws cannot accommodate physical phenomena, and in the academic world this means that those who research into them risk being thought (and treated as) unsound. Yet in science as elsewhere, truth should be our primary concern. In my own case, my conversion to an acceptance of the reality of physical phenomena came over a two-year period of investigating — and observing — poltergeist activity (Fontana 1991, 1992b). Since those days, I have had the good fortune (although in psychical research one tends to make one's own good fortune by going out to look for cases to investigate) to witness physical phenomena with four different groups in conditions in which trickery could be ruled out. Of these I have space only to discuss one, namely the Scole investigation.

The Scole Investigation

The two-year investigation at Scole (a village in Norfolk, England) is fully described by my fellow researchers and myself in a whole issue of the SPR *Proceedings* (Keen, Ellison & Fontana, 1999), and a popular book to which we contributed has been published by the Solomons (G. Solomon & J. Solomon, 1999). The case is also covered at length together with much other evidence for survival in Fontana (2005). The phenomena we witnessed at Scole included all the effects already mentioned, namely lights, materializations, levitations, touches by materialized hands, and the direct voice.

Although most of the phenomena took place in darkness, the spirit lights (for want of a better term) were so bright and in some cases so enduring that at times we three investigators could see each others' faces. Films provided by us and kept in marked canisters through the séances were found afterwards to have pictures, diagrams and messages on them (on one occasion the film was placed in a locked box held in the hands of Walter Schnittger, one of our co-investigators, throughout the sitting), small spirit lights were seen to enter crystals and illuminate them from clearly visible positions inside them, diffused patches drifted around the room, hands as far as the wrists were seen to materialize in the bright spirit lights and to pick up objects from the table, hands touched us on our feet and legs under the table in positions rendered inaccessible by the solid supports on which the table rested, and patches of light took the shape of small robed figures.

I had 16 sittings with the Group, each of them some three hours long, and Montague Keen, Secretary of the SPR Survival Research Committee, even traveled to the USA and Europe with the Group and took part in the successful séances they held in strange rooms and with unfamiliar groups of sitters. Not only were the three of us experienced investigators, Professor Arthur Ellison, former Head of the Department of Electrical and Electronic Engineering at the City University, was an expert in the ways electricity can be misused in the séance room.

A familiar criticism of physical séances is that magicians are never present. In the case of Scole a professional magician, James Webster, a silver medal holder of the Inner Magic Circle (the leading fraternity for magicians in the UK) and a man with 40 years experience of psychical research was present at three sittings, and was categorical that no magician, even if he had unimpeded access to the séance room beforehand in order to hide equipment (in fact the room was searched by us before each sitting) and used accomplices (an impossibility under the circumstances) could possibly duplicate the phenomena he witnessed.

Again what is the relevance of all this for survival? At Scole we found that the communicators, usually speaking through the two entranced mediums who with Robin and Sandra Foy made up the Scole Group but also using the direct voice, showed every sign of consistent individuality throughout the two years, both in terms of their personalities and their vocabulary. They were unfailingly courteous, and unfailingly well-informed on scientific matters and on the history of the SPR. When I asked one of the direct voice communicators if I could shake his hand, he clasped mine immediately and without fumbling, even though at the time the room was in complete darkness (we were often touched with the same accuracy by materialized hands at our request). Rather than to bring through communications from other deceased people, the expressed intention of the communicators was to develop methods of producing physical phenomena without drawing ectoplasm from the mediums, and in this they appear to have succeeded in that at the end of the séances the mediums showed no sign of the exhaustion typical of mediums who supply ectoplasm. Nevertheless, during a séance in the United States, George Dalzell, a Licensed Social Worker in California and a member of the Skeptics Society, considered the evidence he received of his deceased partner important enough to include in his book, in which a chapter is devoted to Scole (Dalzell, 2002).

As with the examples of physical phenomena already given, it would stretch the bounds of credibility to argue that the phenomena at Scole were due to PK, just as it would stretch the bounds of credibility to argue they were the result of fraud. The balance of probabilities is firmly on the side of survival. The communicators appear to be who they said they were, namely deceased individuals who retained their powers of intellect, memory, humor, and compassion, and a strong motivation to communicate the reality of survival.

Instrumental Transcommunication

The same appears to be true for communications received through what is now known as Instrumental Transcommunication (ITC). The term covers all those anomalous communications and messages received through electronic media such as tape recorders, radios, computers, and fax machines. First reported in 1959 by Swedish artist and documentary film make Friedrich Jurgenson, who found extraneous voices on tapes of bird song he recorded for one of his documentaries, the phenomena have increasingly been reported in Europe (particularly Spain, Italy, Germany and France) and the USA. Dismissed initially by some critics as stray radio transmissions misinterpreted by listeners as spirit messages, careful investigation over the years has found this explanation to be inadequate.

Currently, software developed by the FBI for the acoustic analysis of the human voice is being used in order to identify the characteristics of ITC voices, and results indicate that samples of these voices contain anomalies that distinguish them from normal voices. Computer modeling of the shape of the larynxes that would be required to produce these voices were they of human origin has also revealed anomalies that indicate with a high level of accuracy that they are not from this source (Fernándes, 2004). The two ITC methods used most extensively by investigators are EVP (Electronic Voice Phenomena) and DRV (Direct Radio Voice). In the former, a ten-minute or so recording is made of a source of white noise (e.g., running water or the static when a radio is tuned between two stations) during which the investigator asks the occasional question, leaving a subsequent pause each time. The tape is then rewound and played back in the hope that anomalous voices (usually brief and faint) will now be heard during these pauses. In DRV the procedure is similar except that the anomalous voices are now heard to come directly through the white noise (i.e., through the loudspeaker of the radio), potentially allowing two-way conversations to take place (see Senkowski, 1989, for a full description).

In the best DRV examples, the voices are sufficiently clear as to be heard without difficulty. Communicators have given both their own names and the names of investigators. I have been in the studio of Dr. Anabela Cardoso when excellent results have been obtained under controlled conditions. For example, without warning her that I intended to do so, on one occasion I asked the communicators to repeat five simple words after me, which they did successfully, disposing of the possibility that stray radio transmissions were being received (Cardoso, 2003, Cardoso & Fontana, 2002). In a recent experiment at the studio of Marcello Bacci in Italy, conducted by Dr. Cardoso, Professor Mario Festa, Engineer Paolo Presi, and myself, all five valves were removed from the radio that Bacci uses as a source of white noise, yet the communications continued to be heard through the radio loudspeaker. This also disposes of the possibility of stray radio transmissions (Cardoso et al., 2004 — a report of this experiment has also been sent to all leading and popular parapsychological publications).

The physical phenomena yielded by ITC offer further strong evidence for survival. Precautions can be taken against trickery and the receipt and misinterpretation of stray radio transmissions, and voice samples can be acoustically analyzed to detect anomalies incompatible with the human voice. Content analysis can also be undertaken to identify details that indicate communicators are who they say they are. If communications satisfy these various tests, then the explanations reduce once again to survival or to PK. And once again, the former seems the more acceptable. It is unfortunate that prejudice against ITC still exists among some parapsychologists, few of whom have studied the evidence published over the past 25 years. One problem for English speakers is that much of it is in Italian, German, Spanish and French, but the *ITC Journal* now publishes research in English as well as in Spanish and Portuguese, making this evidence more generally accessible.

Conclusion

Physical phenomena in their various forms have been regarded with suspicion by parapsychology for some three quarters of a century. However, for reasons discussed in this chapter, this suspicion has not always been warranted, and has unfortunately led to the neglect of a great deal of evidence strongly suggestive of survival. I am not alone in hoping that the position is now, for good reason, beginning to change.

References

Burton, J. (1948). *Heyday of a wizard.* London and Toronto: Harrap.
Cardoso, A. (2003). Survival research. *Journal of Conscientiology,* 6, *21,* 33–36.
Cardoso, A., Festa, M., Fontana, D., & Presi, P. (2004). The reality of ITC voices scientifically demonstrated on 5th December 2004 during experiments with Marcello Bacci at Grosseto, Italy, Europe. *ITC Journal,* 14–21.
Cardoso, A., & Fontana, D. (2002). Developing a protocol for ITC. *ITC Journal, 12,* 55–63.
Carrington, (1908). *The physical phenomena of spiritualism.* Boston, MA: Small, Maynard & Co.
Carrington, H. (1909). *Eusapia Palladino and her phenomena.* London: Werner Laurie.
Dalzell, G. E. (2002). *Messages: Evidence for life after death.* Charlottesville VA: Hampton Roads.
Dunraven, Earl of (1924). *Experiences in spiritualism with D. D. Home.* Glasgow: Glasgow University Press.
Fernández, C. (2004). Daniel Gulla interviewed by Carlos Fernández. *ITC Journal, 19,* 40–47.
Fielding, E., Baggally, W, and Carrington, H. (1909). Report on a series of sittings with Eusapia Palladino (the Fielding Report). *Proceedings of the Society for Psychical Research, 23,* 306–569.
Findlay, A. (1951). *Where two worlds meet.* London: Psychic Press.
Fontana, D. (1991). A responsive poltergeist: a case from South Wales. *Journal of the Society for Psychical Research, 57,* 385–403.
Fontana, D. (1992a). The Fielding Report and the determined critic. *Journal of the Society for Psychical Research, 58,* 341–350.
Fontana, D. (1992b). The responsive South Wales poltergeist: A follow-up report. *Journal of the Society for Psychical Research, 58,* 225–231.
Fontana, D. (1998). Polidoro and Rinaldi: No match for Palladino and the Fielding Report. *Journal of the Society for Psychical Research, 63,* 225–231.
Fontana, D. (2005). *Is there an afterlife?* Ropley, Hants: O Books/John Hunt Publishing.
Gaskill, M. (2001). *Hellish Nell.* London: Fourth Estate.
Gurney, E., Myers F. W. & Podmore, F. (1886). *Phantasms of the living.* London: Society for Psychical Research.
Home, D. D. (1872). *Incidents in my life.* London: Longmans Green (re-published 1972 by University Books, Secaucus, NJ.).
Houdini, H. (1924). *A Magician among the spirits.* New York: Harper Brothers.
Jahn, R. G. & Dunne, B. J. (1987). *Margins of reality: The role of consciousness in the physical world.* New York: Harcourt Brace Jovanovich.
Keen, M. Ellison, A. & Fontana, D. (1999). An account of an investigation into the genuineness of a range of physical phenomena associated with a mediumistic group in Scole, Norfolk (The Scole Report). *Proceedings of Society for Psychical Research, 58,* 150–452 (whole issue).
Medhurst, R. G. (1972) (Collected by). *Crookes and the spirit world: A collection of writings by or concerning the work of Sir William Crookes, O.M., F.R.S., in the field of psychical research.* London: Souvenir Press.
Moore, Vice Admire W. Usborne (1913). *The voices.* London: Watts.
Podmore, F. (1910). *The newer spiritualism.* New York and London: Putnam.
Price, H. (1930). *Rudi Schneider: A scientific examination of his mediumship.* London: Methuen.
Rhine, J. W. (1954). *New world of the mind.* London: Faber & Faber.
Rhine, L. (1961). *Hidden channels of the mind.* New York: William Morrow.

Rhine, L. (1967). *ESP in life and lab.* New York: MacMillan.
Senkowski, W. (1989). *Instrumentelle transkommunikation.* Frankfurt: F. G. Fischer.
Solomon, G. & Solomon, J. (1999). *The Scole experiment.* London: Pitkus.
Turner, J. (1973) (Ed.). *Stella C: An account of some original experiments in psychical research by Harry Price.* London: Souvenir Press.
Wydenbruck, Countess Nora (1938). *The paranormal: Personal experiences and deductions.* London: Rider.

8. On Apparitions and Mediumship: An Examination of the Evidence That Personal Consciousness Persists After Death

WILLIAM ROLL

William Roll presents an extremely well researched review of the apparition and mediumship literature. His chapter augments some of the material presented in the previous chapter by David Fontana. Dr. Roll shows that a surprising number of people have seen apparitions, and he discusses the normal and paranormal explanations of this phenomenon. With regard to the cases of mediumship, Dr. Roll describes elaborate experiments using mediums, and he painstakingly explains the results, and the implications of those results. Dr. Roll concludes his chapter with some profound statements about the nature of survival, and he presents some testable hypotheses.—Editors

If we suppose that mind may continue without its brain, the question is, what kind of mind? It seems that each of us have two very different minds. The left-brain hemisphere is the seat of a mind that processes sense data and other things sequentially and that can be conscious. It is the mind of language and step-by-step thinking. In contrast, the right hemisphere is the seat of a mind that processes things simultaneously and is unconscious. If you were aware of doing two or more tasks at the same time, the splitting of consciousness might make you unable to manage everyday affairs and could send you to a mental institution.

Since the early days of psychic research the evidence has pointed to the right hemisphere as the brain structure that is principally involved in psi. If we suppose that the psychic mind may operate after death, as it must in order to communicate with other incorporeal minds and with the living, it would apparently be unconscious. On the other hand, if we suppose that it is the conscious, non-psychic mind that survives, it would apparently neither be able to communicate with other departed minds nor with the living. This may be a simplistic way to look at things but before we explore alternatives, let us see what the evidence says.

Apparitions

According to Dodds (1971), the tradition that spirits of the dead haunt their place of death or burial is as old as Plato "and doubtless far older" (p. 190). Dodds was professor of classics at Oxford with a strong interest in psi. To be of parapsychological interest, experiences of apparitions must show evidence of ESP. Such experiences face the same problems of evidence as other forms of spontaneous psi. For an apparition of the dead the possibility of ESP comes up if the apparition resembles a person who once lived, assuming that the percipient did not know the looks of the person. Apparitions with an ESP component are called veridical apparitions.

Apparitions are not rare. Ten percent of the British respondents to the Census of Hallucinations (Sidgwick & Committee, 1894) said that they had seen, heard, or been touched by an entity or object that was not present in an ordinary way. Some 50 years later in a follow-up questionnaire by West (1948), 14% replied affirmatively, and in a study by Palmer (1979) in Charlottesville, Virginia, the figure was 17%. In a survey by Haraldsson (Haraldsson et al., 1977) in Iceland, a surprising 31% had seen apparitions of the dead while 11% had seen apparitions of living people. In contract, Stevenson (1980) had never heard of post-mortem apparitions among the Druses of Lebanon: "Such phenomena should not occur given the immediate rebirth into another body of anyone who dies" (p. 11). On the other hand, changes of gender between incarnations are commonly reported in India and other societies where this is considered possible and Stevenson has examined reports of rebirth.

There are two schools of thought regarding the collection and evaluation of experiences with a psi component, such as apparitions of the departed. One was formulated by members of the British Society for Psychical Research (SPR) in the 1880s and 1890s, the other at Duke University by J. B. and Louisa E. Rhine in the mid-1900s. The Census of Hallucinations (Sidgwick & Committee, 1894) was a survey of 17,000 percipients and asked if the account was firsthand; if it was written or told before the verifying event was known; if the apparition was identified as an actual person; if the relevant details could have been read back into the narrative after the facts; and if the correspondence between experience and event could have been due to chance. The research required much time and effort and the number of published cases declined over the years. L. E. Rhine (1957), whose cases came from letters to the Parapsychology Laboratory at Duke, only required that the writer seem serious and sane.

The American Society for Psychical Research (ASPR; Dale, White & Murphy, 1962) made a request for cases to readers of three successive issues of a Sunday supplement to a newspaper with a readership of several million. Only 1200 responded and the cases were whittled down to a mere 17 by the ASPR — namely that the experience be about an actual event, that there be a witness who testified that the percipient reported the experience before knowing about the event; and that not more than five years had passed between the experience and a written report.

Personal and Local Connections

Edmund Gurney (Gurney & Myers, 1888–1889) found that recognized apparitions of the dead were "local" or "personal." That is, an apparition was seen in an area the person had occupied when living or near someone who had known the person. Sometimes the two characteristics were combined (p. 408). Eleanor Sidgwick (1885, 1923) observed the same. Not all the apparitions were identified as actual people; some were classified as local or personal because of repeated and independent experiences by two or more people in the same place or near the same person.

L. E. Rhine (1957) found 49 reports of visual impressions of the departed. Sixteen were personal since the percipient had known the deceased; in 15 the deceased was unknown to the percipient but was seen in a location he or she used to occupy; and nine were local and personal. Note that only those cases count as evidence of psi where the person seen was unknown to the percipient. Rhine also found eight personal cases of the "bystander" type where the percipient had not known the deceased, but saw the apparition near someone who had. An example:

> The summer school of music which I attended in the summer of 1927 to 1933 was led by Mr. Thomas S, a musician and teacher. During those summers I resided at the house of Mr. Alfred U. He is also musical. Mr. S died in 1940 and the school was discontinued. In April 1950 I spent an evening in Mr. U's home. During the evening a woman friend of his came in with her husband and I was told beforehand that she was psychic. At the end of the evening ... they invited me to play the piano.... I played them Bach's "Sonatina" from the Cantata, "God's Tune is Best." It is a favorite of mine and I knew it was of Mr.

U.... I did not, as I played it, think at all of Mr. S, though I later remembered that this piece was a favorite of his and one we had often heard in the summer school. When I had finished, Alfred's friend, the "psychic" woman who I had never before seen and knew had never heard of either the summer school or Mr. S, immediately spoke up and said, "Oh I saw such a strange thing just now as you were playing." We asked what it was. She had, she told us, seen a strange man standing quite near to me as I played and evidently trying to say something to me. She hadn't caught what it was. We asked her to describe him and she started with his hair and worked down, but had scarcely got to the goatee on his chin before Alfred and I looked at each other, exclaiming in unison, "Mr. S!" There could be no mistake as Mr. S was a very distinguished and unusual looking man.... I, myself, had at one time been fairly close to Mr. S. [Rhine, 1957, p. 39].

Visions of animals and of inanimate structures are also reported. Sometimes apparitions of animals are identified as deceased pets and sometimes not, such as the ghost cats described by Celia Green and Charles McGreery (Green & McGreery, 1975). In two of their cases, the cats were connected to people rather than places, since the cats were seen in different houses occupied by the same people.

Schouten (1979, 1981) thought artifacts (i.e., errors) in reporting might explain the personal connections in the *Phantasms* collection (Sidgwick, 1923) and Sannwald's (1961) collection. Schouten also discusses the relationship between the departed and the percipient. In *Phantasms*, Schouten (1979) found 51.6% reports involving close relatives (spouses, siblings, children, and parents) as against 13.4% with distant relatives. Similarly, there were 32.8% cases with friends and acquaintances versus 2.2% with strangers (p. 420). For Sannwald the percentages for close and distant relatives were 55.9% versus 11%, and for acquaintances and strangers 28% versus 5.1% (Schouten, 1981, p. 22). The figures include trivial events, minor accidents, as well as serious illness and death. Schouten assumed that for all kinds of relationships except when the people were strangers, "the probability of learning of the death of the target person must have been very high and about equal" (1979, p. 420). Restricting himself to death cases, the distributions remained close to what they had been for all cases: 47.4% for close family, 17.8% for distant, and 34.8% for friends and acquaintances (p. 420).

Schouten then considered the possibility that the differences might result from another reporting artifact. The death of a close relative may impress the percipient more than the death of someone else. He therefore separated the cases according to whether the percipient or another person had contributed the case, but found no significant differences. He then asked if people might report a case sooner when relatives were involved than when the apparition represented an outsider. Instead of finding more cases where close family ties linked the two, the figures suggested that the percipients reported more cases when more distant family members or when friends and acquaintances were involved. He speculated that people may be reluctant to talk about the death of a close relative. Schouten's (1981) analysis of the Sannwald collection also did not sustain the hypothesis that the personal link between percipient and departed was a reporting artifact.

Theories for Apparitions

Sidgwick (1885) dismissed the popular view that ghosts, like ordinary matter, occupy and move through space, because it is does not account for the clothes of apparitions. Perhaps the spirits of the dead have matter-like bodies, but it is difficult to suppose that their clothes, and apparitions are invariably clothed, are also made of this material. She thought that an apparition has no real relation to the external world, but is a hallucination resulting from a communication between the spirit of the deceased and the percipient (p. 147). She noted that her theory cannot account for haunting apparitions, that is, for apparitions seen repeatedly in the same locality, for in addition to the hypothetical connection between mind and mind, "in a haunted house we have a *rapport* complicated by its apparent dependence on locality" (p. 147). We have to make the assumption not only that the spirit is interested in a particular house, but that this interest connects the spirit with the mind of a person living in the house while the spirit does not get into similar communication with the same person or with other persons elsewhere. In other words, the theory does not explain why there should be a telepathic communication from the deceased that makes the stranger see the apparition in a particular place but nowhere else.

Sidgwick (1885) points to another possibility:

> ... which I can hardly expect to appear plausible, and which, therefore, I only introduce because I think that it corresponds best to a certain part of the evidence.... It is that there is something in the actual building itself—some subtle physical influence—which produces in the brain that effect which, in its turn, becomes the cause of the hallucination [p. 148].

Gurney (Gurney, Myers, & Podmore, 1886) also had difficulties with what we may call the physical trace theory for local apparitions. In a discussion of the apparition of a man who is dying away from his former home, now occupied by a stranger who sees the apparition there, Gurney speculated that the man's memory of the house brought him into telepathic contact with the stranger, causing the stranger to see the apparition "because the two minds are simultaneously occupied with an identical conception" (pp. 301–302). Gurney noted that if the explanation were true, there should be cases where "a phantom has appeared to [a person] without previous acquaintance, on the ground of some community of ideas and interest between the two, unconnected with any special locality." Gurney knew of no such cases and was faced with the "perplexing problem of the relation of psychical operations to space" (p. 302). Gurney (Gurney & Myers, 1888–1889) advanced a similar theory when he suggested that some cases of local apparitions involve "the survival of a mere image" somehow imprinted by the person in the area where his or her apparition is later seen (pp. 417–418). A related view is sketched by Ernesto Bozzano (1920, p. 164) in his psychometric theory of haunting apparitions.

Collective Apparitions

Most apparitions are seen when the percipient is alone. Tyrrell (1953) found this to be true for about three quarters of the 1,087 visual hallucinations reported in the Census (Sidgwick & Committee, 1894). Of the 283 cases, which occurred when two or more persons were present, 95 cases (about one third) involved apparitions collectively perceived (i.e., seen simultaneously) by at least two persons, but not necessarily by all present. At the time of Tyrrell's study, the number of collective cases had increased to 130 (pp. 76–80). The proportion of collective cases increases further if we follow Hart's (1956) rule that "the additional persons must have been, not merely present, but so situated that they would have perceived the apparition if it had been a physically embodied person" (p. 204). Hart found 46 cases of this type in the literature, 26 of which the apparition was collectively perceived. There is a problem with the collective aspect of some visions. When two or more individuals see an apparition in the same area, the two are usually in close proximity. This raises the possibility that the experience of one individual is communicated to the other by sensory cues.

Gurney (Gurney et al., 1886) proposed that collective apparitions may result from a kind of telepathic infection where the agent influences the primary percipient who in turn transmits the image to the others present. Tyrrell (1953) doubted whether this could result in the realistic placing of the apparition in the perceptual space of the observers. Instead he supposed that the telepathic agent creates a motif that is expressed as an apparition by the "mid-level centers of the personalities of the percipients of such a kind that it causes each to play his part in expressing a collective idea pattern" (p. 125).

Myers (1903/1955) thought that when a phantasm is seen by more than one person in the same place, it is causing a change in that portion of space although not in the matter there. It is therefore not optically nor acoustically perceived but represents an unknown form of perception (p. 75).

Henry Price (1939), a philosophy professor who was my supervisor at Oxford, had a theory of mental images that may account for apparitions. According to Price, images are "persistent and dynamic entities, which when once formed may have a kind of independent life of their own, and may escape more or less completely from the control of their author" (p. 325). To account for local apparitions, Price suggested that:

> ... an image or a group of images might get itself localized in a particular region of Physical Space.... Once localized there, they might continue to be so localized for a considerable period, retaining the telepathic charge which they had at first, though this might gradually diminish in intensity. Suppose a man now enters the room and suppose there is a telepathic affinity between the contents of his mind and the localized images. A telepathic process then occurs which may result in a sense of presence or in "a phantasm located in his ordinary waking visual field" [pp. 325–326].

To extend his theory to collective cases, Price supposed that the telepathic affinity may involve two or more percipients. If the cases on record form a representative sample, they seem either to suggest that post-mortem existence is even more "earth-bound" and "people-bound" than life before death, or that apparitions do not represent the minds of the departed personal but something else, such as the localized images suggested by Price (1949). A localized image is a type of place memory, a concept Price (1940) expounded on in another paper.

Fading over Time

In Gurney and Myers' (1888–1889) discussion of cases from *Phantasms*, they mentioned 211 instances where the time of the experience in relation to the death of the person was known. Of these, 38 occurred before death (19 within 24 hours before death), 134 occurred within the hour before or after death, and 29 between one and twelve hours after death (note that post-mortem apparitions beyond this time are excluded from *Phantasms*). The paper by Henry Sidgwick and Committee (1894) brings in the cases from the Census of Hallucinations. For 92 recognized apparitions of the dead, where the time of the apparition in relation to the person's death was known, 11 occurred during the 12-hour period before death, 50 at the time of death, and 11 during the following 12 hours. The Census thus corroborated the findings from *Phantasms*.

Myers (Gurney & Myers, 1888–89) observed that recognized apparitions decrease rapidly in the few days after death, then more slowly; "and after about a year's time they become so sporadic that we can no longer include them in a steadily descending line" (p. 427). With respect to the cluster of sightings just before the moment of death, Myers suggested that they are probably not due to the event of death as such, but to the coma or delirium preceding death:

> This we say because we have many instances where veridical phantasms have coincided with moment of *crisis*— carriage-accidents and the like — occurring to distant agents, but not followed by death. Accordingly we find that in almost all cases where a phantasm ... *preceded* the agent's death, that death was the result of disease and not of accident [Gurney & Myers, 1888–89, p. 427].

In general, according to the Census (Sidgwick & Committee, 1894, p. 364), apparitions of the dead are less frequent than apparitions of the living, even when we add apparitions seen at the moment of death. In Louisa Rhine's (1957) collection of 825 hallucinatory experiences, only 88 represent deceased persons, while 440 showed the living and 297 dying individuals (p. 17).

On the other hand, Green and McCreery (1975) reported that only one-third of the visions of their informants were of living people (p. 178) while about two-thirds represented deceased persons or animals. With respect to apparitions of the deceased, their cases in general conform to Myers' observation: "The cases reported to us tend to occur most frequently within a week of the death, and the number falls away as the length of time since the death increases" (p. 188).

Again the possibility of sampling artifacts must not be ignored. The more distant in time a person's death, the less likely it is that this person's apparition will be recognized. As the percipients' memories of deceased friends and relatives fade, or as they themselves die, the likelihood that the apparition will be identified is correspondingly reduced. However, this factor is unlikely to be responsible for the sharp decline in the number of veridical apparitions in the course of a few days or weeks, when the percipients' memories of the deceased must still be sharp.

Myers (Gurney & Myers, 1888–1889), speculated that the "power of communication with living persons must lessen as the decedent becomes more remote from earthly life" (p. 476). Whatever the reason, apparitions disappear or become less recognizable soon after death.

Psychological Aspects

In the attempts to determine the nature of apparitions, perhaps the most important question is whether they act in a purposeful manner that cannot be accounted for only in terms of the needs of the percipient. If the apparition shows purpose or interests consistent with the personality of the deceased, this may suggest that it represents this individual.

Sidgwick (1885) found little evidence of "apparent intention consistently carried out by the spirit" (p. 99). With respect to the localized ghosts in her collection "there is a total absence of any apparent object or intelligent action on the part of the ghost" (p. 143). Gurney and Myers (1888–1889) said they had been unable establish a connection between haunting figures and any deceased person (p. 476).

In spite of Gurney's preference for the theory that apparitions are due to the departed, some cases — for instance a recurrent apparition of a dying woman on the cot where she collapsed after a beating by her husband (Gurney & Myers, 1888–1889) — did not so much suggest any continuing local interest on the part of the deceased, "as the survival of a mere image, impressed, we cannot guess how, or we cannot guess what, by that person's physical organism, and perceptible at times to those endowed with some cognate form of sensitiveness" (pp. 417–418).

Non-recurrent apparitions sometimes seem to show autonomy and purpose. In one of Sidgwick's (1885) personal cases a young man who had taken poison by mistake appeared in a dream to his former employer, ostensibly to assure him that he had not committed suicide (pp. 95–98). In the Chaffin will case (Case of the will of Mr. James L. Chaffin, 1927), an apparitional representation of the deceased also came in a dream and indicated where he had hidden his will; similarly, in the Conley dream case (Myers, 1903/1955, pp. 37–40) an apparition of the deceased told where a sum of money could be found.

In evaluating such cases it should be noted, first, that the percipients might have been equally motivated (e.g., to find the will) and second that these are dream cases and that, like ordinary dreams, the semblance of autonomy shown by the dream figure may have been added by the dreamer to the central theme, such as the location of the will, which supposedly could only have been known by ESP. In other words, the presence or absence of motive and purpose shown by the deceased may result from the psychological state of the percipient. If this is normal or near normal, the apparition does not as a rule act in a purposeful manner. If it does act intelligently, we often find that the percipient is in a prolonged altered condition, such as dreaming, near death, or in a mediumistic trance. This does not necessarily mean that the deceased do not exist as independent entities. They might simply find it easier to come through during more extended altered states and for this reason show more evidence of purpose than when the person through whom they manifest is awake. On the other hand, if an apparition represents an entity with its own distinct needs or purposes, it should be possible to find evidence for these.

L. E. Rhine (1960) addressed the issue of motivation in a study of 258 cases that purportedly involved communication from the deceased. Her account included dream or dream-like experiences as well as physical effects ascribed to the deceased, in addition to apparitional experiences. In 181 cases Rhine found the strength of the motive to communicate to be about equal for the living percipient and the deceased; in 43 the motive of the deceased seems stronger, and in 30 other cases, much stronger. It should be noted that these were Rhine's own ratings. Nowadays independent judges would be used. The following is a case that Rhine placed among the 30 cases highly suggestive of the agency of the deceased rather than the percipient. A woman dreamed that the son of a former neighbor came to her and asked, "Will you give my mother a message for me?" and related something insignificant. The woman dismissed the dream because she thought the boy was alive. When she casually mentioned the dream to his mother, the woman said her son had just died. She was convinced that the message was from her son (pp. 18–19).

Regarding these 30 cases, Rhine commented:

> ... although they all seemed to be instances in which the action could much more reasonably be ascribed to the agent than to the percipient, at the same time the percipients in each case would have had some degree of interest in the news, even if, as in the last case above, it would only have been the interest of an acquaintance in the death of a neighbor. On this account, although the cases of this group give a high probability of influence from the deceased, they do not entirely rule out the alternative of production by the percipient [p. 19].

In only one instance — the so-called "shorthand case" — is the motivation clearly stronger for the agent. Reportedly, some pages scribbled by a boy of four turned out to be an old type of shorthand known to his deceased father with a message to the boy's mother about the location of the father's safety deposit box. Rhine tried unsuccessfully to verify the story, and suspected it was fictional. But it illustrates the type of case that would suggest discarnate agency (p. 23).

Haunting apparitions almost never resemble the deceased, but are sometimes mistaken for living occupants (Roll, et al., 1992). In Scandinavia, impressions called *vardøgler*, such as a person's apparition or footsteps that precede the unexpected arrival of the person, also represent living occupants of the home.

In the 18 haunting cases in Sidgwick's (1885) collection (17 local and one personal):

> ... we have no first-hand account of a ghost appearing undoubtedly in the dress of a distinctly bygone age.... Vague costumes, not specially appropriate to any particular period, are somewhat the most numerous ... though in seven or eight of them the dress seems to have been such as would not at all have surprised the percipients if worn by a living person in the daytime [p. 143].

For recognized apparitions of the dead, "the appearance in dress or otherwise is what the percipient was accustomed to associate with the person in life" (Sidgwick & Committee, 1894, p. 365).

The idea, perhaps first voiced by Sidgwick, that the form of apparitions may in part be supplied by the percipient is worked out in Tyrrell's (1953) theory: An apparition of a deceased person is a joint product of the minds of this person and the percipient. L. E. Rhine (1957) however, found no evidence of anyone other than the percipient. She suggested that the percipient, using his or her abilities of retrocognitive clairvoyance, produced a veridical hallucination of the deceased with no help from anyone else, either living or dead.

Heywood (1976) described two local apparitions, which, though non-veridical, suggest that some apparitions may reflect groups of people rather than individuals. During a visit to the House of Commons, Heywood — a writer and advisor to the government — was relaxing on a bench when she became aware of a being, composed of discarnate members of the House, whose task was to influence for good the deliberations of Parliament. She saw no image but had a powerful sense of a presence that towered over the building. She had a similar experience at her son's school, Eton, where she had gone to pick him up.

Conditions that may be apparition-conducive are suggested by Schouten (1981). He found that 59% of the Sannwald cases occurred in dreams against 34.5% in the waking state. In the *Phantasms* study (Schouten, 1979), which excluded dreams, he found a significant prevalence of impressions in the evening (34.5%) or night (24%, dreams excluded) over morning (19.9%) and afternoon (2.6%). Schouten suggested: "This might be interpreted as additional evidence for the hypothesis that less sensorial input facilitates the occurrence of an ESP experience" (p. 428). Near-death conditions also seem to be conducive to experiences of apparitions representing the deceased relatives and friends of the person.

Apparitions with an ESP component do not seem to differ from hallucinations that lack this aspect. In a comparison of veridical cases with hallucinations from psychotic and normal people R. and W. Anderson (1982) saw no significant differences in the form of the experiences. "So far as is known the mental machinery involved in producing hallucinations is the same whether the hallucination is itself classified as benign, morbid, or veridical" (p. 72). Wilson and Barber (1983) found that about four percent of the population are "fantasy prone" which includes the propensity to hallucinate spontaneously or in response to suggestion. The individuals do not necessarily show symptoms of pathology, but may on the contrary be successful artists or members of other professions where imagination is important.

Mediumship

Mediums exist in most cultures and ages, sometimes within the social structure, as shamans, oracles, or priests, and sometimes outside. The first record of a successful session with a medium may be due to King Saul of Israel (Old Testament, I Samuel 28:6–25). Though he had himself forbidden such practices, Saul consulted the Witch of Endor to seek guidance from Samuel, the dead prophet. The medium called up Samuel who predicted Saul's defeat by the Philistines.

The first successful ESP test may also be due to a medium. More than 2,500 years ago King Croesus of Lydia tested the seven principal oracles. We are told that he sent assistants to each oracle and that on a specific day the assistants were to ask, "What is the King of Lydia doing today?" (Dodds, 1971, p. 198). It was a double-blind test since neither subjects nor the experimenters knew the target. Croesus also made sure that a correct response could not be due to chance. On the chosen day he was boiling a lamb and a tortoise in a copper pot. Five of the oracles failed, a sixth produced a near-hit — only the Pythia at Delphi gave a correct response. This did not come from any departed communicator. The dead were locked away in Hades below the crust of the earth, but the gods could hear them. For more than a thousand years, Apollo was said to speak through the Pythia. The medium would go into trance after a series of rituals and on being addressed would reply as Apollo.

Mediumistic research has two aims; first, to demonstrate that there is evidence of ESP by ruling out sensory cues, logic, and chance and, second, to demonstrate that the ESP is due to the departed. There have been three principal procedures for testing mediums, (i) experimental studies, (ii) investigations of haunting, and (iii) studies of drop-in communicators.

Experimental Studies

Tests of mediums have been structured around "sittings," in which the sitter seeks communication from someone deceased with the help of a medium. The medium, in turn, relies on a "spirit control" to reach the departed and receive a communication. It was soon realized that the sitter, knowing about the deceased, might telepathically cue the medium/control to the right responses. "Proxy sittings" were therefore introduced where someone who did not know the deceased attended the sitting in the place of the "absent sitter." Proxy sittings may not have prevented telepathy from the absent sitter, but they probably prevented sensory cues from this person. The possibility remained that the medium's responses were judged correct simply because they fit the circumstances of most people who seek contact with the departed. In other words, the statements may have been true because of inference or chance.

The so-called "book tests" were early attempts to deal with these issues. The procedure is illustrated by a book test Sir William Barrett did with Gladys Leonard (see Thomas, 1922). It was hoped that the late Frederic Myers would come through and tell "Feda" (the medium's control) where a book in Barrett's library could be found that contained a passage reminiscent of Myers. Leonard had never been to Barrett's home. She (or Myers speaking through her control) said that there were some books on the right-hand side of a room upstairs. The statement was correct—a bookcase was on the right-hand side of the drawing room upstairs. The control continued, "on the second shelf, four feet from the ground, in the fourth book counting from the left, at the top of page 78, are some words which he ... wishes you to take as a direct answer from himself to show how much work you have been doing since he passed over."

Myers could not get the name of the "test book," but the cover gave him a sense of "progression." The control added that "two or three books from the test book" were one or two books that would remind Barrett of the studies of his youth. Barrett said he had no idea which books were being referred to, but on returning home found that, in the exact position indicated, the "test book" was George Eliot's *Middlemarch*. The cover of the book clearly showed the name, the latter half, "march," indicating "progression." On the first line at the top of page 78 were the words, "Ay, ay, I remember—you'll see I've remembered 'em all," which seemed highly appropriate since much of Barrett's work since Myers' death had been about survival after death and whether the memories of friends on earth continued with the discarnate.

But the most remarkable part of this book test is contained in the sentence, "two or three books from the test book...." It turned out that their maid, unknown to Barrett, had replaced two novels with two books by Tyndall, *Heat* and *Sound*, which were found exactly in the position indicated. Barrett claimed:

> In my youth I was for some years assistant to Professor Tyndall, and those books were written whilst I was with him, and the investigations and experiments they describe formed "the studies of my youth." A careful investigation of all the other shelves and books yielded nothing even remotely applicable to the test given. Chance coincidence, therefore, cannot account for this, nor can traveling clairvoyance explain the matter, as Mrs. Leonard knows nothing of our house, nor of my early life, with which Mr. Myers was familiar.

It did indeed seem unlikely that sensory cues from Barrett could have guided the medium, but chance coincidence cannot be ruled out unless we can be certain that this test was not selected from many unsuccessful studies.

Sidgwick (1921) addressed the issue of chance coincidence in a study of 532 book tests with Leonard. She found 192 (36%) to be successful or partially successful, 96 to be dubious, and 244 to be total or near total failures. While it seems unlikely that most of the 192 successes could be attributed to chance, some undoubtedly could be. The question is, How many? The issue was explored by Helen Salter (Salter, 1921) in a "sham" book test. Sixty persons were each asked to choose ten books at random, to open each at a specified place (e.g., top quarter of page 60) and there to look for a passage relevant to some topic or person (e.g., "your father"). Of the 1,800 virtual book tests, 85 (less than 5%) were judged successful or partially successful (i.e., the passage was relevant to the person's father) and the remainder as slightly successful or failures.

To make the situation more comparable to the Leonard studies, Besterman (1931) took three of Salter's successful book test responses and matched them against passages in books chosen randomly. Five of the 89 matches (just over 6%) were judged successful or partially successful. The studies of Salter and Besterman were not properly controlled, but they provide an informal comparison to the Leonard results.

The so-called "cross-correspondences" is a collection of data attributed to the deceased, in particular to members of the SPR, who seemed to have devised these tests to prove their own survival. Between the years 1901 and 1932, there appeared in the automatic writings of several SPR mediums disjointed fragments and allusions to literary sources, including Greek and Latin works. The material made no sense until a reference appeared in the scripts to a theme which could then be recognized in the earlier fragments. The scripts also contained remarks or hints that a cross-correspondence was being developed or had been completed.

The mediums had good reputations and no indication of fraud was found. Precautions were taken to prevent the mediums from learning normally about the scripts of the others. Two of the mediums, Mrs. H. de G. Verrall and her daughter, Helen, were living together but apparently produced their scripts independently. However, it is difficult to avoid the possibility that shared environmental conditions might result in common thoughts and associations. This was less likely to happen for the other mediums, Mrs. Coombe-Tennant (known as "Mrs. Willett"), Mrs. Fleming, a sister of Rudyard Kipling who used the name "Mrs. Holland," and Mrs. Piper, especially for the periods when Mrs. Fleming lived in India and Mrs. Piper in the United States.

Could the seeming connections between the scripts be due to chance coincidence or familiar factors? There were approximately 3,000 cross-correspondence scripts with 250–300 words in each script. Symbolic and indirect references were common so chance connections seem possible in this many records. Helen de G. Verrall (1911) and Salter (1958) addressed this issue by having two or more persons freely associate on literary topics. They found frequent commonalities that could usually be traced to issues of the day, such as women's suffrage, or tendencies of educated people to come up with similar trains of thought when presented with the same literary topic. The main feature of the cross-correspondences, however, was usually lacking, namely the spontaneous introduction of an item unconnected with other themes in the script, but related to the script of another medium. Since the topics rarely referred to current affairs to which the mediums might have been exposed, the scripts did seem to show evidence of ESP. Nevertheless, our appreciation of these and the other early studies must be tempered by the recognition that they lack adequate methods of evaluation.

It became clear that a statistical assessment of the chance factor was needed to determine if there was a connection between the statements by the medium and the circumstances of the target. This took several steps (Pratt, 1936, 1969; Pratt & Birge, 1948; Saltmarsh, 1929; Saltmarsh & Soal, 1930–31). In the Pratt research, the targets were living people. A fully satisfactory procedure (Roll et al., 1970) was achieved in a series of tests with the psychic, Lalsingh Harribance. In previous studies of Harribance we had him respond to photos of people in opaque envelopes. The results were not as good as had been expected from informal observations or from his card tests. On several occasions, Harribance gave detailed descriptions which a target person recognized as applying to his or her circumstances, but which were made to a photograph of another target person in the group. It seemed that there might have been a psychometric contamination among the pictures by keeping them together prior to the trials and by running the tests in close succession (a follow-up test was designed to prevent this).

Two series were done — one with ten male targets, the other with ten female targets. The series was done simultaneously, one target a day — a male one day, a female the next. A secretary drew the targets from a larger pool, one at a time, again to avoid contamination. Furthermore, each target was selected only after the last target of the same sex had been run. Another possible source of confusion for the psychic was avoided by using opposite-sex experimenters (i.e., when the target was female, two male experimenters conducted the test, and when the target was male, the experimenters were female).

Harribance had no prior knowledge of any of the targets, and the experimenter who was with him during the test did not know who the target person was for that day. When a target arrived at the Psychical Research Foundation (PRF) for a test, he or she was met in the library building by either a male or female experimenter (we had two small houses on the Duke

University campus). The target person was photographed, asked to outline a personal problem on an index card, and provide a lock of hair. The person was then led to a waiting room in the laboratory building. The undeveloped photo in its original opaque casing, and another opaque envelope with the problem statement and hair, were placed on a table in an anteroom. Then the second experimenter, who had been in the rear of the building with Harribance, retrieved the envelopes. This procedure ensured than neither Harribance nor the second experimenter had contact with the target or any source of information about the person.

Harribance was handed the unopened envelopes and asked to begin (his statements were tape-recorded). The protocols were transcribed and edited by a person who was blind as to the identity of the target. In the editing stage, repetitive statements, remarks that were not about the target, and statements that might bias the results, were removed (e.g., remarks pertaining to the target's clothing that day which could be related to the weather and might thereby help the target identify his or her transcript). Copies of the ten female transcripts were distributed to the ten females with the request that each select the session that most closely corresponded to her circumstances, with second, third, etc., choices. The same was done for the ten males.

The analysis of all 20 responses, according to first choices gave a significantly high probability against chance ($p < .01$), and according to first and second choices combined, an even higher probability against chance ($p < .003$). The scoring on females alone were also significantly high for first choices ($p < .01$), and for first plus second choices ($p < .006$). This research was done more than 25 years ago and as far as I know remains the best-controlled study of its type. Mediumistic work that approaches, but may not have reached, the standard set by the Harribance research has been done in Great Britain (Robertson & Roy, 2004) and in the US (Schwartz, 2002).

Investigations of Haunting

Can psychics aid investigators in determining whether a house reputed to be haunted is in fact occupied by incorporeal entities or energies? Maher and Schmeidler (1975) came up with a satisfactory method. They brought two groups to a house, one consisting of psychics, the other a control group of non-psychics. Each participant walked through the house alone and marked on a floor plan the spots that seemed most haunted and filled out a checklist about the supposed ghost. The responses of the two groups were then compared. The same basic procedure was used by Maher (2000) for a haunted inn, by Maher and Hansen (1992) for a penthouse, a castle in New Jersey (1995), and a newly purchased house that came with a ghost (Maher and

Hansen, 1997). When Maher (1999) combined her five studies, the result for the floor plans was significant (p = .013), but the checklist results were non-significant.

In the meantime, I had asked Maher (Roll, Maher & Brown, 1992) to evaluate the responses of a group of psychics and controls I had brought to a Japanese steak house and to test for electromagnetic anomalies. The manager and employees had reported footsteps, apparitions, cold spots, invisible presences, and physical incidents. The floor-plan and checklist results were non-significant, but Maher found that the areas the occupants felt were especially haunted gave higher electromagnetic readings than the control areas (p = .007). The electromagnetometer proved to be a better detector of ghostly energies than psychics, and I subsequently acquired one. The electromagnetometer and a geomagnetometer have proved invaluable in my studies of haunts (for example, see Roll & Nichols, 1999).

In most investigations of haunted houses where mediums were brought in (Maher & Schmeidler, 1975; Moss & Schmeidler, 1968; Roll et al., 1992; Schmeidler, 1966; Solfvin & Roll, 1978), there was no evidence that apparitions represented deceased persons. Eileen Garrett, who took part in Schmeidler's (1966) study, thought the wife was psychic and that she produced the visual phenomena. Garrett had not met the owners when she toured the house. On the other hand, William Joines and John Artley (Joines et al., 1969) who brought Douglas Johnson to a haunted house, said that the British medium received impressions of what he took to be departed spirits. Notwithstanding the fact that mediums were involved, the haunting apparitions do not differ significantly from other apparitions. As with other local ghosts, we seem to be dealing with images that are anchored in physical space.

Drop-In Communicators

A drop-in communicator is a supposed discarnate personality who emerges spontaneously in a mediumistic session without anyone present having known the entity and without obvious personal or physical links. Unlike mediumistic tests where the researchers choose the targets, the selection of "drop-ins" is made by the medium. Investigations of drop-ins are attempts to determine whether or not the medium's impressions were obtained, consciously or unconsciously, before the sitting through written sources to which the medium had access. Obituaries and such have explained two cases (Podmore, 1897, pp. 131–132; Gauld, 1971, p. 316) and possibly a third (Haraldsson & Stevenson, 1975). Chance matching between information from the mediums and the circumstances of the supposed drop-in accounted for at least one case (Gauld, 1971, p. 320). Perhaps no drop-in is immune to ordinary explanations.

There are only a handful of what I consider fairly evidential drop-in cases. I outline them briefly without going into the evidence for each. In a Russian case (Myers, 1903/1955, pp. 471–473) table raps announced the presence of a 17-year-old girl who gave her name and said she had died in "the hospital" after poisoning herself. The raps were translated using the common code, one rap for "a," two raps for "b," and so on. One of the sitters who knew the head of the local hospital, checked and verified the details. There was then a personal link between the communicator and a person at the sitting.

In the John Wightman case (Tyrrell, 1939), the drop-in came through automatic writing at a sitting in an Oxford college. Wightman, who had been a member of another Oxford college, had died in a shipwreck 50 years before.

In a Dutch case (Zorab, 1939–1940), Klaas Kraaljenbrink, who had lived in Gouda, purportedly communicated during a sitting in The Hague, about 18 miles away. The communicator indicated he had died in a truck accident earlier that year. The distance between the two towns may be too great to be called a "local" link, but it can be assumed that the medium or the sitters had visited Gouda and that the deceased, or people associated with the deceased, had been to The Hague.

In the case of Robert Marie (Stevenson, 1973), two brothers who had fallen in World War I seemed to communicate with a medium some 18 years later. A local link is suggested since the medium had visited some 10 kilometers from the home of the brothers.

Gauld (1971) studied a series of drop-ins that emerged in Ouija board sittings near Cambridge. Mr. G., a member of the SPR, and his wife usually operated the board. In the case of Kate Clarke (Gauld, 1971, pp. 319–320) the information was too general to link to a definite person; in the Mary Cheyne case (Gauld, 1971, pp. 318–319) the sitters might have heard about the deceased by normal means; and in three cases — Edward Druce, Walter Leggatt, and Josephine Street (Gauld, 1971, pp. 301–302, 315–316, 316–318, respectively) — the information could be found in obituaries or news stories that the sitters might have seen. All four communicators had lived in Cambridge so there would have been a local connection.

There were five cases, however, where at least some of the details about the deceased apparently were not available to Mr. and Mrs. G. All five showed local or personal connections to the couple. Duncan Stevens (Gauld, 1971, pp. 295–301) had lived within "fairly easy reach of Cambridge" (p. 301); Robert Fletcher (Gauld, 1971, pp. 302–306) came from the same district as one of the operators of the board; and Gustav Adolf Biederman (pp.306–315) had lived in London, with which we can assume the sitters were familiar.

There may have been another link since the deceased had written a sarcastic letter to the London *Times* in the 1920s about telepathy experiments conducted by SPR members. We do not know if Mr. G. was an SPR member at the time. Nora Hentall (Gauld, 1971, pp. 320–322) had lived approximately 12 miles from the grandparents of one of the operators of the board.

The most tenuous connection is with the fifth drop-in, Harry Stockbridge (Gauld, 1971, pp. 322–327), who came from a city that was once visited by one of the sitters. In all five cases, the Ouija information included the names of the deceased and more or less detailed addresses or other information that enabled Gauld to discover their identities.

The Evidence for Discarnate Communicators

The second main factor that has shaped mediumistic research has been the effort to exclude ESP by the medium as the sole explanation for the results. Barrett's book test was used in a series of studies conducted by Thomas (1922) that attempted to circumvent the possibility that Leonard scanned or "picked" the minds of the living instead of the dead. Usually the evidential information conveyed by an ostensible communicator through a medium is known to some living person — either the person consulting the medium, or to the friends and relatives of that person. It therefore seems possible that the medium uses telepathy to obtain the information from the living and not the departed. Thomas thought that if the medium could obtain information, which was not known to anybody living, this would be evidence for survival.

When clairvoyance tests at Duke University showed that subjects could respond to ESP targets that no one had sighted, it became evident that the book tests could be accounted for in terms of clairvoyance by the medium. That evidence for survival through mediumship can be obtained comes up against the possibility that mediums inadvertently use ESP to pick up information about this world rather than the "other side." Further analysis of the characteristics of mediumistic data may give some clues as to which is the more likely explanation.

Personal and Local Connections

A personal reading is the preferred mode of interacting with a medium but this allows for sensory cues from client to medium that must be avoided in experiments if valid results are to be obtained. Instead of a personal connection, mediums often use an object that has belonged to the target person to get impressions about the person. Objects that are used in this way are called psychometric objects, an unfortunate choice of words since psychometry also refers to psychological measurement. In any case, psychometry has dominated experimental research with mediums, especially proxy sittings where psychometric objects take the place of the absent target.

Leonore Piper was the most thoroughly investigated medium in the early years of psychic research. Most of the work was done between 1885 and 1915 and was a stimulus for survival research. When she attempted to reach a deceased individual, Piper often used an object that had belonged to the person. Sidgwick (1915) quoted Piper's control:

> Objects carry with them a light as distinct to us as the sunlight is to you. The instant you hand us an object, that instant we get an impression of its owner, whether the present or the past owner and often both. [When the impression is not clear] I find ... that almost invariably the object presented to us for information has been of long standing, or otherwise unhandled, untouched, by its owner for a period of long duration, or sometimes it may have been handled often and by a great number of persons. This often causes confusion [p. 624].

Another time the control said that when a person wears or handles an object, it becomes infused with something like magnetic power, which from then on surrounds the object and enables a medium to learn about the person (p. 629).

In the supposed communication with Myers through Leonard (mentioned above), no psychometric object was used. If one of the persons present at the test, in this case Barrett, knew the deceased, an object is not necessary — or rather, another object is not needed. Like apparitions, mediumistic communicators seem to be personal or local, with the psychometric cases a variant of the local type.

As with apparitions, the question is whether personal and local links are inherent to the process or artifactual. Usually a person who seeks out a medium does so in order to communicate with a specific deceased friend or relative. That is, the inquiry comes with a personal link to the deceased. In proxy sittings the personal link does not disappear, but is removed one or two steps. As a substitute for the weakened personal connection, a psychometric object may then be brought to the medium. Usually, this object once belonged to the deceased and, in the better-controlled tests, is concealed in a package or otherwise provides no sensory information. When the medium holds this object, information about the owner, or others who have had contact with it, may come more readily than without it. It is sometimes said that objects have only a ritualistic or suggestive function and do not by themselves increase the flow of information, but there is also the suggestion that a physical object or place may provide a real channel for ESP.

Fading over Time

In an examination of the automatic writings apparently originating from a group of deceased SPR researchers, Lambert (1971) observed, "In cases where messages purporting to come from a named communicator have been received through a series of sensitives over a period of years, the later messages become less and less precise in the matter of verifiable detail, and worthless as evidence of survival" (p. 219).

Lambert found the outer limit of communication to be about seven years:

> Unfortunately [he added] a "communicator" is able to go on sending messages under the same name as before, long after the limit has been passed. One result is that by this date, 70 years after Myers' death, all sorts of unverifiable scripts, unworthy of his intellectual attainments, are liable to be attributed to him, and published under his name [p. 220].

It should be emphasized that Lambert spoke about "a series of sensitives"—not just one. It is to be expected that a medium, who has access to the memories of a communicator, would exhaust them in the course of several sittings, thereby bringing about a reduction of veridical statements, although the memories might continue to exist and be available to other mediums.

Lambert did not find a single case where a decline to zero-information was followed by a return of the ability on the part of the supposed communicator to recall verifiable details of his or her life. This could suggest that the memories of the departed, which emerge during mediumistic sittings, are attenuated over time like familiar memories.

Xenoglossy

Perhaps the most convincing evidence that a deceased individual communicates through a medium persists would be if the communicator spoke a language unknown to the medium. The purported use of an unknown language is "xenoglossy," from *xenos,* the Greek word for "foreigner," and *glossa* meaning "tongue." "Responsive xenoglossy" is the ability to respond appropriately in an unknown language and not just to recite a string of foreign words (so-called "recitative xenoglossy").

Stevenson (1960) has given two examples of recitative xenoglossy: (i) a hypnotized man who spoke Oscan, an Italian dialect from the third-century BC, and (ii) an illiterate servant girl who spoke Hebrew when she had fever. It turned out that the Italian man had unknowingly absorbed the words from a library book that happened to lie open before him, and the servant girl had been employed by a rabbi, who declaimed aloud while she did her housework.

Until recently, the only example of responsive xenoglossy in the professional literature may have been a report of a short conversation in Dutch by Frederik van Eeden (1901–1903) with a deceased friend who purportedly came through a British medium. Unfortunately, the note-taker did not know Dutch, so little of the exchange was recorded.

Stevenson (1976) has investigated two cases where hypnotized American housewives seemed to be mouthpieces — one, a Swedish or Norwegian personality, perhaps from the seventeenth century, and the other, a German, perhaps from the nineteenth century. Aside from speaking languages unknown to the two women, the communicators described themselves as independent personal entities. They did not, however, give detailed information about the times and places in which they had lived, although the German communicator said she had been the daughter of Hermann Gottlieb, a mayor of Eberswalde (Stevenson, 1976, p. 69). When Stevenson checked, he found that the town never had a mayor of that name. Fabrications of this type are typical of hypnotized subjects, and they cast doubt about the discarnate personality as a whole.

Stevenson discounts the memory theory for his two cases because there seemed to have been no occasions for the two women to learn the meanings of the terms they used. Instead he suggested that unidentified discarnate entities spoke through the women. In addition to words in the two languages that were similar to English terms, Stevenson identified 60 words in the Norwegian/Swedish communications and about 120 words in the German communications — the words being used appropriately in conversations with the investigators. The German communicator, however, did not know German word-order and grammar.

Stevenson asked me to listen to one of the tapes from the Scandinavian communicator since I am familiar with Norwegian and Swedish. There was no doubt that the woman introduced Norwegian or Swedish words (31 words on the tape), but I had no way of determining how they were acquired. Although Stevenson favors a parapsychological interpretation, it seems difficult to rule out the possibility that the women had assimilated their knowledge of the foreign terms, perhaps unconsciously, from films, television, or similar sources. Generally speaking, foreign films with English subtitles are a possible source for such skills.

In another case, briefly described by Stevenson and Pasricha (1979), Uttara, a woman in Nagpur, India, manifested a secondary personality, Sharada, who could speak only Bengali, a language ordinarily unknown to Uttara. She also accurately described village life in Bengal in the early nineteenth century and gave the names of a family of which she claimed to have been a member, and which the investigators were able to trace. Uttara had never been to Bengal, which is more than 1200 kilometers from Nagpur, and none of her family spoke Bengali.

Although her knowledge of Bengal and the Bengali language can apparently not be explained in normal terms, her father did have Bengali friends. Thus, in their full report of the case, Stevenson and Pasricha (1980) leave the door open for a normal explanation. Uttara had taken lessons in Bengali script in the eleventh grade and had learned to read some words. Her teacher told the investigators that he had tutored the girl in the Bengali scripts for several months, but not the correct pronunciation which he himself did not know. Stevenson and Parisha say that it is conceivable Sharada had learnt to read and write some Bengali, but had not learnt to speak it. However, she might have picked up the correct pronunciation by overhearing Bengalis speak among themselves in her home, or by seeing Bengali films and plays.

Posthumous Codes and Locks

One means by which a person might show evidence of surviving death would be by communicating a prearranged message. So far, posthumous messages have been revealed too soon or not at all. The contents of Piddington's (1908) sealed message leaked out as a cross-correspondence topic before his death, while those left by Frederic Myers (Salter, 1958) and Sir Oliver Lodge (Gay, Salter, Thouless, Firebrace, Phillimore, & Sitwell, 1955) were never received.

Robert Thouless (1948, 1949) published two short messages in code to which only he knew the keys. If a medium succeeded in receiving the sequences of letters that provided the keys to the messages after Thouless's death, and if no one had succeeded while he was alive, Thouless thought this would be evidence that his surviving mind was the source. His system was an improvement of the earlier tests because it permitted several trials, while an end was put to the attempts to receive Myers' and Lodge's messages once the sealed envelopes were opened. Furthermore, Thouless' method avoided clairvoyance of the message before his death since his keys were not written down anywhere. Thouless died on September 25, 1984. At least eight mediums have attempted to obtain the keys, none of them succeeding (Berger, 1987).

Stevenson (1976) adapted the coded message test by using a padlock, the combination of which (three two-digit numbers) was set by the owner. The owner randomly selected the numbers, and then converted them to six letters, which became the first letters of a six-word sentence. This sentence would serve as a mnemonic device for the owner. Upon death, the deceased owner would then communicate the sentence to one or more mediums so that the locks could be opened. By April, 1980, three owners of locks have died, and trials for the codes of two locks have been made, both of which were unsuccessful (I. Stevenson, personal communication, April, 1980). One owner was feeble and ill when she set the lock and may have made a mistake. The other was Gaither Pratt, who died on November 3, 1979. Several years earlier, he had set a lock and devised a mnemonic sentence (Stevenson, 1976). Following his death, an ESP subject, as well as Pratt's friends and relatives, communicated their impressions of the numbers or sentence to Stevenson, some offering more than one solution. By May, 1980, 30 attempts had been made, none of them successful.

One problem with this procedure may be that the person who attempts to break the lock's code is only allowed one or a few trials to arrive at a response which must be 100% correct to succeed — by chance alone the odds of success are 125,000 to 1 against. There are very few accounts from the research careers of even the most successful mediums where successful identification of a six-digit number was achieved using ESP. On the other hand, repeated card guessing experiments, including tests by Pratt, have reached comparable levels of significance. Similarly, a series of statements by a medium about an absent sitter may reach a degree of accuracy that is highly unlikely by chance; though any single statement is unremarkable.

Psychological Aspects

Mediumistic communications are usually conveyed by written or spoken words. Sometimes drawings and sketches are added, and sometimes the voice of the medium, or expressive gestures, may mimic the communicator, but the focus is usually on the cognitive aspects, and these give the best clues as to the origin of the material. It is rare to find mediumistic communications where the communications strongly suggest the presence of the deceased. This is surprising because such sessions are usually arranged by surviving friends or relatives with the explicit purpose of interacting with the deceased.

However, Myers (1903/1955) tells of a Russian study where the motivation apparently originated from the other side. Myers' report was about a counselor to the Czar, one named Alexander Aksakov, who was a member of the SPR. During experiments with a planchette board by Aksakov's sister-in-law and her daughter, a female drop-in, Schura, came through. The planchette is similar to a Ouija board. Schura, a daughter of an acquaintance of the Aksakovs, had committed suicide after the death of a cousin during a prison escape. Schura shared the revolutionary views of her cousin, so she asked the operators of the board to bring Nikolaus (another cousin) to the sittings so that Schura could dissuade him from his dangerous political activities.

The operators hesitated until February 26, 1885 when Schura wrote, "It is too late ... expect his arrest." They contacted Nikolaus' parents who did not believe that their son was engaged in such activities. But two years later, the young man was exiled because of dissident activities in January and February of 1885. Schura was identified by intimate details, which could not have been known to the operators of the board. As Gauld (1982) noted, the point of the message seemed foreign to the operators of the board, but it made sense to the girl. Gauld also noted that such communications are very rare.

In the drop-in studies of Gauld (1971) himself, the operators of the Ouija also did not seem to have any strong desire for uninvited visitors from beyond. While the group tried to get as much information as they could from the drop-ins, no serious attempt was made to check their identities. It was only because of Gauld's effort several years later that their existence became known. But there also seemed to be no motivation for the drop-ins to visit the Ouija sitters.

Carington (1934, 1935, 1936–1937; Thouless, 1936–1937), studied three pairs of mediums and their spirit controls, Mrs. Leonard and "Feda," Mrs. Garrett and "Uvani," and Mrs. Sharplin and "Silver." It was found that Leonard and Feda, and Garrett and Uvani had significantly matching personality characteristics, whereas Sharplin and Silver showed none.

Tests were also made of two supposed discarnate agents, as they communicated through two different mediums, to see whether they showed similar reactions and therefore might represent the same personalities. The results led to no such conclusion, but were consistent with the view that the communicators were not independent of the mediums.

On the other hand, in a field study of a female medium (Solfvin, Roll & Kelly, 1977), a telemetry unit was used to record her EEG when she seemed to be herself, and when she was taken over by one of her two controls. As it happened, the three personalities showed different patterns. Heseltine and Kirk (1979) in their study of J. G. and her controls, "Hotep" and "Shoalin," also found that the controls had different EEG patterns. (The study did not compare the EEG of J. G. to those of her controls.) Both studies suggest that the personality differences between mediums and controls may be reflected in physiological differences, but this is not to say that the controls existed "outside" the mediums.

Ludwig, Brandsma, Wilbur, Bendfeldt, and Jameson (1972) found marked EEG differences in a case of multiple personality as well as other physiological and psychological differences. Two or more personalities can evidently occupy the same body. This point is also illustrated by split-brain research. According to Sperry (1974), when the corpus callosum, which links the two brain hemispheres, is cut, "two rather separate streams of conscious awareness" emerge (p. 7). Each has "its own private sensations, perceptions, thoughts, and ideas ... its own private chain of memories and learning experiences" (p. 7).

Multiple personalities are sometimes thought to arise from emotions that conflict with the person's self-concept and are therefore cut off from the main stream of consciousness. It seems possible that mediumistic control may be a form of multiple personality. Certainly controls rarely, if ever, provide evidence that they ever existed.

Some studies suggest that communicators, who can be identified as actual persons, may also be forms of multiple personality with the addition of an ESP component. Sidgwick (1900–1901) tells of a sitting with Piper where Richard Hodgson used, as a psychometric object, a manuscript of a Dr. Wiltse. When Piper held the object, Wiltse seemed to come through and relate some details about a psychic experience he had published. He indicated that he was dead, and his body was in water: "But all the time Dr. Wiltse was alive and well and going through no abnormal experience of any kind" (p. 25).

Heywood (1977) says that after World War II, she went to a medium to see if she could pick up something about a friend, a German diplomat who Heywood feared had been killed. The medium gave his Christian name and other details. She said he was dead and that his death was so tragic he didn't want to talk about it. Heywood later discovered that her friend had escaped to England, had married and never been so happy (p. 9).

Murphy (1945) tells of a similar case. Aside from living communicators, personalities often come through with names, addresses, and dates that fit the lives of no one, either living or dead.

Some veridical communicators show confusion about personal identity. Hyslop (1905) cites a case where the communicator mixed together the memories of a deceased man with those of his daughter. In another study, Hyslop (1908) reports that the deceased confused the names of his sister and mother, and another "lost completely the sense of personal identity" (p. 347).

Stevenson (1973) reports a case in which a medium described events from the lives of two brothers as if they were one, and Haraldsson (in Stevenson, 1973) investigated a case where statements about the primary communicator were mixed up with material about the person's father-in-law.

Discussion

I have examined two types of phenomena that have been interpreted in terms of the continuation of awareness after death: (i) apparitions of the dead, and (ii) mediumistic communicators. I considered the evidence each provided for some form of ESP. There are several weaknesses in the material. Non-experimental studies, such as reports of apparitional experiences and drop-in communicators, are particularly subject to the vagaries of human observation and memory. In experimental studies of mediums, adequate methods of evaluation have rarely been undertaken. I do not, however, think that the reported effects can all be dismissed in terms of mistaken observation or memory, sampling artifact, sensory cues, or chance coincidence.

With respect to the question of whether an aspect of the self continues after death, the answer must also be in the affirmative, but which aspect of the self survives is uncertain. The apparitional reports and mediumistic communications do not seem to indicate the type of autonomous or at least semi-autonomous beings we are familiar with from everyday life. Studies of apparitions and mediumistic communicators resembling the departed seem to be evoked by place memories left on (or with) people, places, and objects with which the departed have been in contact during their lives. Studies of psychometry and related research also suggest that we leave traces of ourselves on (or with) people, places and objects in the environment. The traces may affect others and even occasion physical events, but they do not represent our conscious self. On the contrary they seem entirely unconscious.

For a statement to count as an empirical hypothesis, it must be possible not only to support it through verification, but also to specify observations that would prove it false. Can this be done for the survival hypothesis? Stevenson brings in the super or unlimited extrasensory perception hypothesis (i.e., the super-psi hypothesis) as an alternative explanation for evidence suggestive of survival. I find it difficult to take this theory seriously. A theory that can be stretched to meet any contingency is a metaphysical statement rather than a scientific hypothesis. An empirical hypothesis is only that if, in principle, it can be falsified. The two-fold question is: Do we know enough about ESP to formulate a plausible empirical hypothesis, and will this hypothesis provide an alternative to the survival hypothesis?

The established sciences suggest that man is a psychophysical structure. This is indicated also by psi research. The psychological or interpersonal aspect is manifested by telepathic information *from* other people and telepathic effects *on* other people; the physical or impersonal part is manifested by clairvoyant information *from* other physical systems and psychokinetic effects *on* other physical systems. Properly speaking, there seem to be no separate persons or systems; rather, we may be dealing with a kind of field whose parts are more or less closely connected by familiar, and psi, processes. This theory does not provide an alternative to the survival hypothesis; on the contrary, it *is* a survival hypothesis. Since the psychophysical field is not the property of a single individual, it is unlikely to cease existing after their death. If it is hypothesized that the psychophysical field continues after death, we expect a continuation of its interpersonal as well as its physical aspects.

In the past, parapsychologists, including survival researchers, emphasized the psychological and interpersonal aspects of psi at the expense of the physical or impersonal aspects. This view made them ignore the possibility that survival might be related to the physical world — it placed this world outside the reach of direct awareness. It seems possible, however, that consciousness may not be contained within the psychological system, but may also encompass its physical components. LeShan (1969) has noted the frequently striking resemblances between descriptions of the material world by modern physicists and experiences reported by people in "expanded" states of awareness.

William James may have been the first to propose a psychophysical theory for survival. Following the German physicist and psychologist, Gustav Fechner, who proposed that all memory processes are coordinated with material processes, James suggested that after death, memory traces might exist "psychometrically" in the physical systems associated with the person while he was alive. This "system of physical traces" may be activated during a mediumistic session amounting to a "spirit redivivus" of the deceased and of "recollecting and willing in a certain momentary way" (1909, p. 120).

Using this point of departure we may formulate a predictive hypothesis that evidence for the continued existence of surviving memory and physical traces is more likely to appear in the *presence*, rather than *absence*, of physical systems which were associated with the deceased when he or she was living.

The psychological side of the theory also suggests testable hypotheses. In his appraisal of material obtained through Mrs. Piper, James found evidence of "an external will to communicate" mixed with the medium's "desire to personate" (1909, pp. 120–121), but he was unable to determine whether this external will was that of the ostensible communicator or some "spirit-counterfeit." If the will to communicate is associated with a deceased person, we may suppose it is a function of his (*or her*) beliefs, needs, and state of consciousness at death.

Schmeidler (1977) suggests a predictive theory for mediumistic communication according to the person's stated belief in survival before death and *their* desire to communicate. If there is equally good evidence for communication from people with *negative* attitudes to survival and communication, as there is *positive* attitudes, this would tend to falsify the survival hypothesis, while better communications from persons with positive attitudes would tend to verify it.

Our examination of the assumptions underlying the survival hypothesis has taken us back to James' theory of survival. The facts at the time were too few to be convincing either for or against survival: "I remain uncertain and await more facts, facts which may not point clearly to a conclusion for fifty or a hundred years" (James, 1909, p. 121). We have passed the 50-year mark and are approaching the 100-year mark. It seems to me we are well underway to a resolution. We have predictive theories and, thanks largely to Ian Stevenson, a growing body of facts.

References

Anderson, R., & Anderson, W. (1982). Veridical and psychopathic hallucinations: A comparison of types. *Parapsychological Review, 18*(1), 9–13.

Berger, A. S. (1987). Three unrecognized problems in survival research. *Proceedings of Presented Papers: The Parapsychological Association, 30th Annual Convention* (pp. 76–86). Parapsychological Association.

Besterman, T. (1931). Further inquiries into the element of chance in book tests. *Proceedings of the Society for Psychical Research, 40*, 59–98.

Bozzano, E. (1920). *Les phenomenes de hantisse.* Paris: Alcan.

Carington, W. (1934). The quantitative study of trance personalities: Part I. *Proceedings of the Society for Psychical Research, 42*, 173–240.

Carington, W. (1935). The quantitative study of trance personalities: Part II. *Proceedings of the Society for Psychical Research, 43*, 316–361.

Carington, W. (1936–1937) The quantitative study of trance personalities: Part III. *Proceedings of the Society for Psychical Research, 44*, 189–222.

Dale, L. A., White, R. & Murphy, G. (1962). A selection of cases from a recent survey of spontaneous ESP phenomena. *Journal of the American Society for Psychical Research, 56*, 3–47.

Dodd, E. R. (1971). Supernormal phenomena in classical antiquity. *Proceedings of the Society for Psychical Research, 55*, 189–237.

Gauld, A. (1971). A series of "drop in" communicators. *Proceedings of the Society for Psychical Research, 55*, 273–340.

Gauld, A. (1982). *Mediumship and survival: A century of investigation.* London: Heinemann.

Gay, K., Salter, W. H., Thouless, R. H., Firebrace, R. H., Phillimore, M., & Sitwell, C. (1955). Report on the Oliver Lodge Posthumous Test. *Journal of the Society for Psychical Research, 38*, 121–134.

Green, C. E. & McCreery, C. (1975). *Apparitions.* London: Hamilton.

Gurney, E. & Myers, F. W. H. (1888–1889). On apparitions occurring soon after death. *Proceedings of the Society for Psychical Research, 5*, 403–485.

Gurney, E., Myers, F. W. H., & Podmore, F. (1886). *Phantasms of the living* (2 vols.). London: Trübner.

Haraldsson, E. Gudmundsdottir, A., Ragnarsson, A., Loftsson, J. & Jonsson, S. (1977). National survey of psychical experiences and attitudes towards the paranormal in Iceland. In J. D. Morris, W. G. Roll & R. L. Morris (Eds.), *Research in Parapsychology 1976* (pp. 182–186), Metuchen, NJ: Scarecrow.

Haraldsson, E. & Stevenson, I. (1975). A communicator of the "drop in" type in Iceland: The case of Gudni Magnusson. *Journal of the American Society for Psychical Research, 69*, 245–261.

Hart, H. (1956). Six theories about apparitions. *Proceedings of the Society for Psychical Research, 50*, 153–239.

Heseltine, G. L., & Kirk, J. H. (1979). *EEG activity of a trance medium.* Unpublished paper.

Heywood, R. (1976). Illusion — or what? Part 2. *Theta, 4*(1), 5–10.

Heywood, R. (1977). Interview. *New Realities, 9.*

Hyslop, J. H. (1905). The mental state of the dead. *World To-Day* (January).

Hyslop, J. H. (1908). *Psychical research and the resurrection.* Boston: Small, Maynard.

James, W. (1909). Report on Mrs. Piper's Hodgson-control. *Proceedings of the Society for Psychical Research, 23*, 1–121.

Joines, W. T., Artley, J. L. & Cohen, D. (1969). Investigation of a "haunted house." *Proceedings of the Parapsychological Association*, No. 6, 1969.

Lambert, G. W. (1971). Studies in the automatic writing of Mrs. Verrall: Concluding reflections. *Journal of the Society for Psychical Research, 46*, 217–222.

LeShan, L. (1969). Physicists and mystics: Similarities in world view. *Journal of Transpersonal Psychology, 1*, 1–20.

Ludwig, A. M., Brandsma, J. M., Wilbur, C. B., Bendfeldt, F., & Jameson, D. H. (1972). The objective study of multiple personality. *Archives of General Psychiatry, 26*, 298–310.

Maher, M. C. (1999). Riding the waves in search of the particles: A modern study of ghosts and apparitions. *Journal of Parapsychology, 63*, 47–80.

Maher, M. C. (2000). Quantitative investigation of the General Wayne Inn. *Journal of Parapsychology, 64*, 365–390.

Maher, M. C. & Hansen, G. P. (1992). Quantitative investigation of a reported haunting using several detection techniques. *Journal of the American Society for Psychical Research, 86*, 347–374.

Maher, M. C., & Hansen, G. P. (1995). Quantitative investigation of a "haunted castle" in New Jersey. *Journal for the American Society of Psychical Research, 89*, 19–50.

Maher, M. C. & Hansen, G. P. (1997). Quantitative investigation of a legally disputed "haunted house." *Proceedings of Presented Papers: The Parapsychological Association 40th Annual Convention*, 184–201. Parapsychological Association.

Maher, M. C. & Schmeidler, G. R. (1975). Quantitative investigation of a recurring apparition. *Journal of the American Society for Psychical Research, 69*, 341–352.

Moss, T. & Schmeidler, G. R. (1968). Quantitative investigation of a "haunted house" with sensitives and a control group. *Journal of the American Society for Psychical Research, 62*, 399–410.

Murphy, G, (1945). Field theory and survival. *Journal of the American Society for Psychical Research, 39*, 181–209.

Myers, F. W. H. (1903/1955). *Human personality and its survival of bodily death.* Longmans Green: Garret Publications.

Palmer, J. (1979). A community mail survey of psychic experiences. *Journal of the American Society for Psychical Research, 73*, 221–251.

Piddington, J. G. (1908). Fresh light on the "one-horse-dawn" experiment. *Proceedings of the Society for Psychical Research, 30*, 175–229.

Podmore, F. (1897). *Studies in psychical research.* London: Kegan Paul, Trench and Truber.

Pratt, J. G. (1936). Towards a method of evaluating mediumistic material. *Bulletin of the Boston Society for Psychical Research*, No. 23.

Pratt, J. G. (1969). On the Evaluation of Verbal Material in Parapsychology. *Parapsychological Monographs No 10*. New York: Parapsychology Foundation.

Pratt, J. G. & Birge, W. R. (1948). Appraising verbal test material in parapsychology. *Journal of Parapsychology, 12*, 236–256.

Price, H. H. (1939). Haunting and the "psychic ether" hypothesis: With some preliminary reflections on the present condition and possible future of psychical research. *Proceedings of the Society for Psychical Research, 45*, 307–343.

Rhine, L. E. (1957). Hallucinatory psi experiences: II. The initiative of the percipient in hallucinations of the living, the dying, and the dead. *Journal of Parapsychology, 21*, 13–46.

Rhine, L. E. (1960). The evaluation of non-recurrent psi experiences bearing on post-mortem survival. *Journal of Parapsychology, 24*, 8–25.

Robertson, T. J. & Roy, A. (2004). Results of the application of the Robertson-Roy protocol to a series of experiments with mediums and participants. *Journal of the Society for Psychical Research, 68*, 18–34.

Roll, W. G., Morris, R. L., Damgaard, J., & Roll, M. (1970). Free verbal response tests with Lalsing Harribance. *Proceedings of the Parapsychological Association*, No. 7, 21–23.

Roll, W. G., Maher, M. C. & Brown, B. (1992). An investigation of reported haunting occurrences in a Japanese restaurant in Georgia. *Proceedings of Presented Papers: The Parapsychological Association 35th Annual Convention* (pp. 151–168). Parapsychological Association.

Roll, W. G. & Nichols, A. (1999). A haunting at an army post. *Proceedings of Presented Papers:*

The Parapsychological Association 39th Annual Convention, 253–270. Parapsychological Association.

Salter, W. H. (1921). A further report on sittings with Mrs. Leonard. *Proceedings of the Society for Psychical Research, 32*, 1–143.

Salter, W. H. (1958). F. W. H. Myer's posthumous message. *Proceedings of the Society for Psychical Research, 52*, 1–32.

Saltmarsh, F. H. (1929). Report on the investigation of some sittings with Mrs. Warren Elliott. *Proceedings of the Society for Psychical Research, 39*, 47–184.

Saltmarsh, F. H. (1938). *Evidence of personal survival from cross-correspondence*. London: Bell.

Saltmarsh, H. F. & Soal, S. G. (1930–1931). A method of estimating the super-normal content of Mediumistic communications. *Proceedings of the Society for Psychical Research, 39*, 266–271.

Sannwald, G. (1961). *Parapsychischen erlebnissen und personlichkeitsmerkmalen [Relations between paranormal experiences and personality traits]*. Unpublished doctoral dissertation, University of Freiburg, Germany.

Schmeidler, G. R. (1966). Quantitative investigation of a "haunted house." *Journal of the American Society for Psychical Research, 60*, 137–149.

Schmeidler, G. (1977). Looking ahead: A method for research on survival. *Theta, 5*, 2–6.

Schouten, S. A. (1979). Analysis of spontaneous cases as reported in "Phantasms of the Living." *European Journal of Parapsychology, 2*, 408–455.

Schouten, S. A. (1981). Analysing spontaneous cases: A replication based on the Sannwald collection. *European Journal of Parapsychology, 4*, 9–48.

Schwartz, G. (2002). *The afterlife experiments: Breakthrough scientific evidence of life after death*. New York: Pocket.

Sidgwick, E. M. (1885). Notes on the evidence, collected by the Society, for phantasms of the dead. *Proceedings of the Society for Psychical Research, 3*, 69–150.

Sidgwick, E. M. (1900–1901). Discussion of the trance phenomena of Mrs. Piper. *Proceedings of the Society for Psychical Research, 15*, 16–38.

Sidgwick, E. M. (1915). A contribution to the study of Mrs. Piper's trance phenomena. *Proceedings of the Society for Psychical Research, 28*, 1–657.

Sidgwick, E. M. (1921). An examination of book-tests obtained in sittings with Mrs. Leonard. *Proceedings of the Society for Psychical Research, 31*, 241–400.

Sidgwick, E. M. (1923). Phantasms of the living.... *Proceedings of the Society for Psychical Research, 33*, 23–429.

Sidgwick, H. & Committee (1894). Report on the census of hallucinations. *Proceedings of the Society for Psychical Research, 10*, 25–422.

Solfvin, G. F. & Roll, W. G. (1978). An investigation of a "haunted" house in Washington, DC. *Journal of Parapsychology, 42*, 63–64.

Solfvin, G. F., Roll, W. G. & Kelly, E. F. (1977). *Parapsychology Review, 8*(3), 21–22.

Sperry, R. W. (174) Lateral specialization in the surgically separated hemispheres. In *Neurosciences Third Study Program* (pp. 5–19). F. Schmitt & F. Worden (Eds.), Cambridge: MIT Press.

Stevenson, I. (1960). The evidence for survival from claimed memories of former incarnations, Part I: Review of the data. *Journal of the American Society for Psychical Research, 54*, 51–71.

Stevenson, I. (1973). A communicator of the "drop-in" type in France: The case of Robert Marie. *Journal of the American Society for Psychical Research, 67*, 47–76.

Stevenson, I. (1976). Further observations on the combination lock test for survival. *Journal of the American Society for Psychical Research, 70*, 219–229.

Stevenson, I. (1980). *Cases of the Reincarnation Type. Vol. 3: Twelve Cases in Lebanon and Turkey*. Charlottesville, VA: University Press of Virginia.

Stevenson, I. & Pasricha, S. (1979). A case of secondary personality with xenoglossy. *American Journal of Psychiatry, 136*, 1591–1592.

Stevenson, I. & Pasricha, S. (1980). A preliminary report on an unusual case of the reincarnation type with xenoglossy. *Journal of the American Society for Psychical Research, 74*, 331–348.

Thomas, C. D. (1922). *Some new evidence for human survival*. London: Collins.

Thouless, R.H. (1936–1937). Review of Mr. Whately Carington's work on trance personalities. *Proceedings of the Society for Psychical Research, 44.* 223–275.

Thouless, R. H. (1948). A test of survival. *Proceedings of the Society for Psychical Research, 48,* 253–263.

Thouless, R. H. (1949). Additional notes on a test of survival. *Proceedings of the Society for Psychical Research, 49,* 342–343.

Tyrrell, G. N. M. (1939). A communicator introduced in automatic script. *Journal of the Society for Psychical Research, 31,* 91–95.

Tyrrell, G. N. M. (1953). *Apparitions* (2nd ed.). London: Duckworth.

Verrall, H. de G. M. W. H. S. (1911). The element of chance in cross-correspondences. *Journal of the Society for Psychical Research, 15,* 153–172.

West, D. J. (1948). A mass-observation questionnaire on hallucinations. *Journal of the Society for Psychical Research, 34,* 187–196.

Wilson, S. C., and & Barber, T. X. (1983). The fantasy-prone personality: Implications for understanding imagery, hypnosis, and parapsychological phenomena. In A. A. Sheikh (ed.), *Imagery, current theory, research and applications* (pp. 340–390). New York: Wiley.

Zorab, G. (1939–1940). A case for survival. *Journal of the Society for Psychical Research, 31,* 142–152.

van Eeden, F. (1901–1903). Account of sittings with Mrs. Thompson. *Proceeding of the Society for Psychical Research, 17,* 75–115

9. Getting Through the Grief: After-Death Communication Experiences and Their Effects on Experients*

BY STANLEY KRIPPNER

Professor Stanley Krippner describes some incredible cases of After-Death Communications (ADCs), and concludes that the ADC-experient is usually positively rewarded in some way upon having the experience. Often, the experient has a severe debilitating mood of depression or grief dissolved as a consequence of a change of outlook—the experient comes to believe that the deceased is not suffering in any way and is happy. In other cases, relationship issues are resolved, or unfinished business is concluded. Professor Krippner points out that ADCs are clearly therapeutic in nature.—Editors

For three decades I worked with the intertribal medicine man, Rolling Thunder, who lived in Carlin, Nevada. His wife, Spotted Fawn, was an indispensable part of his enterprises, and I was shaken when she was admitted to the Presidio Military Hospital in San Francisco with a diagnosis of terminal cancer. As a Native American, she was entitled to free treatment at a military hospital, and I visited her two or three times a week to alleviate her pain through hypnosis and guided imagery.

My ministrations were interrupted by an invitation to speak at a conference on dreams in Mexico City. While there, I dreamed that I was back

*Preparation of this chapter was supported by the Chair for the Study of Consciousness, Saybrook Graduate School and Research Center, San Francisco, California, U.S.A.

in California, visiting the ranch of Mickey Hart, a drummer for the Grateful Dead, a rock band. Rolling Thunder and his entourage were staying at Hart's ranch while Spotted Fawn was receiving treatment, just across the Golden Gate Bridge. In my dream, I drove into Hart's ranch just in time to see Rolling Thunder and his group driving out, heading back to Nevada. The medicine man had a sober expression on his face, as did his companions. I asked, "Where is Spotted Fawn?"

Rolling Thunder turned his head slightly toward the back of the van. I saw a wooden coffin strapped to the floor of the vehicle and I knew that it contained the remains of his wife. I awakened, wrote down the dream with a heavy heart, and went back to sleep.

That morning, just as I was waking up, I heard Spotted Fawn's voice, "You know, I won't be seeing you anymore." Upon arriving back in the United States, I learned that my beloved friend had passed away that very night (Krippner, 2000). This type of experience has been referred to as an "after-death communication" (ADC) and is one of the topics of interest to parapsychologists, those investigators who study reported experiences and observations that appear to bypass Western science's understanding of time, space, and energy.*

Definitions and Descriptions

The Society for Psychical Research, the first scientific association to study anomalous (i.e., rare and/or puzzling) phenomena, was founded in London in 1882, primarily to study the possibility that the human personality survives death and, at times, can communicate with those still living (Alvarado, 2003; Gurney & Myers, 1898–1899). The Society proceeded to study other topics (e.g., telepathy, clairvoyance, psychokinesis, hypnosis, dissociation) but the original purpose permeated many of its activities and publications (Keely, 2001).

Over a century later, Guggenheim and Guggenheim (1995) coined the term "after-death communication" when they created their "ADC Project" in 1988, initiating the first in-depth study of ADCs. By 2005, they had interviewed some 2,000 people from all fifty U.S. states and all ten Canadian provinces, collecting more than 3,300 accounts from people who believed

*A brief history of Western concepts of life after death has been presented by Flew (1996) and a cross-cultural perspective has been written by Krippner (1989). Roll (1982) has surveyed the evidence for survival, and Wilson (1985) has applied this evidence to reports of spirit "possession," "multiple personalities," and the "spiritualist" movement.

they had been contacted by a deceased loved one (Guggenheim, 2005). Martin and Romanowski (1997) have defined an ADC as "any contact between a living person and the consciousness, spirit, or soul of the so-called dead" (p. 2), and LaGrand (1999) has referred to an ADC (which he prefers to label an "exceptional experience of the bereaved" or an "extraordinary encounter") as a spontaneously experienced contact with a deceased loved one. Guggenheim (2005) also has emphasized that ADCs appear to be "initiated by deceased loved ones, and no psychics, mediums, or devices are involved" (p. 5). ADC experiences range from the uneventful and the non-emotional, to those that are frightening and disturbing, to a larger number that are said to be comforting and transformative.

According to Drewry (2002), the ADC literature cites several types of purported communication, for example, sensing the "presence" of the deceased, hearing words or other utterances of the deceased, telepathically communicating with the deceased, having the sensation of being touched by the deceased, tasting or smelling something associated with the deceased, receiving a communication from the deceased in a dream or other altered state of consciousness, having out-of-body contact with the deceased, receiving a communication from the deceased before knowing of their death, receiving a communication by means of physical objects moving with no apparent external force, receiving a communication through unusual natural phenomena (e.g., rainbows, bird formations), sexual communication with the deceased, communication with the deceased through instrumentation such as radio broadcast activity, and communication with the deceased through a "mystical experience."

LaGrand (1999) has provided an example of one of the rarest of the 16 types, communication by means of an object that moves with no apparent external force. "Janet," the daughter of "Judy," a psychiatric nurse, was clinically depressed because of the recent death of her brother, "Jim," and had to fly home from college. Janet's parents met her at the airport and returned home. Judy brought the family's two dogs in for the night, and joined her husband and daughter in an upstairs bedroom. Moments later, there was a scratching at the balcony door; upon opening it, the three of them were greeted by one of the dogs who dashed in, ears back and tail flying. They concluded that there was no possible way for the dog to have gone outside and jumped 15 feet up to the balcony by itself. Hence, they decided that Jim, although deceased, had "picked up" the dog to get their attention. Judy recalled that she could almost see Janet's depression lifting, and within a few days her daughter was able to return to school (p. 142).

Another category, hearing from the deceased in a dream or other altered state of consciousness, has been illustrated by the renowned psychiatrist,

Stanislav Grof (1988), who wrote an account of some friends who were vacationing in Maine. One of them, "Peter," went scuba diving and never returned. Consequently, his wife, "Penny," had difficulty accepting her husband's death; this was especially problematic because his body was never found. During a psychotherapeutic LSD session with Grof, Penny reported an ADC experience with Peter who explained that he was, in fact, dead. Peter gave Penny specific instructions concerning each of their children and requested that she get on with her life. Peter then asked Penny to return a book that he had borrowed from a friend, giving Penny the friend's name, the title of the book, and the location of the book in their house. All of this information was correct, and Penny returned the book to its owner. After this ADC, Penny was able to accept Peter's death and to begin working through her grief.

Wright (1998) has presented a case of "spontaneous psychokinesis following bereavement" that falls into the category of receiving a communication by means of physical objects moving with no apparent external force. Following the death of her husband, Wright observed lamps flashing on and off, anomalies with the functioning of her electrical appliances, the appearance (in unexpected places) of objects belonging to her late husband, and similar occurrences, many of which took place in the presence of other witnesses.

The following review of ADC literature and its effects on experients omits accounts of so-called "ghosts," "phantoms," "poltergeists," and "shades," unless their purported appearance can be described as a "contact," thus conforming to the definitions of Martin and Romanowski (1997) and LeGrand (1999). Nor does it include accounts of sessions with "shamans" (see Leclere, 2005) or "mediums" (see Schwartz & Simon, 2005) because these sessions are rarely "spontaneous" (LeGrand, 1999). It does not include accounts of contacts with "angels," "aliens," "deities," or strangers, because these do not qualify as "deceased loved ones" (LeGrand); nor does it include material that is "channeled" to the world-at-large because this does not meet the "deceased love one" or the "so-called dead" criteria. Purported voices of deceased persons through mechanical instruments or heard in tape recorded sessions (e.g., Ellis, 1978; Fontana & Cardoso, 2005) are not included in this review unless they were "spontaneously experienced," thus meeting an important aspect of LeGrand's definition.

Finally, the ADC accounts cited in this essay are better classified as "experiences" (subjective verbal reports) than as "events" (verifiable outcomes and activities). Glik (1993) has emphasized the importance of this distinction when a controversial phenomenon is under discussion because it allows participants in the discourse to focus on someone's lived experience rather than to debate the veridicality (i.e., genuineness) of hypothetical "entities," "energies," and the like.

Research Studies with ADC Experients

Although there is a wealth of anecdotal literature (e.g., Dawson, 2000; Duminiak, 2003; LaGrand, 2001; Stevenson, 1995; Wright, 1999), a small number of investigators have systematically studied the impact of ADCs on their experients. At the end of the nineteenth century, the Society for Psychical Research conducted a mail survey seeking responses to the question, "Have you ever ... had a vivid impression of seeing, or being touched, or of hearing a voice; which impression, so far as you could discover, was not due to any external cause?" (Sidgwick, Sidgwick, & Johnson, 1894). The analysis of over 17,000 returned questionnaires indicated that ten percent of the respondents reported a type of "hallucination" that could be considered an ADC.

A century later, Whitney's (1992) survey of ADC experients revealed that age, religious affiliation, and duration of the relationship did not seem to predispose a bereaved person to an ADC experience; however, the bereaved person's emotional involvement with the deceased was a salient factor. The majority of ADC experiences were positive, decreasing the experients' fear of death, increasing their feelings of contact with a "higher power," and lending conviction to the concept of post-mortem survival.

Devers (1988) examined reports of ADC experiences, finding that they were consistent with the nature of the pre-death relationship. Survivors also felt a resolution of their bereavement and most were convinced that the ADC was an actual communication with the deceased. Later, Devers (1994) conducted a follow-up study, finding that some of their bereaved found their belief system challenged by the ACD and that if they did not change their worldview to accommodate post-mortem survival, it was more difficult to resolve the pain resulting from their loss.

Berger (1995) looked into the relevance of belief in survival to the bereavement process. Although many professional counselors regard ADCs as "hallucinatory," Berger found that experients who disregarded this pathological perspective were able to restructure their lives more effectively.

Grimby (1993) queried 14 widowers and 36 widows in Sweden, and found that 82 percent reported "hallucinations" or similar experiences concerning their dead spouses within a month after their death. Yamamoto, Okonogi, Iwakasi, and Yoshimura (1969) interviewed 20 Japanese widows within the first three months of their husbands' deaths in car accidents. Some

90 percent reported sensing the presence of their husbands in some way. Marris (1958) studied 72 widows in London, England, finding that half of them claimed to have sensed the "presence" of their departed husbands. In a study of 293 widows and widowers in Wales, Rees (1971) reported that nearly half the group sensed the presence of their deceased spouses. Further, he found that the experiences were "psychologically helpful" and that there was no indication that they were pathological. Presence of the dead has been explored by several other investigators (e.g., Conant, 1992), sometimes with discrepant results (Lindstrom, 1995).

Krippner and Faith (2001) examined dream reports from 1,666 respondents from six countries; of these, 135 were judged to be "exotic" in some way. To be scored a "visitation" dream, a deceased person had to provide direction or counsel that the dreamer found to be of value; about one percent of the dreams fell into this category, with fewer from the United States than from Argentina, Brazil, Japan, Russia, or Ukraine.

One example of a "visitation" dream came from a Japanese woman: "My father, who died in World War II, appears to me. He gives me advice about my artwork. He gives me specific advice on what to paint and how to do it. He tells me the topics, what brushes to use, and what colors to use" (Krippner & Faith, 2001, pp. 79–80). A woman from the United States contributed another "visitation" dream: "I am visited by a friend of mine from waking life. He had been murdered in waking life and we discuss the conditions under which he was killed. He can fly and I want to fly too. My friend takes me to a street where I can rent wings for 25 cents. I am able to fly with these wings, but then I realize it is my confidence that is keeping me in the air. My friend has taught me a great lesson." In retrospect, this dream appeared to have contributed to the enhancement of the dreamer's self-confidence in waking life (p. 81).

The most voluminous collection of anomalous experiences was initiated by Louisa Rhine in 1948 and was continued by her daughter Sally Rhine Feather. By 2005, the collection exceeded 14,000 reports, many of them ADCs (Feather & Schmicker, 2005). One respondent wrote:

> After my father died, I felt really alone.... My husband had been ill for two years, and ... we [were] badly in debt.... Our car payments were behind three months and ... [someone] came to repossess the car. While I was talking to the man at the front door, I heard my deceased father say, just as clear as my own voice, "Tell him to wait until Friday." Without hesitation, I said..., "Wait until Friday and I'll pay you." He agreed and left.... Thursday afternoon, my dad's lawyer called me and told me to come to his office and pick up a check for $417. The courts had collected from an old account owed my dead father.... When I hung up the phone, I looked up and said silently, "Thanks again, Dad" [pp. 253–264].

This auditory message was not unusual in the Rhine collection; auditory-only "hallucinations" accounted for over half of all "hallucinatory" experiences that appeared to convey veridical information.

Rhine (1960) constantly reminded her readers that even the best "spontaneous" case can be no more than "suggestive" from a scientific standpoint. Even so, some experiences have such a powerful, life-changing effect on experients that they keep referring to the ADC for years (e.g., Lambert, 1968). Others hesitate to discuss their ADCs; one of Arcangel's (2005) informants confided that his deceased wife had warned him about the 2001 terrorist attacks on the United States, illustrating the events "on a big screen." When Arcangel asked if he had told anyone, he replied, "Lord no! They'd think I was loony" (pp. *xii-xiii*).

"Loony" or not, a variety of surveys have been published indicating that substantial numbers of people, from both genders, from a wide age range, and from various socio-economic groups, ethnicities, and nationalities, have reported ADC experiences (e.g., Haraldsson, 1985; Piccini and Rinaldi, 1990; West, 1990). Haraldsson's (1988–1999) survey of Icelanders revealed that 31 percent of the 1,131 people queried felt that they had experienced the "presence" of a deceased person. Greeley (1989) reported that 42 percent of his 1,445 respondents in the United States reported contact with the dead.

Kalish and Reynolds (1973) sent questionnaires to 434 "people of color" in Los Angeles, reporting that 44 percent had experienced ADCs. Although they claimed the ADCs had been generally beneficial to their grieving process, many of the respondents admitted that they were reluctant to discuss their experiences, fearing pejorative reactions. Another Los Angeles questionnaire study was conducted by Burton (1982) who reported that 76 percent of his respondents claimed to have had experienced an ADC. Because his questionnaires had been sent to members of psychic research groups and classes, Burton then sent out 1,500 additional questionnaires to college psychology students in the Los Angeles area; 50 percent of them reported ADCs. Daggett (2005) conducted a qualitative study of ADCs reported by nine men and nine women in the United States, finding that women were more likely than men to discuss ADCs with others.

In 1979, a curious book was published under the title *Phone Calls from the Dead* (Rogo & Bayless, 1979). Its authors admitted that their topic was "bizarre," yet one that deserved attention. They grouped their subsequent collection of cases into three categories: reported phone calls from someone who was deceased; reported "urgent" phone calls about a dead person from a living person (a friend, relative, or someone calling on behalf of the friend or relative, most of whom later denied having made the call); reported phone conversations by the experient with someone who later turned out to be dead, or at least absent from the place of apparent contact.

Many of these cases would fall into the ADC category, including a report from a German experient:

"On ... Monday, I got a telephone call in the evening.... All of a sudden I heard, distinctly and unmistakably real, my [dead] father's voice.... I heard his voice quite clear..., 'I am here.... How is Mommy, how is Mommy?' All of a sudden, the whole things was over and gone." The man's wife was home at the time and heard her husband engaged in conversation, but thought that her husband had received a piece of bad news because he was so shocked that he could not speak for several minutes [p. 78].

Rogo and Bayless concluded that their experients had to be in "just the right frame of mind" before contact could be made, and that "this probably goes for the intelligence making the call as well" (p. 51). Although controversial, even among parapsychologists, one beneficial effect of the book was to assure people having similar experiences that they were not emotionally disturbed or the only one in the world to have had such an experience.

Drewry (2003) interviewed seven research participants who collectively reported some 40 ADC experiences. Phenomenological reduction methods produced eight themes: unexpectedness of the ADC established authenticity for bereaved individuals; cues for recognition were specific to the deceased and reinforced authenticity; bereaved individuals considered the possibility of self-delusion before accepting the experience as valid; after the ADC, bereaved individuals reported relief, comfort, hope, encouragement, forgiveness, love, and/or joy; bereaved completed "unfinished business" with the deceased; bereaved may have reframed the relationship with the deceased; bereaved may have reframed their self-concept and worldview (e.g., a reduction in the fear of death; an awareness of themselves as a part of something transcendent); bereaved may have reframed their concept of God and their relationship with the Divine. Some participants spoke of a "continued relationship"; one woman commented, regarding her late father, that "in many ways we have a more real relationship now than we did when he was alive." A more common response was, "the experience gave me enough grounding so that I could get through the grief."

ADC experiences and adaptive grief outcomes were investigated by Parker (2004) who interviewed 12 people, bereaved for less than one year. As was the case with most of the other investigators, she screened out psychiatric patients and those with obvious mental illness. Of the research participants, 11 experienced positive changes such as personal and/or spiritual growth. Their ADC experiences appeared to have played specific roles and to have fulfilled specific needs within the context of bereavement, especially when they were considered to be veridical in nature. Parker concluded that ADC experiences were not a sign of psychopathology but part of human experience that, in these cases, had facilitated assimilation and/or accommodation of the deaths of loved ones.

The one research participant in Parker's study who had a negative ADC presents an instance where recovery from personal loss was not served. The ADC experience was "terrifying" for her and may have aggravated the grief process. Interview data revealed that her relationship with the deceased had been ambivalent in nature, and that she felt that there was "unfinished business." As a result, she may have suppressed her grief and the ADC, when it occurred, challenged her to face the issues that remained unresolved.

In summary, the available literature has described several types of effects on ADC experients, for example, providing comfort and reassurance that the relationship continues even after death; giving advice and helping survivors solve problems; protecting the experients by giving them appropriate warnings of impending dangers; providing a sense of life purpose and meaning; confirming the hope that there is life after death; achieving closure or concluding "unfinished business"; reducing anger, guilt, and/or anxiety concerning the deceased; demonstrating that the loved one has not forgotten the survivor; providing information not previously known by the bereaved; assisting the survivor to make his or her own transition at the time of death.

This latter function is exemplified by data collected by Osis (1961) who sent 10,000 questionnaires to physicians and nurses who were requested to submit their observations of seriously ill patients. Of the 640 responses (which represented some 35,000 patients), eight out of ten terminally ill patients reported "death-bed visions," half of them of a deceased relative or friend. Upon examining the responses, Osis concluded that medication had not been an important factor regarding the quality of the experiences.

Ethier (2005) would consider a report of this nature as a "death-related sensory experience" (DRSE) if it was "spiritually transforming" and occurred in conjunction with the appearance of a dead family member or other entity (i.e., a "messenger") to someone who was dying. Earlier, Kubler-Ross (1999) had described dying children's visions of family members not known to be dead by the children.

The medial right temporal lobe, hippocampus, and associated limbic lobe structures of the brain are linked to DRSEs and similar experiences (Morse & Perry, 2000). Joseph (2002) has described similar findings from several researchers in a field of study often described as "neurotheology." A brain-based model of these reports was proposed in the 1880s by several of the founders of the Society for Psychical Research (Gurney, Myers, & Podmore, 1886) who proposed that these experiences were constructed by the brain from its own resources (or what might be called "reserve capacities") once the initiating stimulus (e.g., the visitation of a deceased loved one) sets the constructive mechanisms in motion. However, Morse (1994) has commented that even though these types of experiences may be brain-based, this does not lessen their spiritual significance.

Investigators of ADCs have cited a number of "obstacles" that, from their viewpoint, appear to hamper purported "communication" with the deceased. For example, from the alleged standpoint of the deceased, the bereaved often make excessive demands for contact; rather than facilitating communication, these pressures actually hamper it. From the perspective of the living, timing is problematic, as they have no idea when to expect a "message" from "the other side," and feel disappointed if it fails to arrive (Tymn, 2005). Members of the spiritistic religions of Brazil often take a cautionary position on messages from the deceased, believing that some of these "spirits" are not spiritually advanced and are prone to confuse their "astral" existence with the time they had spent on Earth, giving advice that is inappropriate or confusing (Trisker, 1996, p. x). In other words, just because one is dead, one is not necessarily wise!

Nonetheless, the bulk of evidence suggests that ADC experiences (for non-psychiatric experients) are non-pathological, not pathological; natural, not preternatural; and can be useful in helping survivors move through the grieving process. Whether ADCs are veridical, demonstrating the survival of some aspect of the psyche following the demise of one's body, is another matter.

Possible Therapeutic Applications

The Dalai Lama (2002) wrote, "Death is a natural part of life, which we will all surely have to face sooner or later" (p. *ix*) and Paul Tillich (1963) reminded his parishioners and students that "It is our destiny and the destiny of everything in our world that we must come to an end" (p. 103). These verities are easier to accept intellectually than following the demise of a close friend, relative, or lover. However, a few counselors, psychiatrists, and psychological therapists have used ADCs, in one form or another, as part of what has become known as "bereavement therapy" or "grief therapy" (e.g., Kastenbaum, 1978). For example, a procedure inducing "visitation" dreams has been developed by a well-known dreamworker, Robert Moss (2005). His approach purports to enable bereaved people to dream about departed loved ones, attaining a closure that was not possible while they were alive. Arcangel's (2005) collection of "afterlife encounters" was written to assist hospice workers, families in mourning, and other groups who had unanswered questions about the possibility of life after death. Wright (2002) has provided a practical guide for people who are puzzled or even terrified by ADCs; some of her case studies involve an "emotional resolution" to those people harmed while the deceased was alive (Wright, 2005, p. 7). (Wright noticed that there were no examples, in her collection, of murderers communicating with the living, or if there were, they did not admit their crime!)

Based on his experience with bereaved people, LaGrand (1997) has presented several ways that these experiences can be used in grief counseling: ability in expressing emotions about the deceased, accepting the death of the deceased, recalling comforting memories, eliminating unnecessary suffering, finding meaning in the experience, establishing a "new relationship" with the departed loved one, and establishing a new worldview. LaGrand emphasized that the critical issue is not whether the experience can be confirmed or refuted, but how the experience can be used to help people deal with their losses.

While working as a clinical psychologist with Vietnam veterans, Botkin (Botkin, with Hogan, 2005) serendipitously developed a therapeutic approach now known as "Induced After-Death Communication." During a counseling session with a client who was haunted by the memory of a Vietnamese girl he failed to save, the veteran had a "hallucinatory" experience. The girl "appeared" to him, and told the veteran that she was at peace. This single anomalous experience, whatever its nature, allowed the veteran to re-connect with his family and friends, and to terminate his therapy. Botkin advocated "inducing" ADCs with the Eye-Movement Desensitization and Reprocessing procedure (EMDR), a therapeutic modality often used to treat veterans suffering from post-traumatic stress disorder. According to Botkin, these "induced" ADCs have more in common with NDEs (near-death experiences) than do spontaneous ADCs, suggesting a commonality between the two experiences.

Raymond Moody (1992; Moody & Perry, 1993), well known for his investigations of NDEs (Moody, 1975, but see Hovelmann, 1985), once learned about the psychomanteums of ancient Greece, sites for consultation with the spirits of the deceased. Earlier, he had read about the ancient practice of crystal gazing, and attempted to combine the two traditions. The result was a darkened room where the bereaved could look into a mirror while thinking of the loved one; many experients reported seeing images of the deceased and even engaging them in some type of communication.

Hastings and his associates (Hastings, Hutton, Braud, Bennett et al., 2002) designed a research study involving 27 participants who contemplated a deceased "sought" person, and then entered the psychomanteum to gaze into the mirror while thinking of that person. Finally, each research participant discussed and reflected on the experience with one of the investigators. For example, one research participant's sought person was an uncle who had died seven years previously. In his interview, the participant stated, "My uncle's presence was felt but it was slight and somewhat guarded. He repeated, 'Don't worry' and 'Do what's best for you,' which I somehow can't hear enough of."

Hastings and his group collected questionnaire data before the session and several weeks after the session; psychological tests were administered as well. Participants reported that a variety of imagery had appeared in the mirror (e.g., human and animal faces, robed figures, flowers); they also reported experiences involving dialogue, sounds, lights, smells, and/or body sensations. Thirteen participants reported "contact" with the sought person. When the psychological test results were analyzed, statistically significant differences were obtained indicating reductions in bereavement, as well as resolution of participants' incomplete feelings (e.g., loss, grief, guilt, sadness, and the need to communicate with the sought person). Interview data indicated that the psychomanteum experience had a noteworthy and positive impact on participants' lives. These findings coincide with Guggenheim's (2005) observations that most of the experients in his collection of case studies reported a reduced intensity of grief following the ADC experience.

Needless to say, objections have been raised to this type of grief counseling, seeing it as a buttress to "magical thinking," the tendency to accept explanations of natural phenomena that are at variance with those of Western science (Zusne, 1985, p. 689). I have re-defined magical thinking, conceptualizing it as "a tendency to engage in cognitive activity that attributes effects to causes that are indiscernible by means of sensory perception, technological measurement, or logical interference of the type sanctioned by a given community" (Krippner & Winkler, 1996, p. 446). This does not excuse magical thinking from the role it played in the Roman Catholic Inquisition, human sacrifice by the Mayans and Aztecs, and the burial of living people in their rulers' tombs by ancient Egyptians and Chinese high priests. Yet, Taylor (1989) has taken the position that "being realistic" is not always as important in maintaining mental health as is fostering "positive illusions," especially when the latter cannot be falsified.

ADCs as "Exceptional Human Experiences"

The modern Western worldview holds that the physical form and/or personality of a deceased person change and eventually disintegrate. Many advocates of the survival hypothesis take the position that one's form and/or personality do not entirely disappear but, at least partially, survive bodily death (e.g., Arcangel, 2005; Doumette, 1938). An alternative (and non-Western) point of view holds that one is restricted neither to a particular form or personality, but is an integral part of the world's "force-field" as a whole. Most models of life after death fall on a spectrum between these two conceptualizations, the "form" theory and the "field" theory (Roll, 1982, p. 148). The former has been a major influence in psychical research since the early days of the British and American psychical research societies, and assumes that some aspect of one's personality survives bodily death. The latter point of view is commonly encountered in various Eastern philosophies; even those that espouse reincarnation see this series of earthly lives as a preparation for an ultimate merging with a universal "force-field."

At the very least, ADCs can be described as "exceptional experiences" (EEs), a term coined by Rhea White (1995) who has classified scores of unusual reports. However, White reserved the term "exceptional human experiences" (EHEs) for those EEs that have been "potentiated," that is, the experient has accepted the experience as authentic and has identified with it in some way, leading to a personal transformation of some sort. Even though one's social group may deride the importance of the experience, the experient considers it a part of the repertoire of human activity and of his or her own capacities. Supko-McMahon (1987), for example, used White's concept of EHEs to guide her research project involving 50 funeral home directors and their apprentices, many of whom reported anomalous work-related experiences. Some of the EHEs McMahon reported would fall into the ADC category.

Social construction plays an important part in determining the nature of the experience, as each culture has its own parameters of exceptionality. One might speculate that ADCs are so common in some cultures that they do not warrant the label of "exceptional"; in discussing the Huichol people of Mexico, one commentator observed, by Western standards, "all of Huichol life is a kind of well-organized hallucination, for the cosmos they believe and live in bears very little resemblance to the one that Western civilization wakes up to every morning" (p. 38).

White (1997) has taken the position that EHEs provide the insight and the dynamic to move experients from a lesser to a more consciously evolved state of being that expands their awareness of the nature of the cosmos. It is common for EHE experients to move from conceptualizing themselves as a separate skin-encapsulated ego, but EHEs typically make people aware of their oneness with all living beings. This awareness, in turn, leads to an explanatory narrative, or what I have called a "personal myth" (Feinstein & Krippner, 1988). In modern, technological, industrialized societies, the term "myth" has come to mean "fallacy" or "falsehood." However, the word "myth" is derived from the Greek root *mythos*, that is, "tale" or "talk." Far from being falsehoods, these "talking tales" (or mythic narratives) are actually the repositories of enduring insights. Rudnytsky (1988) observed that "the myths of

Oedipus and the Fall may not tell us the way things were; but they do teach us the way things *are*" (p. *iv*).

Mythological narratives typically address existential human issues and have consequences for behavior; they may be cultural, institutional, ethnic, familial, and/or personal in nature. Myth-making played such a key role in human development that Donald (1991) has called "scenario-building" the primary function of the human mind. Until science develops the technology to confirm or falsify the "survival hypothesis," it is up to the experients to dismiss them as "exceptional experiences" that are curious but unimportant anomalies, or to construct them into "exceptional human experiences" and revel in their transformative power.

"Fields," "Forms," and Ironic Science

There are three types of data suggesting the continuation of one's personality after death: reports of direct contact with the dead, reports of indirect contact with the dead, and memories of a purported past life. The first type of data includes reported ADCs and other experiences in which a dead person is purportedly seen, felt, and/or heard (or supposedly communicated with through symbolic sights, sounds, or other phenomena) by an experient or experients (e.g., Rhine, 1960; Wright, 2002). The second type of data includes reports from "mediums" or other psychic claimants (e.g., Gauld, 1971). The third type of data focuses on reports from people who have described an alleged former life (e.g., Matlock, 1990). All three types of data rest on the "form" model of an afterlife and follow in the tradition of Frederic Myers (1903) whose classic book was a study of "human personality and its survival of bodily death."

The term "personality" is used in a number of ways, but most definitions refer to features that characterize an individual and distinguish him or her from others. If the advocates of the "force-field" model are correct, it is difficult to imagine how this point of view could be tested by parapsychologists since it does not involve the continuation of a "personality," "form," or "body" after one's demise. As a result, Stokes (1993) questions the utility of the term "personality" in these discussions because personality features and traits change over time. He prefers the term "self," as it refers to something that "can not be identified with a particular configuration of atoms comprising a physical body" (p. 76). Instead, the "self" (i.e., the entity that thinks one's thoughts, senses one's sensations, feels one's feelings, and remembers one's memories) either is innate or is constructed by reflecting on one's memories and life-history. This capacity to self-reflect might provide "selves" a better chance of becoming part of a "field" than would a "personality," unless the Buddhists are correct in asserting that self-reflection will reveal the illusory nature of "self" (Blackmore, 2004, p. 402), hence, the paradoxical nature of this undertaking.

The systems theorist Ervin Laszlo (2001) has offered a way out of this dilemma. He has used the ancient Hindu term "Akashic field" to refer to a web of "cosmic information" that unites both human and non-human aspects of the cosmos both before and after death. This concept could serve to integrate the "form" and "field" models and lend itself to investigative methods. There were earlier attempts at reconciliation. Gustav Fechner (1836), best known for his pioneering work in psychophysics, held that a "form" may appear when there is an encounter between two or more individuals. If someone "leaves behind ... a treasure of love, esteem, honor, and admiration in [human memory], such enrichment is his [or her] gain in death, since he [or she] acquires the condensed consciousness of the whole earthly estimate concerning him [or her]" (p. 50).

Another way of reconciling the two models has been posited by William Roll (1982), a parapsychologist, who considered both models as credible. The deceased's "form consciousness"" may continue for some time after death, or may become embedded in a particular setting. However, this aspect of oneself may lose its identity over time. One's "field consciousness," on the other hand, may be unlimited by time and space, and therefore be incapable of dying; however, less of one's earthly "personality" would be present in "field consciousness" than in "form consciousness," and might even operate in tandem with members of a like-minded community.

In the meantime, it is apparent that the study of the effects of ADCs on experients has become a scientific enterprise. These effects appear to be benevolent, in general; as a result, the discussion and even the evocation of ADCs could play an important role in grief counseling. But a further question might be asked: Is the study of ADCs *per se* a "scientific" enterprise? When Gertrude Schmeidler (in Rogo & Bayless, 1979), a former president of the Parapsychological Association, was asked this question about purported phone calls from the dead, she answered "yes and no." On the positive side, many of these anecdotes were investigated promptly, were supported by other witnesses or records, and came from people of good reputation. In addition, the case reports "fit in with a prior body of knowledge" (pp. 150–151).

On the negative side, countless cases were never investigated, were the focus of biased researchers, or were studied, but only after a long delay. Many ADC cases, especially the latter, might be the result of coincidence (Stokes, 1997, pp. 62–63) the experient's inference (p. 63), poor memory (e.g., Stokes, 1997, p. 64), or deliberate falsification (Kurtz, 1985; Stokes, 1997, p. 65).

These are possibilities that cannot be ruled out by anyone making a competent examination of the evidence. For example my presumptive ADC from Spotted Fawn may have been coincidental or a result of inference, since I knew her sickness was fatal. It is unlikely that memory distortion played a role, since I wrote down the dream upon awakening, and the morning hypnopompic auditory material as well. As for fraud, it would hardly enhance my academic reputation to admit that I had been the recipient of an ADC!

On the other hand, if telepathy, clairvoyance, psychokinesis, and similar hypothetical capacities exist, could they not account for the anomalous effects noted in many ADC reports (Chiari, 1978; Owen & Sparrow, 1976)? This possibility often is referred to as the "super-psi" hypothesis since it relies on a robust manifestation of one's psychic capacities to manifest itself.

Perhaps the study of the veridicality of ADCs, and of the survival hypothesis itself, provides an example of what Horgan (1999) referred to as "ironic science," a science "that never gets a firm grip on reality and thus does not converge on the truth." Ironic science cannot make the kind of literal, factual statements about the world that can either be confirmed or invalidated through empirical means. Its modes of inquiry and the knowledge derived resemble those of philosophy, literary criticism, and literature itself. "Ironic science," continued Horgan, "is most pervasive in fields that address the human mind" (p. 470).

The renowned physicist Roger Penrose (2005) once acknowledged that science, at best, has provided a decidedly incomplete guide to the laws of nature, and a 2005 issue of *New Scientist* discussed "13 things that do not make sense," ranging from the placebo effect to dark matter (Brooks, 2005). Clearly, ADCs do not make sense when examined through the lens of mainstream Western scientific paradigms. But William James (1902/2002) expressed his customary insight when he wrote that such experiences "forbid a premature closing of our accounts with reality" (p.319).

References

Alvarado, C. (2003). The concept of survival of bodily death and the development of parapsychology. *Journal of the Society for Psychical Research, 67,* 2, 65–95.
Arcangel, D. (2005). *Afterlife encounters.* Charlottesville, VA: Hampton Roads.
Berger, A. S. (1995). *The aristocracy of the dead: New findings in post-mortem survival.* Jefferson, NC: McFarland.
Blackmore, S. (2004). *Consciousness: An introduction.* New York: Oxford University Press.
Botkin, A. I., with Hogan, R. C. (2005). *Induced after-death communication: A new therapy for healing grief and trauma.* Charlottesville, VA: Hampton Roads.
Brooks, M. (2005, March 19). 13 things that do not make sense. *New Scientist,* pp. 30–36.
Burton, J. (1982, April). Contact with the dead: A common experience? *Fate,* pp. 65–73.
Chiari, C. T. K. (1978). Reincarnation research: Method and interpretation. In M. Ebon (Ed.), *Signet handbook of parapsychology* (pp. 313–324). New York: NAL Books.

Conant, R. D. (1992). *Widows' experiences of intrusive memory and "sense of presence" of the deceased after sudden and untimely death of a spouse during mid-life.* Unpublished doctoral dissertation. West Roxbury, MA: Massachusetts School of Professional Psychology.

Daggett, L. M. (2005). Continued encounters: The experience of after-death communication. *Journal of Holistic Nursing, 23,* 191–207.

Dalai Lama, H. H. (2002). Foreword. In S. Rinpoche, *The Tibetan book of living and dying* (rev. ed., pp. *ix-x*).San Francisco: HarperSanFrancisco.

Dawson, L. (2000). *Visitations from the afterlife.* San Francisco: HarperSanFrancisco.

Devers, E. (1987). *Experiencing an encounter with the deceased.* Unpublished master's Thesis. Gainesville, FL: University of Florida.

Devers, E. (1994). Experiencing the deceased. *Florida Nursing Review, 1* (3), 7–13.

Donald, M. (1991). *Origins of the modern mind: Three stages in the evolution of culture and cognition.* Cambridge, MA: MIT Press.

Doumette, H. J. (1938). *Life after death.* Santa Monica, CA: Christian Institute of Spiritual Science.

Drewry, M. D. L. (2002). Purported after-death communication and its role in the recovery of bereaved individuals: A phenomenological study. Unpublished doctoral dissertation, San Diego, CA: California Institute for Human Science.

Drewry, M. D. L. (2003). Purported after-death communication and its role in the recovery of bereaved individuals: A phenomenological study. *Proceedings, Annual Conference of the Academy of Religion and Psychical Research, 2003* (pp. 74–87). Bloomfield, CT: Academy of Religion and Psychical Research.

Duminiak, C. (2003). *God's gift of love: After death communications.* Philadelphia: Xlibris.

Ellis, D. J. (1978). *The mediumship of the tape recorder: A detailed examination of the (Juergenson, Raudive) phenomenon of voice extras on tape recordings.* Pulborough, England: Author.

Fechner, G. T. (1836). *Das Muchlein vom Leben nach dem Tode* [The little book of life after death]. Dresden: Grimmer.

Feinstein, D., & Krippner, S. (1988). *Personal mythology: The psychology of your evolving self.* Los Angeles: Jeremy P. Tarcher.

Flew, A. (1996). Could we survive our own individual deaths? In G. Stein (Ed.), *Encyclopedia of the paranormal* (pp. 729–742). Amherst, NY: Prometheus Press.

Fontana, D., & Cardoso, A. (2005, May). Instrumental trance communication research project. *Paranormal Review,* pp. 17–19.

Gauld, A. (1971). A series of "drop-in" communicators. *Proceedings of the Society for Psychical Research, 55,* 273–340.

Glik, D. C. (1993). Beliefs, practices, and experiences of spiritual healing adherents in an American industrial city. In W. Andritsky (Ed.), *Yearbook of cross-cultural medicine and psychotherapy, 1992* (pp. 199–223). Berlin: Verlag fur Wissenchaft und Bildung.

Greeley, A. (1989). *Religious change in America.* Cambridge: Harvard University Press.

Grimby, A. (1993). Bereavement amongst the elderly: Grief reactions, post-bereavement hallucinations and quality of life. *Acta Psychiatrica Scandanavia, 87,* 72–80.

Grof, S. (1988). *The adventure of self-discovery.* Albany: State University of New York Press.

Guggenheim, B. (2005, June). After-death communication: A new field of research confirms that life and love are eternal. *Abstracts of Presentations, 30th Annual Conference of the Academy of Religion and Psychical Research, Orlando, FL* (p. 5). Bloomfield, CT: Academy of Religion and Psychical Research.

Guggenheim, B., & Guggenheim, J. (1995). *Hello from Heaven!* New York: Bantam.

Gurney, E., & Myers, F. W. H. (1898–1899). On apparitions occurring soon after death. *Proceedings of the Society for Psychical Research, 5,* 403–485.

Gurney, E., Myers, F. W. H., & Podmore, F. (1886). *Phantasms of the living.* London: Trubner.

Haraldsson, E. (1985). Representative national surveys of psychic phenomena: Iceland, Great Britain, Sweden, USA and Gallup multinational survey. *Journal of the Society for Psychical Research, 53,*145–158. Haraldsson, E. (1988–1989). Survey of claimed encounters with the dead. *Omega: Journal of Death and Dying, 19,* 103–113.

Hastings, A., Hutton, M., Braud, W., Bennett, C., Berk, I., Boynton, T., Dawn, C., Ferguson, E., Goldman, A., Greene, E., Hewett, M., Lind, V., McLellan, K., & Steinbach-Humphrey, S. (2002). Psychomanteum research: Experiences and effects on bereavement. *Omega: Journal of Death and Dying, 43,* 211–228.

Horgan, J. (1999). The undiscovered mind: How the human brain defies replication, medication, and explanation. *Psychological Science, 10,* 470–474.

Hovelmann, G. (1985). Evidence for survival from near-death experiences? In P. Kurtz (Ed.), *A skeptic's handbook of parapsychology* (pp. 645–684). Amherst, NY: Prometheus Press.

James, W. (2002). *Varieties of religious experience.* London: Routledge; Taylor & Frances Group. (Original work published 1902).

Joseph, R. (2002). *Neurotheology: Brain, science, spirituality, religious experience.* San Jose, CA: University Press, California.

Kalish, R. A., & Reynolds, D. K. (1973). Phenomenological reality and post-death contact. *Journal for the Scientific Study of Religion, 12,* 209–221.

Kastenbaum, R. (1978). Death, dying and bereavement in old age: New developments and their possible implications for psychosocial care. *Aged Care and Services Review, 1,* 1–10.

Keely, J. P. (2001). Subliminal promptings: Psychoanalytic theory and the Society for Psychical Research. *Imago, 58,* 767–791.

Krippner, S. (1989). Mythological aspects of death and dying. In A. Berger, P. Badham, A.H. Kutscher, J. Berger, M. Perry, & J. Beloff (Eds.), *Perspectives on death and dying* (pp. 3–13). Philadelphia: Charles Press.

Krippner, S. (2000). Spotted Fawn's farewell. In L. Lawson, *Visitations from the afterlife: True stories of love and healing* (pp. 87–88). San Francisco: HarperSanFrancisco.

Krippner, S., & Faith, L. (2001). Exotic dreams: A cross-cultural study. *Dreaming, 11,* 73–82.

Krippner. S., & Winkler, M. (1996). The "need to believe." In G. Stein (Ed.), *Encyclopedia of the paranormal* (pp. 441–454). Amherst, NY: Prometheus Press.

Kubler-Ross, E. (1999). *The tunnel and the light: Essential insights on living and dying with a letter to a child with cancer.* New York: Marlowe.

Kurtz, P. (1985). Spiritualists, mediums, and psychics: Some evidence of fraud. In P. Kurtz (Ed.), *A skeptic's handbook of parapsychology* (pp. 177–223). Amherst, NY: Prometheus Press.

LaGrand, L. (1997). *After-death communication: Final farewells.* St. Paul, MN: Llewellyn.

LaGrand, L. (1999). *Messages and miracles: Extraordinary experiences of the bereaved.* St. Paul, MN: Llewellyn.

LaGrand, L. (2001). *Gifts from the unknown.* New York: Authors Choice Press.

Lambert, G. W. (1968). Two synchronous experiences connected with a death. *Journal of the Society for Psychical Research, 44,* 232–237.

Laszlo, E. (2001). *Science and the Akashic field: An integral theory of everything.* Rochester, VT: Inner Traditions.

Leclere, A. (2005). *Seeing the dead, talking with spirits: Shamanic healing techniques through contact with the spirit world.* Rochester, VT: Destiny Books.

Lindstrom, T. C. (1995). Experiencing the presence of the dead: Discrepancies in "the sensing experience" and their psychological concomitants. *Omega: Journal of Death and Dying, 31,* 11–21.

Marris, P. (1958). *Widows and their families.* London: Routledge and Kegan Paul.

Matlock, J. G. (1990). Past life memory case studies. In S. Krippner (Ed.), *Advances in parapsychological research Volume 6* (pp. 184–267). Jefferson, NC: McFarland.

Moody, R. A. (1975). *Life after life.* Atlanta, GA: Mockingbird.

Moody, R. A. (1992). Family reunions: Visionary encounters with the departed in a modern-day psychomanteum. *Journal of Near-Death Studies, 11,* 83–121.

Moody, R. A., & Perry, P. (1993). *Reunions: Visionary experiences with departed loved ones.* New York: Ivy Books.

Morse, M. L. (1994). *Parting visions: Uses and meanings of pre-death, psychic, and spiritual experiences.* New York: Random House.

Morse, M. L., & Perry, P. (2000). *Where God lives: The science of the paranormal and how our brains are linked to the universe.* New York: HarperCollins.

Moss, R. (2005). *The dreamer's book of the dead: A soul traveler's guide to death, dying, and the other side*. Rochester, NY: Destiny Books.

Osis, K. (1961). *Deathbed observations of physicians and nurses*. New York: Parapsychology Foundation.

Owen, I. M., & Sparrow, M. H. (1976). *Conjuring up Philip: An adventure in psychokinesis*. New York: Harper & Row.

Parker, J. S. (2004). *After death communication experiences and adaptive grief outcomes*. Unpublished doctoral dissertation. San Francisco: Saybrook Graduate School and Research Center.

Penrose, R. (2005). *The road to reality: A complete guide to the laws of the universe*. New York: Knopf Random House.

Rees, W. (1971). The hallucinations of widowhood. *British Medical Journal, 4*, 37–41.

Rhine, L. E. (1960). The evaluation of non-recurrent psi experiences bearing on post-mortem survival. *Journal of Parapsychology, 24*, 8–25.

Piccinini, G., & Rinaldi, G. M. (1990). *I fantasmi dei morenti: Inchiest su una credenza* [Phantasms of the dying: Survey of a belief]. Viareggio, Italy: Il Cardo.

Rogo, D. S., & Bayless, R. (1979). *Phone calls from the dead: The results of a two-year investigation into an incredible phenomenon*. Englewood Cliffs, NJ: Prentice-Hall.

Roll, W. G. (1982). The changing perspective on life after death. In S. Krippner (Ed.), *Advances in parapsychological research* (vol. 3, pp. 147–291). New York: Plenum Press.

Rudnytsky, P. L. (Ed.). (1988). The persistence of myth: Psychoanalysis and structuralist perspectives. New York: Guilford.

Schwartz, G. E., & Simon, W. L. (2005). *The truth about "Medium."* Charlottesville, VA: Hampton Roads.

Stevenson, I. (1995). Six modern apparitional experiences. *Journal of Scientific Exploration, 9*, 351–366.

Stokes, D. M. (1993). Mind, matter, and death: Cognitive neuroscience and the problem of survival. *Journal of the American Society for Psychical Research, 87*, 41–84.

Stokes, D. M. (1997). Spontaneous psi phenomena. In S. Krippner (Ed.), *Advances in parapsychological research* (vol. 8, pp. 6–87). Jefferson, NC: McFarland.

Sidgwick, H., Sidgwick, E., & Johnson, A. (1894). Report on the census of *hallucinations. Journal of the Society for Psychical Research, 10*, 25–422.

Supko-McMahon, J. D. (1987). *Reported spontaneous psi experience in the funeral industry*. Unpublished doctoral dissertation. San Francisco: Saybrook Graduate School and Research Center.

Taylor, S. E. (1989). *Positive illusions: Creative deceptions and the healthy mind*. New York: Basic Books.

Tillich, P. (1963). *The eternal now: Sermons*. London: SCM Press.

Tompkins, P. (1990). *This tree grows out of hell: Mesoamerica and the search for the magical body*. San Francisco: HarperSanFrancisco.

Trisker, D. J. (1996). *Spirits alive! Confrontations with the spirits of Brazil*. New York: Vantage Press.

Tymn, M. E. (2005, September). Obstacles in communicating exist on both sides of the veil. *ARPR Bulletin*, pp. 8–9.

West, D. J. (1990). A pilot census of hallucinations. *Proceedings of the Society for Psychical Research, 57*, 163–207.

White, R. A. (1995). Exceptional human experiences and the experiential paradigm. *ReVision, 18*(2), 18–25.

White, R. A. (1997). Dissociation, narrative, and exceptional human experiences. In S. Krippner & S. M. Powers (Eds.), *Broken images, broken selves: Dissociative narratives in clinical practice* (pp. 88–121). New York: Brunner/Mazel.

Wilson, C. (1985). *Afterlife: An investigation of the evidence for life after death*. London: Grafton Books.

Wright, S. H. (1998). Experiences of spontaneous psychokinesis after bereavement. *Journal of the Society for Psychical Research, 62*, 385–395.

Wright, S. H. (1999). Paranormal contact with the dying: 14 contemporary Death coincidences. *Journal of the Society for Psychical Research, 63,* 258–267.

Wright, S. H. (2002). *When spirits come calling: The open-minded skeptic's guide to after-death contacts.* Nevada City, CA: Blue Dolphin.

Wright, S. H. (2005, June). Evidence of the after-life from after-death communication. *Abstracts of Presentations, 30th Annual Conference of the Academy of Religion and Psychical Research, Orlando, FL* (pp. 6–7). Bloomfield, CT: Academy of Religion and Psychical Research.

Yamamoto, J., Okonogi, K., Iwakasi, T., & Yoshimura, S. (1969). Mourning in Japan. *American Journal of Psychiatry, 125,* 1660–1665.

Zusne, L. (1985). Magical thinking and parapsychology. In P. Kurtz (Ed.), *A skeptic's handbook of parapsychology* (pp. 685–700). Amherst, NY: Prometheus Books.

10. Birthmarks and Claims of Previous-Life Memories: The Case of Purnima Ekanayake*

ERLENDUR HARALDSSON

This chapter is a reincarnation-type case study. Dr. Erlendur Haraldsson gives in-depth coverage of his investigation of Ms. Purnima Ekanayake, who is claimed to have had a previous life as a Mr. Jinadasa Perera, who died in a road accident in 1995—two years before Ms. Ekanayake's birth. Dr. Haraldsson systematically assesses the accumulated statements made of or by Ms. Ekanayake in order to arrive at the truth status of the past-life claim. It is concluded, with only slight reservations, that the case is of an "unusual quality" that suggests a reincarnation interpretation.—Editors

Overview

Children who speak of memories of a previous life may explain birthmarks as related to wounds inflicted upon them in the former life. In this case a girl claims to have been an incense-maker, and to have died in a traffic accident. After a location had been given, an incense-maker was identified whose life corresponded to many of her statements. He had died in a traffic accident two years prior to her birth, and the post-mortem report revealed that wounds had been inflicted on him in the same area as her birthmarks.

*This chapter was originally published as an article in the Journal for Psychical Research, 2000, vol. 64, pp. 16–25.

Introduction

Birthmarks or birth defects are sometimes important features in cases of children who speak of previous-life memories, or are assumed by their family or community to be a specific personality reborn (Stevenson, 1987). A child may explain birthmarks as resulting from wounds inflicted on it in a previous life. In his recent two-volume work on birthmark and birth defect cases, Stevenson (1997a, 1997b) gives a detailed description of 225 cases. Eleven of them are from Sri Lanka.

In Sri Lanka I have investigated around 60 cases of children who speak about events and persons that have been interpreted as related to a previous life (Haraldsson, 1991; Haraldsson & Samararatne, 1999; Mills, Haraldsson & Keil, 1994). In three instances a child made statements relating birthmarks to a previous life, or talked about accidents and injuries in a previous life which were later found to correspond, or were believed to correspond, to birthmarks on the body of a child. One of them is the case of Purnima Ekanayake that I investigated during five visits to Sri Lanka, from September 1996 to March 1999. This involved the interviewing and re-interviewing of numerous witnesses. (For details of the methodology of such an investigation, see Haraldsson, 1991 and Stevenson, 1987).

The Case

Purnima was nine years old when I first met her in September 1996 at her home in Bakamuna, a small town in the Polunnaruwa district of central Sri Lanka. She was still speaking of her previous life, which is unusual at this age because most children stop doing so around the age of five or six. According to her parents she had been speaking of a previous life since she was three years old. She communicated freely with us, took great interest in our exchanges with her parents and sometimes corrected their statements (I had to use an interpreter although Purnima and her father understood some English). She seemed well adjusted and happy in her family. Her schoolbook contains only A's, and she is at the top of a class of 33. All she said was characterized by great clarity. Purnima is a beautiful and charming girl. Her mother told me that Purnima likes clean and beautiful dresses.

Soon after her birth, Purnima's mother noticed a large cluster of hypopigmented birthmarks to the left of the midline of her chest, and over her lower ribs. Even then it occurred to her mother that they might be associated with injuries in a previous life.

Purnima's Statements Regarding an Alleged Previous Life

Purnima's parents paid little attention when she started to speak of past events in 1990. It was not until early in 1993 that they took some interest in her statements and an attempt was made to check the correctness of her statements.

Regrettably, no record was made of Purnima's statements at that time. Hence it is difficult to reconstruct her original statements, and assess which of her present statements might be moulded by facts that she may have learnt after contact was established with her "previous" family. I have listed in Table 10.1 all 20 statements that, according to her parents, Purnima made before the previous family was traced. These statements were collected during several interviews with her parents spread over three years. Purnima also made these statements to the author and his interpreters.

I died in a traffic accident. The first unusual statement that Purnima repeatedly made as a small child was: "People who drive over people in the street are bad persons." Sometimes she would ask her mother: "Do you not also think that persons who cause accidents are bad people?" These were the first indirect statements referring to a previous life. Purnima also made statements about a fatal accident with a big vehicle (*Zoku uahana* usually means a bus or truck). Her mother thinks that this statement first came about (or she started to pay attention to it) after a traffic accident occurred near their home. Purnima's mother was upset about the accident. Then Purnima tried to soothe her by saying: "Do not think about this accident. I came to you after such an accident." She told her mother how she closed her eyes after the accident and then she came "here." Her mother asked if she had been taken to a hospital. "No," she replied. She added: "A heap of iron was on my body."

Purnima related that after the accident she floated in the air in semi-darkness for a few days. She saw people mourning for her and crying, and saw her body up to and including the funeral. There were many people like her floating around. Then she saw some light, went there and came "here" (to Bakamuna).

My family was making incense (Ambiga and Geta Pichcha) and had no other job. Sometimes Purnima spoke of incense-making and said that she had been making Ambiga and Geta Pichcha incense. Purnima's parents thought that she might be speaking of Ambiga because a jewellery firm of that name was advertising on television. Her mother assumed she was mixing something up. They also thought that she might be speaking of Geta Pichcha as there are "geta pichcha" flowers (a variety of jasmine) in their garden. According to her parents Purnima had also stated that members of her family as well as some

Table 10.1— Statements Made by Purnima (According to her Parents) Before First Contact with Her Alleged Previous Family

	Statement	Rating
1	I died in a traffic accident and came here.	+
2	My family was making incense and had no other job.	+
3	We were making Ambiga incense.	+
4	We were making Geta Pichcha incense.	+
5	The incense factory is near a brick factory and near a pond.	+
6	First only our family worked and then two people were employed.	?
7	We had two vans.	+
8	We had a car.	+
9	I was the best manufacturer of incense sticks.	?
10	In earlier life I was married to a sister-in-law, Kusumi.	+
11	The owner of the incense factory, [I] had two wives.	+
12	My previous father was bad (present father is good).	?
13	Previous father was not a teacher as present father.	+
14	I had two younger brothers (who were better than present brothers).	+
15	My mother's name was Simona.	+
16	Simona was very fair.	–
17	I attended Rahula School.	+
18	Rahula School had a two-storied building (not like in Bakamuna).	–
19	My father said, you need not go to school, you can make money making incense.	–
20	I studied only up to 5th grade.	+

Legend: "+" = verified (sub-total: 14)
"–" = incorrect (subtotal: 3)
"?" = indeterminate (subtotal: 3)

outsiders were working for them making incense sticks. She used to walk around with her hands behind her back imitating how she had examined how they were doing their work. We checked the shops in Bakamuna and found only two brands of incense made in Kandy and one from India, no Ambiga or Geta Pichcha incense.

In earlier life I was married to a sister-in-law, Kusumi. Her parents inferred that she had been a man in her previous life. Further statements will be listed and discussed below.

The Search to Solve the Case

At about the age of four Purnima saw a television programme on the famous Kelaniya temple (close to Colombo and nearly 145 miles away from Bakamuna) and said that she recognized the temple. A little later her father, who is the principal of a secondary school, and her mother, who is also a teacher, took a group of schoolchildren to Kelaniya temple, which is a major place of pilgrimage among Buddhists in Sri Lanka. Purnima had not entered school at this time, but was allowed to join the group. In Kelaniya she said that she had lived on the other side of the Kelaniya River, which flows beside the temple compound.

At one time Purnima's father allowed a friend who is a local reporter to meet Purnima, but she was shy and did not speak to him. The reporter had heard of her talking about incense-making and brought along a pack of incense. She examined it and said she could make better incense than that. More he could not get out of her, he told us.

In January 1993 a recent graduate of Kelaniya University, W. G. Sumanasiri, was appointed a teacher in Bakamuna, and he and the principal became acquainted. Sumanasiri spent his working days in Bakamuna and the weekends in Kelaniya, where he had married. They decided that Sumanasiri would make inquiries across the Kelaniya River. Sumanasiri did not meet Purnima until after his inquiries. According to Sumanasiri the principal gave him four or five items to check:

- She had lived on the other side of the river from Kelaniya temple.
- She had been making Ambiga and Gita Pichcha incense sticks.
- She was selling incense sticks on a bicycle.
- She had a fatal accident with a big vehicle.

The item about selling incense sticks on a bicycle was not mentioned to me by Purnima's parents until after my meeting with Sumanasiri when Purnima's father confirmed Sumanasiri's account of these four items. I have not included it in Table 10.1.

Sumanasiri was accompanied by his brother-in-law, Tony Serasinghe Modalige, who is a native of Kelaniya, and another local person. They parked their car at the temple, and took the hand-driven ferry across the river, as it was some distance to the next bridge. They inquired if there were incense-makers in the area. This area is like a spread-out town, but in between there are fields and village-like clusters of houses. In this area they found three incense-makers, all small family businesses. One of them named his brands Ambiga and Geta Pichcha. The owner was L. A. Wijisiri. His brother-in-law and associate, Jinadasa Perera, had died in an accident with a bus as he was bringing incense to the market on a bicycle in September 1985. This was about two years prior to Purnima's birth. Wijisiri's and Jinadasa's home and factory had been 2.4 miles from the ferry and a 5–10 minute walk from the Kelaniya River.

Sumanasiri's visit to the Wijisiri family was very brief. He informed Purnima's father about his findings. A week or two later Purnima, her parents, Sumanasiri and his brother-in-law made an unannounced visit to the Wijisiri family in Angoda. Before going to Angoda they spent a night at Sumanasiri's home in Kelaniya. There, according to her mother, Purnima whispered in her ear: "This incense dealer [she] had two wives. This is a secret. Don't give them my address. They might trouble me."

Wijisiri's Account of Purnima's First Visit to Angoda

When the group came to Wijisiri's house he was not in, but he arrived a short while later. Wijisiri's two daughters were in the house and Purnima met them first. When Wijisiri came walking towards the house Purnima told those around her: "This is Wijisiri; he is coming; he is my brother-in-law." He heard her say this just as he was entering the house. When Purnima said that she had come to see her brother-in-law and sister, he was puzzled and did not realize that she was talking about a previous life. Wijisiri wanted to send them away, saying that those they were asking for were not here. Then, when he thought about it and the little girl started to ask about various kinds of packets and such things, only then was he inclined to believe her story. She alone spoke; no one else said anything. This is how Wijisiri remembered her visit. This account was confirmed by Purnima's father.

Purnima said to Wijisiri that she used to sell these incense sticks. She asked: "Have you changed the outer cover of the packets?" Wijisiri used to change the colour and design every two years or so. She seemed to realize that the packets looked different from the time Jinadasa was working with Wijisiri. Then she talked about the various packets, and about an accident Wijisiri had many years ago (since that time he has been unable to bend his knee). Also that Jinadasa [she] had applied medicine to his knee after the accident. She asked about Jinadasa's friends, such as Somasiri and Padmasiri. Padmasiri is Wijisiri's brother and had gone with him on business on the day Jinadasa met with his accident. They had left home together and had then split up and gone to different places. She mentioned their names. These were the things that convinced Wijisiri.

Purnima also asked about her mother and her (Jinadasa's) previous sister, who is Wijisiri's wife. The sister was abroad working in Saudi Arabia, and the mother was away at her ancestral home. Purnima expressed concern when she learnt that the mother had gone alone to a distant place. Wijisiri's family was still confused. Then Purnima showed her birthmark. She said: "This is the mark I received when I was hit by a bus." Purnima also mentioned the place of Jinadasa's accident, Nugegoda, which is near Angoda, and said that they had moved their home and factory to a different location within Angoda from the time she was with them, which was correct.

From Wijisiri's family we learnt that Jinadasa had in fact had two wives. After several years of living together he had disagreements with his first wife (Wijisiri's sister). He went to south Sri Lanka to sell incense sticks, became acquainted with a lady by the name of Nanda, and left his former family. In the town of Weligama he lived for five years with Nanda and produced incense with a friend, M. Somasiri, who gave us valuable information. (Jinadasa legally married neither of his "wives." According to Sinhalese tradition a man and woman who live together are referred to as husband and wife.) During a visit to Colombo, Jinadasa learnt of Wijisiri's accident, which left him bed-ridden for several months. He then went to Angoda to help. A few days later he met with his accident.

Did Purnima say anything that was incorrect and that did not fit Jinadasa's life? She had said that two vans and a car had belonged to her (Jinadasa). This was a family business so in a way this was correct but formally the vehicles had belonged to Wijisiri. This is the essence of Wijisiri's account of his first meeting with Purnima.

We had been told that Purnima had recognized an old co-worker, Somasiri. He told us that he had come to see her at her first visit. He stood there among a group of people. Then she pointed to him and said: "This is my friend." When Purnima's father asked who that man was, she answered: "This is Somasiri, my friend." Apparently she also recognized Jinadasa's younger sister, G. Violet. She and Somasiri told us that she had pointed to her and said: "This is my younger sister." These were the only names that Somasiri and Violet heard her say during the first visit.

Purnima's Knowledge of Incense-Making

It occurred to us to ask Purnima if she knew how incense is made. Yes, she said and gave us a detailed reply. There are two ways to make it. One uses cow dung, the other is from ash from firewood (charcoal). A paste is made, and then a thin stick is cut from bamboo and some gum is applied to the bamboo stick. Then the stick is rolled over the paste and then something is applied to obtain a nice smell. As far as she can remember they made their incense from charcoal powder. What is charcoal made from and how is it produced? "When firewood is burnt you get charcoal."

We asked Purnima's parents if they knew how incense was made. The father had heard that it was made from cow-dung, but this was the first time he had heard that it could be made from firewood. Her mother knew even less. Godwin, my interpreter, had never heard how incense was made. We later asked Wijisiri to describe to us and show us how they make their incense. Wijisiri did it the way that Purnima had described.

Further Verification of Purnima's Statements

Of the 20 statements listed in Table 10.1, 14 fit the life of Jinadasa (1-5, 7, 8, 10, 11, 13–15, 17, 20), three are indeterminate (6, 9, 12) and three statements (16, 18, 19) are incorrect.

Let us first consider the incorrect items. Jinadasa had attended Rahula School, as we learnt independently from his mother and younger sister. However, our inquiries revealed that this school did not have a two-storied building until the 1980s. It is correct according to his family that Jinadasa attended school only up to 5th grade. However, he was doing odd jobs for a few years until his sister married Wijisiri. Then he took up incense-making, and two years later "married" Wijisiri's sister. Hence the statement that Jinadasa's father had told him to leave school to earn money by making incense cannot be true. The statement that Jinadasa's mother was very fair is not true now, and it seems unlikely that she was earlier.

Some of the correct items have already been described. Regarding item 5: there is a pond within 200 yards of Jinadasa's old residence. The old factory, 21 which was some 100–150 yards down the road, had been demolished and close to it, a neighbor told us, there had been a kiln (brick-making facility), and another kiln is still close by. Item 13: Jinadasa's father had been a poor farmer (hence not a teacher). Item 14: Jinadasa had indeed had two younger brothers (and two sisters).

The indeterminate items: Items 9 and 12 (best maker of incense sticks, and his father was a bad man) we had no way to check. Item 6: first our family worked, then two people were employed. This was primarily a family business but soon they employed people who worked in the factory or in their homes. We could not ascertain when exactly they started to employ people, but gradually up to 30 persons came to work for them in the time of Jinadasa, who was an industrious and popular man.

Most specific are items 3 and 4, stating that the family was making the brands Ambiga and Geta Pichcha. According to Wijisiri this is correct and they showed us packages of both brands. Since the time of Jinadasa the family has started to make two additional brands.

After the two families met, Purnima made some interesting intimate statements about his life with his first wife that she could hardly have learnt from anyone. Unfortunately we saw no way of verifying them.

Purnima's Birthmarks

We have already mentioned that Purnima was born with prominent birthmarks on her lower chest, left of the midline (see Figure 10.1). Her mother noticed them when she was bathing Purnima as baby. Then in a light-hearted way she said to her husband that these marks might be the result of an accident in a previous life. However, it was only when they met Jinadasa's family that the birthmarks became significant. Prior to the contact with that family, Purnima never spoke about details of her injuries nor do her parents remember her associating her birthmarks with her accident. It was not until Purnima's visit to Angoda that she said that the bus's tyres had run over her chest, and pointed across the left side of her chest where she has her birthmarks. Someone in Wijisiri's family then mentioned that Jinadasa had been injured on the left side of his trunk. Purnima's birthmarks were at the same location. Then the case was considered confirmed by both families.

Jinadasa died immediately of the accident. His brother Chandradasa and his sister were called into the mortuary to identify his brother. Chandradasa told us he saw massive injuries from the lower ribs on the left side and up and obliquely across the body, caused by the wheel of the bus as it ran over Jinadasa's body. Later, Sitriyavati, his sister, identified Jinadasa from his face. His body had by then been covered by a sheet.

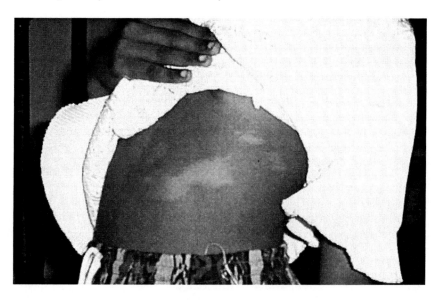

None of the persons involved in this case had seen the post-mortem report. After obtaining permission from the Magistrates' Court of Gangodavilla, which handled Jinadasa's case, we obtained the post- mortem report from the physician, Dr Kariyawasam, who conducted the examination. It gives a detailed description and a sketch of the injuries. They had been massive, particularly on the left side of the chest, where several ribs had been broken. The post-mortem report thus describes the internal injuries:

1. Fracture of the ribs, 1 and 2, 8, 9, and 10, laterally on the left. 1 to 5 anteriorly and 6 anteriorly and laterally, and 7 laterally. 8 and 9 anteriorly and posteriorly, 10 and 11 anteriorly.
2. The liver was ruptured.
3. The spleen was ruptured.
4. Lungs were penetrated by broken ribs.

Externally there was a "grazed abrasion 23" × 10" (58.4 cm x 25.4 cm) running obliquely from the right shoulder across the chest to the (left) lower abdomen." There were lesser injuries on the legs and face.

The chronology of the Purnima case is given in Table 10.2.

Table 10.2 — Chronology of the Case of Purnima Ekanayake	
Date	*Statement*
4 April 1949	Jinadasa Perera is born.
9 April 1985	Jinadasa dies in bus accident in Nugegoda.
24 August 1987	Purnima Ekanayake is born in Bakamuna.
1990	Purnima starts speaking of a previous life at the age of 2 to 3 years.
March 1993	Sumanasiri makes inquiries in Kelaniya/Angoda and meets the family of Jinadasa.
April 1993	Purnima's first visit to Jinadasa's family. Her birthmarks correspond to J's injuries. She is accepted as Jinadasa reborn.
29 August 1993	Article on the case appears in the newspaper Diuaina.
September 1996	EH's first investigation of the case.

Discussion

First, let me summarize the strong points of this case. The locations of the two families are far apart, and the two families were complete strangers. A third party succeeded in finding the person that matched Purnima's statements. Fourteen of seventeen statements that could be checked were found to match the life of Jinadasa, who had died two years before Purnima was born. Purnima's cluster of birthmarks was found to fall within an area of fatal injuries suffered by Jinadasa. Her birthmarks are on the left side of the chest, where most of the ribs broke, and where he is likely to have felt most pain. Also, there is some evidence of knowledge of incense-making that is highly unusual for a child, and which Purnima explains as stemming from her previous life.

This is a good example of a case with different characteristics that fall into a pattern and must be viewed as a whole: memories, birthmarks and, perhaps, how-to-do knowledge. Overall, one can state that the case of Purnima Ekanayake is of unusual quality.

The principal weakness of the case is the fact that no record was made of Purnima's statements before the case was "solved," which occurred three years before the author started his investigation.

This case has some features that are uncommon among Sri Lankan cases. Purnima speaks of memories of a life between death and birth that the author has found only in the case of Duminda Ratnayake (Haraldsson, 1991; Haraldsson & Samararatne, 1999). Purnima's memories have lasted much longer than they generally do. Purnima still spoke freely of her previous life at the age of ten. Purnima's case also has some more common or typical features. Purnima started to speak of her memories at a very early age, and spoke persistently about them. One aspect of her memories was reflected in her play.

Finally, Purnima displays prominently some characteristics that my formal psychological studies have shown to distinguish children speaking of previous life memories from ordinary children (Haraldsson, 1997; Haraldsson, Fowler & Mahendra, submitted). She is highly gifted, has excellent vocabulary and memory, shows some tendency for dissociation, and is less suggestible than most children. She is a demanding child for her parents, is argumentative and independent-minded, wants to be perfect, is much concerned with neatness and cleanliness, and at times is hot-tempered and boastful; in short a vivid and memorable personality.

In a journal article, I hope to present a second birthmark case, that of Chatura Karunaratne. It does not have the principal weakness of this case, as Chatura's statements were recorded by three independent witnesses before a matching previous personality was found. The reader will certainly ask, "Can the facts of these cases be seen as evidence of genuine memories of a previous life?" In the forthcoming article, I will attempt to express my thoughts on that difficult question.

Acknowledgments

I am grateful to the Institut fur Grenzgebiete der Psychologie und Psychohygiene in Freiburg, Germany, which funded most of this research.

Particular thanks go to my interpreters and associates in Sri Lanka, A. B. Ratnayake, Godwin Samararatne and B. A. Rohana Kumara, and to Dawn E. Hunt for thoughtful comments on an earlier version of this manuscript.

References

Haraldsson, E. (1991). Children claiming past-life memories: four cases in Sri Lanka. *Journal of Scientific Exploration* 5, 233–261.

Haraldsson, E. (1997). A psychological comparison between ordinary children and those who claim previous-life memories. *Journal of Scientific Exploration* 1(1), 323–335.

Haraldsson, E., & Samararatne, G. (1999). Children who speak of memories of a previous life as a Buddhist monk: three new cases. *Journal of the Society for Psychical Research*, *63*, 268–291.

Haraldsson, E., Fowler, P., & Mahendra, V. (submitted) Personality characteristics and mental abilities of children claiming previous-life memories: the role of dissociation.

Mills, A., Haraldsson, E., & Keil, J. (1994). Replication studies of cases suggestive of reincarnation by three different investigators. *Journal of the American Society for Psychical Research*, *88*, 207–219.

Stevenson, I. (1987). *Children Who Remember Previous Lives*. Charlottesville: University Press of Virginia.

Stevenson, I. (1997a). *Reincarnation and biology: A contribution to the etiology of birthmarks and birth defects (2 volumes)*. Westport, Connecticut: Praeger.

Stevenson, I. (1997b). *Where reincarnation and biology intersect*. Westport, Connecticut: Praeger.

Section IV: Sociological and Phenomenological Issues

11. What the Channeled Material of Suicides Tells Us About the Afterlife

PAMELA RAE HEATH WITH JON KLIMO

In this chapter, Dr. Pamela Heath and John Klimo present alleged reports of afterlife experiences from suicide victims. The authors do not regard these reports as proof that an afterlife exists. Nevertheless, what is present in such reports is a consistency of phenomenology that speaks to the commonality of humankind's underlying psychology and the "realities" we construct.—Editors

Experiential research can be challenging when your participants are dead. However, if one believes in the possibility of mediumistic channeling, then it is not impossible. Thus, the authors embarked on a recent scholarly examination of several hundred books and magazines published over a period of more than two hundred and fifty years, which contained channeled messages and information said to be from human spirits who have survived physical death and are now existing in a kind of trans-physical afterlife plane of existence. By finding consistent themes across different eras and mediums, it was possible to develop a perspective on what may happen after we die.

Such research is not without its pitfalls. Whenever one uses channeled material one runs into the question of whether such material has been biased or distorted, whether from the source, the inherent process of communication, or the recipient. Such distortions may be deliberate (if the communicating spirit feels an idea is too radical to be accepted by the medium) or inadvertent (if the medium's issues or beliefs get in the way, causing them to place their own spin on what they get). There are other things that can muddy the water. Channeled messages say that the medium's vocabulary and degree of understanding can also limit what is communicated (Austen, 1978). Furthermore, there may be issues related to how much the spirit itself may know, since what beings the channel can connect with may be a function of both the medium's talent and of his or her personality and level of spiritual development.

There are two ways one can try to address these problems. One gets the information from more than one source, and preferably even from different eras and, if possible, cultures. The greater the variety of sources the material is drawn from, the better the chance that the resulting common ground is meaningful. The second method is to supplement and corroborate the channeled information by other forms of data, such as instrumental transcommunication (including electronic voice phenomena or EVPs), out-of-body experiences (OBEs), near-death experiences (NDEs), past life and reincarnation reports, clairvoyance and remote viewing, dreams, lucid dreams, and other altered states of consciousness (ASCs). Although one cannot rule out the possibility that people are copying each other, the resulting consensus within channeled material and across different modalities suggests an impressive degree of commonality of characteristics.

It should be noted that this kind of research takes an experiential approach, as opposed to being proof-oriented. As such, this method considers that, irrespective of the "true" source of the material (of which the truth can never be known), what happens after a person's death can be revealed by using a preponderance of similarities between descriptions and cross-corroboration of the data. Furthermore, where cutting edge topics are involved, such as suicide bombers, people with reputed mediumistic abilities can be engaged to supplement the existing written material.

Suicide is a growing problem in our society, and the experience of these individuals in the afterlife would seem to be of valid concern. There is a surprising wealth of channeled information on this topic — not only from spirits claiming to have committed the act, but also from so-called "spirit guides," deceased friends and family, and impartial discarnate observers. Furthermore, it is possible to compare and contrast the apparent experiences of those who have committed different types of suicides. Thus, we can see whether those who had an otherwise healthy body and took only their own lives, those who were terminally ill and took their life (perhaps with help), and those who deliberately took the lives of others at the same time as their own. This allows us to see how the circumstances surrounding a suicide may influence the purported outcome of that act. The result gives us an interesting perspective on the afterlife.

So, what does the channeled material suggest? The afterlife experience is often spoken of as involving four stages, including: (1) the transition period; (2) a recovery phase; (3) life-review and self-judgment; and (4) spiritual work. Although suicides appear to go through the same stages as those that died through other means, there appear to be some differences, particularly in the smoothness of their transitions or the length of their other stages. It is impossible to say how much this may be due to general factors that may be associated with taking one's own life, such as depression, alcohol, and drugs. Let us look at what suicides may be said to experience in each of these four stages, and what particular pitfalls they may encounter.

The Transition

The transition phase begins as soon as the soul leaves the body. It involves a period of adjustment to the afterlife, including switching from relying on the physical sensory organs to that of consciousness or the subtle energy body. This phase seemed to vary considerably in length and difficulty from one suicide to the next, with some (especially in older channeled material) appearing to be deaf and blind to others in the spirit realm.

One of the commonest initial reactions to death reported by suicides is confusion, which often leads to intense frustration (Mateu 1999; Puryear 1993; Van Praagh 1999). They simply do not understand they have been successful because they still "feel" alive. For example, James Van Praagh (1999) said of a young man who had hung himself, "He can't believe he is dead because he feels so alive. He thinks he screwed something up and is trying very hard to get back into his body through his head. He can't do it, and he is getting very frustrated. He begins to cry!" (p. 170).

There may also be a certain amount of discomfort if they are still emotionally attached to their bodies. Even though they no longer have a body, as they watch what happens to the physical shell left behind, they may feel as if it was happening to them. Kardec (2002) wrote, "One who had committed suicide said to us, 'No, I am not dead,' and added, *'and yet I feel the worms that are devouring my body'*" (p. 159). The length of time that mediums say it takes for the soul to fully separate from the body can be anywhere from hours to days. Perhaps because of this, some sources recommend waiting at least three days before performing cremation.

Most channeled literature agrees that suicides spend at least some time in a dim or misty realm that is often referred to as the "lower astral." This is said to be the plane of existence with the lowest non-physical vibratory frequency. Because of this it is said to be "closest" to that of physical existence on Earth.

Guides are said to try to welcome the newly dead, explain the situation, and try to help them to move to higher levels of existence, where there is more "light." Often these greeters are friends or family that had crossed over before the one being met. Sometimes these may take the form of animals, if those being greeted could have reason to distrust those in human form. Stephen, who killed himself at age fifteen, reported:

> What happens to the suicide is not much different from what happens to someone who dies of old age or in an accident. Your guides and angels are with you at the moment of death.... Your helpers move you to another place and you are met by friends and loved ones who have preceded you — a kind of welcoming party [Puryear, 1993, p. 240].

A number of things can cause problems early on in a soul's transition. Perhaps foremost among these is the suggestion in the literature that suicides and others who die a sudden and violent death may have trouble being able to recognize their greeters. Dresser (1927), Wickland (1974) and others described a number of séances where the dead appeared to be lost in a dark region, unable to see or hear any others around them until their attention was brought to the fact that other spirits were there trying to contact them. Some authors attributed this to the newly dead being mentally fixed on the physical plane, while others felt the problem was due to inadequate development of the astral body's sensory organs. Yet another factor may be a form of coma that suicides are said to experience after their transition. Such spirits may be oblivious to the guides watching over them, waiting for them to awaken so they can try to make contact. Lawrence of Arabia, as channeled by Sherwood (1991), wrote from the afterlife of his experience involving a friend who had committed suicide:

> He was in a kind of stupor and I was told that he might remain in this state for a long time and that nothing could be done about it. We watched over him and were loath to leave him in the misty half-region where he was found.... Suicides often show this long-lasting coma.... I made one such visit and found that he had gone. Knowing the agony of loneliness and "lostness" one can suffer in this region of looming shadows I went immediately in search of him.... I hailed him and he let me come up but it was hard to make him see or hear me. In fact, his body was so ill-developed that his new senses were as yet of little use to him. By some means I got him to come with me and led him into a slightly better region and here he sank down and rested again.... So he sunk again into sleep [pp. 111–112].

Another problem that, fortunately, appears to be mentioned less often in the literature, is one of suicides being stuck because the living are unable to let go of their grief for the individual who died (Barbanell, 1964; Buckley, 1986). Such cases most often involved children and famous celebrities. As medium Chris Fleming noted, "The energy sent out to icons and celebrities can be incredibly strong when it is being done by a lot of people at the same time. It's like a chain that keeps the spirits shackled to our plane. They can't cross over unless we all release them" (C. Fleming, personal communication, July 24, 2005).

Difficulties may also arise if a soul is caught by their physical addictions (Loehr, 1986; Meek, 1980). Even though they no longer have a body, the psychological craving for drugs or alcohol can remain, causing Earth-bound souls to seek out living addicts who will enable them to continue to vicariously continue their habits. George Meek (1980), who obtained much of his information through instrumental transcommunication, wrote:

> A person addicted to hard drugs is in the deepest possible trouble. He will be resistant to any offer of help and will persist in his craving. He will experience torments which equal anything pictured in the old ideas of hell. He may remain in this dreadful condition for what would be centuries of earth time [p. 134].

There appears to be some variation in how the different types of suicide experience this first stage. Traditional suicides frequently appear to be steeped in regret when they cross over. They seem to have more trouble being aware of guides sent to help them and are more prone to spend time in the lower astral. This may relate to left-over psychological baggage — one thing you apparently do take with you into death. Arthur Ford (1974) discussed the issue a number of times, both while alive, acting as an author or medium, and after he died, when he was purportedly channeled by others. He observed that the problems suicides face in the afterlife may relate more to their state of mind than for any moralistic reason, noting:

> The extreme negative, depressed mental state of the suicide at the time of his self-destructive act carries over into the afterlife, placing him at a great disadvantage in making his adjustment. Many times, upon awakening, he does not realise that he has passed over. He may go into an extreme panic upon discovering that he can no longer control his physical body [Ford, 1974, p. 112].

Ford (1974) went on to explain:

> "The mood that drives the suicide to self-slaughter," Meyers wrote through Miss Cummins, "will envelop him like a cloud from which we may not for a long time be able to give him release. His emotional thoughts, his whole attitude of mind sets up a barrier which can only be broken down by his own strenuous efforts, by a brave control of himself, and above all by the call sent out with all strength of his soul to higher beings to bestow succor, to grant release" [pp. 112–113].

The spirit, Acharya, described the problem somewhat differently:

> Because the man suffers so much remorse and because he would give anything
> to get back into his physical body, even though it would mean facing up to
> the consequences, he often refuses to make the effort of will necessary for him
> to get rid of his etheric vehicle ... thus he may remain "earthbound" through
> ignorance, being unable to function properly either in the physical or the
> astral world, feeling the extreme loneliness that exists under these circum-
> stances [Richelieu, 1985, p. 143].

Assisted suicide souls, by contrast, seemed to have few regrets for their
actions (Newton, 1999). Occasionally, there was a mention of lessons cut
short, or time that would need to be made up later, but most seemed to be
at peace with what they had done. Nor did assisted suicides tend to speak of
prolonged or difficult transitions.

There is relatively little available material on the channeled messages of
suicide bombers to draw from. Because of this, any conclusions must be drawn
with caution. Nonetheless, they would appear to go through similar stages in
the afterlife as traditional suicides do. They may not realize they are dead until
greeted by helpers.

> They are confused and annoyed right now.... They expected to be with God.
> They *are* with God. But it's not what they expected.... We allow them to see
> what they would like to see, but the message that comes through is the thing
> that we are showing them. It's not what they expected. And what they need to
> hear is not what they wanted to hear. So, it will be valuable for them [Heath
> & Klimo, 2006].

It should be noted here that allowing souls to initially see the things they were
expecting to find is a common way to make contact. Not only is it used for
suicide bombers, but in any situation where the newly dead have rigid or fun-
damentalist views (Montgomery 1971). Once this connection is made and the
soul had a bit of time to adjust, the guides are then able to start correcting
their charges, to help them understand their true situation.

Some suicide bomber souls appeared to be stuck in a grey or misty zone,
while others made their transitions more readily, greeted by spirits appearing
to them as Holy men or virgins. One medium mentioned that the World Trade
Center attack provided a rather unique transition, not only because of the
numbers that died, but also because of the fact that the perpetrators and victims had such different worldviews. Shaw channeled this message from spirit
guides about those that died September 11, 2001:

> The loss of life from a different place on the Earth and a different perspective
> of those souls had an impact they didn't anticipate when they crossed over....
> It was as if they were all meshed together in a soup, and it didn't seem familiar
> at all.... It was *not* what they anticipated. They felt desperate, as if they were

drowning.... It was a fusion. The same procedure could happen in any explosion. The difference is the soul information and perception of Americans, as opposed to their own countrymen.... It forced them into seeing and feeling something that was different.... It lent them the opportunity for rapid growth because they were thrust into a belief pattern that is almost the reverse of theirs [Heath & Klimo, 2006].

We have seen here that the transition phase can vary considerably between types of suicides. Some appear to be able to see helper spirits immediately, while others wander lost, unable to sense those around them. Assisted suicides as a rule appeared to make smoother transitions than traditional suicides or suicide bombers. Frustration can be a frequent element of the experience, especially as souls struggle to understand that their body is dead, but they are not. Regardless, spirit guides appear to work very hard to help these souls out of their state in the lower astral, and to get them to advance to the next state — that of recovery and healing.

The Recovery Phase

Most modern channelers agree that suicides are not condemned to the lower levels, but are capable of moving forward. Furthermore, it seems clear that they receive spiritual help to do so. All types of suicides (and many who have simply suffered long drawn-out illnesses) seemed to go through a distinct recovery phase. This frequently appeared to involve long periods of sleep. However, it sometimes also involved the use of animal spirits, energy, and peaceful settings that were often referred to as healing centers, where the souls could rest and recover. The spirit of Stephen remembered this experience of recovering in such a healing center (Puryear 1993). His vision was blurred at first, but then formed a sight both comforting and familiar to him. What was interesting here was the use of sleep whenever he remembered something upsetting or stressful. Stephen said:

> I looked around and there was kind of a misty look everywhere, then it got clearer.... I had some vague thought come to me that I had seen somebody hanging on a tree, and I fell back asleep.... I kept waking up and getting afraid and then very gently going back to sleep. Someone came and sat by me. I could hear them talking to me, then I'd go back to sleep. I didn't really want to hear what they were saying [Puryear, 1993, pp. 255–256].

Medium George Anderson also commented on these healing centers and mentioned the use of animals as a form of treatment:

> When souls arrive in the hereafter after having taken their lives, they are immediately taken to a "hospital of reflection." ... It is a place with serene

beauty filled with fields and grass. The only beings there are small creatures, like rabbits and fawns, kittens and puppies. Animals are greatly known both here and hereafter for their ability to heal and their unconditional love. They are used as a kind of therapy for the souls there [Anderson & Barone, 1999, p. 101].

Guides sometimes speak of instilling energy directly as a means of healing their charges. Trio, a group of three spirit guides channeled by Nevada Shaw that claimed to specialize in greeting the souls of terrorists, stated that they would place energy into the essence of souls as a form of healing. They described the energy as follows: "It's like a sound and they feel it in their bodies. It goes down from the top of the body down what you would call the spinal column. It vibrates the body. They may or may not be aware of it" (Heath & Klimo, 2006).

Healing through the installation of energy also appeared to be used in other types of souls. For example, Newton (1999) stated, "Those souls who have developed severe obstacles to improvement are mended by the restoration of positive energy" (p. 59).

Sometimes during the recovery phase, souls were said to have attended their funerals. However, this was by no means universal. Instead, it appeared to be a matter of choice, depending on whether they wanted to go and whether they felt it would be helpful to their recovery. Some spirits worried that going to their funeral would suck them back into old habit patterns and ways of thought, but others spoke of how it could be a healing experience.

The Life-Review and Self-Judgment

After the soul has had some time to recover, they are given the chance to begin their life review and self-judgment. These appear to be tightly integrated together. This is the most consistent and universal stage described, regardless of the culture or era. From Ancient Egyptian writings and the Islamic Book of the Dead to modern channelers, all state that souls must go through this phase before they will be allowed to continue on to a "higher" plane of existence or the opportunity to reincarnate.

A few mediums spoke of this phase beginning as an experience of the soul's life flashing before its eyes, such as one spirit described to Mateu (1999) below:

When I first died, I felt I wasn't dead. No way I could be dead with all the vivid images and pictures of those I loved racing before me in a sudden burst of memory.... Every feeling, thought, and experience I had ever felt in my entire life, I saw in one fell swoop ... a flash of light before my eyes. It was an awesome display of the love I had shared and the people I had touched ... and the pain I had caused [pp. 25–26].

More often, the life-review appeared to be a slow and painstaking process. Souls spoke of having to repeatedly review every aspect of their entire life in order to reach increasingly deeper levels of meaning and understanding. The spirit of Stephen told Puryear that the life-review was too overwhelming to be done all at once (Puryear, 1993). Instead, it is done in stages, considering what was done right and what was not. Furthermore, this phase can be charged with emotion for the spirit:

> At first, it's very emotional because you see all the people you have interacted with, helped, hurt, and forgotten.... What you see about yourself, how you fell short, and what golden opportunities you failed to use, is heartbreaking. You feel such shame, other times anger. Later, there is a little more detachment [Puryear, 1993, p. 236].

As mentioned before, the life review seems to go hand-in-hand with self-judgment. Mateu (1999) channeled another suicide, Alexy, who pointed out that this can be severe. In their own minds they have broken faith by committing suicide. Seeing and feeling the consequences of their actions, and how they affected others, is punishment by itself. Everything is experienced from the viewpoint of others. In this way, a soul comes to truly understand what it was like for those who were harmed by what they had done.

A number of spirits, including Stephen, emphasized that judgment is neither external nor does it always conform to one's prior expectations (Puryear, 1999). Every soul has to judge itself it. This is not to say that souls get off lightly. Instead, as Stephen noted such souls tend to judge themselves quite harshly at first. It is only with time and growing compassion towards themselves that they begin to take a more balanced, and less condemning approach. This process appears to be supervised by guides that are responsible for making sure that the task is performed correctly and completely.

It is an important point that souls do not (or in a few cases are not allowed to) judge themselves using the same belief system as they held while alive. Although intent may be taken into account, if souls have harmed others, even if they believed while alive that they were "right" to do so, then they will be held accountable. There is no get out of jail free card.

Suicide bombers may have a particularly difficult task because like all who die, they have to experience how their actions impacted every other individual whom their actions had touched — not only the usual friends and family, but also those they killed *and the lives of everyone who knew the victims or was in any way emotionally impacted by the act.* They need not go through their victims' entire lives — just that which was cut short, including all the impact that resulted on others. Needless to say, this could be an exhausting process.

In addition to the sheer numbers of lives involved in mass-murder suicide, terrorist souls may have trouble with their life-review for other reasons. First, they have to contend with the often hostile emotions of those left behind, *which they can feel.* The inaccuracy of their expectations can be a second problem, as it can make it harder for souls to adjust to the afterlife. Third, people that live lives full of hatred can have trouble figuring out how to operate in a level of existence that operates based on love. Finally, since one's personality remains unchanged after death, those spirits that were stubborn or belligerent in life may struggle at getting through their life-reviews in a manner that is satisfactory to the guides responsible for supervising the process. This is especially true if they are holding onto deep-seated patterns of lies — which appears to be the case for most suicide bombers. One guide told a medium, "They're saying on an individual level there is a review and even in the review there is an energy of an argumentative discourse, which I think is really interesting. Well, I guess they take that with them" (Heath & Klimo, 2006). Thus, not only the act itself can have repercussions, but also the willingness of the soul to be open-minded and consider other ways of thinking.

Even for an ordinary suicide, there can be a tremendous amount of information for the soul to have to work through and digest. Medium Lauren Thibodeau explained what one such spirit told her:

> It's as if everything that people respond to about his death has to be felt by him. Meaning, he has to take it on a spiritual level and then somehow release. Take it on. Sit with it. Address it. Heal it. And release it. Four steps there. He has to do all that for the anger from everybody. And the judgment of all the people who read accounts like this in the paper [Heath & Klimo, 2006].

It should be noted that the life review and self-judgment phase does not appear to be a matter of choice. It is a mandatory stage that all souls must work through before they are allowed to advance any further. Nor can this period be shortened in any way. However, it may at times overlap with the next stage, that of picking out and performing some form of spiritual work.

Spiritual Work

After their transition, life-review, and self-judgment, many souls of suicides appear to take on some form of self-chosen work. Often, these tasks seem to be considered not only as penance for their act, but also as a way of growing spiritually and preparing for their next incarnation. Unlike the other phases, which appeared to be relatively consistent from one era to the next, this state appeared to show more cultural influence. Although there were a few exceptions, most of the older channeled material stated that reincarnation did not occur and spirits remained at whatever level they were at when they first arrived in the afterlife (Swedenborg, 1984). Swedenborg stated in the 1700s that, "*To eternity, a person stays the way he is*" (Swedenborg, 1984, p. 383). Thus, to this way of thinking, the fourth stage did not exist. Souls were stuck.

This attitude softened in the channeled material of the 1800's as the notions of a loving God and spiritual growth gradually gained acceptance amongst Spiritualist mediums. Cahagnet (1851) wrote:

> "What is the punishment that God reserves for suicide?" "That which he inflicts on all those who do evil, a public reprimand; after that, God renders it impossible for them to do evil, by consigning them to a place apart.... There is no such hell as is depicted on earth; there are places of purification, which are termed places of punishment, because one is there deprived of the sight of God and his divine light; but those who are there are happy" [vol. 1, p. 55].

Contemporary literature addresses the issue of spiritual advancement with considerable optimism, although they note that a soul that has taken its own life may face two problems — completing what should have been his or her expected life-span and the potential increased difficulty of making spiritual progress. While the former issue would always solve itself with time, the latter sometimes seemed to make souls feel they needed to perform a form of self-imposed penance or therapeutic assignment.

Such jobs appear to be entirely a matter of choice; each soul picking out for itself what it feels will be the most helpful for its own development. Often, these souls choose to become greeters, responsible for meeting other newly arrived suicides in the afterlife (Puryear 1993; Wickland 1974). As Anderson put it, "It's like in Alcoholics Anonymous, getting help from somebody who's been through it before" (Anderson & Barone, 1999, p. 129). This appeared to be true not only for traditional suicides, but suicide bombers as well. In addition to missionary work helping others who have committed suicides, these souls will sometimes choose to act as guardian angels for the living. In these cases, they tended to assist loved ones left behind or others at risk for killing themselves. To some extent, this appeared to be the role Stephen played (Puryear, 1993). George Anderson has also mentioned it (Anderson & Barone, 1999).

A number of suicides spoke of the need to reincarnate again. This can be seen as a way of balancing out their previous mistake. On occasion, souls even expressed the idea that they had to factor in other issues, such as a break in the family contract. Johanna Carroll explained:

> You know, we have these sacred contacts as individuals and then collectively, based on past life or whatever the intention of the reincarnation is. I mean, we're all part of a whole. And so, we have the family karma contract that

collectively we all agree to do our part. The suicide creates what's called a tear in the contract. So that part of it, as the collective energy, needs to be healed. Generally what I found is that suicides really do take ... responsibility for that. And as a result, they realize the importance of the family karma contract, that they do need to come back to heal that in another timeline [Heath & Klimo, 2006].

Recent channeled material reflects greater acceptance of reincarnation, and may speak frankly of the souls of suicides using their time in the after-life to prepare for future incarnations. The spirit Hiram explained that most of the spiritual therapy in the afterlife is oriented towards one goal — "getting ready to return again to earth life.... I know that I must return, and I do not mind that. In fact, I welcome it" (Foster 1988, 134).

Only one terrorist spirit claimed to have finished its life review and began working with the souls of those that died through similar means. It is unclear whether this was accurate, since a different medium channeled the message that none of the suicide bomber souls had reached an advanced stage in the afterlife. Because of the small sample size of data, it is difficult to draw any firm conclusions regarding whether these souls have a slower transition and life-review/self-judgment stage, although it seems likely. Nonetheless, once through the life review stage, it would appear that they take on spiritual work in the same manner as do other souls.

Summary

In general, the channeled material of suicides seems to show that, like souls that pass on through other means, they go through the usual transition, recovery, life-review/self-judgment, and spiritual work stages. Where they may differ from other souls, is in a possible prolongation of any or all of these stages, some of which may relate to the suddenness of their deaths or other factors that contributed to their suicide in the first place. The life-review can be particularly problematic if the soul is unwilling to let go of old belief patterns or a lot of people were affected by what happened — such as when suicide is combined with mass murder.

When we look at how the three types of suicide (traditional suicide, assisted suicide, and suicide bombers) compare, we see that there do seem to be differences among them. Assisted suicides may need to spend more time in afterlife healing centers, to recover from their "illness," but appear to have few, if any, regrets and do not seem to become particularly stuck in the lower astral planes. In this sense, their transitions often appear the smoothest of the three groups.

Once the soul of a suicide has finished its transition and has left the lower astral, it may continue to have difficulties during the life-review stage because of the manner of its death. This may be particularly true for suicide bombers, whose lives have touched so many others in negative ways. Also, because people's personalities and feelings are carried over after death, the spirits of suicide bombers, which were described as argumentative, may have a more difficult time letting go of their individual "stories" and seeing their lives from a more spiritual perspective. It should be noted that the life review is not limited to a single pass. Instead, experiences are re-considered and re-evaluated as many times as necessary until it is felt that every possible bit of learning has been wrung from it.

Once the life-review and self-judgment phase was over, suicides often seemed to take on the roles of being helpers to others who want to commit suicide or greeters to those that succeed in taking their own lives. Occasionally, there was talk of how they will have to make up for their suicide during their next life. This was particularly true for those who took their own lives while in a healthy body. Only one suicide bomber soul claimed to have reached this stage. It is unclear whether this was entirely due to the life-review taking so much longer, as was stated by some spirits, or could have been complicated by the smaller sample size. It was difficult to find much channeled material on suicide bomber experiences in the afterlife, since this is a relatively recent topic in the West, and its mediumship is generally treated with hostility in the Muslim world.

One interesting point that the spirits make about both terrorism and traditional suicide is that they represent cases where, either collectively or on an individual level, people feel they were not a part of the greater whole. As one entity put it, they felt "othered." There is an "us" and "them" or "me" and "everyone else" mentality. From the viewpoint of the afterlife, this seems to be regarded as a form of spiritual disconnect. Regardless, the experiences of the two groups seem to be more similar in pattern than that of assisted suicides, who appear to have a relatively "normal" afterlife experience, with smoother transitions and life-reviews no more difficult than that of those who die by other means.

In conclusion, this chapter looked at how the common ground in channeled material, and cross-corroboration of other material, can be used to depict the afterlife experience. It would appear that the souls of suicides go through similar phases to those that died by other means, although they may have somewhat longer, and more difficult, stages. Traditional suicides and suicide bombers in particular may be stuck for longer periods in the lower astral planes, but ultimately they, too, appear to be able to progress to the same healing centers or other beneficial locations that assisted suicides (and those than die by other means) arrive at more quickly. The recovery stage often involves a period of sleep, which seems to vary in length from one soul to the next. At times they may also be given healing energy.

Once souls are strong enough to look at their last life, the life-review and self-judgment phase begins, which in some ways represents only a beginning to the spiritual work that souls take on as a means of advancing spiritually. Many chose to become guides to others who take their own lives, while others act as guardian angels to the living. Only one suicide bomber soul claimed to have finished its life-review and begun work as a greeter for those that are newly dead terrorists.

Ultimately, existence in the afterlife does not appear to be without hope for the suicide. Although the experience may be an unpleasant one for some at first, there appears to be a system set in place, with devoted helpers, to aid them through their transition and recovery. Once the soul is strong enough to move forward, everything else that happens appears to be oriented towards the soul's spiritual growth, and the mastering of whatever lessons were not completed in life, so that future incarnations may focus on other challenges.

References

Anderson, G. and A. Barone. (1999). *Lessons from the light: Extraordinary messages of comfort and hope from the other side.* New York: G. P. Putnam's Sons.
Austen, A. W. (1978). *The teachings of Silver Birch: Wisdom from the world beyond.* 4th ed. London: Spiritualist Press.
Barbanell, S. (1964). *When a child dies.* London: Spiritualist Press.
Buckley, H. (1986). *When you're dead, you're livin.'* San Jose, CA: self-published.
Dresser, Charlotte E. (1927). *Life here and hereafter.* Edited by Fred Rafferty. Facsimile. San Jose, CA: Chase & Rae Occult Book Publishers.
Ford, A. (1974). *The life beyond death: As told to Jerome Ellison.* London: Abacus.
Foster, J. K. (1988). *Epilogue: Souls review their lives after death.* Kansas City, MO: Uni-Sun.
Heath, P., & Klimo, J. (2006). *Suicide: What really happens in the afterlife.* Berkeley, CA: North Atlantic.
Kardec, A. (2002). *The spirit's book.* Translated by Anna Blackwell. Reprint. Las Vegas, NV: Brotherhood of Life Publishing.
Loehr, F. (1986). *Diary after death.* 2nd ed. Grand Island, FL: Religious Research Press.
Mateu, L. (1999). *Conversations with the spirit world: Souls who have ended their lives speak from above.* Los Angeles: Channeling Spirits Books.
Meek, G. W. (1980). *After we die, what then?* Franklin, NC: Metascience Corporation.
Newton, M. (1999). *Journey of souls: Case studies of life between lives.* 5th rev. ed. St. Paul, MN: Llewellyn Publications.
Northrop, S. (2002). *Second chance: Healing messages from the afterlife.* Foreword by John Edward. San Diego, CA: Jodere Group.
Puryear, A. (1993). *Stephen lives! His life, suicide, and afterlife.* Scottsdale, AZ: New Paradigm Press. First published as *From the Turret* (Graphic Stationers and Publishers: Durban, South Africa).
Richelieu, P. (1985). *A soul's journey.* Reprint. Wellingborough, Northamptonshire: Turnstone Press Limited.

Sherwood, J. (1991). *Post-mortem journal: Communications from T. E. Lawrence.* Saffron Walden: The C. W. Daniel Company Limited.
Swedenborg, E. (1984). *Heaven and hell.* Translated by George F. Dole. 3rd Dole ed. New York: Swedenborg Foundation, Inc. First published in Latin (London, United Kingdom) in 1758.
Van Praagh, J. (1999). *Talking to heaven: A medium's message of life after death.* New York: Signet.
Wickland, C. A. (1974). *30 years among the dead.* Hollywood, CA: Newcastle Publishing Company, Inc.

12. Some Observations on Spirit Participation in Medium-Sitter Interaction and Its Organization

Robin Wooffitt

In this chapter, Dr. Robin Wooffitt shows how insights into speech interaction can be gained by a close analysis of the conversations that transpire between medium and sitter. Dr. Wooffitt uses the techniques of Conversation Analysis (CA) to show that conventional transcription techniques lose crucial elements of a conversation, such as pregnant pauses and vocal cues. Skeptics might regard these and other clues as being pivotal in determining a more accurate ratio of normal and ostensibly paranormal origins of the so-called spirit communications, but Dr. Wooffitt warns that the main purpose of CA is to describe how knowledge claims come about through communicative practices.
—Editors

Introduction

There is, undoubtedly, enormous contemporary popular interest in mediumship and demonstrations of post-mortem existence in spirit form. There are several reasons why this may be. High-profile celebrities have been known to consult mediums; perhaps the most famous was Diana, Princess of Wales. Some mediums have been able to take advantage of the recent proliferation of terrestrial and satellite television channels, and have been able to establish successful television careers, thereby increasing not only their own media profile, but also introducing the practices and claims of mediumship to a mass audience. John Edward's *Crossing Over*, for example, is a very popular programme on cable channels in the United States and the United Kingdom. The internet similarly provides resources through which mediums can advertise their services. Finally, some mediums have attained a general celebrity status. The British medium Doris Stokes, for example, was internationally renowned, and able to draw huge audiences to her public demonstrations all over the world. Since her death in 1987, other mediums have been able to develop a large public following. For example, this extract comes from a recent newspaper interview with the Irish medium, Sharon Neill:

> ... Neill is a celebrity psychic in Ireland, with the ability to draw audiences of 2,000 to her live shows, numerous radio and television appearances on her CV and a list of private clients that includes Van Morrison, Ash and Coldplay. In Belfast, people stop her in the street — "It's like being a doctor, everyone wants to tell you about their problems," she says, laughing — and this summer she will become the first spiritualist in 12 years to perform to audiences at the Edinburgh Festival [*The Observer*, 20th July, 2003].

The careers of mediums like Edward and Neill suggest that there is a significant market in the United Kingdom and the Republic of Ireland for large-scale public demonstrations of psychic talents. And the most casual consultation of relevant websites reveals that there are a number of mediums in the UK whose tours of 200 to 300 seater venues around the country seem to be almost continual.

In addition to stage demonstrations, there are various other settings in which members of the public can seek evidence of post-mortem existence from mediums. Mediums can be consulted for one-to-one private sittings. Mediumship forms part of Spiritualist church services, which combine traditional Christian activities, such as prayer and the singing of hymns, with demonstrations of spirit communication from local or national mediums. Mediums can also be consulted in psychical fairs, which are meetings in specially booked rooms in pubs or hotels lasting a short period of time, such as one evening, at which a small number of psychic practitioners — clairvoyants, mediums, Tarot readers, astrologers, and so on — are be available for consultation for a fee, usually between £20 to £35 for a sitting that lasts around 30 to 45 minutes. The emergence, frequency and popularity of psychic fairs further indicates strong contemporary interest in psychic arts more generally.

Mediumship has significantly changed since the Fox sisters began to report the rappings of discarnate spirits. Initially, mediums were able to offer physical evidence of spirit presence:

Some [mediums] specialized in particular effects, whereas others offered a broad repertoire of manifestations. That repertoire might include the materialization of entire spirit bodies — "full form materialization" — in addition to the more commonplace rapping, table tilting, and the emergence of spirit hands. Reports of séances also told of furniture cavorting around the room, objects floating in the air, mediums levitating, musical instruments playing tunes by themselves, bells ringing, tambourines jangling, strange breezes blowing, weird lights glowing, alluring fragrances and ethereal music wafting through the air. From the bodies of some mediums a strange foamy, frothy or filmy substances, dubbed ectoplasm, might be seen to condense [Oppenheim, 1985, p. 8].

Such physical demonstrations, however, are rare in contemporary mediumship. With notable exceptions (for example, the work of the Scole group reported in Keen *et al.*, 1999), the majority of contemporary demonstrations of mediumship are primarily discursive occasions, in that it is through the mediums' words that we are exposed to the spirits. Any proof that is given, any evidence that is provided, is primarily accomplished in the interaction itself: what is communicated between the medium and the sitter or the audience is thus the sole basis from which judgments can be made about the existence of the afterlife, the presence of the spirits and the medium's ability to communicate with them.

This raises an empirical question: how do the spirits participate in mediums' demonstrations of post-mortem existence? That is, how do mediums communicate the presence, words and activities of the spirits during the sitting? In this chapter, I will examine transcripts of recordings of mediums providing one-to-one sittings for individual clients, or in stage demonstrations of spirit agency to larger audiences in theatres and halls. Using a method of analysis of verbal communication which has emerged in sociology, I will describe some highly patterned and recurrent features of the ways in which a range of spirit activities are reported by mediums during sittings and demonstrations.

Data, Methodology and Transcription

The data used in the chapter come from a larger corpus of recordings of naturally occurring interactions between psychic practitioners and members of the public, either singularly or in larger audiences (no data were collected from Spiritualist church services). The data were collected to permit analysis of the generic properties of psychic practitioner-sitter interaction. This project is outlined in more detail in Wooffitt, (2006). The empirical observations which follow were drawn from analysis of a sub-corpus of 10 recordings of medium-sitter interaction. The recordings were made by mediums as part of the sitter's fee, which seems to be increasingly conventional in the UK.

The data were analysed using a conversation analytic methodology. Conversation analysis (CA) has emerged as one of the most powerful qualitative techniques for the analysis of verbal interaction. Introductions to and overviews of CA research can be found in Atkinson and Heritage (1984), Heritage (1984), Hutchby and Wooffitt (1998), and Ten Have (1999). A brief summary of the characteristics of CA research are in order.

Conversation analysis treats talk as social action, in that it focuses on the activities which are accomplished through the design of utterances. It also attends to the ways in which exchanges display robust properties as patterned sequences. CA therefore facilitates analysis of specific kinds of discursive actions through which mediums report the activities of the spirits during medium-sitter interaction.

It is important to emphasize that it is not the goal of Conversation Analytic research to try to arbitrate on the truth or falsity of the content of people's talk. It is merely focused on identifying the organized properties through which talk as social action is produced. It is entirely agnostic as to the truth status of the talk which constitutes social interaction.

In CA research, data are transcribed at a level of detail unusual in social science research, and it is useful to explain briefly the rationale. Research has shown that even apparently minor or trivial aspects of interaction have a significant impact on its subsequent development. CA transcriptions therefore try to capture characteristics of verbal interaction omitted from transcripts which merely record the spoken word. This means not only transcribing what was said, but the way it was said, and making sure that things that might seem messy, "accidental," or ungrammatical are recorded in the transcript and not filtered out in some form of "tidying up" process. To capture these hitherto overlooked features of interaction, CA employs a transcription system, developed by Gail Jefferson, which uses symbols available on conventional typewriter and computer keyboards. The system focuses on, first, the properties of turn taking, such as the onset of simultaneous speech and the timing of gaps within and between turns; and second, it exposes features of the production of talk, such as emphasis, volume, the speed of delivery and the sound stretching.

To illustrate why a detailed transcript is so important, consider the two following extracts. They are two different transcription of the same section of a recording of a medium providing a sitting for a client. The first was done by a trained audio typist using standard forms of punctuation.

EXTRACT (1A). ("M" is the medium, and "S" is the Sitter, or client.)

```
 1    M:   So keep it, maybe you'll know it. Good. Trouble with
 2         ankles. Your ankles have been bothering you or feet,
 3         or someone's feet been bothering them please?
 4    S:   No
 5    M:   Who has had trouble with feet or ankles?
 6    S:   A friend of mine, but
 7    M:   Hang on. Did she talk to you about a sprained ankle or
 8         some ankle problem or getting new shoes..., or trouble
 9         with her feet.
10    S:   A friend of mine had some problem.
11    M:   He's telling me this.
```

Now consider the same data transcribed using conversation analytic conventions.

EXTRACT (1B). (CA transcription. There is an explanation of CA transcription symbols in the Appendix.)

```
 1    M:   so keep it, may┌be you (will) know it.=
 2    S:                  └alright
 3    M:   =good.
 4         (1.5)
 5    M:   mm hm, mm hm
 6         (2)
 7    M:   ((blows air over lips))
 8         (2.2)
 9    M:   mm hm mm
10         (2)          ((M whispering))
11    M:   trouble with ankles. (.) YOur ankles have been
12         bothering, you or feet,
13         (0.2)
14    M:   someone's feet been bothering them (.) please?
15    S:   n:o::,=
16    M:   =who's- who's had trouble with feet.
17         (0.2)
18    M:   or ankles.
19         (1)
20    S:   ah(m) friend of mi:ne but
21         (.)
22    M:   di┌d she┐ (.) ┌talk to yo┐u about hh °hold on° 'h
23    S:     └(but)┘      └(na(r):h: ┘
24    M:   did she talk >t'y'about< sp- (.) a sprained ankle
25         or some (s't've) ankle trouble or getting new
26         shoes for a
27         (.)
28    M:   (fw┌( )┐
29    S:       └a* ┘ (.) friend of mine had some problem,
30    M:   he's telling me this.
```

It is useful to highlight some of the main differences between these transcripts. (What follows is a summary of a discussion from Wooffitt, 2001a, pp. 64–65).

The second version reproduces short utterances and non-lexical contributions which are often omitted from orthographic transcriptions, such as audible breathing, quietly whispered words, and turns known as minimal continuers, such as "mm hm" and "uh huh." All of this detail is lost in the standard transcript which simply provides the words that are said. CA transcripts also capture overlapping talk when two or more parties speak at the same time. In the revised transcript, there are three instances of overlap, in lines 1 and 2, 22 and 23, and in 28 and 29, all of which are unavailable from the first transcript. It is important to detail the participants' precise points of participation as these can implicate subsequent kinds of utterances.

Consider, for example, the spate of overlapping talk on lines 22 and 23. Here, the medium seems to be having some difficulty, in that he has offered a message from the spirits concerning a foot problem but the sitter seems less than enthusiastic about accepting this information. She has volunteered that a friend of hers has had some problem but in lines 20 and 23 is clearly going on to register some doubt that this is what the spirits are referring to. Her second "but" comes in overlap with the medium's "did she." They both stop and then resume at the same moment. In overlap with the medium's "talk to you" the sitter produces an emphatic version of "no': 'na(r):h:." Her overlapping talk is not even recorded in the standard transcript. However, it may have some significance, because immediately afterwards the medium curtails the utterance he was making ("talk to you about ...") and then says, "hold on." So, we can begin to get a sense that his abandonment of that utterance happened fairly swiftly after the sitter's drawn out and definitive "no," and this in turn suggests that it was generated out of his hearing a negative response from the sitter.

Moreover, the "hold on" (incorrectly reproduced in the standard transcript as "hang on"), is said very quietly, and almost whispered. This *sotto voce* production is consistent with other utterances in which the medium is apparently listening and responding to the spirits. This quietly spoken "hold on," then, marks the medium's temporary disengagement from the interaction with the sitter to attend to the spirits. Again, a simple rendering of the words would not capture this performative aspect of the medium's utterances.

CA transcription conventions then, capture a level of detailed information lost in conventional transcription practices, and which may be of analytic interest in that they are consequential to the way in which interaction proceeds.

The Types of Spirit Participation

In this section we will consider the kinds of spirit activity reported by mediums.

Spirit Actions

A medium can claim that the spirit is present at the sitting, and interacting in some way with the sitter: standing behind them, putting their arms around them and so on. Of course, only the medium can see the spirit. In the following extract, the medium proposes knowledge of a physical characteristic of the sitter's dead mother, which is confirmed.

Extract (2). Here, the report of the spirit's interaction with the sitter implies that the medium can see the spirit, which in turn stands as an account for her knowledge of the sitter's mother. And insofar as the medium claims to be able to see the spirit, as opposed to just hearing or sensing it, she is able to provide a demonstration of the extent of her mediumship skills.

Spirits' Discourse

It is common for mediums to claim that they can hear the words of the spirits. These spirit utterances can then be introduced into the sitting to establish the co-presence and agency of the spirits. The spirit's discourse can be paraphrased. For example:

```
M:    hhh was your mum very short.
      (1)
S:    she was ye┌ah
M:              └mm yeah
S:    °yeah°
M:    she's giving you a lovely cuddle
```

Extract (3)

```
M:    does he have a son?=
S:    =yes.
M:    mm (.) he's talking about his so:n.
```

EXTRACT (4). Alternatively, mediums may use direct reported speech to reproduce the very words used by the spirit. In Extract (5), for example, the medium establishes that a spirit with whom he is in contact is the husband of the sitter by reproducing the spirit own words, "I'm her husband," which are indicated in the transcript by the use of speech markers conventional in fictional literature.

```
M:  ˙h >ahm< his father also passed over is
    that corre┌ct,
S:           └ye:s:=
M:  =>because he's talking about his da::d.
S:  y┌es
M:   └and his dad is very stro:ng. (.) his dad was
    a very strong person?=strong willed person and I feel
    there was uhm (0.3) he had very good intelligence. he
    was a very strong-minded. (.) intelligent person
```

EXTRACT (5). Direct reported speech can be use to indicate some aspect of the spirit's personality during the sitting. For example, in the following extract the medium reproduces the spirit's words using increased volume to capture the way in which the spirit is talking, thereby conveying some sense of the personality and desires of the person now in spirit. This personality characteristic is explicitly affirmed in the medium's subsequent talk.

```
M:  Does this make sense to you? In your purse
    or in your bag ┌c'd you┐ picture please
S:                 └ye:s:  ┘
M:  Is this of a man or a male?
    (0.2)
S:  Yes
M:  and isn't that the person you want to contact?
    (0.3)
S:  Yes
M:  hmm ˙hh HHhhhh He is very strong, I am not sure what tuh
    (ki   kuh ˚ku˚)
    (1.3)
M:  is this your husband (.) ┌who passed over please?
S:                           └yes.
    (0.5)
M:  'cause he just said husband "I'm her husband, I'm her
    husband" 'kay? (.) good.
```

Extract (6). Direct reported speech is a key resource by which the medium can establish and convey the personality or behavioral characteristics of the spirit, thereby providing evidence that this is indeed the spirit of a person relevant to the sitter, and further substantiating the broader claim for the postmortem existence of the self with all its attendant traits and idiosyncrasies.

```
M:   So spirit wants me to do a scan on your bo:dy, talk
     about your health, so I'm going to do that okay?  I'm going
     to do this for your health (0.8) Let's see what's going on
     with you. 'hh number one thing is your >mother in spirit
     please?<
     (0.2)
S:   Yes
M:   >'cause I have (n-m) y'r mother standing right over here,
     'hh and she said "I WANna TAlk to HEr and I want to speak
     to her" because 'hh your mother has very lou::d when she
     comes through. 'h she speaks with a=in a very lou:d way=a
     very uhm (.) y'understand very ┌she has to be
S:                                  └ye:s:.
M:   heard, 'h and like this would not happen today
     without her coming through for you.  D'y'┌un'erstand?
S:                                            └'kay
S:   Ye:s.
M:   b'cause she wants to be heard.
```

Extract (7) comes from a sitting with two sitters, a mother and daughter. At the start of the extract, it has been established that sitter 1 is interested in contacting the spirit of her deceased husband. In this extract the medium makes three proposals about the sitter: that she has a bad back, that she is reluctant to discuss certain matters with others and that she is house proud. Immediately after the sitter's acceptance of each of these claims, the medium reports the words of the sitter's husband (now in spirit).

Extract (7). In this short stretch of talk the medium is able to report and establish the spirit's participation in the sitting in such a way that the sitter is presented with the impression that a stable, recognizable and agentic spirit personality is interacting with the medium to make observations about the physical, emotional and behavioral features of the sitter's current life. For example: the spirit's ability to react to earthly events and, to some extent, intervene in them, is implied when the medium reports that the spirit intends to "send her a bit of sympathy" in response to the sitter's acknowledgment that she is has problems with her back.

This also demonstrates the warmth and depth of the spirit's personality, as it is sympathetic to the sitter's medical problem. The benign stance of the spirit if further confirmed in that it is reported as expressing fondness at the sitter's care ("fussiness") about her home.

```
M:    >'ave you 'ad< (.) bit >(o')< trouble with your
      back as well.
      (0.2)
S1:   yes a little bi ┌t
M:               └he says 'ah'd best send
      her a bit of sympathy down" so you understand it,
      ˙hh┌h
S1:      └ye┌s
M:          └coz y'know ˙h y'try to bottle things up and
      you don't always let people get close to you in that
      sense do you
S1:   no.
M:    he says "she can be quite stubborn at times y'know"
      (.)
M:    is that true
S1:   °yes°
M:    an' he knows cz ˙h you are fussy
      about the bungalow aren't
      you ┌girl
S1:       └yes I am
M:    "bless her" he says
```

The Sequential Organization
of Spirit Participation

So far we have noted some of the ways in which, via the mediums' talk, the spirits' participation in the sitting is revealed. In this section, we will consider some of the highly patterned sequential features of mediums' discourse which reveals the agency and presence of the spirits. To do this it is necessary to sketch some of the broader properties of demonstrations of psychic cognition more generally.

All psychic practitioners claim to have some form of special cognition: the ability mentally to communicate with the dead, the ability to understand and predict a person's life via the interpretation of the array of Tarot cards, general psychic and clairvoyant skills, and so on. Through these special forms of cognition practitioners claim to be able to access information about the sitter or client which would not normally be available through the use of the five senses, or which is unavailable in the course of the sitting (Wooffitt, 2001b).

Successful demonstrations of these special powers exhibit some robust properties (Wooffitt, 2000; 2006). In sittings, psychic practitioners will issue a series of utterances, usually (but not invariably) in the form of questions which hint at or imply, that they have access to knowledge about the sitter or their circumstances. If the sitter finds the psychic's utterance to be accurate, or is in some way relevant, it is receipted and accepted with a minimal turn, usually a simple "yes" or "yeah." After the sitter's minimal acceptance or confirmation the psychic practitioner proceeds to a turn in which the now-accepted knowledge is attributed to a paranormal source. For example, the following extract comes from a sitting between a young woman and a psychic who uses the tarot cards.

Extract (8). ("P" is the psychic practitioner)
(Discussing S's plans to travel after graduating.)

```
S:    I graduate in June I'm probably going to work until
      about february ┌so: jus' (.) any old j┌ob    ┌y'know.
                     └RIght okay             └right┘
M:    and are you going to the states,
      (.)
S:    yeah.
M     yea:h, c'z e I can see the old ehm:
      (.)
S:    Hh┌-huh Hah 'h┐
M:       └-statue of ┘ liberty around you,
S:    heh heh h┌e 'hhh
M:             └there you are, there's contentment for
      the future.
S:    oh go┌od
M:         └who's pregnant around you?
```

The question "and are you going to the states" has a propositional character, in that it may be heard as displaying the psychic's current knowledge that the sitter is indeed planning to visit the US. Once this has been accepted it is retrospectively cast as having been derived from the tarot cards: the psychic's utterance "c'z e I can see the old ehm: statue of liberty around you," portrays her prior turn as a consequence of her ability to discern from the arrangement of cards a classic iconic representation of the US, and interpret its relevance to the sitter. Moreover, the turn is initiated with a derivation of "because." This explicitly establishes that the topic of the psychic's prior utterance was generated from the special powers claimed in her subsequent turn.

Once the attributive turn is complete, and the psychic has made a closing remark about the topic of travelling, she initiates another topic with the question "who's pregnant around you?" which, should it be accepted by the sitter, would project the relevance of another attributive turn and further demonstration of special powers.

There is, then, a three-turn sequence which is a vehicle for demonstrations of ostensibly paranormal cognition:

Turn 1	P:	a question which [a] initiates or [b] develops a topic and which proposes a claim about, or knowledge of, the sitter, their circumstances, etc.;
Turn 2	S:	minimal confirmation/acceptance;
Turn 3	P:	the now-accepted information is attributed to a paranormal source

It is noticeable that reports of spirit participation cluster strongly in attributive third turns. Either through direct attribution, or the implication of attribution, the spirits' actions/words are offered as the source of the previously offered and now accepted knowledge claim. Let us reconsider some of the data we have examined earlier in the chapter. For example, in Extract (2a) we first observed how mediums may report the spirit's actions towards the sitter, or some other aspect of the sitting. It can now be seen that this report follows the three turn sequence outlined above.

Extract (2a)

```
T1   M:   hhh was your mum very short.
          (1)
T2   S:   she was ye┌ah
     M:            └mm yeah
     S:   °yeah°
T3   M:   she's giving you a lovely cuddle
```

And in Extract (3a) the paraphrase of the spirit words also displays this patterning.

Extract (3a)

```
T1   M:   does he have a son?=
T2   S:   =yes.
T3   M:   mm (.) he's talking about his so:n.
```

Direct reported speech of the spirits' communications routinely follow this sequential organization. In Extract (7a) we observed three instances; each observes the question — acceptance/confirmation — attribution sequence.

Extract (7a)

```
T1 M:   >'ave you 'ad< (.) bit >(o')< trouble with your
        back as well.
        (0.2)
T2 S1:  yes a little bi┌t
T3 M:                   └he says 'ah'd best send
        her a bit of sympathy down" so you understand it,
        ˙hh┌h
    S1:    └ye┌s
T1  M:        └coz y'know ˙h y'try to bottle things up and
        you don't always let people get close to you in that
        sense do you
T2 S1:  no.
T3 M:   he says "she can be quite stubborn at times y'know"
        (.)
    M:  is that true
    S1: °yes°
T3 M:   an' he knows cz ˙h you are fussy
        about the bungalow aren't
        you ┌girl
T2  S1:     └yes I am
T3  M:  "bless her" he says
```

This three-turn sequence does not only occur in one-to-one sittings. It also
occurs in a range of other communicative contexts (see Wooffitt, 2006, for a
more extensive discussion). To illustrate, though, we can note some instances
from stage demonstration of mediumship. Extracts (9) [a] to [c] come from
notes taken from an ethnographic observation of demonstrations of mediumship to a large audience (200+ people).

Extract (9). ("R" is audience respondent.)

```
[a]
T1   M:  Did he save coins in a jar?
T2   R:  Yes
T3   M:  he says "I want them back"

[b]
T1   M:  have you got a photo in your drawer?
T2   R:  Yes
T3   M:  He's been looking

[c]
T1   M:  You've felt a prod on your shoulder
T2   R:  Yes
T3   M:  She says "that's me"
```

One of the key features of conversation analytic research is that it examines the structural properties of interaction. This is in marked contrast to many other qualitative approaches which examine thematic consistencies in verbal data. The CA focus on the mechanics of interaction is useful in that it provides the basis to draw subtle distinctions between stretches of talk which may be thematically similar. We can illustrate the importance of this by considering the following extract, which begins with the medium reporting on a spirit's happiness.

EXTRACT (10)

```
M:   she's so: happy,
     (0.7)
S:   good.
M:   and so happy to see: (.) everybody, and she brings
     me the beau:tiful colour of violets, (0.2) that lovely
     soft colour of violets, (0.5) which is lovely (.) and
     it's beautifully peaceful (0.3) and uh
     (1.2)
M:   and then (.) she just said don't ↑ever be afrai:d, (0.4)
     don't ↑ever be afrai:d, (0.2) there's nothing to be
     afraid of. (0.7) an(g)uh:,
     (3.3)
M:   (ptch) oh it's lo:vely, (0.2) she just leaned forward and
     put a scarf round  your neck and turned your collar up
     huh huH HUH HAH HAH HAh(n) nn ˙HHH which is a wa(hh)y
     o(h)f  sa(hu)ying, ˙hh (.) ˙h I look after you((ch)huh)
     (ch)hih huh=
S:   =Yeah.
M:   ˙h (ch)Hhu(n) sure she would've always been
     concerned ↑are you warm enough, (w'y-)˙hh hu(n)
```

In Extract (10) there is an instance of the medium reproducing the spirit's words ("she just said don't (*ever* be afrai:d, (0.4) don't (*ever* be afrai:d, (0.2) there's nothing to be afraid of"), and an instance of the medium reporting the spirit's interaction with elements of the physical setting (placing a scarf around the sitter). These are thematically similar to the content of Extracts (3) to (7), and Extract (2), respectively. However, it would be incorrect to assume that they were the same kind of phenomena. This is because the sequential organization of the interaction in Extract (10) is very different to that found in the previous extracts. To explore this, we will focus on the organization of the report of the spirit's activities, and compare it to the report of spirit activity in Extract (2).

The depiction of the spirit's caring behavior in Extract (10) is markedly different to that in Extract (2). In Extract (2), the utterance which reports the spirit's actions occupied the third position of a three turn attributive sequence. But in Extract (10) the report of the spirit's actions does not occupy the same kind of sequential position. Moreover, in this extract the medium goes on to formulate the significance of the spirit's action, stating that it is "a wa(hh)y o(h)f sa(hu)ying, hh (.) h I look after you." This kind of discursive activity is very different to that found in the third turn of the attributive sequence; so, for example, from Extract (2), the report of the spirit's behavior is part of turn which performs the action of demonstrating the use of parapsychological cognition; in this case, the ability to see spirits. Finally, in Extract (10) there is no place in the interaction in which the medium attempts to demonstrate that she has access to paranormal means of cognition.

There is, then, crucial distinction between Extract (10) and those which preceded it. In Extract (10) the medium is describing what she claims she can see. In Extracts (2) to (8) the mediums are performing a different kind of activity: they are demonstrating their possession and use of parapsychological cognition. As such it is an activity which is oriented to and addresses issues of proof and authenticity. These matters are reflected in the design of the three turn attributive sequence. For example, the first turn implied knowledge claim is unattributed. This is the case even when there is an explicit claim that the medium is in contact with a particular spirit, and even when the spirit's words stand as an immediate sequential context for a topic initiating question. There is little acknowledgment that the spirit may be the source of the information hinted at in the question. Extract (11) provides a further example.

EXTRACT (11)

```
M:    a:nd (.) the reason I question that w's because
      I felt her talking about a ma:n. so (.) that was my
      (0.2)
M:    my problem. (.) 'hh so (.) is this lady an aunt
      ⌜or a⌝
S:    ⌊yes.⌋
      (.)
M:    'h and (.) is her husband still here?
S:    no she was a spinster.
M:    she was a spinster then.=a gentleman here that she
      would have been very concerned about,
      (2.5)
S:    only me really
      (0.3)
M:    Well (w)hen in that case (0.2) if:uhm:
      (0.2)
M:    if you were close to her=
S:    =I ws ⌜very cl⌝ose
M:          ⌊and she⌋
      (.)
M:    that's it and she would be concerned
      (0.3)
M:    for you (.) because I knew that it was a man she'd
      left here 'h so that makes sense to me 'hhh and she
      just wanted to give you her love.
T1    colin, who's colin,
```

Here the medium is clarifying a misunderstanding about the spirit's communications. Towards the end of that clarification she reports that the spirit "just wanted to give you her love." Therefore we are entitled to assume that the spirit is co-present in the sitting, or at least interactionally available, although obviously accessible only to the medium. The medium then produces a topic initiating first turn utterance, introducing the topic of a person called Colin. However, there is no indication that the spirit is the source of this information. It is an unattributed (implied) claim. A similar pattern becomes evident if we extend **Extract (10)**.

EXTRACT (10 EXTENDED)

```
M:   she's so: happy,
     (0.7)
S:   good.
M:   and so happy to see: (.) everybody, and she brings
     me the beau:tiful colour of violets, (0.2) that lovely
     soft colour of violets, (0.5) which is lovely (.) and
     it's beautifully peaceful (0.3) and uh
     (1.2)
M:   and then (.) she just said don't ↑ever be afrai:d, (0.4)
     don't ↑ever be afrai:d, (0.2) there's nothing to be
     afraid of. (0.7) an(g)uh:,
     (3.3)
M:   (ptch) oh it's lo:vely, (0.2) she just leaned forward and
     put a scarf round  your neck and turned your collar up
     huh huH HUH HAH HAH HAh(n) nn ˙HHH which is a wa(hh)y
     o(h)f sa(hu)ying, ˙hh (.) ˙h I look after you((ch)huh)
     (ch)hih huh=
S:   =Yeah.
M:   ˙h (ch)Hhu(n) sure she would've always been
     co ⌐ncerned ↑are you warm enough, (w'y-)˙hh hu(n)
S:     ⌊yeah
M:   hu(n) hu(n) ˙hhh a:nduh: (0.2) and (.) her ↓love
     to lesley  because ˙h she's a nice girl she said
     (0.4) a:nd um:
     (10)
M:   swimming.                                        T1
     (2.5)
M:   who's been swimming,                             T1
```

Here the spirit's agency is directly implicated just before the topic initiating questions: the spirit's talk ("she's a nice girl she said") is reproduced as part of the stretch of talk which immediately precedes the introduction of a new topic ("swimming"). But again, there is no statement, acknowledgment or even hint that the source of the information around which the topic initiating turn is built has come from the spirit with which the medium so clearly claims to be in contemporaneous contact.

Topic initiating utterances are therefore designed so that there is no inferable source for the implied knowledge claim, even when the logic of the sitting, and the practitioners' on-going talk, strongly suggests that they have current access to paranormal sources of information. Why might this be?

Mediums, are, by definition, merely the channel through which the spirits and the living can communicate; consequently, they should have no investment in the information they propose or pass on to their sitters. However, any knowledge claim proposed by the medium, however, implicitly, has to be delicately managed. This is because the authority of the medium's claim to have special powers would be compromised were he or she seen to endorse proposals about the sitter which subsequently transpire to be false, or which are unequivocally rejected. There appears to be a strong normative pressure, then, to ensure that knowledge claims proposed by topic initiating questions do not imply or invoke their paranormal source, in this case, the spirits.

Conclusion

In this chapter I have argued that, since the relative decline of physical mediumship, the spirits' participation in sittings is primarily a discursive activity, in that the sitter or client is aware of the presence and conduct of the spirits only via the mediums' reports. To understand spirit participation in contemporary demonstrations of mediumship, then, it is important to examine the interaction between medium and sitter. Consequently, I have described some of the properties of the mediums' discourse through which the spirits' agency, words and activities are introduced into the sitting. In particular, I have focused on a particularly robust and recurrent sequence of turns in which the medium produces a topic-initiating question which implies that he or she is already in possession of some information about the sitter. If this is accepted, the medium then attributes the now-accepted knowledge claim to some aspect of their interaction with the spirit: they can either see the spirit, or hear it. Of course, this is not the only way in which spirit can participate in the sitting; indeed, I have examined one extract in this chapter to illustrate that the spirits' activities can be reported in other ways. However, it is important to stress that the three turn attributive sequence is an important vehicle for the demonstration of a wide range of forms of parapsychological cognition (Wooffitt, 2006), and we should not be surprised that it occurs regularly in medium-sitter interaction.

The properties of the sequence, and thereby the characteristics of the spirits' participation in the sitting, may invite a sceptical interpretation, in that first turn implied knowledge claims are routinely unattributed, and that the spirits are identified as the source of knowledge claims once those claims have been confirmed by the sitter. Although it is intuitively compelling to infer, therefore, that the mediums are simply duping their clients by engaging in a form of cold reading, we should be wary about making such assumption.

In this analysis I have tried to identify some of the discursive practices through which mediums establish the participation of the spirits. The primary sequential structure by which this task is achieved has a defensive orientation in that it operates to underpin the medium's (implicit) claim to have genuine authentic parapsychological abilities. This is achieved in part through the absence of attribution of first-turn knowledge claims and the post acceptance invocation of a spirit source. However, just because we can identify the discursive practices through which matters of authenticity are managed, it is not the case that we can then pronounce those claims to authenticity are thereby false. Studies of authoritative or factual language have shown that reports of even uncontentious states of affairs may be formulated in such a way as to address anticipated sceptical responses (Billig, 1997; Billig et al., 1988; Edwards, 1995; Pomerantz, 1986; Potter, 1996; Wooffitt, 1992). Description of the communicative practices through which knowledge claims are made, attributed, accepted, rejected or revised is not the same as an exposé of linguistic tricks by which a false claim is made persuasive, or through which one person can deliberately mislead another.

Whether the basis for a medium's knowledge claims is spirit contact or by conscious inspection of the sitter's demeanor, that claim still has to be reported and established as factual in the course of the exchange with the sitter. Whether mediums really are communicating with spirits or not, their claims to be in contact with the spirits, and their demonstrations of that link — and, thereby, the participation of the spirits themselves — are irreducibly socially organized phenomena. This chapter has tried to sketch some of the broad properties of this organization.

Appendix: Transcription Symbols

The transcription symbols used here are common to conversation analytic research, and were developed by Gail Jefferson. The following symbols are used in the data.

(.5)	The number in brackets indicates a time gap in tenths of a second.
(.)	A dot enclosed in a bracket indicates pause in the talk less then two tenths of a second.
˙hh	A dot before an "h" indicates speaker in-breath. The more "h"'s, the longer the inbreath.
hh	An "h" indicates an out-breath. The more "h"'s the longer the breath.
(( ))	A description enclosed in a double bracket indicates a non-verbal activity. For example *((banging sound))*
-	A dash indicates the sharp cut-off of the prior word or sound.

:	Colons indicate that the speaker has stretched the preceding sound or letter. The more colons the greater the extent of the stretching.
( )	Empty parentheses indicate the presence of an unclear fragment on the tape.
(guess)	The words within a single bracket indicate the transcriber's best guess at an unclear fragment.
.	A full stop indicates a stopping fall in tone. It does not necessarily indicate the end of a sentence.
,	A comma indicates a continuing intonation.
?	A question mark indicates a rising inflection. It does not necessarily indicate a question.
Under	Underlined fragments indicate speaker emphasis.
↑↓	Pointed arrows indicate a marked falling or rising intonational shift. They are placed immediately before the onset of the shift.
CAPITALS	With the exception of proper nouns, capital letters indicate a section of speech noticeably louder than that surrounding it.
° °	(Degree signs are used to indicate that the talk they encompass is spoken noticeably quieter than the surrounding talk.
Thaght	A "gh" indicates that word in which it is placed had a guttural pronunciation.
> <	"More than" and "less than" signs indicate that the talk they encompass was produced noticeably quicker than the surrounding talk.
=	The "equals" sign indicates contiguous utterances.
[ ]	Square brackets between adjacent lines of concurrent speech indicate the onset and end of a spate of overlapping talk.

A more detailed description of these transcription symbols can be found in Atkinson and Heritage, 1984, pp. *ix-xvi*).

References

Atkinson, J.M. and Heritage, J, (eds.) (1984). *Structures of social action: Studies in conversation analysis*. Cambridge: Cambridge University Press.

Billig, M. (1997). Rhetorical and discursive analysis: How families talk about the royal family. In N. Hayes (ed.), *Doing qualitative analysis in psychology* (pp. 39–54). Hove: Psychology Press.

Billig, M., Condor, S., Edwards, D., Gane, M., Middleton, D. & Radley, A. (1988). *Ideological dilemmas: A social psychology of everyday thinking*. London and Thousand Oaks, CA: Sage.

Edwards, D. (1995). Two to tango: Script formulations, dispositions and rhetorical symmetry in relationship troubles talk. *Research on Language and Social Interaction, 28*(4), 319–50.

Heritage, J. (1984). *Garfinkel and ethnomethodology*. Cambridge: Polity Press.

Hutchby, I., & Wooffitt, R. (1998). *Conversation analysis: Principles, practices and applications*. Oxford: Polity Press.

Keen, M., Ellison, A., & Fontana, D. (1999). "The Scole report." *Proceedings of the Society for Psychical Research, 58*, 151–392.

Oppenheim, J. (1985). *The other world: Spiritualism and psychical research in England, 1850–1914*. Cambridge: Cambridge University Press.

Pomerantz, A. M. (1986). Extreme case formulations: A way of legitimizing claims. *Human Studies, 9*, 219–229.

Potter, J. (1996). *Representing reality: Discourse, rhetoric and social construction.* London: Sage.

Ten Have, P. (1999). *Doing conversation analysis: A practical guide.* London and Thousand Oaks: Sage.

Wooffitt, R. (1992). *Telling tales of the unexpected: The organisation of factual discourse.* Hemel Hempstead: Harvester Wheatsheaf.

Wooffitt, R. (2000). Some properties of the interactional organisation of displays of paranormal cognition in psychic-sitter interaction. *Sociology*, 43(3), 457–479.

Wooffitt, R. (2001a). Researching psychic practitioners: Conversation analysis. In M. Wetherell, S. Taylor, & S. Yates (eds.), *Discourse as data: A guide for analysis* (pp. 49–92). London: Sage, in association with the Open University.

Wooffitt, R. (2001b). A socially organised basis for displays of cognition: procedural orientation to evidential turns in psychic-sitter interaction. *British Journal of Social Psychology*, 40(4), 545–563.

Wooffitt, R. (2006). *The language of mediums and psychics: The social organisation of everyday miracles.* Aldershot: Ashgate.

13. Origins of Belief in Life After Death: The Ritual Healing Theory and Near-Death Experience*

JAMES MCCLENON

James McClenon uses his Ritual Healing Theory to show that our species has evolved a number of mechanisms—genotypes—by which the futurity of the individual in this life is likely to be assured, even after the individual experiences extreme stress and trauma. These experiences can bring about the demise of the individual, but certain individuals, through various psychological and physiological responses, are predisposed to this specific self-protective function. One of Dr. McClenon's studies is featured in this chapter, the results of which support the hypotheses generated from Ritual Healing Theory.—Editors

Overview

This chapter illustrates how ritual healing theory can be tested through analyses of near-death experiences. The ritual healing theory hypothesizes that (1) dissociation/hypnosis genotypes provide survival advantages to hominids exposed to trauma, (2) these genotypes are linked to the incidence of anomalous experiences, (3) ritual healing practices provided survival advantages to those having these genotypes. Anomalous experiences include apparitions, paranormal dreams, waking extrasensory perceptions, sleep paralysis,

*Text regarding analysis of the North Carolina NDE sample will appear in a future volume of the Journal of Near-Death Studies.

psychokinesis, out-of-body and near-death experiences. Such experiences generate beliefs supporting shamanism, humankind's first religious form. Shamanism is based on faith in magical abilities, life after death, and the use of trance for contact with spirits and souls. Resulting shamanic rituals, effective due to placebo and hypnotic effects, provided survival advantages to those with dissociation/hypnosis genotypes. The resulting evolutionary cycle shaped the human propensity for religious sentiment. Cross-cultural and historical analyses of near-death experiences provide insights into the way these experiences shape folk religious belief. Twenty-eight near-death experiences (NDEs) were selected from 1832 anomalous experience narratives gathered in Northeastern North Carolina. Analyses of these NDEs support hypotheses derived from the ritual healing theory.

Introduction

Scholars argue that beliefs regarding life after death evolved with increasing hominid awareness of mortality (Laughlin, McManus, & d'Aquili, 1992; Schumaker, 1990). A typical scenario is that awareness of death increased as the brain's frontal lobes grew larger, providing greater capacity for planning and rational thought. As a result, the theory argues, ancient *Homo sapiens* developed cognitive mechanisms in the temporal lobes, and other parts of the brain, which allowed religious sentiment, thereby reducing fear of death. Belief in an afterlife provided a foundation for shamanism, humankind's first religious form. This model is supported by evidence that shamanism and related altered states of consciousness have a physiological basis (Winkelman, 1992, 2000).

Yet the "fear-of-death" theory is subject to criticism. It fails to specify why shamanism is linked to altered states of consciousness and travel to spiritual worlds. Second, the logic of the theory is uncertain: because fears provide survival advantages, reducing death anxiety does not always increase survival fitness. People who avoid danger tend to live longer than those who lack fear. Third, the theory is not connected to modern knowledge regarding psychopathology. Most modern mental illnesses, obvious survival handicaps, do not seem directly linked to death anxiety. The scenarios devised by evolutionary psychologists explaining post-traumatic stress disorder, depression, suicide, anxiety disorders, autism, sociopathy, bipolar disorder, and schizophrenia do not mention "fear of death" (Gaulin & McBurney, 2001, pp. 297–313). Evolutionary psychologists' explanations are more sophisticated, and more amenable to empirical evaluation, than the "fear of death" theory.

Some evolutionary explanations for religion specify "group selection" processes (Wilson, 2002). Religious groups are thought to have survival advantages compared to non-religious groups. For example, religious rituals may increase cohesiveness and reduce fear during combat. As with death anxiety theories, critical arguments abound. Although the evidence is ambiguous, group selection theorists have not produced strong empirical evidence. They constitute a minority among anthropologists. Many loose ends regarding group selection arguments exist. Primates live in cohesive groups without the benefit of religion. Group selection theories portray no scenario describing how a small amount of religiosity contributed to increased cohesiveness. Second, it is not certain that religion generates cohesiveness. The notion of cohesiveness is derived from Durkheim's theory of religion; historical analysis refutes fundamental assumptions of his theory (Swatos & Gissurarson, 1996). Testing the notion that religion provides "cohesiveness" and an "advantage" is difficult. Religious sports teams seem to have no advantage over secular teams. Third, most evolutionists reject group selection arguments in favor of selection at the gene level. They note that group selection is rare — associated with very specific situations. Group selection models work only in situations where there is little gene flow between groups. Religious groups rarely replace less religious groups. As a result, most evolutionary psychologists reject these theories since gene flow is common (Ridley, 1997, pp. 4–5). Yet group selection should not be completely ignored. Using loose definitions of groups, Wilson (2002) argues that group selection processes occur simultaneously at many levels. The issue has no been completely settled.

The "ritual healing" theory (McClenon, 1997, 2002a), derived from Winkelman's (2000) shamanic paradigm, extends these discussions (see Figure 14.1). This theory argues that hominids with dissociative genotypes have survival advantages should it happen that they are exposed to childhood trauma. These dissociative genotypes were (and still are) linked to the incidence of various forms of anomalous experience — apparitions, paranormal dreams, waking extrasensory perceptions, psychokinesis, out-of-body experiences (OBEs), and near-death experiences (NDEs). Beliefs derived from these experiences provided a foundation for humankind's first religious form, shamanism.

Human evolution should be viewed as a process in which selection of genes was often influenced by cultural processes having physiological basis. Many researchers have found significant correlations between the propensity for dissociation/hypnosis, the incidence of paranormal experience, and beliefs derived from these experiences (Kumar & Pekala, 2001, pp. 275–276; McClenon, 2002a). Experiences generate belief in spirits, souls, life after death, and magical abilities — and these notions form the basis for shamanism (McClenon, 1993, 1997, 2002a). Resulting shamanic rituals, based on

Figure 13.1— Ritual Healing Theory

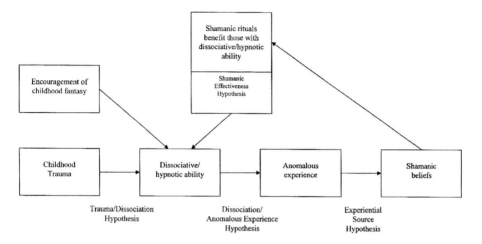

placebo and hypnotic effects, provided greater survival benefits for those with dissociative/hypnotic capacities, causing an evolutionary cycle leading to the modern genetic basis for religiosity. This theory coincides with a growing body of evidence, derived from twin studies, indicating that religious attitude, interests, and practice have a genetic basis (D'Onofrio et al., 1999; Waller et al., 1990).

The ritual healing theory argues that the processes generating religion continue to occur and can be evaluated by social scientists. Folklore collections provide a convenient source of data for testing hypotheses derived from this theory. When people describe apparitions, extrasensory perceptions, out-of-body and near-death experiences, they generate oral religious traditions regarding spirits, souls, life after death, and magical abilities. Analyses of these accounts provide insights into how religious traditions developed among preliterate peoples. This chapter illustrates how the ritual healing theory can be tested through analysis of near-death experiences.

Prevalent Forms of Anomalous Experience

Universal elements within anomalous experience can be determined through cross-cultural comparison. The psychical research literature describes similar accounts of extrasensory and out-of-body experience all over the world. Random samples of students at three colleges in the USA, three colleges in China, and one college in Japan reported anomalous experiences that can easily be classified into similar categories (McClenon, 1994). Anthropology students at Elizabeth City State University, a predominately African-American college, asked friends, family, and neighbors in Northeastern North Carolina, "If you have had a very unusual experience, would you describe it?" Between 1988 and 1997, 1215 anomalous experience accounts were collected. Cross-cultural comparison of accounts allowed identification of naturally occurring categories of anomalous experience (McClenon, 1994, 2002a,b). Categories, listed in order of prevalence, were: (1) apparitions, (2) paranormal dreams, (3) psychokinesis, (4) spiritual healing, (5) rootlore (experiences resulting from rituals derived, in part, from African occult traditions), (6) sleep paralysis, (7) waking ESP, (8) synchronistic events (9) miscellaneous paranormal, (10) occult events (anomalous experiences occurring during rituals or performances), (11) out-of-body experiences, (12) unidentified flying objects (McClenon, 2002a, p. 117). Analyses of these data were published in McClenon (2000, 2002a,b). Between 1997 and 2003, 617 more accounts were collected and sorted into the previously devised categories — indicating equivalent prevalence in most cases.

Cross-cultural analysis implies recurring experiential forms have a physiological basis (McClenon, 2002a). This implies that the physiology of consciousness contributes to general belief in spirits, souls, life after death, and magical abilities. Much evidence supports this claim. Apparitions reported in Great Britain and Hong Kong contain similar "abnormal features of perception" (probably derived from cognitive structures). Ghosts vanish instantaneously, appear in only partial form, and coincide with a relative's death (Emmons, 1982, pp. 75–92; McClenon, 2000). Similar forms of paranormal dreams, waking extrasensory perceptions, out-of-body experiences, psychokinesis, and sleep paralysis are found in narratives from all surveyed populations (McClenon, 1994, 2002a). Most accounts of specific forms are sufficiently similar that, if stories from differing cultures are randomly mixed, the culture of origin for any individual report cannot be determined.

The "physiological basis" argument implies that ancient hominids perceived similar anomalous episodes and that these events led them to similar beliefs in spirits, souls, life after death, and magical abilities. Since anomalous experiences were not distributed normally, the theory implies that those with repeated experiences (who would tend to be more dissociative) became the first shamans.

Shamanism is the collection of religious practices in which practitioners seek to contact spiritual forces through trance in order to benefit those in their hunter/gatherer communities (Eliade, 1964; Winkelman, 2000). Shamanism involves social processes: (1) people perceiving many anomalous experiences develop powerful belief in spirits, souls, life after death, and magical abilities;

(2) after socialization, their belief aids them in performing compelling rituals that benefit others through hypnotic and placebo processes; (3) those more open to these suggestions derive the most benefit.

Previous analyses of collections of anomalous experiences shed light on the relationship between culture and experience. Cardeña, Lynn, and Krippner (2002) provide a general review of the literature pertaining to anomalous experience. Notable studies include Virtanen's (1990) analysis of Finnish spontaneous extrasensory perceptions, Finucane's (1984) historical study of apparitions, Irwin's (1985) discussion of out-of-body experiences, Hufford's (1982) analysis of sleep paralysis cases, and Zaleski's (1987) comparison of European medieval and modern accounts of near-death experiences. This chapter extends this body of knowledge by reviewing (1) cross-cultural and historical comparison of NDEs, and (2) a content analysis of 28 NDEs found in a North Carolina anomalous experience collection (McClenon, 2005).

Historical and Cross-Cultural Analysis of NDEs

Near-death experiences (NDEs) are defined as profound psychological events with transcendental and mystical elements, typically occurring to individuals close to death or in situations of intense physical or emotional danger (Greyson, 2000, p. 315). Moody (1975) identified 15 core features within his NDE case collection: (1) ineffability (difficulty describing the experience), (2) hearing the news of one's death, (3) feelings of peace and quiet, (4) hearing a particular noise, (5) traversing a dark tunnel, (6) feeling out-of-body, (7) meeting others (deceased relatives, friends, religious guides), (8) meeting or experiencing a being of light, (9) perceiving a life review, (10) perceiving a border between life and death, (11) coming back to the body, (12) telling others of the experience, (13) perceiving effects on attitudes toward life, (14) gaining new views of death, and (15) corroboration of information gained from the otherworldly travels.

Since publication of Moody's paradigmatic book, researchers have attempted to determine the exact nature of these "core elements." Moody and others found that no single account contained all 15 elements and, as a result, later researchers created more limited lists. Ring (1980) described five "sequential stages" or "elements." These included (1) feeling peace, (2) body separation, (3) entering darkness, (4) seeing the light, and (5) entering the light. Fenwick and Fenwick (1995) proposed a core containing "the light which is seen, the feelings of peace or joy evoked, the ambivalence about dying — the knowledge that even though you may not want to go, if it is not your time, then you have to return" (p. 159). Sutherland (1992) argues that a "deep structure" exists within

NDEs. People "leave their bodies, pass into an area of darkness, move toward a light, enter a world of preternatural beauty and encounter beings such as deceased loved ones or friends who communicate with them before they return" (p. 30). In general, scholars concur that NDEs have core features, but they cannot agree on the precise nature of these elements. Greyson (1983, 1999) devised a widely used scale quantifying elements thought to define NDEs.

Cross-cultural and historical analysis sheds light on the NDE core. Comparison of NDEs from pre-literate societies, ancient bureaucratic China, feudal Europe, and modern USA reveal that, although NDEs have core features, these episodes are culturally shaped, reflecting experiencers' narrative imaginations.

Kellehear (1996) reviewed NDE accounts from Melanesia, Micronesia, Native America, Aboriginal Australia and Maori New Zealand. He concluded that, although the data imply existence of core elements, similarities are not as great as early researchers assumed. He described features such as a "period of darkness," encounters with "other beings," and the arrival at an "other world." An aged New Zealand Maori described her NDE to King (1985, pp. 87–88), exemplifying the nature of pre-literate accounts:

> I became seriously ill for the only time in my life. I became so ill that my spirit actually passed out of my body. My family believed I was dead because my breathing stopped. They took me to the marae [open space in front of the meeting house], laid out my body and began to call people for the tangi [funeral]. Meanwhile, in my spirit, I had hovered over my head then left the room and traveled northwards, towards the Tail of the Fish [geographical place]. I passed over the Waikato River [and four other places] until at last I came to Te Rerenga Wairu, the Leaping-Off Place of Spirits.... I began to karanga [give a welcoming call] to let my tupuna [ancestors] know I had come.... But a voice stopped me. It was Mahuto [a deceased Maori king, who said] "...go back where you come from until [your ancestors] are ready. Then I shall send for you." So I did not leap off. I rose and returned to my body and my people in Waikato. I passed over all the places and things I had seem on my way. My family and those who had assembled from Washi for the tangi were most surprised when I breathed again and sat up [King, 1985, pp. 93–94].

This account includes NDE core features: an OBE, visit to "other worlds," and mention of a "border" (the leaping off place). It portrays the deep kinship that non-technological people develop with their land (Brody, 2000) and is similar to Native American NDEs reviewed by Wade (2003). Hunter/gatherer accounts differ from those of more complex societies in that they do not include "life reviews" or tunnels (Kellehear, 1996). Hunter-gatherer NDEs reflect the concerns of non-technological people, portraying the afterlife as a utopian extension of pre-agricultural people's normal life.

People in such societies place less emphasis on morality and do not encounter tunnels requiring advanced technology.

Hunter-gatherer NDEs are equivalent to shamanic visions. Typically, shamans, during their initiation, perceive themselves to die after which they travel to outer-worldly domains where they meet spiritual forces. Certain forms of shamanic vision are exactly parallel to NDEs. For example, the Oglala Sioux shaman Black Elk reported an NDE when he was nine years old, an event regarded as his shamanic initiation (Neihardt, 1988/1932, pp. 20–47). Black Elk, and those around him, believed he viewed the same spiritual realms during his NDE that shamans visit during trance. NDEs and shamanic visions fulfill similar functions within non-technological societies; experiencers view spiritual realms, gain insights regarding cosmic mechanisms, and report this information to their listeners. Shamanic vision and NDEs seem to generate equivalent spiritual "transformations."

NDEs within agricultural societies reflect greater cultural complexity. Agricultural, feudal NDEs portray social hierarchy and increased emphasis on morality. For example Chinese Chih-kuai (records of anomalies) include the NDE of Chao T'ai, who lived during the Chin Dynasty (265–420 AD). Chao T'ai died, but revived ten days later to tell of being carried by two horsemen to a large city. There he was required to describe his sins to a magistrate who then ordered him to inspect the waterworks of the afterlife world. During his tour, he viewed deceased people being punished for their misdeeds before rebirth to a new life. He learned the value of rituals performed by the living for the dead. He saw a godly person with beautiful countenance (assumed to be the Buddha), and was told by an overseer that through embracing Buddhist doctrines, one can avoid such punishments. It was then discovered that his "death" was due to a bureaucratic error. He was directed to return to life in order to inform people of the value of rituals performed by the living on behalf of the dead.

This narrative motif, supporting reincarnation, was prevalent in medieval Asia. Asian NDEs portrayed judgment and punishment as a "between life" stage in the reincarnation process. Early stories preceded the acceptance of Chinese "hells," which later became standardized in Chinese folklore by the end of the first millennium (Teiser, 1988a,b). The "between life" punishment motif still exists within some modern Thai NDEs (Murphy, 2001). For example:

> I saw guards hitting the prisoners on the head with an iron hammer. People were being chopped into pieces. They reassembled themselves, and were chopped up again and again, until the karma acquired by killing people was exhausted.... The Yamatoot [servant of the god Yama] took me to another torture chamber. I saw a path made of hot coals. The guard was forcing people to walk this path.... The Yamatoot explained that this path of hot coals was for

those who had too many defilements (Kilesa) and desires (Tanha). We came to another torture area. These prisoners were punished by having their tongues put between red not pincers.... The Yamatoot explained that they were being punished like this because, during their lives, they were liars and slanderers [Murphy, 2001, p. 173].

Feudal European NDEs were parallel to those found in medieval China (McClenon, 1991, 2002a; Zaleski, 1987). For example, the monk Bede, in his *Ecclesiastical History of England*, completed in 731, wrote that Drythelm "died" in 696 AD of a severe illness. Drythelm revived the next day and described his experience. He stated that he had met a man "of shining countenance" who led him through an enormous valley. There he observed tortured souls being thrown from one side of the valley to the other — with ice on one side and flames on the other. Drythelm's guide explained that this was a temporary situation, that these individuals could be released through masses, prayers, alms, and fasts performed by the living on their behalf. Later, Drythelm traveled to a beautiful realm filled with happy people — which his guide explained was merely a holding area for the slightly imperfect — that the actual kingdom of heaven contained far greater fragrance and light. After Drythelm returned to his body, he distributed his property, retired to a monastery, and began a life of devotion, austerity, fasting, and frequent cold baths.

European NDEs from the twelfth and thirteen century portray similar features:

Typically the visionary is told, after viewing purgatorial torments and mistaking them for the punishments of the damned, that there are far worse sights to come ... he sees souls tossed between fire and ice ... and he finds paradise surrounded by or on top of a wall ... and after a brief taste of heavenly joys, he is compelled against his will to return to life ... and after he revives, his newly austere mode of life testifies to the authenticity of his vision [Zaleski, 1987, p. 33].

As with the Chinese Chih-kuai stories, medieval European NDEs emphasized rulers, hierarchies, morality, and benefits of rituals performed for the dead. The theme and tone of these accounts differ markedly from hunter/gatherers' NDE portrayals of rural utopia. Various common features within feudal Chinese and European NDEs seemingly reflect similar hierarchical, moral social structures.

Modern NDEs are often vague regarding after-life architecture but tend to be more positive-minded than medieval accounts. For example, a respondent in North Carolina reports:

I had an out of body experience. I was under anesthesia. I felt out of it. I felt my body rise above me. I could see myself from the ceiling. I couldn't believe it. Many people thought that my experience was a result of the anesthesia, but I don't think so. I felt like I was in heaven [McClenon, 2004, case #12].

This story lacks medieval motifs regarding hierarchical structuring, judgmental obstacles, tests, and purificatory torments. It, like most modern Western NDEs, has elements reflecting the importance of the individual in post-industrial society. As in the past, many respondents perceive qualities within the experience that compel belief (in the example case, the speaker felt "in heaven" even though there was no mention of heavenly symbols). Some Western NDErs describe self-conducted "life reviews," without judgment by an authority figure. They encounter few barriers to heaven and most find their experience to be extremely positive. Modern "transformations" following the NDE typically differ from those described in medieval accounts — the NDEr becomes more "spiritual" rather than penitent. Such reactions reflect optimistic, democratic, "healthy-minded" principles while medieval transformations seem derived from fear of punishment. Modern NDErs do not retire to monasteries to begin lives of devotion, austerity, fasting, and frequent cold baths, as did Drythelm.

As a result of these differences, Zaleski (1987) concluded that, "the otherworld journey is a work of the narrative imagination. As such it is shaped not only by the universal laws of symbolic experience, but also by the local and transitory statutes of a given culture" (p. 7). Yet it would be incorrect to assume that NDEs are totally produced by experiencers' cultures. Analyses of NDE accounts portray a more complex process. Although experiences are shaped by culture, they generate theological innovations. Drythelm's story illustrates this process; it reflected the European hierarchical social structure, but provided seeds for theological innovation — images of transition stages between death and heaven. At the time of Drythelm's NDE, the word "purgatory" had not come into usage since this concept was not theologically acceptable. His vision reflected the changing social forms of his era and, as a result, it was a pre-curser of future theological change. As feudal society became more complex, with multiple layers, its images of heaven and hell reflected this increasing complexity, hierarchy, and bureaucratic structure.

In parallel fashion, Chinese and Japanese NDEs introduced theological innovations while mirroring social complexity (McClenon, 1991). The histories of Pure Land Buddhism in China and Japan illustrate this argument. The Chinese Taoist scholar T'an-luan (476–542 AD) miraculously recovered from a serious illness and described seeing a golden gate open before him. The powerful quality of this vision caused him to seek a religious explanation and, after gathering many Taoist texts, he met the Buddhist monk Bodhiruci (circa 530). Bodhiruci revealed to him a Buddhist text, translated from the Sanskrit scriptures as early as the second century that described a near-death scenario. T'an-luan discarded his Taoist scriptures and spent the rest of his life propagating Buddhist Pure Land doctrines; the idea that the Buddha of the

West (Amitabha/Amida) meets believers at death and escorts them to a special heavenly realm (Ch'en, 1964, p. 344).

T'an-luan popularized Pure Land doctrines by advocating repetitive chanting, a method suitable for lay people. Extensive chanting triggers altered states of consciousness and those with trance skills experienced Pure Land visions during their lives. Believers also discovered, as predicted by scriptures, that people would see the Pure Land when close to death. Buddhist leaders encouraged transcribing these experiential accounts and the resulting collections reveal core features equivalent to those found by modern researchers (McClenon, 1991, 1994). Feudal and modern NDEs include transition stages, meetings with deceased people, contacts with spiritual entities, and visions of beautiful heavenly realms. For example, the Ching-t'u-lun, a document compiled shortly after Tao-ch'o's era, contains twenty NDE accounts. In one story, a butcher, on his deathbed, "first had a vision of hell, whereupon he was terrified into chanting the name of Amida; he then had a vision of Amida offering him the lotus seat, and passed peacefully away" (Becker, 1984, p. 60).

Changes in NDE motifs over time illustrate how culture and experience influence each other and how accounts contribute to cultural innovation. For example, early Japanese medieval collections included images parallel to Chinese "between-life" heavens and hells but, with the introduction of Pure Land Buddhism, later stories described journeys to the Pure Land (Becker, 1981, 1984; McClenon, 1991, 1994). As Pure Land Buddhism became established, NDE accounts provided standardized images of the afterlife, establishing folk religious traditions and motifs (McClenon, 1991).

Claims of "corroboration" contribute to NDEs' power to shape folk religious traditions. Both Asian and European accounts included elements indicating that narratives were not merely dreams, but reflected theological truths since experiencers reported earthly events later verified as true. In parallel fashion, modern anesthetized surgery patients describe seeing medical procedures while out-of-body, and medical personnel later confirm these events.

Modern accounts sometimes include scientific investigations of paranormal claims. Sabom (1998), for example, described a woman who reported a collaborative NDE that occurred while her EEG was totally flat, with auditory-evoked potential ceased, and blood completely drained from her brain. Ring and Cooper (1997, 1999) collected cases of congenitally blind people who reportedly "saw" during their out-of-body and near-death experiences.

When NDErs tell their stories to others, they contribute to their society's folk religious system. Such NDEs constitute forms of shamanic vision. Just as shamans modify their audience's beliefs through magical performance, NDErs sway opinions through story-telling skills. NDErs are like shamans in that they often gain certainty regarding the after-life and, like shamans, their stories result in theological innovations thought to be psychologically therapeutic.

Content Analysis of a Narrative Collection

Analysis of NDEs within the North Carolina (NC) anomalous experience collection allowed testing of ritual healing theory hypotheses. Fox (2003) provides a model for analysis of NDE collections. Twenty-eight afterlife accounts were identified using Fox's (2003) selection strategy based on Moody's (1975) elements. Fox (2003, p. 247) distinguishes "crisis" experiences, in which the account involves the possibility of death and "non-crisis" experiences, where that possibility is not present. He compared the incidence of Moody's "core features" within crisis and non-crisis accounts and found equivalent frequency (Fox, 2003, p. 247). This finding implies that NDEs are not generated through mechanisms related to a dying brain, but through visionary processes.

Hypotheses

The 28-case NC afterlife experience collection contained 22 crisis cases, 5 non-crisis accounts, and 1 deathbed vision. These cases were evaluated using the five hypotheses derived from the ritual healing theory.

1. The Biological Basis of NDEs: Any large collection of NDE narratives should reveal core features reflecting the biological basis of this experiential form. The incidence of features can be counted through scales based on the work of Moody (1975), Ring (1980), and Greyson (1983).

2. The Source of NDEs: Shamanism vs. Dying Brain: One explanation for the physiological basis of NDEs is that these episodes are the result of a dying brain. The ritual healing theory offers a counter-hypothesis — that NDEs are equivalent to shamanic visions (McClenon, 2005). The ritual healing theory argues that comparison of crisis accounts to non-crisis accounts should reveal equivalent incidence of core features as measured by Moody, Ring, and Greyson.

3. The Cultural Shaping of NDEs: Just as shamanic visions are shaped by the experiencer's culture, NDEs are hypothesized to reflect the experiencer's culture. Exploratory analysis of the predominately African-American NC collection should reveal a different ratio of positive/negative emotions than found by Fox (2003) in his British sample and different percentages of NDE types than found by Greyson (1990) in his USA sample.

4. The Shamanic Nature of NDEs: Much evidence supports the argument that NDEs are a form of shamanic vision (Green, 1996, 1998, 2001; Ring, 1989; Serdahely, 1991). The ritual healing theory predicts that the type of person who reports an NDE is more likely to report other forms of anomalous experience. It also hypothesizes that NDEs, and other anomalous experiences, motivate some experiencers to seek shamanic skills. As a result, these people play shamanic roles, performing magical services for others. These hypotheses can be investigated qualitatively through analysis of cases coinciding with these predictions.

5. The Social Impact of NDEs: The ritual healing theory argues that audiences hearing NDE stories tend to increase their belief in life after death. Qualitative analysis of stories deemed most interesting by listeners, and the impacts attributed to these stories, should shed light on the process by which folk religion is created through oral transmission of experiential accounts.

Findings

1: The Biological Basis of NDEs: Table 13.1 compares the incidence of NDE core features found by Fox (2003), Ring (1975), and Greyson (1983) to the incidence found in the NC collection. Although the NC collection revealed a lower incidence of core features, the existence of these elements in the NC sample supports the hypothesis.

Table 13.1— Comparison of Fox (2003), Ring (1980), Greyson (1983) Sample Mean Scores to North Carolina Sample Mean Scores

Scale Measuring Core Features	Average Score Reported in Previous Samples	North Carolina Sample
Fox (2003; using Moody's, 1975, scale)	Crisis: 3.30	Crisis: 2.80
	Non-crisis: 2.90	Non-crisis: 2.90
Ring (1980)	1.46*	1.16
Greyson (1983)	16.48	3.78

Note: Average incidence of NDE elements was determined by summing proportions of "core experiencers" reporting each "stage," provided by Ring (1980, p. 40)

2: The Source of NDEs: Shamanism vs. Dying Brain: Table 13.2 compares average scores using Moody, Ring, and Greyson scales applied to crisis and non-crisis accounts. As found by Fox (2003), average scores associated with crisis and non-crisis accounts did not differ significantly.

Scale	Coder scores mean (n = 27)	Crisis experience mean (n = 22)	Non-crisis experience mean (n = 5)	t (crisis vs. non-crisis)	df	p (crisis vs. non-crisis)*
Moody (1975)	2.83	2.81	2.87	-0.06	25	.95
Ring (1980)	1.16	1.18	1.07	0.48	25	.64
Greyson (1983)	3.78	3.69	4.13	-0.32	25	.76

Note: Small sample sizes make inferential tests of significance problematic. Relatively large differences in means are required to achieve statistical significance. For example, if the five non-crisis Greyson NDE scores were proportionally reduced so that their mean was 1.32, or increased to create a mean of 6.96, the associated *t* would achieve significance at the .05 level (two-tailed test)

3: The Cultural Shaping of NDEs: The NC sample revealed somewhat higher incidence of negative emotion (30% of crisis emotion incidence, 80% of non-crisis emotion incidence) than was found by Fox (18.75% of crisis emotions, 13.40% of non-crisis emotions). The types of NDEs in the NC sample differed markedly from those reported by Greyson's (1990) International Association for Near Death Studies (IANDS) members: 42.7% of the IANDS accounts were "transcendental," 41.6% "affective," and 15.7% "cognitive." Only three individuals scored high enough on Greyson's (1983) NDE scale to allow a subscale classification; in all cases, these were "transcendental." Within this "transcendental" motif, NC respondents reported an out-of-body experience and travel to a heavenly realm where they spoke with relatives or Jesus. They reported virtually none of the distortions of time that contributed to IANDS cognitive NDEs. Seventy-five percent of the IANDS respondents stated that their experience included the feature "everything seemed to be happening all at once; or time stopped, or lost all meaning" (Greyson, 1990, p. 156). No NC account revealed this feature.

Qualitative analysis portrays the element in the NC collection causing these stories to differ from other collections: a higher percentage of anxiety regarding out-of-body travel. Three non-crisis respondents stated that their anomalous sensations caused them to become highly anxious (they thought that they might be dead). Two respondents described sleep paralysis incidents. For example, "I awoke in a deep sweat. My eyes were open but I could not move. I looked above at the ceiling and I saw myself, my spirit, before my very own eyes. I remember praying, asking the Lord what was happening. I felt my heartbeat dropping and I began to panic."

4: The Shamanic Nature of NDEs: The ritual healing theory hypothesizes that NDEs are one of the forms of anomalous experience that provide a basis for shamanism. It predicts that any large collection of NDEs should include stories portraying shamanic processes: people who have a tendency to experience anomalous perceptions, are healed by spiritual processes, and become healers themselves.

One case in particular illustrates the shamanic biography. While in the hospital, a 30-year-old female perceived an NDE that included feelings of peace, OBE, meeting others, seeing the light, coming back, telling others, effects on life, new views of death, and corroboration. She reported that she had been considered a "special" child due to the many apparitions she perceived when young. She remembered frequent conversations with a deceased uncle when she was five years old (before she realized he was dead). She told of apparitional visits by a deceased grandfather and a precognitive dream of a shooting in her neighborhood. She described a waking extrasensory perception that foretold a relative's death. She reports many precognitive dreams: a wake that corresponded exactly with later events, a miscarriage experienced by a woman at her work, a trip to Richmond for a medical appointment, and a bald stranger whom she later recognized as her brother's attorney (even though he wore a hairpiece). She described a series of precognitive dreams regarding winning numbers in the Maryland lottery. She won small amounts on three occasions and her cousin won a larger sum by playing a number she provided (McClenon, 2002a, p. 139). These experiences made her certain of spiritual forces, life after death, and her own magical abilities. She acquired a reputation in her community as a spiritual healer/advisor — a person whose prayers were often answered. As a result, people often asked her to pray for them. Her NDE contributed to her beliefs:

> ... it's like this, [Jesus] touched my hand and it's like — now, no matter what happens, I really know He's there for me. It's made a difference for me — how I think — how I treat other people.... I ask Him for guidance and I try to take the steps as he guides me. But I don't worry about anything because I don't need to. I know that I'm only going to be here for a little while and when I go, I know there is going to be complete peace. I'm not afraid of dying.

People who have multiple otherworldly experiences tend to develop certainty regarding spiritual affairs. For example, a 53-year-old male described a non-crisis OBE that included 6 of Moody's core features and scored 7 on Greyson's NDE scale. His first experience alarmed him, but after repeated experiences, he came to believe that he could control his perceptions:

Since this occurrence, I have had this same thing happen to me several times. From these experiences, I feel that it is possible that the dying process may have some human choice involved in it. I feel that it may allow you to ultimately control your final destiny. Even though we are overpowered by the stresses of everyday life, the light that I saw makes you think and see that Jesus has given us a final escape route from the truly unbearable aspects of life. It is ultimately up to us to use this wisely for the betterment of all concerned.

The idea of control is at the heart of shamanism. The shaman gains control of his cognitive processes and, as a result, is able to visit spirit worlds and win concessions from spiritual forces. Those who have frequent anomalous experiences often feel they have magical abilities they believe they can use to benefit themselves and others. For example, an adult male described repeated OBEs. He knew his mother was sick and purposefully attempted to "visit" her spiritually:

> You may not believe this, but I tell you every word of it is true. For years I have had this ability to leave my body to go and visit someone who may be in trouble or who is dying. When my mother was dying I went to visit her, not in person but spiritually.... I went in my room and got down on my knees like I was praying. The next thing I knew I was with my mama. We talked and talked about all those good times we used to have and she told me that she was going to be all right and to go back to myself and not grieve because she was going to be in heaven and would be watching down over me. When I came back everybody was around me and they told me I must have passed out. I looked at them and said, "No, I was with mama." [His father supported his story by noting that his son had described many valid anomalous experiences in the past and that the reported experience had coincided with his wife's death within 15 minutes.]

These cases illustrate a pattern found around the world. Those who experience frequent anomalous events develop powerful beliefs and tend to perform shamanic roles within their communities. The ritual healing theory argues that the physiological and social processes that created shamanism are still occurring today.

5. The Social Impact of NDEs: The ritual healing theory argues that audiences are changed by hearing reports of NDEs, and that these stories shape religious beliefs. This process was documented when interviewers were asked to summarize their reactions to each informant's story and by asking coders to identify those stories they found most interesting.

Qualitative analysis of these results provides insights into processes by which some stories gain wide distribution, affecting folk beliefs. Although respondents provided a variety of opinions — from strong skepticism to absolute belief — most typically, they expressed belief in the validity of the NDE accounts:

When people hear that someone has died and come back to life, they often label the person as crazy. But, if you think about it, Jesus died and came back to life. If you believe that then why is it so hard to believe that another human could not do the same?

I had never given any thought to these types of things. I was very interested in what Mrs. M. had to say because it just seemed so unreal. While she was talking, I got goose bumps. I felt spooked thinking that it really happened. It made me think that when we die, our spirits, or souls, really leave the body, and not just die with our mortal beings. I had always believed in life after death because of religious reasons, but there's a difference in believing something and hearing that it has actually happened.

Student coders were asked to list the three stories they found most interesting and to describe why they were attracted to those particular stories. Four stories received four or more votes: (1) the woman who reported an extremely large number of anomalous perceptions which included an NDE, (2) the man who claimed to engage regularly in out-of-body travel and who visited his mother as she died, (3) a woman who had a vision of hell and heaven, and (4) a man who saw deceased relatives immediately before he died (classified as a deathbed vision and not included in the analysis).

Student essays provide insight into why certain stories were found most interesting. Coders were attracted to the idea that some people control their anomalous perceptions — a concept central to shamanism. Some coders stated that the hell/heaven vision represented their own religious beliefs and they evaluated this story as particularly valid. Coders also selected the deathbed vision as interesting due to the empathy this story elicited (the story went into much detail describing the suffering of a dying man). Although this story was presented in a rambling, unorganized style, coders stated that they identified with the storyteller's grief, a process that helped them also feel the storyteller's joy when the man glimpsed his deceased relatives before dying.

Student essays revealed how people use their own experiences, coupled with emotional processes, to evaluate these stories. Essayists often noted that personal life histories made specific stories more appealing. For example, various female students (some of whom had children) found one story to be particularly powerful: a young woman reported an NDE while suffering childbirth complications. In her vision, she chose life on earth rather than entrance to heaven so that she could raise her newborn child. The coders' evaluations reveal how certain stories provide healthy ways for people to think about problems they face — for example, stress associated with child rearing.

The coders' comments reveal the differential impact of anomalous accounts; some stories were found to be much more interesting than others. Social processes govern the selection process by which anomalous accounts are granted greater weight. It would seem that specific apparitional accounts of the resurrection of Jesus played an extremely important role within Christian theology, while certain Asian NDEs shaped Buddhist folk belief.

Within modern Western folk traditions, NDEs seem to be gaining greater importance, contributing to a form of ecumenical folk belief. People in multiethnic societies benefit from folk belief systems that encourage religious tolerance. The after-lives portrayed in most modern NDEs are tolerated far more than those advocated by Christian denominations prevalent in Northeastern North Carolina. In a way, NDE accounts play a shamanic role in modern societies, portraying healthy, innovative ways of thinking about life and death.

Conclusions

Cross-cultural, historical comparison of NDE accounts and a content analysis of a North Carolina NDE collection support hypotheses derived from the ritual healing theory. NDEs have core features, implying a biological basis. They seem derived from a process related to shamanism rather than one derived from a dying brain. Like shamanic visions, they are shaped by the experiencer's culture, revealing aspects that differ among cultures. They are part of a process by which some people take up shamanic roles and, as a result, they shape folk religious traditions.

References

Becker, C. B. (1981). The centrality of near-death experience in Chinese Pure Land Buddhism, *Anabiosis, 1,* 154–171.

Becker, C. B. (1984). The Pure Land revisited: Sino-Japanese meditations and near-death experiences of the next world. *Anabiosis, 4,* 51–68.

Brody, H. (2000). *The other side of Eden: Hunters, farmers, and the shaping of the world,* New York: North Point Press.

Cardeña, E., Lynn, S. J., & Krippner, S. (2002). *Varieties of anomalous experience: Examining the scientific evidence.* Washington, DC: American Psychological Association.

Ch'en, K. (1964). *Buddhism in China: A historical survey.* Princeton, NJ: Princeton University Press.

D'Onofri, B. M., Eaves, L. J., Murrelle, L., Maes, H. H. Spilka, B. (1999). Understanding biological and social influences on religious affiliation, attitudes, and behaviors: A behavior genetic prespective, *Journal of Personality, 67,* 953–984.

Eliade, M. (1964). *Shamanism: Archaic techniques of ecstasy,* London: Routledge.

Emmons, C. F. (1982). *Chinese ghosts and ESP: A study of paranormal beliefs and experiences.* Metuchen, NJ: Scarecrow Press.

Fenwick, P. and Fenwick, E. (1995). *The truth in the light: An investigation of over 300 near-death experiences,* London: Headline.

Finucane. R. C. (1984). *Appearances of the dead: A cultural history of ghosts.* Buffalo, NY: Prometheus Books.

Fox, M. (2003). *Religion, spirituality and the near-death experience.* New York: Routledge.

Gaulin, S. J. C. & McBurney, D. H. (2001). *Psychology: An evolutionary approach.* Upper Saddle River, NJ: Prentice Hall.

Green, J. T. (1996). Journeys into the light: Near-death experiences as an ecstatic initiation. *Shaman's Drum*, pp. 49–54.

Green, J. T. (1998). Near-death experiences, shamanism, and the scientific method. *Journal of Near-death Studies, 16*, 205–222.

Green, J. T. (2001). The near-death experience as a shamanic initiation: A case study. *Journal of Near-Death Studies, 19*, 209–225.

Greyson, B. (1983). The near-death experience scale: Construction, reliability, and validity, *Journal of Nervous and Mental Disease, 171*, 369–375.

Greyson, B. (1985). A typology of near-death experiences. *American Journal of Psychiatry, 142*, 967–969.

Greyson, B. (1990). Near-death encounters with and without near-death experiences: Comparative NDE scale profiles, *Journal of Near-Death Studies, 8*, 151–161.

Greyson, B. (1999). Defining near-death experiences, *Mortality, 4*, 7–19.

Greyson, B. (2000). Near-death experiences. E. Cardeña, S. J. Lynn, and S. Krippner (Eds.), *Variety of anomalous experience: Examining the scientific evidence* (pp. 315–352). Washington, DC: American Psychological Association.

Hufford, D. (1982). *The terror that comes in the night: An experience-centered study of supernatural assault traditions*, Philadelphia, PA: University of Pennsylvania Press.

Irwin, H. J. (1985). *Flight of mind: A psychological study of the out-of-body experience*. Metuchen, NJ: Scarecrow Press.

Kellehear, A. (1996). *Experiences near death: Between medicine and religion*. Oxford: Oxford University Press.

King, M. (1985). *Being Pakeha: An encounter with New Zealand and the Maori renaissance*. Auckland, New Zealand: Hodder & Stoughton.

Kumar, V. K. & Pekala. R. J. (2001). Relation of hypnosis-specific attitudes and behaviors to paranormal beliefs and experiences: A technical review. In J. Houran & R. Lange (Eds.), *Hauntings and poltergeists: Multidisciplinary perspectives* (pp. 260–279). Jefferson, NC: McFarland.

Laughlin, C. D., Jr., McManus, J., & d'Aquili, E. G. (1992). *Brain, symbol, and experience: Toward a neurophenomenology of human consciousness*. New York: Columbia University Press.

McClenon, J. (1991). Near-death folklore in medieval China and Japan: A comparative analysis. *Asian Folklore Studies, 50*, 319–42.

McClenon, J. (1993). The experiential foundations of shamanic healing, *Journal of Medicine and Philosophy, 18*, 107–127.

McClenon, J. (1994). *Wondrous events: Foundations of religious belief*. Philadelphia: University of Pennsylvania Press.

McClenon, J. (1997). Shamanic healing, human evolution, and the origin of religion, *Journal for the Scientific Study of Religion, 36*, 345–54.

McClenon, J. (2000). Content analysis of an anomalous memorate collection: Testing hypotheses regarding universal features, *Sociology of Religion, 61*, 155–69.

McClenon, J. (2002a). *Wondrous healing: Shamanism, human evolution, and the origin of religion*. Dekalb, IL: Northern Illinois University Press.

McClenon, J. (2002b). Content analysis of an anomalous experience collection: Evaluating evolutionary perspective, *Journal of Parapsychology, 66*, 291–315.

McClenon, J. (2004). Unpublished after-life experience collection.

McClenon, J. (2005). Content analysis of a predominately African-American near-death experience collection: Evaluating the Ritual Healing Theory. *Journal of Near-Death Studies, 23*, 159–81

Moody, R. (1975). *Life after life*. Atlanta: Mockingbird.

Murphy, T. (2001). Near-death experiences in Thailand. *Journal of Near-Death Studies, 19*, 161–78.

Neihardt, J. G. (1988). *Black Elk speaks: Being the life story of a holy man of the Oglala Sioux*. Lincoln, NE : University of Nebraska Press. (Original work published 1932).

Ridley, M. (Ed.) (1997). *Evolution*. New York: Oxford University Press.

Ring, K. (1980). *Life at death: A scientific investigation of the near-death experience*. New York: Coward, McCann & Geoghegan.

Ring, K. (1984). *Heading toward Omega: In search of the meaning of the near-death experience.* New York: William Morrow.

Ring, K. (1989). Near-death and UFO encounters as shamanic initiations: Some conceptual and evolutionary implications. *ReVision, 11,* 14–22.

Ring, K. (1990). Shamanic initiation, imaginal worlds, and light after death. In Gary Doore (Ed.). *What survives? Contemporary explorations of life after death* (pp. 204–215). Los Angeles, CA: Tarcher.

Ring, K. (1992). *The omega project: Near-death experiences, and mind at large,* New York: William Morrow.

Ring, K. & Cooper, S. (1997). Near-death and out-of-body experiences in the blind: A study of apparent eyeless vision, *Journal of Near-Death Studies, 16,* 101–47.

Ring, K. & Cooper, S. (1999). *Mindsight: Near-death and out-of-body experiences in the blind.* Palo Alto, CA: William James Center for Consciousness Studies.

Sabom, M. (1998). *Light and death: One doctor's fascinating account of near-death experiences.* Grand Rapids, MI: Zondervan.

Schumaker, J. F (1990) *Wings of illusion.* Buffalo, NY: Prometheus.

Serdahely, W. J. (1991). Were some shamans near-death experiencers first? [Letter]. *Journal of Near-Death Studies, 9,* 255–257.

Sutherland, C. (1992) *Reborn in the light: Life after near-death experiences,* New York: Bantam.

Swatos, W. H., & Gissurarson, L. R. (1996). *Icelandic Spiritualism: Mediumship and modernity in Iceland.* New Brunswick, NJ: Transaction Publishers.

Teiser, S. F. (1988a). *The ghost festival in medieval China.* Preincton, NJ: Princeton University Press.

Teiser, S. F. (1988b). Having once died and returned to life: Representations of hell in medieval China. *Harvard Journal of Asiatic Studies, 48,* 433–464.

Virtanen, L. (1990). *That must have been ESP!* (trans. J. Atkinson & T. Dubois). Bloomington, IN: Indiana University Press.

Wade, J. (2003). In a sacred manner we died: Native American near-death experiences, *Journal of Near-Death Studies, 22,* 83–115.

Waller, N. G., Kojetin, B. A., Bouchard, T. J., Jr., Lykken, D. T., & Tellegen, A. (1990). Genetic and environmental influences on religious interests, attitudes, and values: A study of twins reared apart and together. *Psychological Science, 1,* 138–142.

Wilson, D. S. (2002). *Darwin's cathedral: Evolution, religion and the nature of society.* Chicago: University of Chicago Press.

Winkelman, M. (1992). *Shamans, priests and witches: A cross-cultural study of magico-religious practitioners.* Tempe, AZ: Arizona State University Anthropological Research Papers #44.

Winkelman, M. (2000). *Shamanism: The neural ecology of consciousness and healing.* Westport, CN: Bergin and Garvey.

Zaleski, C. (1987). *Otherworld Journeys: Accounts of Near-death experiences in medieval and modern times.* Oxford: Oxford University Press.

Section V: Conclusions

14. *Where Do We Go from Here?*
LANCE STORM

This chapter is a summary of all of the 13 chapters in this book. The author considers the different ideas presented in those chapters. Reaching a consensus proves to be an exercise dependent upon making concordant those issues that are discordant between the various schools of thought, as well as drawing out the omissions of the various authors' chapters. The 13 chapters are also considered in terms of the language used by the authors.—Editors

Introduction

Where do we go from here? Humankind has long asked this question. Is there a way to an answer without having to wait until one's actual death? If physical demise is the only way to find out, and if indeed there *can* be an answer waiting to be heard (perceived?) by a disembodied personality sufficiently identical with the personality before it left the body, then that which survives will get an answer in the affirmative. The alternative is no response at all.

But as an author faced with an editorial responsibility, where do *I* go from here? Has enough material been presented in the preceding chapters to reach a conclusion? Before this book was written, there were already a number of answers floating around that indicated a kind of survival, but we want to go beyond the specious compromises proffered by the likes of R. W. Hood and R. J. Morris (1993), where survival can be achieved via methods that are "biosocial" (everlasting life is achieved through our children), "creative" (our works survive us), "natural" (we are each part of an eternal whole), or even "mystical" (communion with a higher power). Even the hoped-for but ephemeral mystical experience pales by comparison to a life hereafter with the Deity — especially if an epiphany in this life may be, as Jung proposes, a mere (by comparison!) encounter with what he calls the Self, the so-called Central Archetype, the "God-image" as he refers to it.*

So, let us consider the proposition — that a certain substance has the capacity to survive bodily death, as is given in our religions and some of our philosophies. The answer to the question of a life hereafter might be nearing the affirmative because much of the evidence presented in the preceding chapters could stand as evidence for survival, regardless of the fact that it could also stand as evidence for phenomenologies other than survival such as normal but rare neuropsychological brain functions, or even super-psi. After all, what is to qualify as evidence? There are extreme skeptics who deny survival, who also happen to balk at the mere suggestion that anything could be paranormal. Perhaps, for the opened-minded amongst us, we have enough material to form *an* answer, even if it is not *the* answer for which many might wish. For example, an OBE (see Moreman, Chapter 2) may really be an experience *outside* the body, or it may be an inside-body experience (an IBE — or more characteristically, a lucid dream, a meditative experience, or a fantasy-state such as is embodied in Braud's term "mythopoetic"), but both explanations — OBE and IBE — are not mutually incompatible with one another.

Consider another example — that of reincarnation (see Haraldsson, Chapter 10). Perhaps the relatively "new" personality of an infant child can reproduce memories of a past life, and/or exhibit marks or "scars" corresponding to wounds incurred in that past life — we may be able to speak of mental and physical remnants that can be adopted by, or transferred to, a new host. But what if the memories and marks result from super-psi (super-ESP and super-PK)? Maybe some living agent telepathically planted the memories, or the child accessed the information telepathically or clairvoyantly. Maybe the same

---

*Jung (1958) equated the god-image with the Self, which he defines as the totality of the personality (consciousness and the unconscious): "It is only through the psyche that we can establish that God acts upon us, but we are unable to distinguish whether these actions emanate from God or from the unconscious. We cannot tell whether God and the unconscious are two different entities. Both are borderline concepts for transcendental contents. But empirically it can be established, with a sufficient degree of probability, that there is in the unconscious an archetype of wholeness.... [S]trictly speaking, the God-image does not coincide with the unconscious as such, but with ... [this] special content of it, namely the archetype of the Self" (para. 757).

living agent used super-PK to manipulate the gene code or organs of the child to produce markings and "scars" that "match" those of the postmortem individual — though we must ask for what purpose. But if we were going to ask that question, it would be mandatory to ask why a non-living agent (a disembodied soul) would do such a thing to a person. Why burden a host with "past wounds"— especially a small child? Either way, the super-psi hypothesis does not preclude the possibility of genuine reincarnation, and *vice versa* (cf. Braud, Chapter 4.) Other examples, in which both survival and super-psi are each suitable as explanations, include drop-in communications (i.e., uninvited "spirit" communication at a séance) and trance mediumship (see Chapters 7 and 8).

There would be a need for researchers to entertain and follow up avenues of empirical inquiry that might differentiate between these alternative explanations. How might the super-psi hypothesis better explain, for example, the phenomenology of the reincarnation-type case than does the straight-out hypothesis that something like a soul reincarnates? In fact, the super-psi explanation works nicely for the "soft" evidence like trance mediumship, drop-in communication, cross correspondences, and the like, but one needs a very flexible mind to accommodate the "hard" evidence like the reincarnation-type range of phenomena (i.e., scarring, birthmarks, and deformations, etc.) and transplant cases (where an organ donor's personality adjuncts itself to the recipient's personality). Ultimately, Stephen Braude (2003) calls upon the *Argument from Crippling Complexity*— super-psi in its simpler form appears to involve accessing multiple sources of information from an extremely complex causal nexus, which Braude argues becomes impossible to mediate. So, on the basis of parsimony, Braude rules that the scales are tipped in favor of the survival hypothesis.

However, it is suggested here that, as in the OBE case, so also with reincarnation-type cases, etc., alternative explanations for each type of phenomenon are mutually exclusive. Besides, that which is a workable truth for one person is often nothing more than opinion for another. So, in perhaps presenting so much inconclusive evidence in this book, we have nevertheless advanced a little because no one can exclusively defend or refute one hypothesis in favor of another on the basis of interpretations and reinterpretations of the evidence, especially if it requires the application of Ockham's Razor. If a believer or a skeptic is to be taken seriously, he or she would need to find better "evidence" than an argument, and/or something better than the flourish of a hand wielding a time-honored cutting implement used for the express purpose of performing philosophical surgery rather than arriving at the truth.

That being said, we need to determine whether this book's chapters cohere into a sensible and serviceable whole, or merely present as nothing more than a fragmented potpourri of disparate research findings. So, let's begin our review of the chapters.

The Review

We start with Chandler's contribution (Chapter 1) because the best place to start is at the beginning, and that is where Chandler starts. The question of survival may have been around in our remote past, though the form of that "question" at one time was (no doubt) more tacit, implicit, unexpressed. With the advent of language, the question could be voiced, and the answer was in the affirmative — our ancestors did believe in life after death. But Chandler asks if that belief emerged only from our ancestors' conscious fear of their own mortality. Apparently, there was a mindset amongst our ancestors that indicates that if there was an attitude of fear, it was fear of the dead, rather than fear of death (cf. McClenon, Chapter 13). Thus, Chandler undermines many a paleoanthropologist's viewpoint that our ancestors were afraid of death and therefore invented the afterlife as an ego defense mechanism — a kind of denial of extinction.

The argument is a strong one, but fear of the dead is an issue that needs further consideration — it is largely an *irrational* fear. Our ancestors feared (or revered at best) perilous mountaintops, gaping chasms, and the darkness of forests and caves — and they feared them not just because they were afraid of falling from great heights, or because these places were the abodes of ferocious animals, but also because they believed those unfathomable places were "occupied" by spirits. On that basis, the "specter" or visiting apparition that might haunt the bereaved remains a puzzle to us. Why should it haunt?* I did say one would not *rationally* fear dark forests, caves and other unknown realms, but of course we know from the psychodynamic theories that we project our innermost, often rational, fears onto the unknown, and that *does* result in irrational fears. These fears are often not in our conscious awareness. So emerges our fear of spirits, demons, specters, and ghosts, and thus do we have an alternative, more likely source of fear of the dead — it is the fear of that which is unconscious, and that is a wretched, if not crushing state of affairs indeed for the species *Homo sapiens* that prides itself on its reason, its culture, its sophistication, its technology, and its temporal and psychological "distance" from ancestors who didn't know any better.

Chandler argues that the "egoic soul" (or "Trickster") refuses to let go its desire for immortality, in this life and in the afterlife, which suggests that the soul survives, but does not want "to move on"— hence, it haunts.

How far are we actually removed from our ancestors? Perhaps not very far, but it is worse still for the survival hypothesis if it can be shown that those entities that occupy the afterlife are all really in our heads. Are ghosts nothing more than artifacts of the psyche? We moderns may say so, but knowing that a ghost is a product of one's psyche does not make one any less fearful of it. So why did our ancestors not fear death? It would seem that the more positive NDEs and OBEs might assuage that fear — ND- and OB-experients could relate their pleasant encounters to others in the tribe, thus giving them an optimistic take on the death experience (cf. McClenon, Chapter 13).

But in modern times, things are very different. In our large cities, where community has all but disappeared, ND- and OB-experients rarely share their stories in mainstream society. Pedagogy tends to end outside the school grounds and the workplace. With our culture in such a state, it is a small but *necessary* step from this current stage in our cultural evolution, to the next stage where we attempt the implementation of an afterlife of sorts in this world. It is *necessary* because we have to assuage our fear of death somehow, for if the "denial of death" hypothesis criticized by Chandler is true of any culture it is true of ours, not those of the past. What kind of substitute for the afterlife can we implement, and how?

For many people, the denial of death has set so hard, a new cultural practice has emerged. It is a revival of an old Egyptian practice, but with a twist — it is the mummification of the living, not the dead. As Chandler points out, we now "preserve" ourselves in any number of ways with creams, balms, exercise, advances in medicine, and what not, and many want to live longer than ever before, simply to escape the ultimate truth — for many, the ultimate nothingness — that awaits us all. Broderick (2005) has elaborated on what could be done using other similar methods of preservation — "cryonic suspension in expectation of eventual medical repair, rejuvenation, indefinite life extension, uploads, a transformative transition to some posthuman condition we can scarcely yet imagine" (p. 9). Modern science and medicine give us the possibility of sustaining even longer that same personality that struggles with special diets and endless hours in the gym. But is that the only hope we have — not a life beyond the grave, but a life that cheats death for some undetermined time? A life encoded on something not much more sophisticated than magnetic tape — a life in an electronic dream world. Should we not erase, rewind, and reconsider?

Notwithstanding the possibility that these options are, or may one day be open to us, scientific survival is not the same thing as metaphysical survival, for the former gives no guarantee that the brain won't eventually suffer some degree of irreparable decay during its cryogenic suspension, or the personality won't be damaged within its silicon exo-skeleton. I somehow doubt that our entrepreneurs of tomorrow will be interested in fostering a survival technology that is the safest or most reliable, or even the most logical, or easiest to realize. The technology of physical- and personality-preservation most likely to be endorsed will be the one that promises the greatest financial yields for its developers and investors. If ever an ideology existed that would most likely underscore a drive to an immortality of sorts it would be capitalism! The personification of death, Joe Black (played by Brad Pitt in Martin Brest's 1998 movie *Meet Joe Black*), thought death and taxes was a "strange pairing." The pairing is apt, but with only slight modification, perhaps death and money is more appropriate for the modern and postmodern world. Perhaps we would not be surprised either by the sad truth that survival in the future may be a privilege of those who have the money, just as it was for the pharaohs of old.

A clearer vision of how things were meant to be for humanity beyond corporeal life really requires a wiping clean of the mirror of disillusionment that currently haunts many a postcivilized individual. Perhaps we may find an answer in the former values that have depreciated so much over the centuries. But have too many of us grown tired of these philosophical and religious notions? Can there be any hope for such viewpoints in the current era? These are questions we may infer from the final words of Chandler's chapter.

In Chapter 2, Moreman reminds us that the mystical tradition provides its own argument for survival — it is experiential rather than evidential. The mystic merges with everything — the relative self meets the Absolute Other. Moreman makes it very clear that the idea of a re-emerging self (a "realization of the true essence of the self" — p. 37) has nothing at all to do with the Western misconception of an obliterated self.

Mysticism, a "universal human experience" (p. 38), is open to all, but clearly not all of us are having mystical experiences. Moreman claims that mystical experience is something earned or needed rather than something one falls into by chance or happenstance. But in what sense is a realized self in this life (which results in nirvana, or union with God or the Absolute, etc.) the same self as the self in the afterlife? Moreman tells us that the individual self merges with the Universal Mind — as Moreman states: "the individual is lost in terms of its individualized nature" (p. 44). Not quite obliteration, but nothing near survival of unique identity either. But again, Moreman points out that belief in the survival of identity stems from a Western ego-driven desire that cannot in itself inform us about the true nature of the afterlife.

There's room in mysticism for a more impartial viewpoint that gives more support to the super-psi hypothesis than does Braude (2003). Mysticism implies that there is an interconnectedness between all humans, living and dead, at a spiritual level, that implies psi and super-psi processes. But as

all humans are physical beings, there is no way of proving that this interconnectedness effect is not dependent upon physical determinants (such as our
various organs), so, to be critical, interconnectedness is a human experience
that does not necessarily imply survival of self—even more so if self merges
with the so-called Universal Mind.

Moreman concludes by reminding us that there is a deeper transcendent
meaningfulness in the human experience that also underlies the whole cosmos, so that mysticism is an inherently optimistic approach, and an answer
to, the survival question. But just when some hope might be restored by the
argument from mysticism, we are reminded of more technical issues in Chapter 3. Moreman's chapter is partly an historical and cross-cultural review, and
this approach is necessary, but Stokes (see Chapter 3), in the same vein as
Moreman, is the first author in our collection who actually considers survival
from a multi-factorial point of view that goes into the critical detail entailed
in the inherent complexity of the self-construct. That essence of our being
could be a persisting self ("consciousness that persists from our birth to our
death"— p. 48), an I-thinker (the "entity that thinks one's thoughts"— p. 50),
a self or mind in the dualistic sense that exists outside our brain, a "Shin" (an
entity that is not mind, but soul-like, and is able to interact paranormally
with, and control the mind and body), or mini-Shins (little delusional entities —"a multitude of fields of consciousness, with many of them under the
illusion that they are the 'executive module' controlling the entire body"— p.
65). And all the other possible selves are presented: (i) split off sub-parts of
consciousness, (ii) multiple consciousnesses, (iii) constantly constituting and
re-constituting selves, and (iv) hierarchies of selves. Chapter 3 presents a
mind-field of selves, or do I mean a minefield? Which self is to be preferred,
and on what basis? Stokes comes to a delicately considered conclusion — consciousness survives.

Let us then entertain the idea of a "field of pure consciousness," as proposed by Stokes, much like the "contentless awareness" proposed by Braud's
fictional Erica (see Chapter 4).* But Erica pointed out that consciousness has
becomes reified. Perhaps we should think in terms of "consciousing" and forget about "consciousness" as a thing that "exists" and therefore as a thing that
has form and substance and a possible future. After all, it is that prejudice in
our thinking that may be forcing us to deal with the ramifications of survival
of consciousness and the related dimensions of mortality and immortality, the
finite and the infinite, the immanent and the transcendent. Consider, for
example, the following dialog between Mr. Spock and Dr. McCoy in the
episode "Spock's Brain" (Cronin, 1968-1969) from Gene Roddenberry's *Star*

See also Rao (2002).

Trek series, where Spock has his brain removed from his skull by way of a highly sophisticated surgical technique:

> Spock: I seem to have a body that stretches into infinity.
> McCoy: Body? Why, you have none!
> Spock: Then what am I?
> McCoy: You are a disembodied brain.
> Spock: Fascinating. Activity without end, but no volition....
> Unfortunately, I do not know where I am.

If we remain suspended in our disbelief, and assuming that this scenario is something like the real life experience that a "disembodied brain" might expect, what must it be like for consciousness — or for pure egoic personality to be more specific?* I imagine it is much worse (or much better depending on what one wants or expects). Spock's predicament, if transferred from his brain to that of his consciousness only, is exacerbated by more general considerations of what it is that constitutes Spock's consciousness in the first place. Neither soul nor spirit have any (or all) of the qualities of matter, so how do we conceptualize the non-substantial? At least Spock is still defined as a person, but only from within the context of him being a brain — he retains his identity *because*, not in spite of the fact that, he is still an entity, a brain.

Regardless of the problem of reification, the idea of a "contentless awareness" or "contentless consciousness" *does* mean there would be a survival of sorts, but that idea does not allude to the brand of survival we in the Christian West have been sold for centuries. Apropos to this line of thought is the psychodynamic view of consciousness, which sees human consciousness as depending on an ego† if the experience of consciousness is to make any real sense because ego brings the non-experiencing Self into the third dimension of objective reality (see Chapter 4, p. 83). Imagine if the afterlife view shared by billions was to be superseded by a new version of survival (one that denies the survival of a personal identity comprised mainly of personality components and memories accumulated over a lifetime). There will be many dissatisfied and disgruntled believers in the world, most of whom will certainly resist the radical nihilistic idea of the kind of omniscient non-existence that the ego-less self or ego-less consciousness must, and will always experience, if it can be called experience.

*Insofar as Spock's brain is undamaged, perhaps his situation could occasion brain events characteristic of some types of NDE and OBE.

†I will use the term "ego" in deference to "self" as used by Stokes (see p. 48) so as not to confuse the vernacular "self" with Jung's Self, which Jung originally capitalized to avoid confusion. As Stokes and others use the word "self," the small "s" self is essentially the same as ego, or "I," or "personal identity." Jung's Self, on the other hand, is the "totality of the psyche," which by his definition includes consciousness, thus embracing the ego, and the unconscious.

However, we still do not have a solid reason to accept even the possibility of the survival of a contentless consciousness if the self is concomitant or co-extensive with a living human being that cannot in itself survive bodily death. Jung defined "the Self" as the totality of the psyche — "the unity of the personality as a whole" (Jung, 1971, para. 789), but what if the totality, the wholeness of Self was, or must be inclusive of the physical body? There seems to be evidence suggesting that the physical body is essential to the totality. While Spock's disembodied brain may be a wholeness of sorts, what are we to make of brain-damaged individuals? What of those suffering acute and irreparable brain lesions, complete or partial severance of frontal lobe executive functioning (to be taken here as isometric with ego-functioning)? What of the intellectually disabled and incapacitated? What of those languishing in the last devastating throes of Alzheimer's Disease where, by all accounts, the identity is all but gone? What of those in coma? Where is the ego — the center of the field of consciousness — that endeavors to hold all parts together and prohibit fragmentation? With no center, there can be no sense of an "I" — an identity — that can relate to the world and others. Many who come out of coma, for example, report nothing of their experiences during their long "absence," which is not dissimilar from the reports produced by those of us who wake up each morning from sleep where no dreams are remembered.

Stokes (see Chapter 3, p. 55) attempts a resolution with Thalbourne, but they are resting here on theories taken from medical literature and current parapsychological theory. We, in this final chapter, are after answers concerning identity — or, if preferred, consciousness, or soul — and we want to know where either may reside. Multiple levels of experience by multiple consciousnesses within the brain, are not united, and that is a serious problem. Unification, it seems, would be imperative in the Great Beyond if one were to feel complete in oneself. If a split-off part of one's psyche enjoys an existence outside one's ego-awareness, what is one to think of its existence? Does that split-off part know it exists? Would it ultimately be "forced" to re-unite with one's ego-consciousness or identity in the afterlife?

So, again, we must wonder what happens to the intellectually challenged in our communities where we can hardly talk of a complete, or viable, or functional ego complex. Perhaps a witnessing but impersonal consciousness may be all those challenged individuals can hope to get in the afterlife. But for those cases, we can hardly imagine how identities can be formed *ex nihilo* when they lack, completely or partially, the starting point that we all take for granted — a life on earth with memories and experiences. But, of course, that wouldn't matter *if* Braud and Stokes are right. We might imagine the experience of one such case going from this world into the afterlife, as being like birth for the first time, or like coming out of a coma — or better, waking from a strange, cloudy netherworld comprised of dimly-formed incomprehensible images and murmurings, into a new brighter world that is clearly perceived, but related to nothing previously experienced while alive. In fact, that would be no different than what we, each with our own relatively well-formed ego complex, could or might expect. For the underprivileged of whom I speak, a contentless, ego-free consciousness is likely to be an adequate, if not good compromise given the alternatives. Certainly, it is the best they can hope for (if they can hope!). Perhaps it is all we can hope for too, and perhaps it is all we should reasonably expect.

These scenarios are likely to cause some cognitive dissonance and emotional disturbance amongst those who hold more formal (or less formal?) views of what is to be expected in the afterlife. But what are people's beliefs based on anyway? Hallucination? Delusion? Chapters 5 and 6 are studies of exactly these kinds of phenomena.

Thalbourne (Chapter 5), in his two-part study, investigated relationships between proneness to hallucination and (a) veridical visionary experience, (b) hearing the voice of a dead person, and (c) sensing a ghost. If survival experiences are the result of hallucination, then we can expect to find strong relationships between hallucination-proneness and these three variables — especially sensory experiences with non-living entities. In both studies, Thalbourne showed that the relationships were all rather weak, indicating that hallucination does not necessarily explain survival-type experiences in every case. Thalbourne concluded: "those who argue that having veridical visionary experience, hearing the voice of a dead person, and sensing ghosts are merely the result of hallucinations find only a little support for this position in this study" (p. 104).

Boyd and Zimbardo (Chapter 6) showed that the time after death — the transcendental-future — is thought of as being the time when "reunion with deceased loved ones, eternal life, reincarnation, the avoidance of eternal damnation, and the elimination of current poverty, pain, suffering, and shame" (p. 109) takes place. The transcendental-future exists as a kind of "foreign land that [one] can never visit" (p. 121), not while one is still alive anyway. And the one thing that holds true for those who believe in an afterlife, is equally true for those with a transcendental-future belief system — there are no "reality checks" that might serve to undermine one's motivations in this life, but "negative events can be interpreted as divine tests, such as those endured by Job, and positive events can be construed as rewards for proper behavior. Both can be interpreted as markers on the path to enlightenment, and can therefore be positive reinforcers" (p. 121).

Boyd and Zimbardo also point out that "for many people without material success in this lifetime, existence is made bearable by creating illusions"

(p. 123). But we need to weigh Boyd and Zimbardo's conclusions against that of Thalbourne — paranormal belief about the afterlife (i.e., the transcendental-future) may emerge from experiences that are not necessarily "created illusions" — the products of delusional or hallucinatory states of mind. While Boyd and Zimbardo note that traditional religious belief and New Age beliefs are responsible for transcendent-futures comprised of positive illusions, it should be noted that belief systems are responsible for the negative illusions as well. At first take, one might consider the creation of these so-called "illusions" to be an unethical practice, were it not for the fact that the world's great religions, unlike some money-oriented New Age philosophies, were founded on true and worthy ideas and inspirations — or that is what we are led to believe — even if they produced some weird and wonderful, and even downright morbid afterlife scenarios (see again, Chapter 1). However, regardless of anyone's say-so, what "baggage" we can realistically expect to dump, and what we can expect to take with us, is still anyone's guess — only the religions with their respective dogma seem sure about this, which is what Boyd and Zimbardo are saying, but their data suggest it is no longer irrational to believe such dogma.

But I have to ask, what contents of our personality need purifying, and what would be left after that process? In this life, we have to acknowledge that our cultural (including religious) heritage is not only responsible for the noblest triumphs of the human spirit, but is likewise responsible for our greatest depravities. But those fates are also the legacy of our phylogenetic evolution. On the basis of those two factors, being given the belief that some special reward or place awaits one is small potatoes compared to what may be involved in one's afterlife evolution. We may expect to lose the mostly physical attributes that define us — along with the reflexes, fixed action patterns (i.e., instincts) and the basic drives — but how much psychological content can be stripped away before we are no longer what we hold ourselves to be? Chapters 7, 8, 9 and 10 give ideas as to what might remain of us in the afterlife. It appears there are contents that can be witnessed, if not measured.

Fontana (Chapter 7) discusses three major phenomena that have been observed. These are (i) spirit energies experienced during séances, (ii) direct voice phenomena through mediumship, including foreign languages (i.e., xenoglossy),* and (iii) Instrumental Trans-communication (ITC), which is another form of spirit message, usually received through electronic media

---

**Note that Braude (2005) argues that there are perfectly normal explanations for xenoglossy. He argues that research into second-language acquisition that appears to be paranormal, undermines the survivalist position. Linguistic proficiency can be achieved with "very little effort, input or support," while "prodigious" abilities "may lurk under the surface, awaiting an appropriate fertile ground for expression" (p. 124).*

such as TVs, radios, and computers. In the case of spirit energies, Fontana tells us that there has been occasional fraud. We can make the allowances that Fontana suggests, and grant that mediums do not always cheat, but we only know they cheat when they are *caught* cheating. Since we do not have reliable success rates for mediumship, we cannot even say which, or what proportion of the phenomena are genuine. Nevertheless, reports of some cases, such as Eusapia Palladino (at her most credible best) and D. D. Home, seem to be beyond reproach.

But what are we to make of "table levitations, raps, touches by spirit hands, movement of objects, ringing of bells, and materializations of spirit hands" (Fontana, Chapter 7, p. 129)? Can some discarnate entities do no more than focus their energies on inanimate matter? On that basis, how can we rule out conventional PK explanations? Even direct voices, which are not so easily explained as fraud, are less difficult to explain if one accepts that a combination of dissociation and super-psi is sufficient.

Finally, ITCs are often dismissed as artifacts of electronic media, but Fontana points out that analyses of the "spirit voices" reveal unusual characteristics not associated with the normal human voice. There is a strong case for further ITC research because it offers a level of objective analysis not so readily attainable in mediumship studies. Unfortunately, it is not often taken seriously — even by parapsychologists.

Roll (Chapter 8) presents a meticulous and comprehensive review of the apparition and mediumship literature. Though it is not exhaustive, most of the major aspects and types, as well as critiques and criticisms, of research into apparitions and mediumship are covered. Roll argues for survival, but he is not sure which aspect of the self survives. Generally, he is concerned that parapsychologists have taken the wrong path, or better, have missed a golden opportunity to explore aspects of our ontology, our being, that have become marginalized. The "physical or impersonal aspects [of psi]" have been overlooked because the "psychological and interpersonal aspects" get all the attention (p. 169).

We cannot ignore Roll's point here — the unconscious dualistic mindset of most psychologists and parapsychologists maintains an oftentimes-unhealthy split that is far from being healed. To paraphrase Roll, the question is, Are we seeing ourselves, and our place in the world, as outsiders or insiders? Perhaps, there are no "separated systems," but of course that implies that we need a theory that covers or unites all systems. Roll's "psychophysical field" is the suggested means by which all things are inter-connected, and Roll maintains that it continues beyond this life — "If it is hypothesized that the psychophysical field continues after death, we expect a continuation of its interpersonal as well as its physical aspects" (p. 168). But proposing another hypothesis still leaves the question unanswered.

Focusing less on the phenomena, and more on the consequences of the phenomena, Krippner (Chapter 9) describes some incredible cases of After-Death Communications (ADCs), and concludes that the ADC experient is usually positively rewarded in some way upon having the experience. Often, the experient has a severely debilitating mood of depression or grief dissolved as a consequence of a change of outlook — the experient comes to believe that the deceased is not suffering in any way and is happy. In other cases, relationship issues are resolved, or unfinished business is concluded.

For the most part, ADCs are clearly therapeutic in nature and clinicians and mental health professionals are seeing the benefits of the ADC as a means of treating the bereaved. ADCs may be regarded as "exceptional" in nature (White, 1995, would refer to them as "Exceptional Human Experiences" if the experience is personally transformative). However, ADCs are evidence more of transformations in this life than of what we might undergo in the next. More compelling material comes from Chapters 10 and 12.

Chapter 10 presents a reincarnation-type case, but readers are left to make their own decisions about what the phenomenology of the case means. And there is room for doubt over the evidence, which comes mainly as retrospective reports after the previous personality was identified. Studies are now coming out that have written records made before the personality is objectively identified by researchers — for example, see Keil and Tucker (2005). The other problem with reincarnation-type cases is that super-psi and dissociation have not been ruled out, and nor has possession (which may or may not indicate survival). Nevertheless, in essence, the past-life events in Purnima Ekanayake's life, and the phenomena reported in the three chapters that precede Haraldsson's chapter, give strong support to some kind of paranormal hypothesis, but which one? All we can say is that these four chapters present a perplexing body of evidence, but as I have asked above, how do we judge that evidence?

I argued earlier that the most salient point to emerge from consideration of the evidence was that such a consideration would not preclude mutually exclusive multiple viewpoints. Certainly, in the cases of some mediumistic phenomena, sightings of apparitions and ghosts, etc., the phenomenology of many of these contents bring up my earlier hypothesis that many could be projections. And Braud (Chapter 4) speaks of these contents as being the "productions of the personifying, dramatizing, mythopoetic tendencies of our 'unconscious minds'— ways of communicating with ourselves in the service of providing needed lessons and satisfying important wishes" (p. 87). But the boundaries of conscious and unconscious experience are not clearly defined, so that the argument from projection may never be completely convincing, nor may it ever be proved because the unconscious is, to all practical purposes, unlimited. Furthermore, many spirit communications, especially those of profound veracity, suggest something other than projection — either survival or super-ESP, while some of the physical phenomena that have been reported suggest either survival or super-PK.

While the argument from reincarnation-type cases is clearly not to do with projection, and while some weight can be given to the arguments from possession and dissociation that explain reincarnation-type phenomena, I consider these arguments poor substitutes for the argument from super-psi. But even so, I believe that at this point super-psi is looking to be itself a poor alternative hypothesis to the survival hypothesis simply because it doesn't explain why there are not more reports of the same reincarnated personality, and even if small children could use super-psi and glean the vital information from living sources, I cannot see motive in them to act as they do. Thus am I also forced to rule out conscious and deliberate impersonation, as I cannot see why a child should claim so vehemently that he or she is that reincarnated person.* The super-psi hypothesis, however, more readily explains transplant cases than reincarnation-type cases — recipients of donors' organs may wonder about their donors, and they may even feel compelled to use psi to find out something about them, even if it results in temporary or permanent changes in personality. (Note too, that in these types of transplant cases we cannot rule out the possibility of cell memory, which is not a survival-like phenomenon.)

We may now wonder if we are any closer to a solution to the survival problem, but at this stage an attempt at a solution would be premature as our review is not yet complete. So, what does the phenomenological approach offer us?

Heath with Klimo (Chapter 11) describe a consistent four-stage passage of experience for suicides ostensibly "passing over": (i) transition, (ii) recovery, (iii) life review and self-judgment, and (iv) spiritual work. Even across many cultures and using a variety of sources, these four stages describe a commonality of experiences by suicides — (i) the "soul" leaves the body, and adjusts to its new non-physical environment, (ii) some kind of spiritual help is given by individuals living or dead so that the suicide may recover from their trauma, (iii) the soul considers what it has done and evaluates its deeds, and finally, (iv) the soul attempts to advance spiritually (although Heath and Klimo point out that cultural differences were found at this stage — for example, the soul

---

*On the issue of identity, it is possible that small children easily and unconsciously identify with alien personalities, wherever they may reside, just as a young child's still-forming ego-complex is vulnerable (indeed facilitates) unconscious identification with family members — particularly stronger personalities such as mother and father.

may or may not reincarnate depending on whether the reincarnation concept exists in a given culture).

From this analysis we learn that humans worldwide are pretty much in agreement about what the afterlife experience of suicides is all about (i.e., the material is so thematically consistent that it lends itself very well to structuralization and generalization), but one might take issue with this analysis because it depends on channeled material only. We cannot be sure how much wish-fulfillment there is in our channelers, and that is something that is not only likely to exist in a vast number of cultures that are separated temporally and geographically, but is most certainly going to color constructions of the afterlife experience. Note, however, that Heath, with Klimo, was not attempting to prove that an afterlife exists.

Wooffitt (Chapter 12) argues that a closer look at the structural components of conversations that transpire between medium and sitter is in order. Only then can we get an idea as to how afterlife knowledge claims are "made, attributed, accepted, rejected or revised" (p. 239). Though that may be the main point of conversation analysis (CA), there is no doubt that skeptics will only see such fine analyses as a subtle means of fraud-spotting (specifically cold reading). However, Wooffitt points out that it is not the purpose of CA to provide "an exposé of linguistic tricks by which a false claim is made persuasive" (p. 239). Given what I am about to say in the next section about the origins and constructions of many of the words and terms parapsychologists use in their everyday conversation and scientific writings, it is arguably advisable to question the conscious intent, or otherwise, that underscores the use of those very words and terms.

McClenon (Chapter 13) takes us closer still to the personal experience involved in afterlife phenomena and he is not afraid to reduce the experience to a thing primal, crucial, pivotal, indispensable, in the otherwise humdrum existence of a mere mortal that would, likely as not, blunder his or her way through life without purpose or hope of salvation. McClenon holds the opinion that "NDEs appear to be gaining greater importance" (p. 259). This statement may only refer to a specific sub-population because McClenon's finding is not supported by Chandler (Chapter 1), who claims that society is fragmenting under the weight of lost religious and folk belief, including belief in an afterlife. At least, as Chandler points out, it is not fear of death that is a problem anymore — it is fear of life, especially amongst the young (again see, Chapter 1, pp. 26–28). If McClenon is right, then a return to religious experience is not only a must, it is imperative that it be brought into practice through ritual healing, just as the NDE serves its own purpose. This change in our culture may see a revision of current attitudes towards life here — now, and in the hereafter.

By way of an aside, McClenon's review goes a little further than the shamanic experience. He presents a considerable number of studies showing how belief in an afterlife just happens to rest hand-in-hand with experiences of other paranormal phenomena — specifically experience of ESP and PK. And with the weight of evidence supporting the psi hypothesis (see Thalbourne & Storm, 2005), it is not putting the cart before the horse to say that people experience psi phenomena and that's why they believe in it. If run-of-the-mill paranormal phenomena are directly substantiated in people's experience, and they are proved not to be delusions exclusively explicable within some kind of medical or psychological framework, it may be highly presumptive and counterproductive to refute the super-psi hypothesis, and even the survival hypothesis, on the grounds that they too are accounts of delusional experiences.

So to answer my earlier question, What does a phenomenological approach offer us? — it appears that (in essence) McClenon and Wooffitt only add to the arguments of Krippner, and Boyd and Zimbardo — the purposes served by notions, experiences, and talk of survival, are as important as the issue of survival *per se*. They give us a greater insight into survival phenomenology as it pertains to our cultural heritage, which not only broadens our understanding of the afterlife phenomenon, but also is crucial to our survival in the here and now. Right alongside that expanded viewpoint, sits the case for a paranormal hypothesis that might explain the material presented in the evidential chapters (Chapters 7 to 10) because it seems that such a hypothesis is appropriate. However, no conclusion can be drawn at this stage as to whether a super-psi or a survival hypothesis can stand on its own. In fact, I have argued throughout this chapter that multiple viewpoints were feasible (in the next chapter, I will challenge this position). At this point, I take a necessary digression because I believe that something other than the apparent anomalous nature of afterlife phenomena, but equally pertinent to it, needs consideration.

The Language

Secular versus Archaic/Religious Terminology

Throughout the preceding 13 chapters, the basic afterlife concept was considered in mainly secular (including scientific) terms, but it is surprising how often the various putatively scientific discourses reverted to, and even depended on, a terminology that has its roots in an archaic, even religious past. It is not the aim of this chapter to single out specific examples — the reader will recall the more salient instances anyway. Suffice it to say, these accounts were not solely reducible to second-hand reports or hearsay, but often were denoted in the words of the authors, or were connoted in conceptions that might otherwise be described using religious or archaic terminology. In parapsychology, this trend began in the early days of psychical research. The religious viewpoints of the early psychical researchers were inherent in the so-called secular ideas of those researchers. Traditional religious beliefs in the immortality of the human soul, meant that if the soul survived, and assuming that the soul was the personality — a semblance of its former self — then it made good sense to try to prove that mediumship, channeling, and spirit communication, were genuine events (or not), and that they would therefore indicate survival (or not) of that personality. From the start, psychical research really was a search for the human soul.

The fact is, survival is an ancient idea, but there is no need to single out modern parapsychology for continuing this adherence to archaic concepts — it merely finds itself in the same situation as other disciplines. However, a viewpoint ostensibly presented as being exclusively secular can be seen as an attempt to strip the idea of survival from its historical and religious background in order to reach a considered scientific (i.e., objective) conclusion about survival. Ultimately, it is an attempt that fails. The main reason is that our culture, all cultures, are steeped in a religious past. It is our heritage, and our legacy. It is the spur of our relentless quest for knowledge and understanding of who we are, and why we are here. It prompts our whole epistemological drive to research and theorize the way we do.

It may be of no import whatsoever to some readers to raise this fact that our science is based on archaic and religious ideas — indeed for some, it is not quite the revelation it might first appear to be. But it may be of interest to readers to point out that while I am at ease using the adjective "archaic" in a conventional way (referring to the primitive, or ancient, or even antiquated), my use of the adjective "religious" to describe these ideas makes me feel rather uncomfortable. It might be wise at this point to mention that my discomfort is ameliorated by the fact that I use the word "religious" not so much in a dogmatic or doctrinal sense, but more in the original Latin sense of *religare*, which means something like binding to the source of numinosity or sense of awe (Edinger, 1986; Wyld & Partridge, 1968). Indeed, I would prefer to use the Jungian adjective "archetypal" to describe these ideas — religious ideas are archetypal ideas — but my dissenters would be in their rights to say I was merely substituting one mystery with another. I would beg to differ, primarily because Jung did not place archetypes in some kind of otherworld outside direct human experience (one of his major goals was to educate people in the knowledge of ownership of their psychic contents instead of projecting them), but I would be severely off the topic of this chapter, not to mention the theme of this book, if I pursued this argument.

While we may argue that (i) the various treatments of the dead (e.g., burial, entombment, mummification, etc.), or (ii) treatments related to the dead (e.g., ritual healing, mourning, prayer, memorial service, etc.), or (iii) experiences of the dead (e.g., visions, auditions, communications with discarnate entities, etc.), or (iv) the various understandings about being dead and existing in the afterlife (i.e., belief in spirits and survival in some form or other) are not necessarily the *products* of religion *per se*; the reader will appreciate the fact that we do not have to accept the opposing viewpoint that nearly all religions *absorbed* into their structure, *post hoc*, the phenomenology of the dying, and the dead, and departure into a "future-life." We can entertain the idea that these "treatments," "experiences," and "understandings," and religion as we know it, evolved together and that they therefore cannot be separated. It is as much a conundrum in its two-fold phenomenology as the chicken-and-egg paradox, but it is eminently serviceable in that dual inseparable form.

The main advantage of this conception is that we can eliminate the argument over invention or discovery. We can thus see that archaic/religious ideas, such as survival, may have emerged from an inner psychic reality (given by an inherited predisposition), and that makes them *discoveries* of preformed elements in the psyche, while at the same time they are *inventions* in the formal sense because they bear all the hallmarks of (a) being culturally specific and therefore original (not copied), (b) having irrupted into consciousness as if from the imagination, but actually from deep structure (brain or otherwise), and (c) having been inferred from some other experience.

A second advantage is that we can refer to, and revere religious ideas without prejudice because they are immutable at a core level, and we can rely on that immutability when we make conjectures (for example) about survival, and what it is that might survive. And one does not have to be religious in the canonical or denominational sense to appreciate or validly apply these ideas to theoretical speculation or research into (say) survival. Thus I return to my major thesis that it is apparent that there cannot be an exclusively secular viewpoint about afterlife conceptions. Instead, all and sundry viewpoints are expressed in a muted archaic or religiously-derived vernacular that is hybridized or merged with expressions and terms that are couched in the topical parlance of anthropology, psychology, and the language of the arts and sciences.

Consider the key modern-day term "psyche," and its archaic counterparts such as *spirit, mind, soul, anima*, etc. The word "psyche" has essentially the same meaning, but all these words carry an enormous critical mass of religious/archaic overtone. Psyche (Greek: *psukhē* meaning breath, life, or soul) is the soul, spirit (Latin: *spiritus* = breath), or mind, in each of us — it is weightless, colorless, and amorphous. Psychology was originally the study of the mind or soul of humans and animals. Speaking of animals, the concept of animation, derives from the Latin word *anima* (living being), which is related to the Greek word *ánemos* (wind), and harkens back to a pagan idea that animals were alive because they had an invisible life force like a wind blowing inside them that accounted for their movement. All animals, mice to men, have this same life force. And when an animal dies, something (otherwise called its life) is now considered finished, missing, gone, vaporized, from this worldly plane.

Other terms have their histories: personality (Latin: *persona*, from an older Etruscan word *persu* = actor's mask, part), identity (Latin: *idem* = same), and consciousness (Latin: *conscius* = know or aware). Anyone who considers him- or herself as having identity and consciousness is really saying that they feel themselves to be the same from one moment to the next, and they have knowledge of this fact, or they are aware that they play a part like an actor, which is maintained over the course of their life. This feeling may only be enforced, or given expression, by one's corporeality. On the physical plane, the part a person plays is really expressed from within their body. One term in particular, "consciousness" (as discussed earlier), means more now than just knowing or being aware, but has become reified for many psychologists and parapsychologists. That is, consciousness has been given manifest form like many transformations spoken of in the religious canons — it is identified with the personality as being who one is, though many would argue that this view is over-determined (see again, Chapter 4).

Perhaps the neutral term "discarnate entity" has some scientific credo, but then it is the offspring of the Latin *dis* + *caro* = "to be apart from flesh." And an entity is merely a *thing* (Latin: *ens* = thing), which is scientifically meaningless to our purpose. So, the typical discarnate entity would be a thing separated from the flesh, so once again we have the idea of a soul or spirit. Even the highly regarded modern scientific concept of energy (Greek: *en ergeia* or "inside [the] work") is an age-old idea (e.g., *mana* = supernatural or magical power), and the term finds itself quite commonly deployed by New Age theorists who use it to describe the nature of the spirit or soul that putatively crosses over — "We are all just energy, and energy cannot be created or destroyed!" Analysis of words gives us clues to the ideas embedded in language, but does that really get us to the point of identifying what it is that may survive our bodily demise? Psyche, soul, spirit, personality, identity, consciousness, and discarnate entity — all these are terms that relate in an oppositional or negative sense to something positive and corporeal (i.e., they are not like flesh). They are like psi phenomena — always defined in terms of what they are not. That is the only meaning the terms ever had, and by that meaning, they only obliquely refer to the nature of what might survive in the afterlife.

Given the archaic, religious, and historical roots of our language, our scientific constructions of that which survives are barely different from the archaic, religious, animistic notions of our pagan ancestors. Any conceptualization, now or from the past, is an inherently archetypal idea that gives structure to our culture, and the cultures of our remote ancestors.

With the waters of the survival question muddied by the complications of the meanings and derivations of our words *and* the way we use language, we necessarily move to a consideration of that which survives in terms of language anyway because we cannot abandon the attempt to produce convincing scenarios about what a life hereafter could be like — and to simplify things, we would like to confine ourselves to a unique discourse if possible. As I said, whichever discourse we settle on also depends on, indeed is driven by, ideas of what it is that is supposed to survive — ego, self, spirit, soul, personality, consciousness, energy, life-force, or otherwise. Even outside that limitation, we end up with a *scenario*— not the *reality*. That unfavorable outcome results from a rule that applies to science in general — the old Socratic rule that we can never know anything because language is an abstraction of what really is; it is a symbolic venture into the world of the real. Likewise, Kant expressed a similar sentiment when he spoke of the "phenomenal" world, which we know (because we witness it with our senses and create it in language) as not being anything remotely isometric with the so-called "noumenal" world that we cannot know — the world as it really is. It would surely follow that the possible reality of survival — the reality of an afterlife — is, first, a phenomenal experience that, second, can only be exactly known insofar as it can be exactly expressed in language, and we have seen that language is not precise.

On the one hand, to take the minimalist (received) approach, and say that something survives the mortal body — call it what you will — and to add that it survives somewhere beyond this world, has been sufficient in itself to satisfy the demands of a vast majority of people on this planet. The profound truth is that those many people have indeed found satisfaction through their various discourses, notwithstanding the fact that those discourses may have had their origins in any number of experiences, many of which have been the subject of this book. And as Chandler points out in regard to the postcivilized youth, not to have the belief that often emerges from transpersonal experience, or not to be able to experience the transpersonal by one's own will just at a time when there is a most crucial need for it, bars access to the meaning of one's life, which is tantamount to losing one's life.

On the other hand, if the specific natures of that "something" and that "somewhere beyond" are required before the scientifically inclined are satisfied, and I am only giving heed to the opposing viewpoint — i.e., the optimalist (empiricalist) approach — then we may have a hung jury because there is too much disagreement amongst the investigators to reach a consensus. Many a protagonist of the scientific view expects a great deal more than someone else's discourse to sway them one way or another.

Unfortunately, what still stands outside both viewpoints is the reality of the limitations of language — it reveals as much as it conceals. As long as the something and the somewhere remain inexpressible, or limited when expressed in language, or the conceptions of both cannot be understood by all, or are understood in different ways, there can be no answer, or no single answer to the question of survival.

In spite of that controversial claim, since the various conceptions of survival exist in our many faiths, religions, and beliefs (in their concordant and contradictory forms), and these are venerated by billions of people in any given culture, it follows that these conceptions must exist and be venerated for good reason. Indeed, the benefits of culturally devised afterlife conceptions have already been indicated (cf. the main points expressed in Chapters 6, 9, 11, & 13). But I would venture further that the good reason might transcend its purpose in this life. Consciousness, as a creative factor, whether it is as a brain- or a mind-state, may have a far greater reach than heretofore imagined. Can consciousness ("consciousing" or being conscious) go so far as to have influence beyond this life? And if so, would it not surely have to change to the degree that it no longer creates at an individual level? I would answer Yes to both questions. After all, a single-purpose merging of consciousness would be an *a priori* necessity in a domain where the egotistical goals of flesh-and-blood individuals would logically and intuitively no longer have right of place — a split-minded universal consciousness would be incompatible in a transcendent universe, just as the immanent universe we know can only exist at all if opposing forces are held in balance. As long as those choices of consciousness do not, of necessity, include unconscious ego-serving — and most afterlife protagonists would agree there is no room for egos in the afterlife (or Heaven, at any rate) — the individual may not only make up his or her own mind, thereby creating his or her own life, but may indeed, by that process, be making up and creating his or her own afterlife. If so, then the only remaining question, and perhaps one that is more important than the question of survival, is: Can the billions of us, in a likeminded manner, imagine (or does it even make sense to imagine) what we *should* want the afterlife to be like? I will return to this question in the next and final chapter.

References

Braude, S. E. (2003). *Immortal remains: The evidence for life after death.* New York: Rowman and Littlefield.
Brest, M. (Director) (1998). *Meet Joe Black.* Los Angeles, CA: Universal Studios.

Broderick, D. (2005). Afterlife as science fiction. *The New York Review of Science Fiction, 17*(7), 1, 6-9.

Cronin, L. (Writer) (1968-1969). *Spock's brain.* Los Angeles, CA: Norway Production/Paramount Television.

Edinger, E. F. (1986). *Ego and archetype.* New York: Penguin.

Hood, R. W. Jr., & Morris, R. J. (1983). Toward a theory of death transcendence. *Journal for the Scientific Study of Religion, 22,* 353-365.

Jung, C. G. (1958). *Psychology and religion: West and east.* Princeton, NJ: Princeton University Press.

Jung, C. G. (1971). *Psychological types.* Princeton, NJ: Princeton University Press.

Keil, J. H. H., & Tucker, J. B. (2005). Children who claim to remember previous lives: Cases with written records made before the previous personality was identified. *Journal of Scientific Exploration, 19,* 91-101.

Rao, K. R. (2002). *Consciousness studies: A cross-cultural perspective.* Jefferson, NC: McFarland.

Thalbourne, M. A. & Storm, L. (Eds.). (2005). *Parapsychology in the twenty-first century: Essays on the future of psychical research.* Jefferson, NC: McFarland.

White, R. A. (1995). Exceptional human experiences and the experiential paradigm. *ReVision, 18*(2), 18-25.

Wyld, H. C., & Partridge, E. H. (1968). *Webster universal dictionary.* Routledge and Kegan Paul.

15. A Solution: Radical Survivalism

LANCE STORM

In this final chapter, the author makes an attempt at formulating a new interpretation of survival based mainly on the ideas put forward by the various contributors in the previous chapters.—Editors

In the previous chapter I suggested that super-psi and survival might only be two ways of looking at the same thing. The reader needs to recall the oft-told analogy of the elephant that is approached by blindfolded Indians. Each Indian brings his two hands into contact with a different part of the elephant and describes it from personal experience — one grasps the trunk and concludes that an elephant is like a snake; another grasps the tail and concludes that an elephant is like a rope. Other Indians give their interpretations. Researchers in parapsychology, every scientist, each one of us, is like one of those Indians grasping at paranormal phenomena, and then trying to describe it in terms that derive from personal experience. Although sometimes we are lucky and reach a consensus, oftentimes we come across phenomena that force pluralistic or multiple viewpoints upon us. For example, the wave nature and the particle nature of light in quantum physics are two different ways of looking at one and the same phenomenon. That is how the universe is, and paranormal phenomena, survival specifically, may be no exception.

The chapters in this book present virtually all the phenomena about survival that we can manage and need to consider in one book. I have considered the objective findings and the many subjectively derived beliefs and ideas about survival whether or not they were based on direct experience of putatively discarnate entities or related phenomena. The main theme of the survival hypothesis, proponents of which were in the majority, seems to be pitted against the sub-theme of the super-psi hypothesis, the latter of which tended to be conspicuous by its absence, though a number of authors did discuss the issue (viz., Braud, Fontana, Moreman, and Roll).

Fontana (Chapter 7) lays the argument from complexity against super-psi, but Moreman (Chapter 2) argues that a super-psi model that incorporates mystical experience explains the uncharacteristic practical skills and foreign language usage of mediums as phenomena we could expect to see if a living mind had access to a Universal Mind. Unfortunately, dissociation and telepathic interaction are sufficient in themselves to undermine the need for help from a mind of that order, though we can maintain the psi component to a lesser degree.

In agreement with Fontana, Roll (Chapter 8) presents the argument from falsifiability, which goes back to the days of Karl Popper (1963)—*any test of a theory is an attempt to falsify it.* Roll does not think the super-psi hypothesis can be falsified because a "theory that can be stretched to meet any contingency is a metaphysical statement rather than a scientific hypothesis" (p. 168).

Braud (Chapter 4), however, considers the super-psi hypothesis in a fair-minded manner: "we don't know the range or limits of what might be possible through psi in the living, so it would be unwise to place limitations on it in the face of such ignorance" (p. 87). Braud goes further and adds: "I saw no reason for psi in the living not to be mixed with the actual existence of some afterlife process..." (p. 87). Braud proposes that "living psi" can enmesh with, or be triggered by life remnants or a "surviving residuum" (to use Braud's term), and the fragmentariness of these anomalous experiences are given structure in and by the personifying and dramatizing capacity of the psyche — the "mythopoetic" dimensions of our "unconscious minds," to paraphrase Braud.

On the one hand, we can think in an alternativist* manner where we can hold two essentially contra-posed ideas about a single phenomenon, though these ideas are capable of "working" in unison: thus, paranormal information acquisition and physical action can come from (i) living sources *or* (ii) some kind of surviving substance. On the other hand, we can tread a middle-path between the two hypotheses: thus, all minds maintain their existence even after death in some kind of mind or "psychophysical field." But a third perspective is possible. We can consider a complete merger of the two (or more) major inter-related components. Indeed, we can consider a far-reaching form of the survival hypothesis, which I term radical survivalism — a model which proposes that all events and all beings after their demise (along with all their experiences) are preserved or sustained as forms of knowledge

*"Alternation is the ability to alternate in one's belief according to context" (Edwards, Ashmore, & Potter, 1995, n8).

or information, and that cognition and super-cognition facilitate access to these constant or continuous forms. But before this model can be explained in greater detail, three things must be done.

First, I go beyond the multiple process notion of super-psi that involves complex information scanning, etc., to a more subtle form — the "magic wand version" proposed by Stephen Braude (2003), because I find it to be dramatically similar to, and indeed supported conceptually by, two theories of psi — one posited by Jung (1960; namely synchronicity) and the other by Thalbourne (1981, 2004; namely psychopraxia).

Regarding magic-wand super-psi, Braude (2003) proposes that "(a) psi agency requires nothing more than an efficacious need or wish (under favorable conditions), and (b) given such an efficacious need or wish, virtually *anything at all* can happen" (pp. 36–37). There is no need for "complex search procedures" as proposed in other psi theories. Unfortunately, Braude later contradicts himself when he says "super-psi explanations require, at least for the best cases, multiple sources of information — hence, several distinct causal connections between the psychic subject [e.g., a medium] and the world" (p. 305). He then inappropriately uses the radio analogy to explain the super-psi process, thus undermining the criterion of "efficacious need." He also introduces a causal factor (a so-called "causal nexus") that bespeaks, and belies on his part, a kind of mechanistic understanding, or mechanical conceptualization, of the psi process. No surprise that he ultimately dismisses super-psi on parsimonious grounds (cf. Moreman, Chapter 2).

Jung, on the other hand, eliminated both efficacious need (at least conscious need) and mechanical causality from his theory. Further, he regarded synchronicity — the acausal connecting principle that linked inner and outer events (thus incorporating ESP and PK) — as being necessarily contingent upon "absolute knowledge." In regard to accessing knowledge that is ordinarily beyond the limited ego complex (i.e., not mediated by the sense organs), but which appears in so many synchronicity experiences, Jung (1960) claimed that it is "not a conscious knowledge as we know it, but rather a self-subsistent 'unconscious' knowledge which I would prefer to call absolute knowledge" (para. 931). Synchronicity may be explained by a kind of "meaningful orderedness," which leads Jung to hypothesize the existence of an independent meaning as given by absolute knowledge of these events.*

Similar to Braude's initial proposition, Thalbourne's psychopraxia theory, proposes that the self-complex adopts a pro attitude (or desire for a particular

---

*I will not delve into the factor of meaningfulness because it extends beyond the compass of this book (cf. Chapter 2). However, for my purposes, an objective synchronicity is a viable hypothesis as embodied in such paranormal forms as ESP and PK (see Storm, 1999, for an argument to this effect).

outcome) that may be conscious or unconscious (the stronger pro attitude winning out), and that this outcome is achieved provided that a sufficient condition is met that may be comprised of any number of conditions deemed necessary for the effect to take place.* Therefore, a psychopractic effect must start with a pro attitude on behalf of the living self. Thalbourne posits that if it is not found in the living participant, we must look elsewhere. Sources of pro attitude might include individuals aware of the task at hand (say, in a laboratory where we may therefore hypothesize that an experimenter effect may exist), or even discarnate entities.

None of the three theories — even magic-wand super-psi — necessarily depends on cybernetic process (*pace* Braude), where systematic information scanning or searching may be considered crucial, as is the case in normal information acquisition. Thus, they all can (or do) eliminate the need for elaborate detailed explications of the psi process. While it may also be said that synchronicity and psychopraxia can both be put forward as super-psi contenders that challenge the survival hypothesis, only Braude gave some consideration to supplanting the survival hypothesis with the magic-wand super-psi hypothesis before he abandoned the latter hypothesis (out-of-hand, to my way of thinking). I have no intention of exclusively defending the super-psi hypothesis, or using the above theories to that end, but I am not intent upon defending conventional notions of survival either — hence the term radical survivalism. My aim is to apply what we already know about psi to the issue of survival — specifically, but not limited to, the fact that psi has not yet been proved to be governed by issues of complexity (for example, see Storm & Thalbourne, 2003, for an argument to this effect).

The complexity factor can undermine conventional cybernetic models of psi process (see the extensive review of psi theories by Stokes, 1987, and by Irwin, 2004), and even more so, the argument from crippling complexity seems to stand in the way of the super-psi hypothesis as an alternative to the survival hypothesis, primarily giving reason for Braude to abandon it on parsimonious grounds. But as I have already argued, magic-wand super-psi, taken at face value, cannot be threatened by complexity. Furthermore, super-psi requires only some kind of paranormal process from living agents, whereas hard-line survivalism clearly stipulates some kind of paranormal process involving *non-living* agents, so I put it to the reader that survivalism posits one more level of complexity than the super-psi hypothesis — if we are to

*Note therefore that causal relations are implied in the arrangement of the sufficient condition, but we cannot make the judgment that psychopraxia (and therefore super-psi) necessarily involves the kind of complexity (i.e., a "causal nexus") that Braude thinks is necessary in explaining some intriguing and intricately detailed cases of survival phenomena.

make a ruling based on parsimony (and Braude has missed this point), it is the argument from super-psi that wins the day.

However, if the complexity argument cannot stand, and if it can be reasonably argued that the principle of parsimony need not be applied so rigidly (cf. Foster & Martin, 1966), if at all, then both the super-psi hypothesis and the survival hypothesis can be sustained. Thus, the second step towards radical survivalism requires abandonment of the principle of parsimony. I regard this principle as primarily a mere philosophical convenience in many cases, and in the case of magic-wand super-psi, Braude misapplies it anyway. At the same time, since we have no grounds for applying the principle of parsimony, I do not argue that people now have a choice between superpsi and survival. It is not my intention to provide belief options here.

The third and final requirement for radical survivalism is to draw from (and if necessary, modify) the theories of Braude (2003), Jung (1960), and Thalbourne (2004), and merge those ideas with the super-ordinate conceptions suggested by our contributors — especially Moreman, Stokes, Braud, and Roll (Chapters 2, 3, 4, and 8, respectively). If we accept that the synchronistic process (information reception via ESP or PK) requires the existence of absolute knowledge (after Jung) with access via (magic-wand) super-psi (after Braude) or psychopraxia (after Thalbourne), and if we regard action (normal or paranormal) as being goal-oriented (after Thalbourne), we can say that the agency (activity and intervention) involved in survival experiences (NDE, OBE, visitation by discarnate entity, etc.) is primarily the same thing as *manifested access to an ostensibly unlimited pool of information, experiences, actions, and events, which fall under the super-ordinate category of absolute knowledge* (cf. the key theoretical arguments of Moreman and Roll in their respective chapters).* Motive or pro attitude may be derived from conscious or unconscious goals on the part of the agent (after Thalbourne), but we clearly need to go beyond the idea of an agent who is *active* in holding motives, and propose that many individuals are not really (or always) agents as such because they can be passive when they have a survival experience. We should be free to say that some special individuals do not seek contact with remnants or residuals or elements of personalities (here or in the hereafter), but are merely born that way, or they are affected or disaffected by

*I am uneasy with conceptions that refer to "mind" beyond the corporeal person (such as "Universal Mind") because they imply identity, and they extend beyond the phenomenological evidence of the survival literature. Likewise, the term "field" as such (e.g., "field of consciousness' or "psychophysical field") introduces phenomenological considerations that demarcate it from the conventional understanding of a field per se as is given, for example, in the discipline of physics where fields are generally properties of matter. (See also footnote on p. 292.)

happenstance — they are nothing more than likely candidates or "plausible conduits" (cf. Moreman's argument from meaningfulness — p. 44).

Whereas mediumship and channeling may indicate active process on the part of the medium or channeler, there are many cases in the survival literature that suggest that psi experients are more likely to be passive victims (some forms of reincarnation are cases in point).* This proposition needs elaboration by analogy. While Western philosophers may say that a loose tile in a roof falls on the head of one of two men because the man who is hit happened to be walking in the path of the falling tile, Eastern philosophers will ask why it was him and not the other man that was hit. There may be factors in the sorry man's life that explain his "victimization" (these factors interest the Eastern philosopher and many a transpersonal or psychodynamic practitioner), but we have to recognize that chance also explains much in our world (this type of explanation interests the Western philosopher). That which befalls a person may be the result of chance factors. We are not compelled to explain all cases of everyday accident or misfortune in terms of the personal quotient (i.e., in terms of active agency). Nor should we feel compelled to explain all cases of psi experience in the same way. Thus, we cannot assume that *all* paranormal processes require active-agent motivation on the part of the psi experient, or on the part of any other entity, living or proposed to be dead, that one cares to posit. This formulation may adequately explain those peculiar and disturbing cases of reincarnation referred to on page 290.

The matter of intention or motivation *per se* is not, in point of fact, the most pressing issue of radical survivalism that needs addressing. The greater issue concerns the nature of absolute knowledge, and indeed the term "absolute knowledge" may be rather blunt and misleading. Note that I draw parallels between absolute knowledge and information, including information related to experiences, actions, and events, insofar as absolute knowledge refers not only to subjective knowledge, but to all objective information in the universe, though from the empirical evidence, there may be limits to that universe. Nevertheless, beyond the printed words and pictures, outside electronic media, past all that was ever witnessed or executed and thus seen, or heard, or felt, or thought, or done, we cannot be sure what *final* form knowledge/information actually takes, or where it exists. Even though we know that brains, matter, space, etc., might be good starting points, it is clear that once a thing is known by way of experience of one form or another (e.g.,

---

*Readers should re-consider the phenomenology of Ekanayake's experiences (Chapter 10). More disconcerting examples can be found in the reincarnation literature (for example, see Keil & Tucker, 2000; Stevenson, 1993). For my part, I find it difficult (and a needless task) to appropriate meaningfulness to, or in, a re-incarnated wound remnant.

via the sensory modalities or by paranormal information acquisition), knowledge (or information, and these terms might as well be considered interchangeable) has autonomy by dint of it being organized in some such way that it is perceived by living beings who are then capable of interpreting that knowledge or information. The interpretation may be subjective and possibly inaccurate, but it may well be incomplete only, and therefore not necessarily lacking in some degree of objectivity. For example, an array of chess pieces (itself an individual information unit comprised of sub-units of information such as the chess board, knights, rooks, etc.) provides different interpretations dependent upon who is perceiving it — a grandmaster may clearly see checkmate in so many moves (and so much more), whereas an infant will see toys with which to play (and so much more). In either case, the knowledge/information exists.

In addition, and perhaps even more anomalous is the fact that knowledge/information may never be extinguished — even if the chessboard and the pieces, in our example, are destroyed.* We may now say that (a) all events including human experience (existence and action) create knowledge/information, (b) this knowledge/information has autonomy, and (c) humans participate in giving this knowledge/information its autonomy — in a sense, humans participate in the "design" of the cosmos (here I touch on my point made in the closing paragraph of Chapter 14). If we substitute "fields of consciousness" for absolute knowledge, I can agree with Stokes that "fields of consciousness ... may play a fundamental role in ... the design and creation of the universe itself" (p. 48). But how can I justify the equivalence of absolute knowledge with fields of consciousness, or even a single unified field of consciousness? Do I need to justify it?

It seems to me that if many researchers insist that consciousness can exist, as many of our authors have claimed in preceding chapters (and let us suspend the argument from reification for the moment), then so too can absolute knowledge. Personally, it is beyond me what consciousness is supposed to be, or mean, outside the knowing entity that I have referred to in the previous chapter as the ego-complex. Perhaps my confusion is merely semantically based — some researchers might regard the ego-complex (the "I"-identity) and pure consciousness as the same thing. If we dispense with the ego concept, it is easy to adopt the panpsychist view and say that a plant has consciousness, and even emotion, motivation, and volition for that matter, as is given

*Note that I acknowledge that this conjecture is arrived at by philosophical induction because I assume the veracity of retro-cognition, synchronicity experiences, and some survival experiences. Note, however, that philosophical induction is a hallmark of our sciences. Induction is nothing more than establishing the truth status of a phenomenon, what Jung refers to as "statistical truth" (for details, see Storm, 2005, p. 295).

in the literature (Buck, 1988, makes a strong case to that effect, albeit a controversial one). However, the panpsychist type of pure consciousness, some forms of which appear to exist without the capacity to give account of their functioning, without the capacity of relatedness to their being and the being of others, is perhaps a concept to which I cannot relate. Indeed, this is the problem that Moreman raises and critiques (see Chapter 2). But my problem is not based on an egoistic Western prejudice about survival of the individual — it merely derives from the problem of how and why a paradoxically *unconscious* pure consciousness (and that is where the argument logically takes us) could access absolute knowledge.

My mindset may limit my imagination, but then I would prefer to regard all beings and all events as contents and constituents of absolute knowledge *in-process* rather than appeal to the New-Age conception that we, and all we do, are "energy" because at least absolute knowledge implies form and structure. Energy, since it would require a myriad of differentiated forms that can be mediated in some way to make any informational sense, must be of a lower order than absolute knowledge, or even consciousness, whatever form either may ultimately take. In any case (as discussed in Chapter 14), the term "energy" creates problems of a semantic nature. However, relativity theorists tell us that energy, as well as matter and spacetime, constitute the fabric of the universe. But if energy, matter, and spacetime are all inter-related at some fundamental level, in some fundamental way, the question of order is still paramount. Again, can I justify the equivalence of absolute knowledge with fields of consciousness, or even a single unified field of consciousness? In trying to arrive at a clear conceptual framework of what it is that might survive (absolute knowledge, consciousness, etc.), we can be no wiser because the entities are beyond our empirical, and (for some) conceptual grasp.* Nevertheless, I will continue with my model, and state that other forms of knowledge may exist, and these would include things impossible to know by other than paranormal means. As Stokes says: "if psi phenomena exist, this is an indication that minds may have nonlocal aspects and direct access to a 'higher dimension' or at least a wider region of spacetime than is encompassed by the brain" (p. 53). This is a standard understanding amongst parapsychologists of a dualistic persuasion, but I quote Stokes here because it parallels the conception I have of absolute knowledge. However, I do not hold that the brain, or some

---

*It is unfortunate that we depend so much on terminology, such as "knowledge," "consciousness," "mind," "information," "field," "energy," and "matter" because they create very misleading notions. These are all conceptual entities and do not really create the kind of certainty that finite beings might demand. My experience is that we simply do not have, and cannot get, unanimity on the meanings of any of these terms. Again, the problem of language arises as was discussed in Chapter 14.

sub-component of the brain, is necessarily limited in spacetime (I will amplify this point shortly), and I would also say that the "higher dimension" might as well be called absolute knowledge and dispense with conceptions of place or location altogether.

By the evidence, and within the constraints of our epistemology, it is claimed that we can access absolute knowledge but I, as an empiricist, cannot propose in doctrinaire terms (a) how it might exist, (b) why it exists, or (c) and where it exists. The simple truth is, I do not have cause (from evidence or theory) to propose a how, or a why, or a where. Libraries are places that contain knowledge, and we know how and why, but there is no justification to extend that analogy to the concept of absolute knowledge, so I will not attempt it. What I can say is that absolute knowledge (irrespective of one's ontological viewpoint) may be, in part, constituted in the matter of the universe in all its forms, which therefore includes the fabric of living beings (i.e., brain structure, DNA, etc.). In the human capacity, absolute knowledge includes memories, ideas, thoughts, and feelings, and the products of the unconscious functions and processes (including the mythopoetic), and all other such actions, the determinants of which are not fully-specified in any field given the complexity of human personality. On that basis, many so-called survival experiences may have to be considered on a case-by-case basis as is recommended by Braud (Chapter 4).

We might now consider whether conventional conceptions of surviving entities (ghosts, apparitions, spirits, souls, consciousnesses, discarnate or disembodied personalities, etc.) are necessary to radical survivalism,* since Braud has suggested that the mythopoetic device can perform the function of identity creation — certainly, it is not suggested in either term "life remnant" or "surviving residuum" that either should be a knowing or self-aware entity, any more than should nail clippings or the hair on the floor of a barber shop, which can equally be regarded as remnants or residuals.

To pursue this thread further, we may, for example, consider our dream-lives or other altered states of consciousness (ASCs) in which identities are created all the time.† In the psychodynamic tradition, a factor is acknowledged (which we may broadly call unconscious process) that is capable of producing vast panoramas and vistas of often other-worldly brilliance during these ASCs, populated by "living" beings of every possible and impossible

*This is a controversial supposition, and I am loath to apply the principle of parsimony in this instance. Not that there is no good reason why it might not be applied but, by my own rule, I will not be selective.

†We should entertain the possibility that such identities are, or may also be, created in fantasies, alien abduction experiences, visions, NDEs, OBEs, lucid dreams, etc.— all contents of which fall within the category of the mythopoetic.

morphology, acting out their parts in scenarios and stories that range from the everyday/ordinary to the epic/mythological. Here we meet individuals we may never know — that may never have existed, and may never come into existence — they may in fact be symbolic aspects, anthropomorphic (and even theriomorphic) representations of our own personalities and those of others. But they may, on the basis of absolute knowledge, even be inner manifestations of past, present, and future individuals who may have been, or are, or will be real (i.e., may have corporeality) one day. And anything that has happened, or will happen, to these individuals could (within reason) be expressed during these ASCs.

All these events can be mythopoetic formulations courtesy of the psyche and absolute knowledge. All the psyche needs is the material, which can be sourced by normal and paranormal means. As Jung has said of dream and fantasy material, it is "autonomously selected and exploited by the psyche, with the result that the rationality of the cosmos is constantly being violated in the most distressing manner" (Jung, 1953, para. 186). In our rational world, the intangible forms we meet in the various altered (and not so altered) states of consciousness often do distress us, just as ghosts and apparitions may frighten us. In these ASCs, as it happens, it is the case that — however awesome and impossible, irritating or soothing they may be — experiences of these forms are very often attributable to our selves. Many of these forms have dubious origins. They appear in waking life through trance states and mediumship, they appear in dreams and fantasies, and ostensibly "scientific" terms are used to describe them, some professions (often appropriately) categorizing them as nothing more than delusion and hallucination (however, see Chapters 5 and 6).

The study of paranormal phenomena has been referred to as "ironic science" (see Krippner, Chapter 9). The discipline of parapsychology, however, cannot be so easily dismissed as ironic science, and many researchers are convinced that there is evidence of survival. They have made some keen judgments and sensible statements about the phenomena in question, in the same way as many physicists have made formal claims about certain subatomic processes that still cause dispute in their discipline. Empirically, though, I must now say that we only have survival-*like* phenomena as "evidence" of survival because, by that evidence, the only statement we can make with absolute certainty is that it is *living* beings who claim to have survival experiences. That is, it is not yet safe to say survival-like phenomena are the same thing as evidence of survival. As a result, these statements can have one, and only one meaning in radical survivalism — we simply cannot extend our concepts to an afterlife, and as such radical survivalism, while it does propose a survival of sorts, does not propose survival in the conventional sense.

I have considered the data and suggested a radical form of the survival hypothesis—a form that interprets the human experience of survival-like phenomena wholly in terms of living beings. However, we may only be halfway towards a convincing radical survivalism given such cases as that of Pam Reynolds (Williams, 2005). Here we have an example of a completely brain-dead individual who had an aneurysm that had to be excised. There was a reasonable chance of success, but:

> this operation, nicknamed "standstill" by the doctors who perform it, required that Pam's body temperature be lowered to 60 degrees, her heartbeat and breathing stopped, her brain waves flattened, and the blood drained from her head. In everyday terms, she was put to death. After removing the aneurysm, she was restored to life. During the time that Pam was in standstill, she experienced an NDE. Her remarkably detailed veridical out-of-body observations during her surgery were later verified to be very accurate. This case is considered to be one of the strongest cases of veridical evidence in NDE research because of her ability to describe the unique surgical instruments and procedures used and her ability to describe in detail these events while she was clinically and brain dead [Williams, 2005].

This is one of the few cases where objective measures were taken before, during, and after the NDE—a situation imperative in the process of validating that the NDE is not a phenomenon that occurs only *before* or *after* clinical death, which some researchers consider to be the only times during which the brain can still function mythopoetically (i.e., in a hallucinatory, dream-like, or fantasy manner). Blackmore, for example, is convinced that

> it is very difficult to pin down the time when [the NDE] happens. I think that it is more likely that the experiences are happening when you go into unconsciousness and when you are coming out—in those borderline states in which we know all kinds of strange hallucinations and peculiar feelings happen anyway [Blackmore, quoted in Broome, 2002]

The problem here is that Pam Reynolds' consciousness was maintained against all physical evidence to the contrary, and this is only one event that undermines Blackmore's assumption concerning the times at which NDEs supposedly occur.

One compelling theory that has been around for more than a decade—a theory that may explain consciousness during brain death—has been put forward by Hameroff and Penrose (Hameroff, 1994; Hameroff & Penrose, 1996). Their theory describes the quantum processes that transpire at the subatomic level within the microtubules, or cylindrical structures that make up, and give shape to, the neurons. Our conventional understanding about neurons is that information transfer is essentially comprised of multiple all-or-nothing events of neuronal firing, otherwise known as action potentials. But neurons are so extremely intricate in themselves that conventional wisdom about neuronal functioning is an oversimplification to say the least. Hameroff claims that deep in the core of the neuron, microtubules are working like microscopic quantum computers,* which allow for the super-positioning effects that conglomerate to form consciousness, and convey information and therefore knowledge. Hameroff (1994) claims that

> consciousness should be viewed as an emergent property of physical systems. However, although consciousness has its origin in distributed brain processes it has macroscopic properties — most notably the "unitary sense of self," non-deterministic free will, and non-algorithmic "intuitive" processing — which can best be described by quantum-mechanical principles [p. 91].

I would venture to say that the "non-algorithmic intuitive process" implies or includes paranormal process, but we need not concern ourselves with this issue at this time. What is key here is whether or not consciousness can be a property that descends into, and has its beginnings in the deepest structures of the brain.

Hameroff proposes that quantum functioning within the microtubules, by way of a complex process of entanglement and super-positioning, can take place in the clinically dead brain. At this deep fundamental level of consciousness there exists meaningful informational wavelike-forms that literally leak out of the non-functioning microtubules because the normally coherent microtubules can no longer contain that information simply because microtubular metabolic processes have ceased. But instead of being dissipated or lost, the process of quantum coherence or entanglement ensures that the information is maintained in its original integrated form. Consciousness is simply relocated (externalized) since it is no longer contained within any kind of cellular structure (particularly the microtubules, and therefore the neurons, and therefore the brain), thus accounting for the veridicality inherent in so many NDE reports.

Some part of personal identity, it seems, has its origins in consciousness, but that is not to equate the two. So just as a library, for example, is not the same thing as the librarian or a humble borrower of books, the layperson may find it a difficult step to go from entangled conglomerates of information to a personal identity, a personality, a soul, or *my* consciousness as distinct from

*Readers unfamiliar with quantum processes as understood and taught in standard physics textbooks need know only that quantum mechanics describes such subatomic phenomena as "super-positioning" (e.g., the overlapping of two wave forms without interference), "entanglement" (i.e., subatomic particles interacting in unison), and "non-locality" (i.e., entanglement between spatially separated systems)—see also, Chapter 3, p. 63. These phenomena are at odds with the Newtonian cause-and-effect paradigm that currently and sufficiently explains the material world that we experience in our day-to-day lives.

your consciousness. And by all accounts, this neural basis for emergent consciousness has come nowhere near to being proved as yet, but nor has it been refuted according to Atmanspacher (2004). Nevertheless, the theory is not without its detractors (Grush & Churchland, 1995). Irrespective of the uncertainty, I must hark back to Roll's earlier statement (and important concession): "It seems possible ... that consciousness may not be contained within the psychological system, but may also encompass its physical components" (p. 169).

What effect does a quantum-dependent theory of consciousness have on radical survivalism? In fact, one main component is affected — super-psi may not be a paranormal effect but merely a normal effect that we can expect to see under extra-ordinary conditions (e.g., NDE states) where a particular form of quantum process is facilitated. Let us call super-psi something else — perhaps "super-cognition" or "super-perceiving" are preferable terms. Other than that, the main components of the model are not affected at all because I am not attempting to elaborate upon the constituents of consciousness, nor am I concerned whether the "I"-identity can be maintained in death — I am not even concerned as to whether or not it really is consciousness that Hameroff and Penrose are proposing exists at that fundamental level. But I would argue in defense of their theory that, fundamentally, the construct of a quantum-dynamic information-base that Hameroff and Penrose describe may well be phenomenologically isometric with the absolute knowledge construct that Jung proposes, and which I consider necessary for the model described here.

The mythopoetic component of the model would be primarily a macro (brain) process more than anything else, although the symbolic and archetypal constituents of the mythopoetic process may have their roots (at least partially) at that fundamental level proposed by Hameroff and Penrose. On that basis, the rudiments of survival-like experiences most likely have their origins at some quantum level, but the experience *in consciousness* must take place in a pseudo-dead brain. After all, the most frustrating phenomenology about the NDE is that near-death is not death — it is *near* death. Pam Reynolds may have had paranormal experiences during her NDE (she observed, from above, doctors sawing through her skull, and she recalled conversations between nurses and surgeons with startling word-for-word accuracy), but she did not have a so-called RDE (real-death experience). We cannot conclude that her brain was dead *per se* during her NDE. Since revival was possible we have to assume that the vast majority of her brain cells were not dead, even if some number of cells may have died during standstill (i.e., during clinical brain death). We know that brain surgery is severely constrained by time limits of the order of 4 to 6 minutes (certainly not more than

10 minutes) — otherwise real brain death ensues. Until a "discarnate" entity really is discarnate, and is proved to be *permanently* discarnate, we cannot conclude that consciousness (in any of the forms described thus far) survives in the conventional sense, even if absolute knowledge (or Hameroff's and Penrose's quantum-dynamic information-base) does.

In summary, radical survivalism is comprised of three main components — absolute knowledge, super-psi (or super-cognition or super-perceiving), and mythopoetic construction. The model proposes that: (i) super-psi is not governed or restricted by arguments from crippling complexity, or the laws of causality, or the principle of parsimony, (ii) theoretically, all events, and the characteristics that all beings have, along with all their experiences are preserved as absolute knowledge after the demise of the corporeal form *for some time unspecified**;(iii) absolute knowledge can be accessed by conscious beings, (iv) such access is facilitated by the super-psi process, but normal processes may be sufficient in themselves, (v) involvement in such processes can be active or passive and (vi) the mythopoetic function (though not essential) facilitates these processes, resulting in the manifestation of survival-like experiences.

Conclusion

The key question asked in Chapter 14 was, Can the billions of us, in a likeminded manner, imagine what we *should* want the afterlife to be like? As many of our authors suggest, it may be that we can. Taking one simple conception (viz., the afterlife), quite real and self-evident for some, but for others, a conception that may need a great deal of faith and study before belief becomes knowing, we can go from that conception to the suggestion that we are involved in the design of the hereafter. If we aren't now actively involved in designing that future as we *should* imagine it to be, then we *should* start now.

This proposition seems to be no more than what believers in survival already believe they know — that if one was born and existed in the world, then the events of that existence are maintained. However, by the evidence, we cannot say for how long, but it appears that some form of the essence (or major components) of those who have lived, was maintained after their demise — that form being perceivable in every possible meaning of the word.

**It may be, as is proposed by Hameroff and Penrose, that these non-corporeal components exist as quantum formulations and on that basis they may be described as "entangled" and are accessible to conscious beings, but only under specific and usually rare circumstances such as are given in the various ASCs.*

And perhaps that future form may primarily be as we designed it to be. That belief logically extends from the conception of absolute knowledge (in whatever form one imagines that conception to take, and for want of a better term). On that basis, our purpose here may be just as important as our purpose hereafter. That is a more sobering thought than has been offered by even our greatest faiths. And it is a clarion call to all living beings, insofar as they have consciousness, to re-consider and re-evaluate the meaning and importance of their lives, and the lives of others, because the sense of the question of survival will be informed by those actions, and the answer is only going to be understood in the context in which the question is posed. So, at the risk of sounding jejune, if one has no knowledge of another's context, and one is asked, "Do we survive bodily death?" then even a simple answer like "Yes" will probably be unclear.

References

Atmanspacher, H. (2004). Quantum approaches to consciousness. In *Stanford Encyclopedia of Philosophy*. Retrieved September 6, 2005, from <http://plato.stanford.edu/entries/qtconsciousness/#5>

Braude, S. E. (2003). *Immortal remains: The evidence for life after death.* New York: Rowan and Littlefield.

Broome, K. (Producer/Director) (2002). *The day I died.* Bristol: BBC.

Buck, R. (1988). *Human motivation and emotion* (2nd ed.). New York: John Wiley & Sons.

Edwards, D., Ashmore, M., & Potter, J. (1995). Death and furniture: The rhetoric, politics, and theology of bottom line arguments against relativism. *History of the Human Sciences, 8*(2), 25–49. Reprinted in M. Gergen & K. J. Gergen (Eds.) (2003). *Social construction: A reader.* London: Sage.

Foster, M. H., & Martin, M. L. (Eds.) (1966). *Probability, confirmation, and simplicity: Readings in the philosophy of inductive logic.* New York: Odyssey Press.

Grush, R., & Churchland, P. S. (1995). Gaps in Penrose's toilings. *Journal of Consciousness Studies 2,* 10–29.

Hameroff, S. R. (1994). Quantum coherence in microtubules: A neural basis for emergent consciousness? *Journal of Consciousness Studies, 1,* 91–118.

Hameroff, S., & Penrose, R. (1996). Orchestrated reduction of quantum coherence in brain microtubules: A model for consciousness. In S. R. Hameroff, A. W. Kaszniak, & A. C. Scott (Eds.). *Toward a science of consciousness: The first Tucson discussions and debates* (pp. 507–540). Cambridge, MA: MIT Press.

Irwin, H. J. (2004). *An introduction to parapsychology* (4th ed.). Jefferson, NC: McFarland.

Jung, C. G. (1953). *Psychology and alchemy.* Princeton, NJ: Princeton University Press.

Jung, C. G. (1960). *The structure and dynamics of the psyche.* Princeton, NJ: Princeton University Press.

Keil, J. H. H., & Tucker, J. B. (2000). An unusual birthmark case thought to be linked to a person who had previously died. *Psychological Reports, 87,* 1067–1074.

Popper, K. (1963). *Conjectures and refutations.* London: Routledge and Kegan Paul.

Stevenson, I. (1993). Birthmarks and birth defects corresponding to wounds on deceased persons. *Journal of Scientific Exploration, 7,* 403–410.

Stokes, D. M. (1987). Theoretical parapsychology. In S. Krippner (Ed.), *Advances in parapsychological research 5* (pp. 77–189). Jefferson, NC: McFarland.

Storm, L. (1999). Synchronicity, causality, and acausality. *Journal of Parapsychology, 63,* 247–269.

Storm, L. (2005). A socioempirical perspective on skepticism about psi. In M. A. Thalbourne & L. Storm (Eds.). *Parapsychology in the Twenty-First Century: Essays on the future of psychical research* (pp. 275–304). Jefferson, NC: McFarland.

Storm, L., & Thalbourne, M. A. (2003). Perceived complexity, perceived task difficulty, and other states of mind: The influence of mental states on psi outcomes. *Journal of the American Society for Psychical Research, 97*, 155–74.

Thalbourne, M. A. (1981). *Some experiments on the paranormal cognition of drawings with special reference to personality and attitudinal variables.* Unpublished Ph.D. thesis, Department of Psychology, University of Edinburgh, Scotland.

Thalbourne, M. A. (2004). *The common thread between ESP and PK.* New York: The Parapsychology Foundation.

Williams, K. (2005). People have NDEs while brain dead. In *Near-death experiences & the afterlife.* Retrieved September 5, 2005, from <http://www.near-death.com/experiences/evidence01.html>

About the Contributors

John N. Boyd received a degree in economics from UCLA and his Ph.D. in experimental psychology from Stanford University. After serving as director of scientific affairs at Alertness Solutions, an international human factors and performance-related consulting firm, Dr. Boyd joined Yahoo! in the spring of 2002 as the first researcher dedicated to the investigation of the user experience of online advertising. His seminal work on this topic has been highlighted in numerous internal and external forums. Dr. Boyd's initial focus on advertising has since expanded to include research manager roles for both Platform and Network Services groups. Beyond the confines of his current research, his broader interests lie in exploring the Internet as a social medium and discovering how traditional psychological principles can be used online to change behavior in pro-social ways.

William Braud earned his Ph.D. in experimental psychology at the University of Iowa in 1967. At the University of Houston, he taught and conducted research in learning, memory, motivation, psychophysiology, and the biochemistry of memory. At the Mind Science Foundation in San Antonio, Texas, he directed research in parapsychology; health and well-being influences of relaxation, imagery, positive emotions, and intention; and psychoneuroimmunology. Currently, Dr. Braud is professor and research director at the Institute of Transpersonal Psychology in Palo Alto, California, where he directs doctoral dissertation research, and continues research, teaching, and writing in areas of exceptional human experiences, consciousness studies, transpersonal studies, spirituality, and expanded research methods.

Keith Chandler pursued his undergraduate education at Washington University in St. Louis, Missouri, and his graduate studies as a Woodrow Wilson fellow at the University of Chicago. He left academic life in 1953 and pursued a career in business. In 1955 he married a talented artist and designer, Muriel McCarthy, and the couple moved to Jamaica in 1970 where they founded a highly successful *batik* art and fashion industry that continued until Muriel's death of lung cancer in 1990. During that time, Keith Chandler also pursued a career as an independent scholar, publishing numerous journal articles, but after his wife's death he devoted himself full time to his intellectual passion — philosophy. His published works include *Beyond Civilization* (1992, 2001), *The Mind Paradigm* (2001), *PSI: What It Is and How It Works* (2001), and *The Android Myth* (2002). In 1998, he sold his home in Jamaica and now resides in Miami, Florida.

David Fontana is a past president of the Society for Psychical Research (SPR), and currently life vice president and foundation chairman of the SPR's Survival Research Committee. He has published over 100 scientific papers and some 30 books (six of which were specially commissioned by the British Psychological Society). Until recently he was distinguished visiting fellow at Cardiff University, and now holds the first chair in transpersonal psychology in the UK at Liverpool John Moores University. He has edited or served on the editorial board of a number of leading psychology journals, including *The Transpersonal Psychology Review* and the *British Journal of Psychology*. He is a member of the Parapsychological Association, and has written widely on many aspects of psychical research, with particular emphasis on the question of survival of physical death. He was co-author of the *Scole Report*, which details the most extensive investigation into physical phenomena conducted in the UK for many years. His latest book *Is There an Afterlife?* (2005) surveys much of the best evidence for survival, emphasizing its convincing nature. Currently he is engaged with Dr. Anabela Cardoso in a major investigation into instrumental transcommunication (ITC), funded through the SPR.

Erlendur Haraldsson is professor emeritus of psychology at the University of Iceland in Reykjavik. He is an active researcher on paranormal phenomena with numerous publications in scientific journals. Since the late 1980s he has conducted extensive investigations in Sri Lanka, India, and Lebanon, of children who claim to remember a previous life. Dr. Haraldsson is the author of four books that have appeared in many languages, among them *At the Hour of Death*, a unique study of deathbed-visions that he wrote with Karlis Osis, and *Miracles Are My Visiting Cards* on the phenomena associated with Sai Baba.

Pamela Heath received her medical degree from the University of Texas Medical Branch at Galveston in 1980 and is board certified in anethesiology. She practiced at multiple locations, including twice serving as the chief of anesthesia and spending two years working on the Navaho reservation before returning to school to receive her doctorate in psychology specializing in parapsychology in 1999 from the American School of Professional Psychology,

Rosebridge campus. She is an associate member of the Parapsychological Association and on the board of directors for the California Society for Psychical Research. Dr. Heath continues to practice medicine part time, in addition to working with the Office of Paranormal Investigations and writing. Her publications include the book *Into the Psychokinetic (PK) Zone: A Phenomenological Study of the Experience of Performing Psychokinesis*, and she has been published in the *Journal of Parapsychology*.

James Houran has a Ph.D. in psychology (University of Adelaide), and is an author, public speaker and 15-year veteran in the field of research and clinical psychology. He has received several grants in support of his research in parapsychology and anomalistic psychology. Dr. Houran has authored or co-authored over 100 journal publications and his work has been featured in several media outlets and programs including the Discovery Channel, A&E, the BBC, *New Scientist*, and NBC's *Today* show. He recently edited *From Shaman to Scientist: Essays on Humanity's Search for Spirits* (2004) and is the co-editor of the modern day classic anthology, *Hauntings and Poltergeists: Multidisciplinary Perspectives* (2001). Dr. Houran recently served as an instructor of clinical psychiatry at Southern Illinois School of Medicine. He is currently the vice president of Integrated Knowledge Systems, Inc., a research and online testing consulting firm.

Jon Klimo holds a doctorate in psychology from Brown University. He has been working full-time teaching in different doctoral programs for the past 31 years. He is currently associate professor of psychology at the American Schools of Professional Psychology, Argosy University, San Francisco Bay Area Campus, in Point Richmond, California. From 1974 to 1982, he was a professor at Rutgers University, where he was the founding director of the Creative Arts Education Program. He is a member of the Parapsychological Association and for seven years, at Rosebridge Graduate School of Integrative Psychology (1991–1998), he designed, developed, and was chief instructor in one of only two doctoral-level academic specialization programs in parapsychology in the United States. Dr. Klimo has chaired some 200 dissertation committees, and he has researched, taught, publicly presented, and published in the areas of parapsychology, alternative medicine, consciousness studies, new paradigm thought and new science, metaphysics and the transpersonal domain. He wrote what is widely considered the definitive study on the phenomenon of channeling—*Channeling: Investigations on Receiving Information from Paranormal Sources* (1998). He is currently finishing a book with co-author Pamela Heath titled *Suicide: What Really Happens in the Afterlife?*

Stanley Krippner, Ph.D., is Alan W. Watts Professor of Psychology at Saybrook Graduate School, San Francisco. He is a fellow in three APA divisions, and former president of two divisions. Formerly, he was director of the Kent State University Child Study Center, Kent, Ohio, and the Maimonides Medical Center Dream Research Laboratory, Brooklyn, New York. He is co-author of *Extraordinary Dreams* (2002) and co-editor of *Varieties of Anomalous Experience: Examining the Scientific Evidence* (2000). Dr. Krippner has conducted workshops and seminars on dreams, hypnosis, and/or anomalous phenomena in 24 countries and at the last four congresses of the Interamerican Psychological Association. He has given invited addresses for the Chinese Academy of Sciences and the Russian Academy of Pedagogical Sciences. In 2002, he was awarded the American Psychological Association's Award for Contributions to International Psychology.

James McClenon is a professor of sociology at Elizabeth City State University (North Carolina). He is the author of many journal articles pertaining to the sociology of unusual experiences and the author of three books: *Deviant Science: The Case of Parapsychology* (1984), *Wondrous Events: Foundations of Religious Belief* (1994), and *Wondrous Healing: Shamanism, Human Evolution, and the Origin of Religion* (2002). He has studied shamanism in Okinawa, Taiwan, Korea, Thailand, Sri Lanka, and the Philippines. His research areas include anomalous experience, shamanism, the sociology of the paranormal, and spiritual healing.

Christopher M. Moreman earned his first degree in classical studies from Concordia University in Montreal (1997) before traveling to the U.K., where he completed an M.A. in the study of mysticism and religious experiences from the University of Kent at Canterbury (1999). He acquired a growing interest in the mystical traditions of the world, particularly those of Buddhism and Taoism. Dr. Moreman has a Ph.D. in religious studies from the University of Wales at Lampeter (2004). He is presently an assistant professor at St. Francis Xavier University in Nova Scotia, Canada, and he has also taught at Indiana University of Pennsylvania and the Thomas More Institute in Montreal. Dr. Moreman has taught a variety of courses in world religions, Buddhism, mysticism, new religious movements, death and the afterlife, and religion and the paranormal. He is a member of both the Society for Psychical Research and the American Academy of Religion, where he co-chairs the program unit, Death, Dying, and Beyond.

William G. Roll received his B.A. from the University of California at Berkeley, a B.Litt and an M.Litt from Oxford University, and a Ph.D. from Lund University. The M.Litt thesis was about Roll's ESP experiments; the

Ph.D. thesis was an examination of parapsychological findings suggestive of the survival of human personality after death. Dr. Roll has written four books, including *The Poltergeist* (1972), and *Unleashed: Of Poltergeists and Murder* (2004), which he co-wrote with Valerie Storey. He has also written several book chapters and more than 200 research papers. Dr. Roll has appeared on the television series *Unsolved Mysteries,* and other television documentaries. He received the Distinguished Career Award from the Parapsychological Association in 1996, and the Tim Dinsdale Memorial Award from the Society for Scientific Exploration in 2002.

Douglas M. Stokes is a frequent contributor to the literature on parapsychology. His publications include the book *The Nature of Mind* (1997), as well as numerous articles, chapters and book reviews in the *Journal of Parapsychology,* the *Journal of the American Society for Psychical Research, Skeptical Inquirer,* and the *Advances in Parapsychological Research* series published by McFarland. He served as associate editor of the *Journal of Parapsychology* for several years. He is a magna cum laude graduate of Harvard University and earned a Ph.D. in experimental psychology from the University of Michigan. Dr. Stokes has worked as a psychological researcher, a parapsychological researcher at J. B. Rhine's Institute of Parapsychology, a teacher of mathematics, and a psychotherapist. He is currently a management consultant with the firm of Sullivan, Cotter and Associates, Inc., in Detroit. Dr. Stokes lives in Ann Arbor, Michigan, with his wife and daughter.

Lance Storm earned a B.A. (Honors) in psychology (1998) and a Ph.D. in parapsychology (2002) at the University of Adelaide, South Australia. He has published in *Psychological Bulletin,* the *Journal of Parapsychology* and the Jungian journal *Quadrant.* He is the editor of the *Australian Journal of Parapsychology,* in which he regularly publishes, and is a member of the Parapsychological Association and the Australian Institute of Parapsychological Research. He is a co-recipient, with Dr. Michael Thalbourne, of the D. Scott Rogo Award for Literature (2002). In 2003, he was awarded the Gertrude R. Schmeidler Student of the Year Award for work in parapsychology. He is co-editor with Dr. Michael A. Thalbourne of the book *Parapsychology in the Twenty-First Century* (2005). Currently, as a research fellow, he is conducting parapsychological research in the School of Psychology, University of Adelaide, where he assisted Dr. Thalbourne in establishing the Anomalistic Psychology Research Unit.

Michael A. Thalbourne obtained his B.A. (Honors) degree at the University of Adelaide, South Australia, in 1976, and his Ph.D. in parapsychology at Edinburgh University in 1981. He has been published in all the major English-speaking parapsychological journals, and has written the widely used book *A Glossary of Terms Used in Parapsychology* (1982). He is a member of the American and British Societies for Psychical Research, and the Parapsychological Association. Dr. Thalbourne is president of the Australian Institute of Parapsychological Research and was founding editor of its journal, the *Australian Journal of Parapsychology*. His most recent publications are the second edition of the above-mentioned *Glossary* (2003), and the parapsychological monograph *The Common Thread Between ESP and PK* (2004). He is co-editor with Dr. Lance Storm of the book *Parapsychology in the Twenty-First Century* (2005). He is currently a research fellow at University of Adelaide, where he is also the director of the Anomalistic Psychology Research Unit.

Robin Wooffitt is a senior lecturer in the Department of Sociology at the University of Surrey, UK. His research interests are conversation analysis and discourse analysis, and social science responses to anomalous human experiences. Dr. Wooffitt has written many journal articles on the topic of conversation analysis and related areas, and he is the author of a number of books, including *Conversation Analysis and Discourse Analysis: A Comparative and Critical Introduction* (2005), and *The Language of Mediums and Psychics: The Social Organization of Everyday Miracles* (2006). He is currently a Perrott Warwick Researcher with the Koestler Parapsychology Unit at the University of Edinburgh, where he is examining verbal interaction between experimenter and subject in the Ganzeld procedure.

Philip G. Zimbardo is internationally recognized as the voice and face of contemporary psychology through his widely seen PBS-TV series *Discovering Psychology*, his media appearances, best-selling trade books on shyness, and his classic research work, *The Stanford Prison Experiment*. Professor Zimbardo has been a Stanford University professor since 1968, having taught previously at Yale, NYU, and Columbia University. He has been given numerous awards and honors as an educator, researcher, and writer, and for service to the profession. Among his more than 350 professional publications and 50 books is the oldest current textbook in psychology, *Psychology and Life*, now in its 17th edition. His current research interests are in the domain of experimental social psychology. Professor Zimbardo has been president of the American Psychological Association, and chair (2005) of the Council of Scientific Society Presidents (CSSP) representing 63 scientific, math and technical associations with 1.5 million members.

Index

panexperientialist theory of consciousness 64
panpsychism 62, 63, 291, 292
paranormal: controversy of 5; and hallucination 95; and meaning 44 45; as a problem 40
Parapsychology 5, 40, 47, 111, 128, 139, 279, 285, 294; attitude towards 5
parsimony, law of 265, 289, 293, 298
Paul (apostle) 22, 23
Penrose, R. (physicist) 189
Phantasms of the Living (book) 132, 145, 148, 152
Phone Calls from the Dead (book) 180
physical trace theory 146
Piper, L. (medium) 155, 161, 167, 169
PK (psychokinesis) 5, 51, 52, 130, 132–134, 136, 138, 139, 177, 244, 246, 264, 265, 274, 276, 278, 287, 289
Plato 143
Podmore, F. (psychical researcher) 132
Pope, representative of God 22
postcivilization 26
post-mortem survival 178; *see also* life after death
Price, H. H. (philosopher) 34, 35, 148
Princess Diana 222
Princeton Engineering Anomalies Research Unit (PEAR) 130
Psychical Research Foundation 156
psychokinesis *see* PK
psychomanteum 6, 42, 78, 184, 185
psychometry 161, 168
psychopraxia 287, 288, 289
Purnima Ekanayake (reincarnation-type case) 194–205, 275

quantum interconnectedness 40, 63
quantum physics 40, 131, 285

radical survivalism 286, 288–290, 293–295, 297–298
Raynolds, P. (psychologist) 92
reincarnation 10, 32, 36, 69, 79, 85, 86, 92, 93, 109, 186, 208, 217, 218, 249, 264, 265, 272, 275, 276, 277, 290; *see also* Purnima Ekanayake
religion, and cohesiveness 244
religious belief, associations with 108
Rhine, J. B. (parapsychologist) 128, 130, 143, 180
Rhine, L. E. (parapsychologist) 130, 143, 144, 149, 150, 151, 152, 179, 180
Rhine Feather, S. (parapsychologist) 179
ritual healing theory 242, 243, 245, 253, 254, 256, 257, 259
Roll, W. G. (biography) 304
Roman Empire 22

St. Augustine 23
Salter, H. (psychical researcher) 155
Samuel (Book of) 32, 153

Schiller, F. C. S. (pragmatist) 37, 41
Schmeidler, G. (parapsychologist) 188
Schnittger, W. (psychical researcher) 137
scientism 28, 38
Scole Investigation 130, 136, 137, 138, 224
self: as continuing 48; downloaded 50; hierarchy of 59; as "I-thinker" 50 269; as illusion 49; multiple (split) 58; persisting 48, 49, 50, 269; as personality 187; as pure consciousness 49, 51, 65; and quantum theory 57, 63, 66; as "Shin" 52, 53, 54, 55, 56, 57, 269; as mini-Shin 65, 66, 67, 68, 69, 70, 269
Shakespeare, W. (playwright) 11, 29
shamanism 243, 244, 253, 254, 256, 257, 258; definition of 246
Sheol 21, 35
Sidgwick, E. (psychical researcher) 144
Skeptics Society 138
Sloan, J. (medium) 135, 136
Society for Psychical Research (SPR) 129, 134, 135, 137, 143, 155, 159, 160, 162, 165, 175, 178, 182
spirit actions 228
spirits' discourse 228
spiritualism 217
split-brain findings 54
split-brain research 61, 166
SPR *see* Society for Psychical Research
Stevenson, I. (psychical researcher) 34, 69, 143, 158, 162–165, 167, 168, 170, 195
Stokes, D. (medium) 223
Stokes, D. M. (biography) 305
Storm, L. (biography) 305
Sufism 39
suicide 208, 276; channeled material of 207–221; mass-murder & suicide bombers 216, 218, 219; stages after (life review) 214; stages after (recovery) 213; stages after (spiritual work) 216; stages after (transition) 209
suicide bombers 212
super-psi hypothesis 6, 36, 38, 41, 42, 43, 87, 168, 189, 264, 265, 268, 274–276, 278, 285–289, 297–298; argument against (i.e., crippling complexity) 265, 288, 298
Swedenborg, E. (theologian) 217
synchronicity 44, 83, 246, 287, 288, 291
Synesthesia 105

Taoism 12, 39
Tartarus 22
Tattersall, I. (paleoanthropologist) 15, 17
Thalbourne, M. A. (biography) 305
thanatophobia (fear of death) 16
Thibodeau, L. (medium) 216
Thouless, R. H. (psychologist) 52, 53–55, 65–67, 164, 166
Tillich, P. (theologian) 12, 183
time perspective, definition of 109
tombs 21, 185
transcendental-future 120; and learning theory

DATE DUE
